Foundations of a Sociology of Canon Law

Judith Hahn

Foundations of a Sociology of Canon Law

 Springer

Judith Hahn
University of Bonn
Bonn, Germany

Funding Information: Ruhr University Bochum

ISBN 978-3-031-01793-3   ISBN 978-3-031-01791-9   (eBook)
https://doi.org/10.1007/978-3-031-01791-9

Translation from and revised version of the German language edition: "Grundlegung der Kirchenrechtssoziologie: Zur Realität des Rechts in der römisch-katholischen Kirche" by Judith Hahn, © Springer Fachmedien Wiesbaden GmbH 2019. Published by Springer VS. All Rights Reserved.

Translator's Note

The following text is the translation and amended version of the first edition of the German original by Judith Hahn entitled *Grundlegung der Kirchenrechtssoziologie: Zur Realität des Rechts in der römisch-katholischen Kirche* which was published by Springer in 2019.

The English text is, I believe, more than the sum of its parts. This is true at a basic level insofar as some additional passages were added by the author to supplement the English language version. But it is also true at the linguistic level. It is common wisdom among writers and translators alike that form and content are indivisible, and that a faithful rendering from one language to another requires a translator to possess a firm footing in the disciplines being translated. Yet embarking on the translation of a work at the confluence of multiple academic disciplines as on this occasion certainly surpassed my rudimentary knowledge of the subject matter at hand. I am therefore grateful to the author for her forbearance in the translation of quotations, her attention to ensuring the accuracy of terminology, and her general support in the task of uniting linguistic form and academic content. This project was extremely challenging, but it is in the challenge that the enjoyment and satisfaction lie. The result is a new work in English in which language and content have been united at least as much by the author as by the translator. As a consequence, although it has been a collaborative endeavour at the linguistic level, this book still indisputably bears the clear hallmark of the author. There is therefore good reason to believe it will be as informative and readable in English as it is in German.

Acknowledgements

Writing a book is a highly individual and to some degree also a deeply personal endeavour. Its success depends on one's own interests, personal style, daily form, physical condition, mental endurance, background knowledge, and subjective judgement. And yet any study of this kind is also a communal effort, brought into being thanks to the support of others who have contributed to its success in a whole host of ways. This is particularly true in the present case, not least because writing a book about sociology as a theologian and canonist without any higher sociological education is no self-evident undertaking. This endeavour would therefore have been inconceivable without those who have supported my efforts to bring sociology, theology, and canon law together by contributing their knowledge and criticism to this interdisciplinary study. As a theologian and canonist, I came into contact with matters sociological in the course of my education, but acquired only modest theoretical and methodological knowledge in the field. My path to the sociology of law lay in private study, encouraged and supported by others. During a fellowship which took me to the Käte Hamburger Center for Advanced Study "Law as Culture" in Bonn in 2015–16, I became familiar with and learned to appreciate the "classics" of sociology and of the sociology of law which have left their thumbprint on my study.[1] I would like to single out Marta Bucholc for particular thanks as one colleague whose sociological and legal scholarship has impressed me greatly and from whom I have learnt a significant amount about how to read the sociological classics, appreciate their impulses for developing current sociological theories, and apply them to understand more of the law. Over the past couple of years, I was also fortunate to make the acquaintance of theologians who fruitfully work in the intersection of sociology and theology. I want to mention Bryan Froehle, Palm Beach Atlantic University, and Wim Vandewiele, KU Leuven, both sociologists and practical theologians and experts on the empirical research of the Roman

---

[1]E.g. Durkheim (1960); Weber (1978); Ehrlich (1936); Pound (1923); Llewellyn (1940); Geiger (1964); Carbonnier (1974); Bourdieu (1987); Dworkin (1998).

Catholic Church. Their sociological view of the church has helped me to sharpen my perception of the institutional structures which constitute the church.

Since my first tentative steps, I have studied numerous recent contributions to the sociology of law, from ground-breaking theories, such as Niklas Luhmann's theory of society,[2] through individual studies often on very specific matters, to the many obligatory textbooks and considerable body of literature which has been written for students of law and of sociology. Reading these books was almost always a stimulating experience, and not infrequently an enjoyable one. In preparing my book, I noted repeatedly and with considerable gratitude that there are valuable general overviews of the sociology of law which provide access to the field for readers from outside the sociology of law. Two books that impressed me greatly are worthy of mention here by way of example: Susanne Baer's sociology of law *Rechtssoziologie* (2021), now in its fourth edition, and Gerhard Struck's book of the same title (2011). Both are well suited for students who wish to learn more about the sociology of law, but also for all those who are interested in critical and reliable interdisciplinary introductions to the sociology of law with a practical bent. As a matter of fact, I cite these texts relatively seldom in my book. To surmise from this that I had learnt little from them would be a mistake. Indeed, I am indebted to these authors for helping me to form a systematic understanding of what constitutes law in fact. Their contributions provided the impetus for my thoughts on what the sociology of canon law can learn from the general sociology of law, and are therefore of immeasurable value for my study.

Many thanks go to my former colleagues in Bochum and my new colleagues in Bonn. What unites us at both Faculties of Catholic Theology is that our work is focused on a theology which is interested in reality. In consequence, sociology partners theology in many of our approaches. I am very grateful to find myself in such good company. Much deserving of mention at the Bochum Chair of Canon Law is Andrea Hartwig, whose support was of great value to me, particularly during times in which I withdrew into my studies to finish a book.

As always, I am most grateful to Robert John Murphy for his indispensable assistance; this time, in any case, I am grateful to him not only for carefully proofreading my manuscript, but for preparing the English version of this book by translating it from the original German and by carefully proofreading the additions which I made in the English version.[3] This is the fifth book which we have worked on together. Whilst our cooperation has most certainly played its part in improving my English step by step, I am still rather clueless about how to publish in English without Robert Murphy's support.

I dedicate this book to Thomas, who suffered the most from my constant chattering about it.

---

[2] E.g. Luhmann (1969; 1977; 1986; 2004; 2014).

[3] See Hahn (2019).

Bibliography

Baer, S. (2021). *Rechtssoziologie: Eine Einführung in die interdisziplinäre Rechtsforschung* (4th ed.). Nomos.

Bourdieu, P. (1987). The force of law: Toward a sociology of the juridical field. *The Hastings Law Journal, 38*, 814–853.

Carbonnier, J. (1974). *Rechtssoziologie* (Schriftenreihe zur Rechtssoziologie und Rechtstatsachenforschung 31). Duncker & Humblot.

Durkheim, É. (1960). *The division of labor in society* [1893] (G. Simpson, Trans.). The Free Press.

Dworkin, R. (1998). *Law's empire*. Hart Publishing.

Ehrlich, E. (1936). *Fundamental principles of the sociology of law* (W. L. Moll, Trans., with an introduction by R. Pound). The Harvard University Press.

Geiger, T. (1964). *Vorstudien zu einer Soziologie des Rechts* (mit einer Einleitung und internationalen Bibliographie zur Rechtssoziologie von P. Trappe). Luchterhand.

Hahn, J. (2019). *Grundlegung der Kirchenrechtssoziologie: Zur Realität des Rechts in der römisch-katholischen Kirche*. Springer.

Llewellyn, K. N. (1940). The Normative, the Legal, and the Law Jobs: The Problem of Juristic Method. *Yale Law Journal, 49*, 1355–1400.

Luhmann, N. (1969). *Legitimation durch Verfahren* (Soziologische Texte 66). Luchterhand.

Luhmann, N. (1977). *Funktion der Religion*. Suhrkamp.

Luhmann, N. (1986). *Die soziologische Beobachtung des Rechts*. Suhrkamp.

Luhmann, N. (2004). *Law as a social system* (Oxford socio-legal studies, F. Kastner, R. Nobles, D. Schiff & R. Ziegert, Eds., K. A. Ziegert, Trans.). Oxford University Press.

Luhmann, N. (2014). *A sociological theory of law* (M. Albrow, Ed., E. King-Utz & M. Albrow, Trans.). Routledge.

Pound, R. (1923). *Interpretations of legal history*. The Macmillan Company.

Struck, G. (2011). *Rechtssoziologie: Grundlagen und Strukturen*. Nomos.

Weber, M. (1978). *Economy and society: An outline of interpretive sociology* (G. Roth & C. Wittich, Eds.). University of California Press.

Contents

Chapter 1
Introduction

Abstract The study is the first book to present a sociology of Roman Catholic canon law from the perspective of canon law studies. By modelling a theoretical sociology to study canon law with the aim of better understanding the function and reality of the law in the Roman Catholic Church, it follows the methodology of a descriptive sociology as applied frequently in the sociology of law. The study receives the manifold approaches to a sociology of the law and discusses their merit in contributing to a sociology of canon law. In drawing on empirical findings from the sociology of law and the sociology of religion, the study substantiates its theoretical arguments by drawing on knowledge about both the reality of the church and the reality of law.

Keywords (Roman Catholic) canon law · Canon law studies · Roman Catholic Church · Sociological theory · Sociology of law · Sociology of canon law · Sociology of religion · Theology

This book is a sociology of canon law. It seeks to comprehend the *reality* of canon law. It is a book about ecclesiastical law *as it is*—and not about how canon law might be or should be. It focuses on the canon law of the present day, and not on its glorious past. By taking this approach, my study is also an experiment. It is a product of canon law studies. However, unlike most contributions by scholars of canon law, my study does not comment on canon law with the purpose of showing its merits and demerits in regulating ecclesiastical issues. Instead, it attempts to study the legal reality of the church. Of course, as a canonist I am not trained to analyse this reality from the outside as a sociologist would. Instead, by arguing from the viewpoint of canon law studies, my study represents an approach which is devoted to examining the law of the church from "within," that is from the point of view of theology as an academic discipline which seeks to understand the connection between God, faith, and the law.

I view canon law studies as being part of theology. As a theo-legal discipline, it is unique insofar as it examines the law of the church from the perspective of theology and from the perspective of legal studies. In my opinion, its essential interdisciplinary shape also requires canon law studies to become proficient in using the tools of

© The Author(s) 2022
J. Hahn, *Foundations of a Sociology of Canon Law*,
https://doi.org/10.1007/978-3-031-01791-9_1

the sociology of law. To understand canon law as it is we must learn to analyse its reality with the help of sociological theory and methodology. This helps us to understand canon law somewhat better; but it also helps us to understand more of theology. As canon law studies is theology, a canonist's sociology of canon law is also a contribution to the debate on the status of sociology in theology and on the value of sociological findings for theology. The following introduction seeks to provide a little more clarity to this interdisciplinary field by locating the sociology of canon law at the intersection of the disciplines of canon law studies, theology, and sociology.

1.1   Canon Law Studies as Theology

In the academic culture in which I spent my formative years, canon law studies was and remains a subdiscipline of theology. It is the discipline which studies the law of the church as a law rooted in church and which is designed to serve ecclesiastical purposes. Theology understands the concrete earthly church as an embodiment of the heavenly church. Canon law studies is therefore tasked with clarifying how the organisation and legal structure of the earthly church as fact connects with the heavenly church as norm. Hence, similarly to ecclesiology, canon law studies engages in scholarly study about the church. However, it focuses in particular on the earthly church as fact which takes on a concrete form with the help of norms, and, in particular, legal norms. In consequence, one may understand canon law studies to be a continuation of ecclesiology. Canonist Robert Ombres put this finding as follows, "Canon law may be usefully understood as applied ecclesiology."[1] This statement acknowledges the connection between law and ecclesiology; and it also highlights the reason why canon law studies is essentially perceived as practical theology. Hence, in contrast to other suggestions made by practical theologians about why canon law is a practical discipline, I propose understanding canon law studies as a discipline of practical theology not so much because it studies the law as a field of ecclesial practice, but because it studies the legal structure of the church as the practical embodiment of the heavenly church. Canon law studies, I would like to suggest, is practical theology because it analyses how the church as norm becomes fact, and does so with the help of those facts which we call "norms." I will return to this thought in Sect. 2.1.11.

The classification of canon law studies as theology has become manifest in two tasks assigned to canon law studies after the Second Vatican Council, as canonist Sabine Demel points out. Demel states that it is the task of canon law studies to consistently analyse two problems. First, canon law studies constantly has to ask whether there are new theological findings which prove to be legally relevant—and must consequently be adopted into canon law. Second, canon law studies has to

---

[1] Ombres (2016, p. 137); see also Doe (1992, p. 336).

constantly review existing law to establish whether it adequately expresses the current findings of theology.[2] If it is the task of canon law studies to understand the legal order of an organisation which provides its members with law to structure the social but which is also relevant for salvation, then canon law studies cannot rely solely upon the arguments of legal philosophy, history, and sociology to understand the law as a social phenomenon. For canon law, reference to its own traditions and to analogous norms in the secular legal system is most certainly enlightening. Nevertheless, the roots and reasons of canon law must also be grounded in theology. Post-conciliar canonical thought is therefore in a constant search for a theologically grounded foundation of canon law. This requires canon law studies to have a solid grounding in theology. However, its essential interdisciplinary structure also requires canon law studies to be familiar with legal studies as a source of knowledge about the law and about legal methodology. This dual perspective of theology and legal studies has led to heated methodological debates among scholars of canon law still seeking agreement on where to locate the discipline and how to outline its theory and methodology. Different points of view collide. It is a matter of lively debate whether canon law studies is a legal discipline with legal methods,[3] a theological discipline with legal methods,[4] a theological discipline with theological methods,[5] or a theological-legal discipline with both theological and legal methods.[6] None of these approaches appears to be fully convincing inasmuch as they either undermine the character of canon law studies as theology or as a legal discipline, or muddy the waters with respect to methodology. With a view to these problems one approach stands out, as I find. Its most prominent proponent was canonist Winfried Aymans. Aymans focused his attention on the genuinely theological character of canon law studies without losing sight of the fact that theology is not methodologically monistic, but is reliant on the methodological resources of other disciplines. Aymans consequently defined canon law studies as a discipline of theology, albeit one which relies upon legal methods, yet doing so in the interest of and within the boundaries set by theology.[7] I agree with Aymans in this respect but want to open up his approach a little more, as I will suggest shortly.

---

[2] See Demel (2012, p. 15).

[3] E.g. Fürst (1977, pp. 500–501); Hervada (2004, pp. 57–68).

[4] E.g. Eichmann and Mörsdorf (1964, p. 36).

[5] E.g. Corecco (1994, p. 16).

[6] E.g. May and Egler (1986, pp. 17–22); Sanders (2000, p. 394). For overviews of the complex methodological debate in canon law studies see e.g. Cattaneo (1993, pp. 52–64); May (1999, p. 92 fn 2); Graulich (2006, pp. 248–249); Neudecker (2013, pp. 467–468).

[7] See Aymans and Mörsdorf (1991, p. 71); Aymans (1995, p. 370).

1.2   ...Using Methods of Legal Studies

In line with Aymans's definition of canon law studies as theology which uses legal methods in the pursuit of canonical knowledge, canon law studies avails itself of legal methodology to study the legal shape of the church. This choice of methodology is not the only way to proceed, but it is necessary if canon law studies seeks to claim with any justification that it can shed light on canon law *as law*. In order to understand what canon law is, canon law studies must have legal methods at its disposal as part of its methodological repertoire. But what is *the* methodology of the law? We cannot really refer to legal methodology as though it were a single concept. This is because questions of legal history, foundation, philosophy, dogma, language, and sociology all require a methodology of their own. Studying the law therefore requires a plurality of methods. This is evident in canon law studies inasmuch as it employs text-hermeneutic and linguistic methods of interpretation for its legal exegesis; employs philosophical and analytical approaches to studying the foundations of canon law, its underlying principles, and the relation between law and justice in its study of legal dogma, theory, and philosophy; employs historical approaches to studying legal history; and employs social theory and social research in its sociology of law to study the social reality of the church and its law.[8] My study is about precisely the latter sociological dimension of canon law studies.

1.3   ...Using Methods of the Sociology of Law

As a sociology of canon law by a canonist, my book is a canon law study and as such a theological endeavour, yet an endeavour using methods taken from the *sociology of law* to gain theological insights. This finding underscores the essential interdisciplinarity of the sociology of canon law as a field of research. Admittedly, this interdisciplinarity might not appear particularly exotic from the perspective of the sociology of law, as this discipline always stands at the intersection between several disciplines: it has links to general sociology, empirical social research, and legal theory. In the following I will therefore outline what these links mean for the sociology of canon law.

1.3.1   The Sociological View of the Law

The first point that I feel compelled to make is that the relationship between the sociology of law and general sociology is a rather fraught one. And it is likewise not easy to draw a clear line between the two. General sociologists tend to look at the

---

[8]On the "non-legal" aspects of canon law studies see also May and Egler (1986, p. 25).

role of the law in their study of groups, such as societies or communities, and to examine the law as a social phenomenon. In contrast to general sociology, the sociology of law has a narrower focus, as it focuses specifically on the law. In this light, legal scholar David Schiff describes the sociology of law as the "sociological study of specific legal phenomenon [sic], e.g. specific legal situations or the social relations associated with certain legal rules".[9] In trying to identify the social significance of the law, sociologists of law tend to focus their attention on the legal system, its professionals ("lawyers, judges, the jury, the officials of a legal system"), and the places of the law ("the court room, the solicitor's office, the jury room"[10]). There are several approaches to exploring the interplay between the law and society from the perspective of the sociology of law. Socio-legal scholar Manfred Rehbinder categorises them as follows: One may either reference legal norms and examine the degree to which they influence group behaviour, or study group behaviour to ask what norms it is based on, or refer to the legal authorities' behaviour and study the institutions responsible for upholding the law in order to identify situations in which the legal authorities react to certain types of social behaviour and sanction breaches of law.[11] Rehbinder finds all of these perspectives important for gaining a sociological understanding of what the law is and how the law functions. However, those often highly focused studies by the sociology of law tend to overlook the interplay between society and the law, as Rehbinder also notes. This interplay is more an issue for general sociology, even though general sociologists tend not to be primarily interested in law. Nevertheless, David Schiff's list of the foremost general sociologists in whose work the law played a significant role includes inter alia Émile Durkheim, Eugen Ehrlich, Max Weber, and Karl Marx.[12] Other names also spring to mind; this certainly not exhaustive list might also include Michel Foucault, Pierre Bourdieu, Niklas Luhmann, and Jürgen Habermas. Schiff believes that if one's intention is truly to comprehend the law, it is necessary to take both perspectives into account, namely the specialist interests of sociologists of law with their focus on legal phenomena, and the study of the law as a normative phenomenon with an enormous impact on society, as undertaken by general sociologists. Scholarly enquiry into the law has always rested, as Schiff states, on a *dual* approach: first, on the question of what constitutes the social ("what is society?"), and, second, on the question of what brings about the legal reality which confronts us as members of social groups ("what is law?").[13]

---

[9] Schiff (1976, p. 294).

[10] Schiff (1976, p. 294).

[11] See Rehbinder (2014, p. 38).

[12] See Schiff (1976, p. 295).

[13] Schiff (1976, p. 297).

1.3.2 Empirical Approaches to the Law

However, delving into the field of the sociology of law, one encounters some disagreement about what constitutes the right approach to this endeavour. One major difference of opinion revolves around the status of *empirical* approaches in the sociology of law. Its theories and methodologies necessarily have to reflect that the sociology of law deals with the reality of law. This explains its interest in empirical social research.[14] Many of its representatives therefore understand the sociology of law as an empirical field of scholarly enquiry which draws on methods used in empirical sociology in order to study the social reality of the law. However, empirical approaches do not necessarily involve *experimental* methods. Legal scholar Martin Shapiro made this point when he described the difficulty of conducting simulated and experimental research on the law under laboratory conditions as the "impossibility of putting laws and nations in test tubes and bubble chambers."[15] In addition, field research methods have also frequently proven inadequate, despite the finding that some sociologists of law such as Rüdiger Lautmann have been successful in demonstrating that participant observation can yield quality results at the highest level. Lautmann's famous study, entitled *Justiz—die stille Gewalt* [*Judiciary—The Silent Force*],[16] in which he documented his observations on the decision-making methods of judges, has become a classic piece of empirical research on adjudication. The study is rare and special as Lautmann, a scholar with both legal and sociological training, was able to conduct his research from his own position as a judge, and was therefore practically invisible as a sociologist for his fellow judges. Lautmann admits that his study would be virtually impossible to replicate under current conditions. Whilst it was possible in the early 1970s for a sociologist and qualified lawyer to work as a judge for a while in order to pursue his research, sociologically trained lawyers today would find it very difficult to occupy the position of a judge for a short period of time, at least in the German judicial system, due to the current terms of recruiting tribunal staff. Sociologist Thorsten Berndt, for instance, who in his 2010 study documented the self-perceptions and self-images prevalent among German judges, could not rely on the method of participant observation to do so, but had to rely on interviews as his method of choice. It is therefore clear that the circumstances of the time play at least some part in determining what is methodologically feasible. These challenges place a burden of responsibility on the sociology of law to identify the most appropriate empirical methods for engaging in empirical research on the reality of the law. Sometimes an

---

[14]E.g. Blankenburg (1975). Blankenburg's volume is a compilation of socio-legal contributions which were written based on the methods of observation, interview, and documentary analysis. On the empirical methods used in the sociology of law see also Carbonnier (1974, pp. 176–195, for documentary analysis, and pp. 196–230, for empirical data collection); Röhl (1987, pp. 105–118); Rehbinder (2014, pp. 48–64); Baer (2021, pp. 279–290).

[15]Shapiro (1981, p. VII).

[16]First edition 1972; second edition 2011.

experimental approach is possible and expedient; sometimes textual analysis and comparative study make more sense. Martin Shapiro shares this view. In his study *Courts* he used comparative law research to examine the idiosyncrasies of various judicial systems. Shapiro, for his part, described his approach as "a substitute for the experimental method"[17]. Whilst admitting the limited effectiveness of this substitute, Shapiro regarded it as without alternative as an experimental approach was not an option for his research.

1.3.3 Law as Doctrine, Law as Practice

The importance of empirical studies might be evident for the sociology of law; yet it is not uncontroversial. Sociological approaches which understand the law primarily as a social practice are clearly drawn to empirical methods. Yet approaches which examine the law primarily as a *doctrine* have trouble warming to them; sociologist of law Jean Carbonnier subsumes these theories from the sociology of law under the heading of "philosophies of the sociology of law".[18] Similar feelings of reticence towards empirical studies are, however, not exclusive to philosophical approaches in the sociology of law, but also exist in legal studies in general. A brief look into legal practice reveals this reticence as well, as most legal practitioners hold sociological knowledge in rather low esteem. Socio-legal scholar Roger Cotterrell, commenting on the results of empirical studies, states that everyday legal life constantly relies on non-legal expert opinions, for instance in the form of medical, psychological, or technical reports; however, lawyers seldom refer to sociological findings and, if they do, they tend to do so with scepticism. Cotterrell suspects the reasons behind this in the fact that the social sciences—in contrast to the other non-legal disciplines which legal studies draw on—cast doubt on legal expertise because they offer a *competing narrative* about social reality, as Cotterrell suggests, "Social scientific and legal knowledge compete in the interpretation of social relationships".[19] Whilst lawyers understand themselves as intermediaries between legal doctrine and social practice, social scientists tend to be more sceptical about the relevance of doctrine as a force for shaping social practice. Cotterrell therefore sees the roots of this conflict between the law and sociology in the tensions between approaches which take a doctrinal view of law, and those which view law primarily as a social practice. However, these antipathies among legal practitioners have not led to their complete loss of interest in the social sciences, according to sociologist Doris Mathilde Lucke. Lucke believes that legal practice operates in two moves. Whilst the law uses its expertise to make itself immune to infiltration by other fields of scholarship, at the same time it also embraces the selective expertise it needs from other fields by drawing that expertise into the legal domain. Hence the law digests external expertise, but in the mode of

---

[17] Shapiro (1981, p. VII).

[18] Carbonnier (1974, p. 21).

[19] Cotterrell (1984, p. 209).

appropriating it. Lucke explains, "In a sophisticated combination of operating a *closed shop* policy in relation to its own knowledge, and keeping an *open source* policy towards outside knowledge, it has become possible for the law to appropriate the knowledge of other disciplines in something akin to annexation and, stripped of its disciplinary identity beyond recognition, to pass it off as its own."[20] Hence, the law overcomes its coyness towards the social sciences, according to Lucke, by assimilating sociological knowledge. However, lawyers tend to take this knowledge seriously only if it appears to be genuinely legal. Sociological knowledge must therefore conceal its sociological roots to find acceptance within the realm of the law. Lucke observes, "The more it conceals its sociological identity, the more sociology increases its potential to bring about change. . . . In the end, the lawyers can then not only say they already knew everything *themselves*, but that they have also—and always—known it *better*."[21]

1.3.4   Dogmatic and Empirical Approaches

The sociology of law is closely aligned with legal studies, and particularly with its subdiscipline of legal theory.[22] The educational backgrounds of socio-legal scholars often reflect this proximity, as many of these scholars happen to have sociological and legal training. Hence, sociologists of law are often also legal scholars.[23] Nevertheless, the relationship between sociology and legal studies is anything but harmonious. Niklas Luhmann speaks of an ambivalence in the relationship between the disciplines.[24] In a similar vein, legal realist Karl Llewellyn notes that it is hard to reconcile the two, stating, "The two realms of thought and discourse mix no more

---

[20] Original quote, "In einer raffinierten Verbindung aus einer—auf das eigene Wissen bezogenen—*closed shop*-Politik—und einer—auf fremdes Wissen bezogenen—*open source*-Politik wurde es . . . möglich, sich das Fachwissen anderer Disziplinen annexionsartig anzueignen und es, seiner fachlichen Identität bis zur Unkenntlichkeit entkleidet, als das ureigene auszugeben", Lucke (2010, p. 83).

[21] Original quote, ". . .entfaltet soziologisches Wissen sein praxisveränderndes Potenzial umso wirkungsvoller, je mehr es seine fachliche Identität verliert. . . . Am Ende haben die Juristen dann nicht nur alles *selbst*, sondern vor allem alles—und zwar immer schon—*besser* gewusst", Lucke (2010, p. 83).

[22] For an approach which conceives of legal philosophy, legal theory, and the sociology of law as being intrinsically interlinked, see Kunz and Mona (2006).

[23] In the revised 2011 edition of his 1972 book *Justiz—die stille Gewalt* [*Judiciary—The Silent Force*] Rüdiger Lautmann describes his own formation as a legal scholar and sociologist and his biographical development as shifting between jurisprudence and sociology. Most fascinatingly, Lautmann asks what influence these two perspectives exerted on his own study. He also recollects the irritations which his dual qualification in law and sociology caused, particularly among other lawyers, see Lautmann (2011, pp. 10–12, 22).

[24] See Luhmann (1986, p. 9).

comfortably than oil and water".[25] We may detect this conflict also by studying the academic backgrounds and self-conceptions of socio-legal scholars within their disciplines. Manfred Rehbinder noted this by stating that it is possible to place sociologists of law into two categories, those who understand themselves more as legal scholars, and those who understand themselves more as sociologists.[26] In a similar vein, Jürgen Habermas identified a dualism between normative and objectivist approaches to the law, which he found highly problematic, noting,

> Tossed to and fro between facticity and validity, political theory and legal theory today are disintegrating into camps that hardly have anything more to say to one another. The tension between normative approaches, which are constantly in danger of losing contact with social reality, and objectivistic approaches, which screen out all normative aspects, can be taken as a caveat against fixating on one disciplinary point of view.[27]

Within legal studies there is some similar disharmony in the field of legal theory, namely between those legal theories which are anchored in legal dogma on the one hand, and legal theories rooted in empirical observations and sociological findings on the other. Doctrinal or dogmatic normative theories of law conceive of the law as a system derived from legal doctrine, as the conceptual result of the rules, principles, and values underlying the law, as Roger Cotterrell explains, stating, "By normative legal theory I mean theory which seeks to explain the character of law solely in terms of the conceptual structure of legal doctrine and the relationships between rules, principles, concepts and values held to be presupposed or incorporated explicitly or implicitly within it".[28] According to normative legal theories, the law arises out of doctrine and only acquires its significance as law in doing so. However, David Schiff rightly points out that the underlying doctrinal basis of legal theorists who argue along these lines is by no means homogenous. It is actually dependent on philosophical decisions such as whether to align oneself with a natural law, positivist, or realist school of thought. Schiff explains the consequences of these differences with regard to normative theories of law by stating,

> Natural law philosophy searches for an a priori legitimacy for legal phenomena and involves studies into the ideas of justice, nature, etc. Positivist legal philosophy involves the study of the identification of legal phenomena, their normative structure and validity in human, if not empirical terms. Realist schools of legal philosophy are concerned with the interpretation of laws in terms of social or psychological facts, replacing the normative by the causal.[29]

However, irrespective of the philosophical approach chosen to establish a doctrine of the law, there is one demerit that all of these approaches share, as Cotterrell maintains. The problem is that all dogmatic approaches towards the law only really hold water if one's viewpoint does not venture beyond the legal system itself, and only really make sense to legal professionals who are participants in the doctrinal

---

[25] Llewellyn (1940, p. 1356).

[26] See Rehbinder (1963, p. 470); see also Carbonnier (1974, pp. 18–20).

[27] Habermas (1996, p. 6); see also Carbonnier (1974, p. 274).

[28] Cotterrell (1983, p. 241).

[29] Schiff (1976, p. 297).

debates about the law. In contrast, empirical theories of law have attempted to study law, including legal doctrine, in its historical context and with regard to its social meaning. Cotterrell explains this approach by noting, "By empirical legal theory I mean theory which seeks to explain the character of law in terms of historical and social conditions and treats the doctrinal and institutional characteristics of law emphasized in normative legal theory as explicable in terms of their social origins and effects".[30] Cotterrell believes that empirical legal theories also permit outside observers to understand aspects of the law without necessarily having participated in the doctrinal debates about the law. The consequence, however, is that empirical legal theories tend to exist at one remove from legal professionals and their practice, even though it is precisely this practice which provides empirical theories of law with a basis for drawing conclusions about the reality of the law.

In arranging legal theories as he does, Cotterrell clearly adopts Luhmann's observation that legal scholars and legal professionals view law from the *inside*, whilst sociologists tend to view it from the *outside*.[31] Whilst legal scholars view law primarily as doctrine, sociologists consider it a social practice. At the same time, however, Cotterrell also points out that Luhmann's interdisciplinary observation has *intra*disciplinary parallels, insofar as it is not only the disciplines of legal studies and sociology that are in dispute about the primacy of doctrine or empirical facts; these fault lines also extend across legal studies and the sociology of law themselves, dividing legal theories or sociologies of law according to whether they prefer a doctrinal or empirical starting point for approaching the law. These conflicts have a history. The problematic relationship between doctrinal approaches and those empirical or sociological approaches more focused on reality were to no small degree influenced by the socio-legal scholars of the past. Eugen Ehrlich, for example, as one of the founders of the sociology of law, provoked doctrinal thinkers in the foreword to his *Fundamental Principles of the Sociology of Law* by claiming that the legally immanent workings of the law, namely legislation, adjudication, and administration are actually fairly immaterial for the development of law.[32] Of far greater influence is society, as Ehrlich claimed. Consequently, the sociology of law, in studying the reality of law, is actually the true scholarly field of legal study, according to Ehrlich.[33] Ehrlich's thesis unleashed a controversy which culminated in a serious confrontation between himself and legal positivist Hans Kelsen in 1915, which became known as the "Kelsen-Ehrlich debate."[34] "Debate," it must be said, is a rather friendly term to describe the fury with which Kelsen responded to Ehrlich's thesis, whereas Ehrlich felt misunderstood and hurt by his fellow disputant's harsh attacks. Their controversy might serve as an emblematic example of the deep rifts

---

[30] Cotterrell (1983, pp. 241–242).

[31] See Luhmann (1986, pp. 19–20; 2004, p. 59); on this subject also Sandberg (2016, pp. 66–77).

[32] See Ehrlich (1936, p. XV).

[33] See Ehrlich (1936, p. 25).

[34] See Kelsen and Ehrlich (2003).

between doctrinal and sociological legal theories. In modern-day legal studies here in Germany, this rivalry plays out primarily to the detriment of the sociological approaches, because legal studies frequently puts more emphasis on normative doctrinal approaches. As a consequence, the sociology of law suffers in the broader landscape of legal studies due to its precarious status in the canon of the various fields of legal study, with their primarily dogmatic footing. In Germany, its relegation to the periphery of legal scholarship is reflected in the training given to law students, in which sociological issues, at present, occupy only a subordinate position.[35] However, cultivating a dualism of doctrinal and sociological legal theories might prove to be detrimental to both approaches, as it might lead to blind spots in knowledge about the reality of the law. It is therefore most interesting to note that for Roger Cotterrell and other scholars seeking to comprehend the reality of the law, dogmatic *and* empirical approaches are equally valuable in the quest to obtain a viable understanding of law. Their mixed approaches contain the idea that those seeking to grasp the law in all its complexity must possess a knowledge of legal doctrine as well as of legal practice. Cotterrell believes that legal theories often suffer from the underrepresentation of one or the other of the two perspectives. He believes the solution to this problem lies in educating legal theorists to be at one and the same time trained experts in doctrine who view the law from the inside, and experts schooled in sociology who view the law from the outside. Cotterrell approaches this duality from a sociological perspective, proposing, "The legal sociologist must become a lawyer in order to challenge or go beyond lawyers' conceptions of law."[36] In addition, giving legal experts a grounding in sociology might prove to be just as expedient. The above-mentioned phenomenon—that many modern-day socio-legal scholars have received a legal and a sociological education—is an opportunity to overcome the mutual suspicions that exist between those who advocate dogmatic approaches, and those who advocate sociological approaches to the law.

1.3.5 Pure or Applied Sociology of Law

One aspect of the debate between legal studies and the sociology of law about whether to start with doctrine or with practice in the process of understanding law has been the long-standing question about what *purpose* is served by seeking to understand the reality of law.[37] The question behind this issue is whether plumbing the depths of legal reality is seen to be a descriptive or a normative undertaking. In research by German-speaking scholars, this is a bone of contention between two approaches, namely the merely descriptive approach of the *sociology of law*—as a

---

[35] See Röhl (1987, p. 1); Machura (2010, pp. 382–383).

[36] Cotterrell (1983, p. 244).

[37] See Rehbinder (1963, pp. 470–471).

distinct socio-legal school—and the normative endeavour of *sociological jurisprudence* in the tradition of Eugen Ehrlich (who nevertheless stated himself that the sociology of law was a mere "science of observation").[38] Jean Carbonnier makes a similar differentiation between the more academic pure sociology of law and the more practical applied sociology of law and tries to find a synthesis between the two, noting—in slightly flamboyant wording—,

> The truth belongs to itself. It may be useless or even detrimental, but does not forfeit an inch of its truthfulness. Therefore, the sociology of law could content itself with being a pure science which finds its raison d'être in its scientific function. But it wants to be more, wants to assume a practical function and to become an applied science. Even more than sociology in general, it has a desire to serve because it finds itself in the situation to socialise with lawyers whose knowledge is fully focused on practice, and who would find it ungraceful to understand jurisprudence as a purely luxurious undertaking.[39]

The approach taken by the sociology of law—or Carbonnier's pure sociology of law—seeks to discover more about the reality of law unimpressed by heteronomous interests such as improving the law. It is mainly a descriptive approach which seeks to comprehend how law and reality are reciprocally pervasive, without deriving any normative claims from its findings.[40] Carbonnier understands it as the task of a pure sociology of law to provide knowledge about law, to explain law, and criticise it.[41] "The sociology of law benefits—itself," writes Niklas Luhmann, adding, "One may hardly expect any benefit from sociology for legal practice."[42]

In contrast, sociological jurisprudence—or the applied sociology of law, according to Carbonnier—serves a normative purpose, namely improving the law, primarily legislation and adjudication, by understanding its social context, meaning, and functioning. Its practical purpose has its roots in the debates surrounding empirical law research ("*Rechtstatsachenforschung*"), with its roots in Eugen Ehrlich's work. Empirical law research enjoys greatest influence in Anglo-American legal circles due to the major relevance of legal practice for the development of common law. The most renowned exponents of sociological jurisprudence include legal scholar Roscoe Pound as well as Supreme Court Justices Oliver Wendell

---

[38] Ehrlich (1936, p. 473).

[39] Original quote, "Das Wahre genügt sich selbst. Mag es auch unnütz oder gar schädlich sein, so verliert es doch keinen Zoll seiner Wahrheit. Die Rechtssoziologie könnte sich folglich damit begnügen, eine reine Wissenschaft zu sein, die eine volle Daseinsberechtigung in ihrer wissenschaftlichen Funktion findet. Sie will aber noch mehr sein, eine praktische Funktion übernehmen und eine angewandte Wissenschaft werden. Sie empfindet sogar in noch viel stärkerem Maße als die allgemeine Soziologie dieses Bedürfnis zu dienen, weil sie von ihrer Lage her gezwungen ist, mit den Juristen zu verkehren, deren Wissenschaft ganz auf die Praxis ausgerichtet ist, und die es als eine Schande empfinden würden, wenn die Jurisprudenz eine reine Luxuswissenschaft wäre", Carbonnier (1974, p. 252); for Carbonnier's definition of pure and applied sociology of law see Carbonnier (1974, pp. 231–290).

[40] See Raiser (2007, p. 7).

[41] See Carbonnier (1974, pp. 235–251).

[42] Original quote, "Die Rechtssoziologie nützt—sich selbst"; "Ein Nutzen für die Rechtspraxis ist von Soziologie kaum zu erwarten", Luhmann (1986, p. 44).

Holmes and Benjamin Cardozo. Their conception of law is primarily functional and instrumental. Law should demonstrate social utility and be judged accordingly. Roscoe Pound, in one of his famous quotes, spoke pointedly of "jurisprudence . . . as a science of social engineering".[43] As a consequence, sociological jurisprudence is not an interpretive sociology in the strict sense of Max Weber,[44] but a school of thought in legal theory which, like other validity theories, seeks to pave the way for the *advancement* of the law. In doing so, however, it does not seek answers in the prepositive normative sphere as prepositive theories of the law do, or in positive law as positivist theories do, but seeks them on a prepositive *descriptive* level. With this in mind, socio-legal scholar Gunther Teubner questions whether sociological juris-prudence can really be considered a sociological field of enquiry or if it is actually more of a genuinely legal field, as Teubner finds, "The constructs of sociological jurisprudence . . . are hybrid creatures which the legal process produces with author-ity borrowed from the social sciences."[45]

1.3.6   Interdisciplinary Fields of Research

As these references show, we may not place the sociology of law within any single discipline without compromising the complexity of its fields of enquiry. In Anglo-American research, therefore, the diverse approaches contributing to the sociology of law are frequently collected under one common heading of *Law and Society* or under the banner of *socio-legal studies*. As collective endeavours of scholars from various backgrounds these fields are proof that socio-legal questions frequently overlap with those of political science, economics, ethnology, anthropology, psy-chology, and the historical sciences. One related cultural studies approach to law is to perceive *law as culture*.[46] Niklas Luhmann was one of the first scholars to point out that law is a generator of culture, noting, "The law is one of the many areas in which social communication not only takes place, but communicates extensively about itself. This creates, to some degree epigenetically, cultural assets, which are consistently in use and being replicated, reproduced, and modified."[47] Legal scholar Bernhard Losch describes the culture that law gives rise to as "that section of the

---

[43] Pound (1923, p. 152).

[44] See Weber (1978).

[45] Original quote, "Die Konstrukte der soziologischen Jurisprudenz . . . sind hybride Kreaturen, die der Rechtsprozeß mit von den Sozialwissenschaften geborgter Autorität produziert", Teubner (1990, p. 140).

[46] E.g. Cotterrell (2004, pp. 1–14); Mezey (2001, pp. 35–67); Gephart (2006); Losch (2006); Witte and Striebel (2015, pp. 161–198); Olson (2017, pp. 233–254); Reimer (2017, pp. 255–270).

[47] Original quote, "Das Recht ist einer der vielen Bereiche, in denen gesellschaftliche Kommunikation nicht nur abläuft, sondern extensiv über sich selbst kommuniziert. Dabei entsteht, epigenetisch gewissermaßen, Kulturgut, das ständig in Gebrauch genommen, repliziert, reproduziert und abgewandelt wird", Luhmann (1986, p. 11).

totality of culture … which contains the elemental and universally valid rules of order and communication which can, where necessary, be compulsorily enforced."[48] Whether his understanding of law as a rule system that can be imposed by force truly bears scrutiny is a discussion which I will take up in Sect. 2.1.6. Nevertheless, Losch does make the indisputable point that law occupies a unique place in cultures. However, viewing law as culture in this way, as Losch continues, poses a twofold challenge. It challenges cultural studies to engage in the cultural criticism of law, and it challenges legal studies to engage in the legal criticism of culture.[49]

1.3.7   *Sociological Research on Canon Law*

Its multidisciplinary embedding gives the sociology of law a particularly high degree of connectivity with other fields, among them the sociology of canon law. However, at the same time, its pluridisciplinarity makes the field of the sociology of law into something of a minefield, as evidenced by the conflicting views mentioned about its methodology and the purpose of its research. So whilst the sociology of law is integrative and unites research methods of different provenance, it also demands that those involved in the debates on the sociology of law clarify their standpoint with regard to their theory and methodology. A similar challenge confronts the sociology of canon law, which must reconcile a sociological approach to law with a normative theory of law. One way of dealing with this dilemma is Roger Cotterrell's proposal, which suggests averting conflicts between sociology and legal studies by entrusting the sociology of law to scholars equipped with both a solid grounding in sociology as well as in law. Placing the sociology of canon law in the hands of researchers versed in sociology and canon law studies would be equally beneficial to canon law studies as it seeks to comprehend the reality of canon law in the light of its normative legal theory and its practical shape. The main stumbling block, however, is the dearth of people equipped with a training in both canon law studies and sociology. Further research on canon law in the nexus between legal dogma and legal practice is therefore much to be desired. The consequence of this state of affairs is that sociological approaches to canon law are scarce. Those few contributions that do exist are frequently sociologists' studies and not authored by canonists; one example is sociologist Simon Hecke's fabulous 2017 book on legislation and the legal structure of canon law.[50] It is worth noting, however, that some canonists—such as Werner Böckenförde, Norbert Lüdecke, and Georg Bier—pursue their work with a sociological bent. Their work on canon law exhibits a clear interest in sociology,

---

[48] Original quote, "denjenigen Ausschnitt aus der Gesamtheit der Kultur …, der die elementaren und allgemeingültigen Ordnungs- und Kommunikationsregeln enthält, die notfalls auch zwangsweise durchgesetzt werden können", Losch (2006, p. 34).

[49] See Losch (2006, pp. 207–230).

[50] See Hecke (2017).

even if this is not their main line of enquiry. Instead of gathering data about the reality of law in the church themselves, these authors are receptive to data from the sociology of religion.[51] As a consequence, they confront the law with reality[52]—however, and even more often, they confront reality with the law.[53] Norbert Lüdecke's most recent book is a profound description of how the German bishops have dealt with the Catholic laypeople's constant demands for church reform which have been voiced repeatedly and with increasing insistence since the Second Vatican Council.[54] Lüdecke explains why many of the lays' present hopes of church reform seem rather futile from the perspective of canon law. He suggests critical Catholics study the law to recognise the structural foundations upon which the church is constructed with the aim of better understanding how the church is shaped by its law and why this connection is so resistant to reform. Whilst Lüdecke himself is very critical of how church authorities have instrumentalised the law to hermetically enclose the church in a way which defies reform, he regards it as his duty as a canonist to explain canon law's function in this respect without imposing his own opinion on others. As a canonist, Lüdecke sees it as his mission to inform his readers about the legal order of the Catholic Church and its functioning without permitting his own opinion to dominate. That is clearly an approach which accords with a descriptive sociology. Hence, even though authors such as Lüdecke and Bier do not explicitly acknowledge the sociological significance of their contributions to a sociology of ecclesiastical institutions, their studies are—upon greater scrutiny—clearly discernible as sociologically relevant. As insights on the interrelationship between the law and the reality of the church, these studies contribute to the sociology of canon law. It would therefore be inaccurate to speak of a sociological vacuum in canon law studies, even if specifically sociological contributions are rare.

1.3.8 Theological and Canonical Considerations

Canonists' reticence to contribute to the sociology of canon law is understandable, as the academic spectrum of canon law studies has only limited connectivity with sociological studies. The sociology of law plays virtually no role in canonists' training. Among the canonical treatises which students of theology and canon law study and which canonists cite as key objects of their research, the sociology of canon law does not appear at all. Canon law studies takes a primarily doctrinal and systematic approach to the legal order of the Catholic Church. Canonical treatises include the study of the seven books of the Code of Canon Law (the main legal

---

[51] E.g. Lüdecke and Bier (2012, p. 93).

[52] E.g. Böckenförde (2006b, p. 147).

[53] E.g. Böckenförde (2006a, pp. 121–124); Lüdecke and Bier (2012, pp. 13–14, 27, 175, 188–189, 191–192, 204, 237–239).

[54] See Lüdecke (2021).

source of global law of the Roman Catholic Church promulgated in 1983; hereinafter abbreviated to: CIC/1983): the general norms of canon law, its constitutional law, sacramental law, the teaching function of the church, property law, penal law, and procedural law. In addition, canon law studies draws on legal theory and legal philosophy by studying the foundations of canon law and legal theology, incorporates an historical perspective on the law by studying the history of canon law, and examines canon law in relation to other legal systems, particularly in relation to the state as expressed in the law of state and church relations. It is therefore most apparent that canon law studies is actually deeply involved in interdisciplinary bridge-building, not least by examining canon law in the context of theological, philosophical, historical, jurisprudential, and comparative approaches to law. This finding makes the absence of a bridge to sociology all the more striking. Most studies in canon law fail to address the aspect of legal reality at all, or deal with it only marginally. This becomes clear upon inspecting the handbooks and introductions to canon law studies. Whilst some of their authors point out that canon law must eventually come to terms with its limited effectiveness in modernity—which is a sociological observation—,[55] most of them pass no comment on this problem and on other sociological issues at all. My remark is only an observation, and not a lament or reproach. And neither do I want to suggest that canonists are careless about or ignorant of the reality of canon law. Admittedly, a small number of canonists give the impression that they are not interested in the reality of canon law because this would call into question the traditional grandeur of canon law and touch upon sensitive areas of their own professional identity. However, I find that most canonists I know do not belong to this group. Most of my colleagues are actually deeply interested in knowing more about the reality of the law which they study. Yet they do not believe this field of enquiry lies within their own professional remit, mostly because we canonists, as mentioned, lack a repertoire of sociological theory and methodology as the result of our limited training. Adding to this is the fact that canonists must overcome a twofold feeling of estrangement before they can engage with sociological issues, as they must endure the same tensions between the more dogmatic and the more sociological approaches to law to which I alluded in my previous considerations. For canon law studies, these tensions are exacerbated by the somewhat problematic relationship between theology and sociology, one of the relics of Neo-Scholastic anti-empiricism, which had a marked effect on canon law studies and continues to influence it today. This problematic Neo-Scholastic inheritance exists throughout the theological disciplines, but is particularly burdensome for the normative theologies, such as moral theology and canon law studies. For canon law theory, the consequence is that it has to date largely drawn its main thoughts and theories from dogmatic theology whilst largely overlooking legal practice, leaving an *empirical* knowledge gap about ecclesiastical practice, but also a theoretical knowledge gap with regard to the theoretical and theological implications of ecclesiastical practice. What significance the legal practice of the

---

[55] E.g. Demel (2014, pp. 21, 45); Brosi (2013, p. 19).

church has for the theory of canon law is therefore largely unanswered. This situation has not changed much despite the church discovering after the Second Vatican Council that ortho*doxy* and ortho*praxy* are inseparable, thereby attributing to ecclesiastical practice a dogmatic significance. So if we assume that the legal practice of the church as part of this larger frame of ecclesiastical practice has dogmatic significance too, it is glaringly obvious that it should become an object of canon law research. With the aim of allowing theology to learn more not only about the practice of the church, but also about the dogmatic value of this practice, theologians have increasingly come to ask themselves over the past couple of years how to go about connecting sociology and theology.[56] Fundamental theologian Magnus Striet, for instance, recently outlined the significance of sociology for theology. Striet finds that it is no longer possible to claim an understanding of social actors without reference to sociology. Insofar as we have to conceive of the church as a social actor and as composed of manifold social actors, we must also learn to analyse the church—in the interests of theology itself—by using a sociological repertoire.[57] As a theological discipline, canon law studies shares this interest. We are therefore invited to rely on sociological theories and methodologies to provide us with a point of access to studying the reality of canon law. In doing so, we acknowledge a conception of canon law which accepts that modern theological thinking must be mindful of orthodoxy and orthopraxy not only to understand practice but to argue convincingly with regard to orthodoxy, too. There is no doorway to orthodoxy without an understanding of practice. Most obviously, the task of reflecting on the connection between doctrine and practice is one which canon law studies cannot leave to other disciplines such as the sociology of religion. Instead, it is an integral part of canon law studies itself as a field of theological research which is committed to understanding the law of the church in the light of modern theology.

1.3.9 Descriptive and Normative Interests

Locating the sociology of canon law within the research landscape of canon law studies also serves to provide an answer, albeit an indirect one, to the question about what purpose we serve by studying the reality of canon law. Both approaches which I have introduced—namely the descriptive approach represented by the sociology of law in a narrower sense which seeks to understand what law is, and the normative approach represented by sociological jurisprudence which seeks to better understand

---

[56] On the relation between theology and sociology see e.g. Striet (2014a); on the significance of empirical approaches for theology see e.g. Müller (2006, pp. 216–220); Campbell-Reed and Scharen (2013, pp. 232–259); on the significance of empirical approaches for *practical* theology see e.g. Werbick (2015, particularly pp. 497–598).

[57] See Striet (2014b, p. 17).

the law itself with the aim of improving it—are legitimate approaches to a sociology of canon law. Furthermore, the two approaches to the sociology of law are not mutually exclusive and may even complement each other, as legal scholar Thomas Raiser convincingly argued.[58] For the sociology of canon law, they might represent two incremental steps, reflecting the dual purpose of a sociology of canon law: Whilst understanding more about the reality of canon law entails utilising the descriptive methods of the sociology of law, the knowledge hereby acquired about the reality of canon law may then serve to constitute the basis for normative considerations. Both steps are of genuine interest to canon law research. Whilst it might be conceivable to locate research on the reality of canon law within the sociology of religion, it would be inconceivable for any discipline other than canon law studies to research the connection between the reality of canon law and its legal theory, doctrine, and norms with its descriptive interest in understanding their relationship better and with its normative thrust towards improving the legal theory, doctrine, and norms based on this knowledge.

1.4 Approaching a Sociology of Canon Law

My book serves as an introduction to the sociology of canon law. Due to its narrow focus, I have limited my study to the *descriptive* concerns of a sociology of canon law. Under the hermeneutic and methodological umbrella of the sociology of law in general, I will take a first step on the path to acquiring a deeper understanding of the legal reality of canon law.

1.4.1 Theories in Monographic Form

A project of this kind can be approached in a number of different ways. In the preface to his textbook *Rechtssoziologie* [*Sociology of Law*] Klaus Röhl, for example, identifies three common approaches to producing a monographic study on the sociology of law.[59] One could, as Niklas Luhmann did most prominently, start by formulating a comprehensive theory and then supplement it with empirical knowledge. One might also start with empirical data and collate empirical research findings irrespective of the plurality of theories underlying them. Or one could gather the diverse approaches to the sociology of law and use them to provide an overview of the academic spectrum of contributions; indeed, this is the approach taken by many

---

[58] See Raiser (2007, p. 8).
[59] See Röhl (1987, p. V).

textbooks on the sociology of law.[60] The second and third approaches are not realistic options in my case. There is currently no established field of a "sociology of canon law" which studies the reciprocal influence of canon law and ecclesiastical reality. Empirical research examining the law of the church is also rare.[61] Hence, there is neither a broad base of sociological theory which may provide a theoretical basis for understanding phenomena of canon law, nor is there a body of empirical data on canon law to be compiled which might deliver greater sociological insights. I have therefore come to the conclusion that developing a comprehensive introduction to the sociology of canon law is only possible at the current time by following the first approach proposed by Röhl and by blending it with the other approaches. Hence, I will attempt to formulate a sociological theory of canon law. I will do so by gathering and discussing theoretical approaches to the sociology of law put forward by other scholars and by referring to the empirical findings procured by others to test the relation of my theory to reality. In doing so, I hope to provide an overview of the relevant questions under discussion in the sociology of law and to show their relevance for canon law and canon law studies. My study therefore sets out to understand what "law" is or can be in church. It surveys the functions of law in church. It asks how ecclesiastical legal institutions contribute to fulfilling these functions. It examines the conditions underlying the legal validity of canon law. It discusses the problems surrounding the ecclesiastical legal subjects' recognition and acceptance of canon law. It studies the phenomenon of compliance and, even more so, of non-compliance. It speculates about the future of a legal order which has been rapidly losing its effectiveness in recent decades. At present, we may ask ourselves whether the canon law of the future, should it exist, will still have a claim to being canon "*law*." We should ask ourselves what conditions have to be met to retain this claim. A sociology of canon law today is well positioned to suggest some answers to these questions already in the here and now.

1.4.2 Learning from Existing Research

It is certainly not my intention to propose an overarching theory such as Luhmann's systems theory. Instead, my work represents a humble experiment which tries to forge, from existing socio-legal research, a sociological theory of canon law which examines the relation between canon law and the reality of the church. To this end, I have surveyed the literature and findings of the sociology of law, which has been

---

[60] E.g. Cotterrell (1984); Röhl (1987); Kunz and Mona (2006); Raiser (2007); Struck (2011); Rehbinder (2014); Baer (2021).

[61] One example from canon law studies is Andreas Weiß's interview-based study of the permanent deaconate, see Weiß (1992), and his unpublished study on judicial decision making in ecclesiastical marriage annulment procedures (see Weiß, 1995). Another example is the empirical study which I conducted together with Thomas Schüller and Christian Wode on the reporting of issues related to canon law in the media: see Hahn et al. (2013a); Hahn (2013b; 2015).

endeavouring to clarify the relationship between law and society for over a hundred years, to establish the degree to which these works may contribute to a better understanding of canon law. Under these circumstances, my approach requires a preliminary remark: Studying the diverse sociologies of the law shows that these studies tend to focus almost exclusively on *state* law. In drawing on them, my approach proceeds from the assumption that the sociology of canon law is capable of learning from studies about state law; I will examine this challenge in greater detail in Sect. 2.2.4. My approach is of course only plausible if one considers canon law and state law to be comparable to some degree. If we understand canon law to be an order which serves the Catholic Church as a religious organisation on a spiritual mission, this begs the question whether there is enough comparable data to compare canon law with law which organises plural societies and secular states. Many idiosyncrasies of canon law might suggest otherwise, as examples might illustrate. Canon law theory, for example, understands canon law as serving the church and its members with regard to their earthly goods, but also with regard to their spiritual well-being and their salvation. Canonical penal law prohibits and sanctions practices which are unacceptable to the faith community and incompatible with a life of faith. These ideas and purposes are fairly alien to secular state law. Because canon law exists to serve a religious community and its very specific purposes, it is not per se evident why a sociology of canon law benefits from sociological studies on state law. Nevertheless, because canon law and state law overlap in many ways, it is fair to assume that mutual learning is possible. One may for instance observe that canon law fulfils similar functions to state law. This is particularly obvious with regard to its functions of creating order and solving conflict. One key commonality that both legal systems share at the foundational level is due to their character *as law*, namely that they are both *positive* laws. Canon law is positive law. Just like state law, it is made by human beings. Although canon law sometimes speaks of "divine law" and refers to norms deriving directly from God, this does not change the fact that positive canon law is the result of human legislation. This is also true for those norms which have their roots in divine law. Their roots may lie in the prepositive realm, but they become positive canon law through processes of human legislation. This characteristic of canon law, that it is positive and human just like all law, allows us to assume that it shares many commonalities with other law, religious and secular alike. This commonality makes it comparable even with modern state law. So while canon law as the law of the church has a markedly different purpose to state law, the two are similar enough in their origins in human legislation, in their structure deriving from this origin, and in their function of providing human groups with order and with access to organised conflict resolution to invite comparison, as I want to suggest. Adding to this is the observation that questions of validity and effectiveness of law are also key issues for canon law, as much of its "success" or "failure" to provide the church with order and with feasible instruments of conflict resolution depends on its legal subjects' willingness to abide by the law. Canon law studies therefore has an interest in understanding the conditions under which legal subjects accept laws and the conditions under which they reject them. It needs to know why individuals abide by the law or disregard it. Identifying these and other similarities between canon law and state law helps us to understand the law of the church. It therefore seems to me both plausible and adequate for a sociology of canon law to learn from the general sociology of law.

1.4.3 Selecting Sociological Theories

My study draws on a number of theoretical works on the sociology of law. Proceeding in this way by building on existing material makes it necessary to identify criteria to determine which approaches to use, and which to set aside. I decided to give approaches consideration based on how well they are suited to understanding canon law *as law*. I did not choose approaches simply because they discuss religious law—very few actually do—but mainly because they do not exclude religious law as a variety of law, whether they discuss it or not. Admittedly, it is a risky strategy upon which to base a discussion on the proposition of canon law being in fact law, as this is already a preliminary decision of a theoretical nature. Approaching the sociology of law in the light of legal theory places the quest for sociological knowledge into a normative mould. But at the same time, it is virtually impossible to avoid such theoretical decisions, as Thomas Raiser finds insofar as he views a dual theoretical framing of the sociology of law as a necessity: on the one hand, the sociology of law, as Raiser states, has always drawn its theory from the theories of general sociology, which enables it to discuss society including its legal dimension.[62] On the other hand, it draws its theory from the theory of law, enabling the sociology of law to discuss law and matters juridical, including the dogmatic background of law.[63] In a similar vein, I allowed myself to be guided by canon law theory in the process of selecting suitable socio-legal approaches for my study. Admittedly, this is a limitation from the outset. Yet this decision seemed necessary if I was to make reliable statements about canon law and its unique legal characteristics. I therefore excluded avowed monistic approaches to the sociology of law, which consistently align the law with statehood. Most certainly, these approaches can be highly instructive about the development of law in modernity. But they are not well suited as a theoretical foundation for understanding non-state law such as the law of religious communities. From my point of view, we may only find a constructive link between the sociology of law and canon law theory in sociological approaches which are at least open to the idea of non-state law. But conversely, selecting sociological theories based on legal theory also means relying on a legal theory which adopts a favourable stance towards the sociology of law. For me, this meant referencing a legal theory which is theoretically open to the sociology of law. In order to meet this requirement, my study draws on a theoretical approach to law which places ecclesiastical practice

---

[62] See also Carbonnier (1974, p. 17).

[63] See Raiser (2007, p. 9).

at the heart of its considerations.[64] As I mentioned above, I am not interested in ecclesiastical reality alone; I also consider practice to be a key contributor to theory-building. Deploying a practice-orientated theory of this kind in order to probe the usefulness of sociological approaches for the purpose of developing a sociology of canon law therefore seems not only possible, but expedient. Knowledge about what theoretically and theologically constitutes the law of the church therefore served as my basis for defining criteria to decide whether a socio-legal theory is suitable for enhancing our understanding of canon law in its interaction with the life of the church.

My study draws on a range of socio-legal contributions including works from legal studies, general sociology, politics, organisation theory, and institutional theory. The two latter perspectives are particularly instructive about the church as an organisation and institution. It would be possible to create an entirely separate sociology of law for the church based on organisation sociology.[65] The church clearly exhibits many characteristics which are typical for organisations, such as bureaucratic consolidation, formalisation, and specialisation. Jurisprudence and law and society scholar Brian Tamanaha observes that these are typical for legal communities taking on an organisational shape in the nineteenth and twentieth centuries, noting, "The shift to regular payment tied to offices, growth of legal education institutions, specialization of legal knowledge, creation of specialized courts, and so on, were not unique to state law but aspects of commensurate developments across society."[66] These typical organisational elements in the field of law are also clearly manifested in the Catholic Church; indeed, some of them have existed for longer in the Catholic Church than in many other religious communities. The typical organisational effects of consolidation, formalisation, and specialisation such as the establishment of professional legal offices, institutions for legal training, and specialised court systems have existed in church at least in some degree since the twelfth century. Organisation theory and sociology therefore have a part to play in my study, even if they are not my primary focus. Neither is my study a comprehensive sociology of canon law *institutions*. As a study which seeks to lay the groundwork for a sociology of canon law, my book does not seek to scrutinise adjudication in church in greater depth, neither does it posit a specialist sociology of ecclesiastical administration or legislation.[67] It goes without saying, however, that the sociology of ecclesiastical legislation does have a role to play in discussing how canon law comes into being. And it is impossible to speak of the practical consequences of canon law without recourse to ecclesiastical adjudication and administration. I will touch upon these topics, but not as an exercise in developing my own institutional theory of canonical institutions. However, future studies might undertake this task.

---

[64] E.g. Hahn (2012a; b; 2014a; b; 2019).

[65] On understanding religious communities as organisations e.g. Petzke and Tyrell (2012); on the organisational challenges of the Catholic Church e.g. Gabriel (1989).

[66] Tamanaha (2017, p. 119).

[67] On this classification in relation to state law see Rehbinder (2014, pp. 135–201).

1.4.4   Learning from Empirical Data

In addition to drawing on existing theoretical works on the sociology of law, my study also draws on the *empirical* findings of others. Whilst their knowledge does not necessarily provide any direct answers to issues of canon law, it does frequently ask the right questions which are relevant for canon law, too. For example, Rüdiger Lautmann's renowned study *Justiz—die stille Gewalt* [*Judiciary—The Silent Force*] does not provide any insights into *ecclesiastical* adjudication and judicial decision making, but it does clarify which questions would be most enlightening to ask of ecclesiastical adjudication, too, and suggests methods which might be useful for the sociology of canon law to study these questions. Because my study is not an empirical study, it does not test any of these empirical methods, nor does it provide any answers to questions asked of canon law which require an empirical mode of enquiry. Instead, my study is merely a starting point which provides a theoretical basis for future empirical projects that aim to address these issues. In my study, the survey of empirical studies procured by other scholars primarily serves to establish the plausibility of my theoretical findings. Empirical findings might help to determine the degree to which a theory relates to reality. In my book, empirical studies from the sociology of law fulfil this test function of determining the degree to which my sociological theory on canon law relates to the legal reality in church. Empirical studies of the sociology of religion and, in particular, of church sociology, fulfil a similar function. These studies, which examine the life of the church, frequently touch upon legal aspects of ecclesiastical life, too.[68] They address matters of legal relevance, even if they do not study the law *as law* but as a part of the social reality of the church. These studies are therefore a rich source of knowledge for the sociology of canon law.

Distilling the relevant information from them is sometimes an arduous process, albeit a rather insightful one. The following finding might serve as an example. It derives from the famous empirical study on American Catholicism *American Catholics Today*, prepared by a group of church sociologists; I will discuss the study in greater detail in Sect. 5.2.3. *American Catholics Today* examined a number of issues including the degree to which Catholics in the United States agree with the magisterial teachings on sex and gender and ecclesiastical marriage and family doctrine.[69] The study showed that the vast majority of respondents *did not* endorse the magisterium's teachings. For the sociology of canon law, which examines the reception of *legal* norms, these findings on the acceptance of *moral* norms are most interesting. We cannot, however, simply take these findings on the church members' non-endorsement and non-compliance of moral norms out of their context and readily apply them to the law. Yet there is reason to suspect that this knowledge of the Catholics' stance towards ecclesiastical moral norms tells us something about their handling of legal norms as well. The scepticism of many church members

---

[68] E.g. D'Antonio et al. (2007); MDG-Trendmonitor (2010; 2021).

[69] See D'Antonio et al. (2007, pp. 95–104).

towards the official church's moral standards suggests that there is also a low level of acceptance of legal norms, particularly of those which have received much public criticism. *American Catholics Today* does not provide any empirical data to prove this claim exactly. But it does provide empirical data on moral norms which allow for an educated guess with regard to legal norms. In a similar vein, in the newest MDG-Trendmonitor of 2021, a huge empirical study on Catholicism in Germany, 70% of Catholics questioned in representative interviews stated that they find the church tends to stick with outdated norms.[70] Yet again, the study makes no particular mention of *legal* norms. Nevertheless, it does provide us with some hints how German Catholics at present perceive of canon law. Hence, while studies in church sociology do not usually provide direct results for the sociology of canon law, they often provide us with strong indicators of the legal reality in church. They are therefore of indispensable help in demonstrating the plausibility of my sociological theory, which I will elaborate in the following.

Bibliography

Aymans, W. (1995). Die wissenschaftliche Methode der Kanonistik. In W. Aymans (Ed.), *Kirchenrechtliche Beiträge zur Ekklesiologie* (Kanonistische Studien und Texte 42). Duncker & Humblot.

Aymans, W., & Mörsdorf, K. (1991). *Kanonisches Recht: Lehrbuch aufgrund des Codex Iuris Canonici, vol 1: Einleitende Grundfragen und Allgemeine Normen.* Ferdinand Schöningh.

Baer, S. (2021). *Rechtssoziologie: Eine Einführung in die interdisziplinäre Rechtsforschung* (4th ed.). Nomos.

Berndt, T. (2010). *Richterbilder: Dimensionen richterlicher Selbsttypisierungen.* Springer.

Blankenburg, E. (Ed.). (1975). *Empirische Rechtssoziologie.* Piper.

Böckenförde, W. (2006a). Neuere Tendenzen im katholischen Kirchenrecht: Divergenz zwischen normativem Geltungsanspruch und faktischer Geltung. In N. Lüdecke & G. Bier (Eds.), *Freiheit und Gerechtigkeit in der Kirche: Gedenkschrift für Werner Böckenförde* (Forschungen zur Kirchenrechtswissenschaft 37, pp. 111–131). Echter.

Böckenförde, W. (2006b). Zur gegenwärtigen Lage in der römisch-katholischen Kirche: Kirchenrechtliche Anmerkungen. In N. Lüdecke & G. Bier (Eds.), *Freiheit und Gerechtigkeit in der Kirche: Gedenkschrift für Werner Böckenförde* (Forschungen zur Kirchenrechtswissenschaft 37, pp. 143–158). Echter.

Brosi, U. (2013). *Recht, Strukturen, Freiräume: Kirchenrecht* (Studiengang Theologie 9, überarbeitet und mit einem Beitrag zum deutschen Staatskirchenrecht ergänzt von I. Kreusch). Theologischer Verlag Zürich.

Campbell-Reed, E. R., & Scharen, C. (2013). Ethnography on holy ground: How qualitative interviewing is practical theological work. *International Journal of Practical Theology, 17,* 232–259.

Carbonnier, J. (1974). *Rechtssoziologie* (Schriftenreihe zur Rechtssoziologie und Rechtstatsachenforschung 31). Duncker & Humblot.

Cattaneo, A. (1993). Die Kanonistik im Spannungsfeld von Theologie und Rechtswissenschaft: Zur gegenwärtigen Diskussion über Epistemologie und Methode der Kirchenrechtswissenschaft. *Archiv für katholisches Kirchenrecht, 162,* 52–64.

---

[70] See MDG-Trendmonitor (2021, p. 46).

Corecco, E. (1994). Theologie des Kirchenrechts. In L. Gerosa & L. Müller (Eds.), *Ordinatio fidei: Schriften zum kanonischen Recht* (pp. 3–16). Ferdinand Schöningh.

Cotterrell, R. (1983). The sociological concept of law. *Journal of Law & Society, 10*, 241–255.

Cotterrell, R. (1984). *The sociology of law: An introduction.* Butterworths.

Cotterrell, R. (2004). Law in culture. *Ratio Juris, 17*, 1–14.

D'Antonio, W. V., Davidson, J. D., Hoge, D. R., & Gautier, M. L. (2007). *American catholics today: New realities of their faith and their church.* Rowman and Littlefield.

Demel, S. (2012). Wer interpretiert wen? Der Codex Iuris Canonici als „Krönung" des Konzils. *Herder Korrespondenz*, special issue 2, October 2012, 13–18.

Demel, S. (2014). *Einführung in das Recht der katholischen Kirche: Grundlagen—Quellen— Beispiele* (Einführung Theologie). Wissenschaftliche Buchgesellschaft.

Doe, N. (1992). Toward a critique of the role of theology in English ecclesiastical and canon law. *Ecclesiastical Law Journal, 2*, 328–346.

Ehrlich, E. (1936). *Fundamental principles of the sociology of law* (W. L. Moll, Trans., with an introduction by R. Pound). The Harvard University Press.

Eichmann, E., & Mörsdorf, K. (1964). *Lehrbuch des Kirchenrechts auf Grund des Codex Iuris Canonici, vol 1: Einleitung, Allgemeiner Teil und Personenrecht* (11th ed.). Ferdinand Schöningh.

Fürst, C. G. (1977). Vom Wesen des Kirchenrechts. *Communio, 6*, 496–506.

Gabriel, K. (1989). Möglichkeiten und Grenzen kirchlicher Organisation in der individualisierten Gesellschaft. In Schweizerisches Pastoralsoziologisches Institut (Ed.), *Konfessionelle Religiosität: Chancen und Grenzen* (pp. 52–67). NZN.

Gephart, W. (2006). *Recht als Kultur: Zur kultursoziologischen Analyse des Rechts* (Studien zur europäischen Rechtsgeschichte 209). Klostermann.

Graulich, M. (2006). *Unterwegs zu einer Theologie des Kirchenrechts: Die Grundlegung des Rechts bei Gottlieb Söhngen (1892–1971) und die Konzepte der neueren Kirchenrechtswissenschaft.* Ferdinand Schöningh.

Habermas, J. (1996). *Between facts and norms: Contributions to a discourse theory of law and democracy* (W. Rehg, Trans.). The MIT Press.

Hahn, J. (2012a). "Gesetz der Wahrheit": Rechtstheoretische Überlegungen im Anschluss an aktuelle päpstliche Äußerungen zur Rechtsbegründung. *Archiv für katholisches Kirchenrecht, 181*, 106–128.

Hahn, J. (2012b). Die Ansprache des Papstes im Deutschen Bundestag: Gedankenanstoß für Überlegungen zur Kirchenrechtsbegründung. In G. Essen (Ed.), *Verfassung ohne Grund? Die Rede des Papstes im Bundestag* (Theologie kontrovers, pp. 91–105). Herder.

Hahn, J. (2014a). Lehramt und Glaubenssinn: Kirchenrechtliche Überlegungen zur einer spannungsreichen Verhältnisbestimmung—aus aktuellem Anlass. In M. Knapp & T. Söding (Eds.), *Glaube in Gemeinschaft: Autorität und Rezeption in der Kirche* (pp. 182–212). Herder.

Hahn, J. (2014b). Recht verstehen: Die Kirchenrechtssprache als Fachsprache—rechtslinguistische Probleme und theologische Herausforderung. In T. Schüller & M. Zumbült (Eds.), *Iustitia est constans et perpetua voluntas ius suum cuique tribuendi* (Beihefte zum Münsterischen Kommentar 70, pp. 163–198). Wingen.

Hahn, J. (2015). Zwischen Wirken und Wirkung: Die Kirche—Glaubensgemeinschaft in Rechtsgestalt in der Medienöffentlichkeit. In J. Rist (Ed.), *Staat und Kirche: Über Geschichte, Konzeption und Praxis eines spannungsreichen Verhältnisses* (Theologie im Kontakt, Neue Folge 2, pp. 147–165). Aschendorff.

Hahn, J. (2019). *Church law in modernity: Toward a theory of canon law between nature and culture* (Cambridge Law and Christianity). Cambridge University Press.

Hahn, J., Schüller, T., & Wode, C. (2013a). *Kirchenrecht in den Medien.* UVK.

Hahn, J., Schüller, T., & Wode, C. (2013b). Kirchenrecht in den Medien: Analyse der Berichterstattung in den Nachrichtensendungen von ARD und ZDF. *Communicatio Socialis, 46*, 479–493.

Hecke, S. (2017). *Kanonisches Recht: Zur Rechtsbildung und Rechtsstruktur des römisch-katholischen Kirchenrechts.* Springer.

Hervada, J. (2004). *Pesamientos de un Canonista en la hora presente* (2nd ed.). Navarra Gráfica Ediciones.

Kelsen, H., & Ehrlich, E. (2003). *Rechtssoziologie und Rechtswissenschaft: Eine Kontroverse (1915/17)* (Juristische Zeitgeschichte, Kleine Reihe 7, mit einer Einführung von K. Lüderssen). Nomos.

Kunz, K.-L., & Mona, M. (2006). *Rechtsphilosophie, Rechtstheorie, Rechtssoziologie: Eine Einführung in die theoretischen Grundlagen der Rechtswissenschaft.* UTB.

Lautmann, R. (2011). *Justiz—die stille Gewalt: Teilnehmende Beobachtung und entscheidungssoziologische Analyse* (2nd ed.). Springer.

Llewellyn, K. N. (1940). The normative, the legal, and the law jobs: The problem of juristic method. *Yale Law Journal, 49,* 1355–1400.

Losch, B. (2006). *Kulturfaktor Recht: Grundwerte—Leitbilder—Normen.* Böhlau.

Lucke, D. M. (2010). "Unwissenheit schützt vor Strafe nicht:" Wissen und Wirkung im Recht. In G. Wagner (Ed.), *Kraft Gesetz: Beiträge zur rechtssoziologischen Effektivitätsforschung* (pp. 65–90). Springer.

Lüdecke, N. (2021). *Die Täuschung: Haben Katholiken die Kirche, die sie verdienen?* Wissenschaftliche Buchgesellschaft.

Lüdecke, N., & Bier, G. (2012). *Das römisch-katholische Kirchenrecht: Eine Einführung* (unter Mitarbeit von B. S. Anuth). Kohlhammer.

Luhmann, N. (1986). *Die soziologische Beobachtung des Rechts.* Suhrkamp.

Luhmann, N. (2004). *Law as a social system* (Oxford socio-legal studies, F. Kastner, R. Nobles, D. Schiff & R. Ziegert, Eds., K. A. Ziegert, Trans.). Oxford University Press.

Luhmann, N. (2014). *A sociological theory of law* (M. Albrow, Ed., E. King-Utz & M. Albrow, Trans.). Routledge.

Machura, S. (2010). Rechtssoziologie. In G. Kneer & M. Schroer (Eds.), *Handbuch Spezielle Soziologien* (pp. 379–392). Springer.

May, G. (1999). Kirchenrechtswissenschaft und Kirchenrechtsstudium. In J. Listl & H. Schmitz (Eds.), *Handbuch des katholischen Kirchenrechts* (2nd ed., pp. 90–101). Pustet.

May, G., & Egler, A. (1986). *Einführung in die kirchenrechtliche Methode.* Pustet.

MDG-Trendmonitor. (2010). *Religiöse Kommunikation 2010, Kommentarband I: Erkenntnisse zur Situation von Kirche und Glaube sowie zur Nutzung medialer und personaler Informations- und Kommunikationsangebote der Kirche im Überblick. Ergebnisse repräsentativer Befragungen unter Katholiken sowie der Gesamtbevölkerung* (im Auftrag der MDG Medien-Dienstleistung GmbH durchgeführt vom Institut für Demoskopie Allensbach in Zusammenarbeit mit Sinus Sociovision, Heidelberg). MDG Medien-Dienstleistung GmbH.

MDG-Trendmonitor. (2021). *Religiöse Kommunikation 2020/21: Einstellungen, Zielgruppen, Botschaften und Kommunikationskanäle* (im Auftrag der MDG Medien-Dienstleistung GmbH durchgeführt vom Institut für Demoskopie Allensbach, Sinus Markt- und Sozialforschung GmbH). Herder.

Mezey, N. (2001). Law as culture. *Yale Journal of Law & the Humanities, 13,* 35–67.

Müller, K. (2006). Vox Dei? Zum theologischen Status von Umfragen. *Lebendige Seelsorge, 57,* 216–220.

Neudecker, G. (2013). *Ius sequitur vitam—Der Dienst der Kirchengerichte an der Lebendigkeit des Rechts: Zugleich ein Beitrag zur Vergleichung des kanonischen und staatlichen Rechtssystems* (Tübinger Kirchenrechtliche Studien 13). LIT.

Olson, G. (2017). Introduction: Mapping the pluralist character of cultural approaches to law. *German Law Journal, 18*(2), 233–254.

Ombres, R. (2016). Justice and Mercy: Canon law and the sacrament of penance. In F. Cranmer, M. Hill, C. Kenny & R. Sandberg (Eds.), *The confluence of law and religion: Interdisciplinary reflections on the work of Norman Doe* (pp. 131–143). Cambridge University Press.

Petzke, M., & Tyrell, H. (2012). Religiöse Organisationen. In M. Apelt & V. Tacke (Eds.), *Handbuch Organisationstypen* (pp. 275–306). Springer.

Pound, R. (1923). *Interpretations of legal history*. The Macmillan Company.

Raiser, T. (2007). *Grundlagen der Rechtssoziologie* (4th ed.). UTB.

Rehbinder, M. (1963). Max Webers Rechtssoziologie: Eine Bestandsaufnahme. In R. König & J. Winckelmann (Eds.), *Max Weber zum Gedächtnis: Materialien und Dokumente zur Bewertung von Werk und Persönlichkeit* (pp. 470–488). Westdeutscher Verlag.

Rehbinder, M. (2014). *Rechtssoziologie: Ein Studienbuch* (8th ed.). C. H. Beck.

Reimer, F. (2017). Law as culture: Culturalist perspectives in legal theory and theory of methods. *German Law Journal, 18*(2), 255–270.

Röhl, K. F. (1987). *Rechtssoziologie: Ein Lehrbuch*. Heymann.

Sandberg, R. (2016). A sociological theory of law and religion. In F. Cranmer, M. Hill, C. Kenny & R. Sandberg (Eds.), *The confluence of law and religion: Interdisciplinary reflections on the work of Norman Doe* (pp. 66–77). Cambridge University Press.

Sanders, F. (2000). Theologie + Rechtswissenschaft = Kirchenrecht? In A. Leinhäupl-Wilke & M. Striet (Eds.), *Katholische Theologie studieren: Themen und Disziplinen* (Theologische Einführungen 1, pp. 380–397). LIT.

Schiff, D. N. (1976). Socio-legal theory: Social structure and law. *The Modern Law Review, 39*, 287–310.

Shapiro, M. (1981). *Courts: A comparative and political analysis*. The University of Chicago Press.

Striet, M. (2014a). *"Nicht außerhalb der Welt": Theologie und Soziologie* (Katholizismus im Umbruch 1). Herder.

Striet, M. (2014b). Sich selbst als geworden beschreiben wollen: Theologie und Soziologie. In M. Striet (Ed.), *"Nicht außerhalb der Welt": Theologie und Soziologie* (Katholizismus im Umbruch 1, pp. 13–32). Herder.

Struck, G. (2011). *Rechtssoziologie: Grundlagen und Strukturen*. Nomos.

Tamanaha, B. Z. (2017). *A realistic theory of law*. Cambridge University Press.

Teubner, G. (1990). Die Episteme des Rechts: Zu erkenntnistheoretischen Grundlagen des reflexiven Rechts. In D. Grimm (Ed.), *Wachsende Staatsaufgaben—sinkende Steuerungsfähigkeit des Rechts* (pp. 115–154). Nomos.

Weber, M. (1978). *Economy and society: An outline of interpretive sociology* (G. Roth & C. Wittich, Eds.). University of California Press.

Weiß, A. (1992). *Der Ständige Diakon: Theologisch-kanonistische und soziologische Reflexionen anhand einer Umfrage*. Echter.

Weiß, A. (1995). *Wahr und gerecht? Studien zur Theorie und Praxis richterlicher Entscheidungsfindung im kirchlichen Ehenichtigkeitsprozess* (Habilitation thesis, Faculty of Catholic Theology, unpublished). University of Tübingen.

Werbick, J. (2015). *Theologische Methodenlehre*. Herder.

Witte, D., & Striebel, C. (2015). Recht und Macht bei Bourdieu und Foucault, oder: Wie selbst aufgeklärte Machtanalysen des Rechts dessen Kulturalität ausblenden. *Sociologia Internationalis, 53*, 161–198.

Chapter 2
Law Through the Lens of Sociology

Abstract Religious law such as canon law is studied best by applying a pluralist theory of the law which, besides the states, accepts other groups—such as confederations of states, contracting parties, or religious communities—as producers of law. However, applying the concept of legal pluralism requires clarification about what constitutes "the law." Niklas Luhmann understood law as those communications operating on the basis of the binary code "legal"/"illegal". Creating "law", according to Luhmann, is the process of institutionalising those expectations concerning what constitutes "legal" behaviour. Luhmann's approach may be connected with others which understand the law as a certain kind of doctrine rooted in and connected with institutions. Whilst all normativities share doctrinal qualities, it is only the law which employs institutions to provide for doctrinal consistency and, most importantly, the justiciability of its doctrines.

Keywords Legal monism · Legal pluralism · Max Weber · Coercion · Niklas Luhmann · Systems theory · Behavioural expectation · Doctrine · Knowledge system · Institution · Justiciability

It is the task of the sociology of law to study the law and how it engages with the social reality of a group. With this in mind, it is worth recalling David Schiff's observation that socio-legal scholars must always be at pains to answer two questions at once: one pertaining to *society*, and one pertaining to its *law*.[1] It is the task of sociologists of law to study the influence of law on the social life of groups, such as societies or communities, as well as the influence of social reality on the law. Whilst the one explores the organisation and control of a social group by and through law, the other examines the social conditions within which the law comes into being and evolves. This also points at the connection between law and *power*, which I will discuss in Sect. 4.1.

---

[1] See Schiff (1976, p. 297).

2.1 Sociological Views of the Law

In order to study law and how it interacts with the social life of a group, it is first necessary to study the social reality in which one believes the law to reside, in order to clarify which phenomena are encompassed by "law." This includes the process of identifying the social group whose normative order it is that constitutes the law, thereby identifying the legal community which is integrated by law. The sociology of law identifies a number of different ways by which groups can qualify as legal communities. As a consequence, sociology understands "law" in several different ways.[2]

2.1.1 Legal Monism and Pluralism

Exponents of a *monistic* understanding of the law consider there to be a single source of norms we call "law," namely the state. According to monistic theories, in modernity the state is the only source of norms of a truly legal nature; we may therefore also speak of an etatist concept of the law.[3] A monistic-etatist definition of "law" therefore excludes all legal phenomena from "law" which originate from non-state agents, such as religious communities. Contributions by canonists arguing that canon law is indeed "law" can therefore be seen as ripostes to monistic incursions. Their arguments have left their mark on the theory of canon law.[4] The debate about the nature of canon law primarily revolves around the question about whether it is possible, when speaking of canon law, to speak of "law" in a *proper* sense or whether it is necessary to speak of it in an *analogous* sense.[5] Understanding canon law as analogous law can mean two different things, as canonist Ludger Müller observed.[6] It might on the one hand mean understanding it as analogous to state law. In this case, state law constitutes a univocal concept of law; canon law then exists analogously to this concept. Canonist Antonio Rouco Varela notes, for example, that canon law shares many characteristics with state law, so drawing an analogy seems possible. Speaking of the "law" of the church is therefore justified and necessary, according to Rouco Varela.[7] On the other hand, explains Müller, one

---

[2] See Cotterrell (1983, pp. 244–247); Röhl (1987, pp. 212–222).

[3] See Röhl (1987, p. 219).

[4] E.g. Sobański (1986, pp. 3–15).

[5] E.g. Müller (1991); Orsy (1992, pp. 141–142); Rouco Varela and Corecco (1998, particularly pp. 62–79).

[6] See Müller (1991, p. 13).

[7] See Rouco Varela and Corecco (1998, pp. 64, 74–76). However, somewhat contrary to this statement Rouco Varela also calls canon law a law "sui generis." It would be misleading to understand canon law as a further specimen of the genus "law" to which state law also belongs. Instead, it would be more adequate to understand it as a proper law of its own see Varela and Corecco (1998, pp. 64, 73).

might understand "law" itself as an analogous concept in order to use it as an umbrella term for all legal practices which we might then also refer to as "law."[8] Such an approach understands state law and canon law in the same way as analogous law, because they are both analogies based on the analogous concept of "law." Müller, however, rejects both positions. He believes canon law is not analogous law.[9] This is because claiming such would impute that canon law is essentially different to law in general. Instead, canon law is true law, according to Müller, albeit with its own unique characteristics. Müller finds canon law to be a law *sui generis* and a true realisation of "law," just like all other forms of law such as state law, contract law, or international law.[10] His premise is that the concept of law is univocal because it contains the essential *DNA* of law which is common to all legal systems. At the same time, he also concedes that this DNA is difficult to define, and that it requires interdisciplinary dialogue between legal studies, philosophy, and theology to clarify what actually constitutes the DNA of "law."[11] I find Müller's position rather plausible from the perspective of legal theory. Whilst I agree that it is difficult to define what makes the law (I will attempt a definition in the course of this section), plausible definitions do exist, I find, which allow us to assemble different legal traditions into a single univocal concept of "law." However, settling the discussion on the true or analogous legal character of canon law for canon law legal theory is not of critical importance for my study, because my book focuses on the sociology of law and not on legal theory. In this study, I can therefore leave the question aside as to whether it is more convincing to understand canon law as law in a true or analogous sense. In venturing beyond this theoretical issue, it is of interest from the perspective of the sociology of canon law to note that, irrespective of whether one understands there to be a univocal or analogous general concept of "law," both approaches seek to reject the monistic claim to a concept of "law" that is solely fulfilled by state law. Insofar as both approaches understand the general concept of "law" as being superior to canon law *and* state law, they actually support canonical approaches which seek to correct the monistic claim of state law which has become dominant in some fields of legal discourse.

It is most helpful to note, in any case, that canon law studies is not alone in contesting the limitations that go along with monistic claims. In this endeavour canon law studies is supported by many voices from the sociology of law. Eugen Ehrlich, one of the founding fathers of the sociology of law, was an early critic of monistic reductionism, stating that it seriously misjudged not only religious law but also other phenomena of non-state law.[12] Ehrlich was keen to point out that "law" develops and unfolds independently of state intervention. He believed in a *pluralist* concept of the law which included other groups besides the state as producers of

---

[8]E.g. Corecco (1981, pp. 435–436).

[9]See Müller (1991, p. 116).

[10]See Müller (1991, p. 1170); see also Rouco Varela and Corecco (1998, p. 64).

[11]See Müller (1991, p. 118).

[12]See Ehrlich (1936, pp. 15–16).

legal norms. We might think of the law of confederations of states, of contract law, which emerges from an agreement between contracting parties, of legal customs which crystallise into customary law, or of the laws of religious groups that unite the members of religious faith communities.[13] Just because the law that emerges from these various agents and in these various groups is highly heterogeneous does not mean that it has nothing in common, as the legal scholar Otto von Gierke already argued at the beginning of the twentieth century. Despite the obvious differences between the producers of legal norms, von Gierke observed that if one "scrutinises social beings with the eye of legal studies, one may discover a common basic principle of legal structuring permeating all social law."[14] Von Gierke's thesis, which already enjoyed prominence in the socio-legal debates of the twentieth century, has been gaining currency in recent years. This is because the sociology of law, as a consequence of globalisation, has observed a pluralisation of the law in various social spaces.[15] It is noticeable in the way international law has infiltrated into state law, for example in questions of human rights, or in the superimposition of transnational or international law onto national law, as in the field of commercial and business law. At the same time, the debate about the status of particular law in national legal systems is becoming increasingly topical, for example with respect to the role of indigenous law in national law or in the discussion about integrating religious laws into secular legal systems in the context of the migration debate.[16] In short, legal pluralism is a factor which will come to play an increasingly important role in an increasingly globalised world. As Gunther Teubner states, this has recently served to add some weight to the theory of legal pluralism. Whilst the theory started out by examining colonial law and the law of colonised groups, the focus has now changed to prioritise the legal structures of different ethnic, cultural, and religious groups within the modern nation states.[17] Nowadays, the main focus of legal pluralism is on legal phenomena at the global level. Nevertheless, my study is primarily interested in legal pluralism on a more local level, namely the phenomenon of religious law embedded in the legal systems of modern states. However, as Roman Catholic canon law claims global validity for Catholics across the world, studying the reality of canon law through a sociological lens requires both to focus on global and local issues by asking how local Catholics process global canon law to become a legal reality at the local level.

---

[13] E.g. Gurvitch (1960, pp. 41–42); Schiff Berman (2005, pp. 1105–1145).

[14] Original quote, "bei der rechtswissenschaftlichen Betrachtung der gesellschaftlichen Lebewesen ein gemeinsames Grundprinzip der juristischen Struktur zu erkennen, das sich durch alles Sozialrecht zieht", Gierke (1902, p. 33); from today's point of view with regard to supra-, trans-, and subnational law see Schiff Berman (2005, p. 1111).

[15] E.g. Voigt (1999/2000); Schiff Berman (2005, pp. 1105–1145); Tamanaha (2017, particularly pp. 151–193).

[16] E.g. Reuter (2014); Bottoni et al. (2016); Wittreck (2016); Schuppert (2017).

[17] See Teubner (1996, p. 257).

2.1.2 Ubi communitas ibi ius

"*Ubi societas ibi ius*" is an ancient proverbial phrase expressing the finding that societies generate their own legal orders even when they are not organised into sovereign states. Canonists of the *Ius Publicum Ecclesiasticum* absorbed this idea into canon law theory. Members of this school argued that the church, as an institution with quasi-state power, naturally has a legal structure. When the church had to constrain its quasi-state-like ambitions in the twentieth century, the approach of the *Ius Publicum Ecclesiasticum* lost some of its plausibility. Nevertheless, although the church was not able to prevail in its power struggle against the modern nation states, the axiom of "*ubi societas ibi ius*" has lost none of its power of persuasion. Instead, the axiom continues to provide food for thought in the present debates on what constitutes the law. It is particularly in the light of current approaches such as legal pluralism where it is most relevant. Whilst we might not conceive of all ethnic, cultural, or religious groups as "societies," we might perceive them as groups structuring their communal life with norms of a legal nature. Hence, if we look out for legal phenomena, we may discover an essential tendency not only in societies but also in communities—following Ferdinand Tönnies's differentiation—,[18] to create order in the form of legal structuring. In light of this finding, "*ubi societas ibi ius*" has not lost its plausibility, and simply needs broadening into "*ubi communitas ibi ius*."

Ius Publicum Ecclesiasticum's rereading of "*ubi societas ibi ius*" implies a closeness to the natural law doctrine of the church, as it suggests understanding the production of "law" as a "natural" inclination among groups. It conceives of the inclination to create law as a natural aspect of human social interaction. This ecclesiastical theory enjoys some support in secular theory. Niklas Luhmann, for instance, makes an observation with similar implications, stating, "Like knowledge, law emerges in a rudimentary form in all social systems, without recourse to the official law posited and sanctioned by the state—thus in organizations, families, groups that exchange postage stamps, neighborhood relationships, and so on. No system can manage cognitive or normative expectations for any length of time without knowledge and law emerging."[19] If we follow Ehrlich, Luhmann, and others, and accept that we are indeed dealing with "law" in manifold expressions of social norms, then this lends weight to the theory of legal pluralism which accepts that "law" is also created by a significant number of non-state agents in parallel to state law. The way we look at these plural versions of law is however frequently skewed, states Brian Tamanaha, because legal theory in particular—in its quest to discover what constitutes "*the* law"—misleadingly insinuates that law is a *single* object. Contrary to that proposition, Tamanaha remarks,

---

[18] See Tönnies (2001).

[19] Luhmann (1995, p. 331).

Thus posed in singular terms, theorists have striven to find a set of elements for a single correct notion of law, their minds closed to the possibility that there might be multiple forms of law. . . . There are multiple manifestations of law, each with a collection of characteristics, none essential or necessary, and much variation amongst them. One must be open to a multiplicity of conventionally recognized forms of law to see this.[20]

2.1.3   Spatial and Individual Pluralism

If we assume that there are indeed multiple forms of law, we may come to find that legal subjects are not solely the addressees of a single legal order, but are regularly the subjects of multiple laws. There is both a plurality of law with regard to *space*, where legal subjects are confronted with the demands of various legal orders in spaces in which several jurisdictions overlap, and a plurality of law with regard to personal affiliation, inasmuch as legal subjects are confronted with the demands of plural legal orders as a consequence of their various different roles, as citizens, as members of religious communities, and as insurance policyholders.[21] Canonist Silvio Ferrari recently stated that some tensions that exist between state law and religious law may result from the fact that state law is largely organised based on the principle of territoriality, while religious communities tend to subject their members to their law personally, that is with regard to their capacity as members of the respective community.[22] This observation is certainly true for canon law. Whilst canon law also relies heavily on the principle of territoriality when organising the inner structure of the church, it initially addresses its subjects as *members* of the church and, thus, as persons belonging to the church as a religious community (e.g. canons 11, 96, 205 CIC/1983).

The sociological considerations on legal pluralism are also helpful for determining the status of canon law in its relationship with other legal orders. A pluralist understanding of law lends itself well to a sociological study of canon law. It makes it possible to understand the church as a producer of law. And it allows the study of canon law in parallel to other legal orders to which it has a sometimes constructive, sometimes conflictive relation. Legal scholar Gary F. Bell surveyed this relationship in an enlightening contribution about the status of Roman Catholic canon law in Singapore. He examined the mostly harmonious co-existence of the two legal orders, but also the potential conflicts between state law and canon law in the light of the pluralist paradigm.[23] This paradigm permits us to understand the members of the Roman Catholic Church as legal subjects of multiple legal systems that can complement and support each other at times, but which can also end up competing with each other.

---

[20] Tamanaha (2017, pp. 76–77).

[21] See Baer (2021, pp. 110–113).

[22] See Ferrari (2016, pp. 7–8).

[23] See Bell (2012, pp. 1–37).

2.1.4 The Problem of Panjurism

Even though a pluralist understanding of law makes sense from a socio-legal perspective and from the perspective of the sociology of canon law, we should still note that pluralist approaches are not entirely free of arbitrariness. If we assume that "law" develops out of all kinds of social relations, this begs the question how to tell "law" apart from non-legal norms. The primary question is whether it is possible to make this distinction at all. And, if it is, then the question arises *how* to make it. One approach is to accept all norms as "law" which are conventionally acknowledged as "law" by a certain group.[24] Brian Tamanaha advocates this point of view. He notes, "Law can be anything, can take any form and serve any function, legal officials and/or people conventionally recognize."[25] Tamanaha believes his approach also settles the problem of arbitrariness. This is because, in contrast to what one might expect, the criterion of a group *recognising* norms as "law" does not necessarily result in the arbitrary bloating of "law," as Tamanaha observes. Whilst the law of the European Union, canon law, or sharia law are widely accepted as being "law," the public does not understand the rules of street gangs, universities, or sports clubs as law, as Tamanaha maintains.[26] This is the case because we regularly do not understand agents such as street gangs as possessing the "deontic powers" necessary for creating "law." Here, Tamanaha draws on legal philosopher John Searle's theory that views institutions as producers of norms because of the deontic power ascribed to them.[27] Whilst we accept the idea of the European Union or religious communities as exercising legal deontic powers when they formulate laws, we do not generally view street gangs, universities, or sports clubs as possessing legal deontic powers, as Tamanaha argues,

> Universities and sport leagues are not collectively recognized as 'legal' systems and do not have the legal deontic powers exercised by legal officials. The members of these very organizations do not typically view their own rule system as 'law', which they recognize they are subject to. Their rule systems do not establish basic rules and social intercourse, are not backed by organized physical force, and make no general claims of justice and right. Hence rule systems in general are not legal systems per se.[28]

One might discuss if Tamanaha is really right to assume that street gangs, universities, and sport leagues are not recognised as producers of law and lack the deontic powers to create law. I doubt that Tamanaha's examples are ideal for proving this point. Diana Villegas's ground-breaking study on "mafia law" of organised crime in Columbia, for instance, helps to see that in the light of the legal pluralism paradigm we should not easily dismiss agents such as street gangs as producers of legal orders

---

[24] See Röhl (1987, pp. 215–216).

[25] Tamanaha (2017, p. 150).

[26] See Tamanaha (2017, pp. 48–53).

[27] See Searle (2010).

[28] Tamanaha (2017, p. 54).

or rather "illegal legal" orders, as Villegas proves.[29] However, we may leave Tamanaha's concrete examples aside at this point to focus on his argument that rule systems are not legal systems when they are not acknowledged as legal systems. Tamanaha's criterion for determining what constitutes law, namely that "law" is what people consider to be law, results in a rather fluid understanding of "law." This is something that Tamanaha freely concedes, but he does not consider this problematic. In his view, the decisions which classify rule systems as "law" are actually rather contingent and open to change. Nonetheless, these decisions, as fragile as they appear, are also in fact remarkably stable, as Tamanaha concedes.[30] Most of today's secular legal scholars, for instance, accept canon law rather unquestioningly as "law," even though from their point of view there might be reason to doubt its character as law. Once normative orders are accepted as "law," it seems that they tend to qualify as "law" as long as they do not provide a major reason to question this classification.

Understanding "law" as a matter of conventional acceptance does however raise the spectre of arbitrariness at least in one respect, because defining law in this way attributes certain agents with the power to define what is law, as legal ethnologist Franz von Benda-Beckmann states, most interestingly with a sideways glance at the power of definition as exercised by legal studies. Some "law" is in fact "dogmatically and politically privileged as 'legal' by legal science",[31] according to von Benda-Beckmann, while other law is less privileged. However, if a legal order lacks this privileged status in the eyes of legal studies, this does not necessarily mean that it is less "legal" than law which enjoys acceptance as "law."

Benda-Beckmann's criticism enjoys some support in the sociology of law, albeit in a slightly reversed way. His criticism of the proposition that law is not "law" if it is not recognised as such by certain authorities is reflected in the socio-legal debate about whether, conversely, all normativity is "law" if it *is* acknowledged as such. Such an all-encompassing understanding of law is referred to in some areas of the sociology of law as "panjurism"[32] and is rejected by many scholars as problematic. Panjurism is problematic for the sociology of law primarily because it makes "law" as its subject matter such a diffuse phenomenon. If any normative practice can be understood as "law" simply by being considered to be such, then the concept of law loses some of its definitional precision. In this light, it is no longer possible to make a clear distinction between law and other social norms. Klaus Röhl remarks, "A pluralist definition of law leaves virtually nothing for society to contrast it with. It might be useful for ethnologists, small group researchers, or legal historians. But it has no place in the modern sociology of law."[33] Röhl's criticism reflects similar problems deriving from the approach which understands *law as discourse*, that is "as

---

[29] See Villegas (2018).

[30] See Tamanaha (2017, p. 77).

[31] Benda-Beckmann (2002, p. 69).

[32] A term coined by Jean Carbonnier: see Carbonnier (2001, p. 25).

[33] Original quote, "Ein pluralistischer Rechtsbegriff läßt kaum etwas übrig, was man dem Recht als Gesellschaft gegenüberstellen könnte. Er mag für Ethnologen, Kleingruppenforscher oder

a particular way of reasoning and problem-solving",[34] as Roger Cotterrell explains. Two problems might derive from this approach: on the one hand, interpreting law as a form of discourse might show a tendency to miss the binding and obligatory nature of law. On the other hand, conversely, this approach cannot prevent the "juridification" of other discourses as there is no clarity about where the limits to legal discourses lie and what it actually is that limits them.

2.1.5 Law as a Coercive Order

In seeking to resolve the problem of how we may identify law under a pluralist understanding of law, a number of approaches are useful in finding criteria which distinguish law from other forms of social norm. One classic approach is that of Max Weber, which focuses on the enforceability of law and its coercive character as an essential identifier of law. Weber writes, "We shall speak of law . . . in all those cases where the validity of a norm consists in the fact that the mode of orientation of an action toward it has some 'legal consequences'; i.e., that there are other norms which associate with the 'observance' or 'infringement' of the primary norm certain probabilities of consensual action guaranteed, in their turn, by legal coercion."[35] This aspect of coercion is constitutive of law, as Weber notes. We may only understand as law those norms which rest on the potential for coercion exercised by a *coercive apparatus*. Weber defines,

> 'Law,' as understood by us, is simply an 'order' endowed with certain specific guarantees of the probability of its empirical validity. The term 'guaranteed law' shall be understood to mean that there exists a 'coercive apparatus' . . ., that is, that there are one or more persons whose special task it is to hold themselves ready to apply specially provided means of coercion (legal coercion) for the purpose of norm enforcement.[36]

Weber is clear that coercion may take a number of different forms, such as physical force or psychological compulsion. He also emphasises that it is not only the coercive apparatus of the state which is capable of enforcing law, but also coercion as institutionally exercised by various groups addressing their own members or even third parties. Weber explains,

> The means of coercion may be physical or psychological, they may be direct or indirect in their operation, and they may be directed, as the case may require, against the participants in the consensual group (Einverständnisgemeinschaft) or the association (Vergesellschaftung), the organization (Verband) or the institution (Anstalt), within which the order is (empirically) valid; or they may be aimed at those outside.[37]

Rechtshistoriker nützlich sein. Für die Rechtssoziologie der Gegenwart ist er verfehlt", Röhl (1987, p. 219); see also Tamanaha (1993, pp. 192–194).

[34] Cotterrell (1983, p. 246).

[35] Weber (1978, p. 313).

[36] Weber (1978, p. 313).

[37] Weber (1978, p. 313).

Whilst in modernity it is the state which exercises a monopoly on coercion by violence,[38] besides the law of the state there is also "extra state law" issued by other groups, which often enforce their law through nonviolent coercion.[39] For Weber, this coercion in its various forms, and especially the enforcement of law through a coercive apparatus, is *the* key criterion that distinguishes law from other normativities which are free from coercion, such as customs and conventions.[40] Weber defines *custom* as something acquired through training and as habitual behaviour which individuals engage in unthinkingly. Custom therefore operates without any coercion, based on the group members' natural compliance with norms to which they are accustomed. On the contrary, Weber understands *convention* "to exist wherever a certain conduct is sought to be induced without, however, any coercion, physical or psychological, and, at least under normal circumstances, without any direct reaction other than the expression of approval or disapproval on the part of those persons who constitute the environment of the actor."[41] Hence, compliance with conventional norms is dependent on some pressure being applied by the group in the form of approval or disapproval of certain behaviour. However, it is only in "law," according to Weber, where this pressure takes the form of physical or mental coercion.

2.1.6 Criticism of Coercion Theories

Weber's theory found widespread support among many scholars of sociology and of law, but it also drew criticism. Roger Cotterrell for one identifies a key weakness in Weber's argumentation being that anybody who seeks to understand coercion as constitutive of "law" is also obliged to differentiate between legal coercion and other forms of coercion, which is no easy task.[42] In addition, not every legal matter has at its disposal a coercive apparatus; one need only think of much of constitutional law. Nevertheless, law such as constitutional law which is not directly backed up by coercion is frequently no more difficult to implement and enforce than law which has direct recourse to Weber's coercive apparatus, such as penal law, as Cotterrell states. Legal scholar Paul Schiff Berman adopts a similar stance in his research, which focuses on the consequences of globalisation for law. He observes that law, and primarily global law, which is less constrained by nation states or territory than traditional state law, can no longer be clearly defined by referring to a power of coercion. Whilst traditional views of law have defined the law by referring to *sovereignty*—as a set of norms emanating from a sovereign equipped with the

---

[38] See Weber (1978, p. 314).

[39] See Weber (1978, pp. 316–319).

[40] See Weber (1978, pp. 319–325).

[41] Weber (1978, p. 319).

[42] See Cotterrell (1983, p. 250).

power of coercion—, sovereignty is no longer the key root of law in the context of globalisation, as globally effective law does not necessarily arise from sovereign powers. Gunther Teubner follows a similar line of argument and speaks of "stateless global law"[43] when referring to the interconnected and dense regulatory system under which multinational companies operate. The first steps towards creating this system were already evident in the age of colonialism, as Brian Tamanaha notes in reference to the legal authority of the East India Companies, "In the past, private companies have acted as de facto political sovereigns. The Dutch East India Company fought wars, entered treaties, seized land and administered territories. The British East India Company operated similarly, seizing control of much of India from Mughal rule".[44] It is therefore possible, and even more so today, to identify phenomena of transnational or international law which exist without being rooted in state sovereignty. Tamanaha also views the European Union as constituting a key challenge to the claim that law is essentially dependent on state sovereignty.

A further point of discussion deriving from this issue is the question of *who*, under the conditions of globalisation, is best suited to fulfil the legislator's role. Schiff Berman no longer views national or transnational legislators as the nuclei around which global law crystallises. The function of producing law, he believes, has to some extent been taken over by courts responsible for settling transnational and international issues. As a consequence, when examining the effectiveness of law he suggests focusing to a greater extent on the influence of judicial decisions, stating, "jurisdiction might actually be a better model than sovereignty for understanding how law operates in an interconnected world."[45] The question remains, however, as to how suprastatal courts can enforce their decisions if not on the basis of the type of coercion traditionally exercised by states. Schiff Berman sees their effectiveness rooted in the fact that their decisions are effective *de facto*. They play a major part in international trade relations, exert influence on the actions of transnational players and on national adjudication, and—most interestingly—frequently do so with low levels of coercion. Schiff Berman believes their power resides in "rhetorical persuasion, informal articulations of legal norms and networks of affiliation that may not possess literal enforcement power".[46] These alternative powers to create legal realities, Schiff Berman admits, do not speak against the significance of coercion for law. They do prove, however, that the law is not always and consistently intertwined with coercion. Schiff Berman acknowledges, "Coercive power obviously exists, and it is certainly an important (and often the dominant) factor. Yet the mere articulation of norms . . . may have significant though less obvious, persuasive power."[47] This finding suggests that the coercive dimension of law might be less significant for the constitution of law than Weber assumed, with neither being fully

---

[43] Teubner (1996, p. 256).

[44] Tamanaha (2017, p. 162).

[45] Schiff Berman (2005, p. 1144).

[46] Schiff Berman (2005, p. 1144).

[47] Schiff Berman (2005, p. 1144); see also Teubner (1996, p. 270).

insignificant for the functioning of law. This explains why sociologists of law who hold fast to coercion often adopt differentiated positions on coercion theory. Sociologist Georges Gurvitch, for example, believed that every law allows for coercion as a *possibility* but does not necessary apply or even claim it.[48] Current research has drawn some attention to this reluctance of legal orders to actually apply coercion. Legal scholar Christoph Möllers commented on this finding by pointing out that the functionality of normative orders makes it necessary to refrain from the rigid enforcement of norms and the consistent sanctioning of norm violations, because constant coercive practice would be a repeated reminder of the limits of the very same order. Möllers notes with regard to the law, "The actual employment of force imposes too obvious limitations to the legal order."[49] The fact that the state frequently fails to act, says Möllers, should not merely be interpreted as its inability to pursue all breaches of law, but as an open decision not to sanction some breaches of law "because enforcement could, factually and normatively, entail too high a price to be paid."[50] Other scholars such as Eugen Ehrlich, in turn, do not even accept the potential for coercion as constitutive of law. According to Ehrlich, law "can do" coercion, but it is not coercion nor the possibility of coercion that constitutes legal orders. Ehrlich cites an aphorism ascribed to French statesman Charles Maurice de Talleyrand to illustrate the problem of founding law on coercion or its possibility, noting, "The French express the thought that the state cannot permanently base its right upon might in the very expressive words: *On peut tout faire avec les baionettes, excepté s'y asseoir.*"[51] This picture is even more powerful in Ehrlich's original German wording, as Ehrlich slightly changes Talleyrand's aphorism. He translates it as the impossibility of *sitting* on bayonets, instead of conjuring the image of *leaning* on them. So while he considers coercion as an effective means for enforcing the law, he doubts that law based solely on coercion or the possibility of coercion could ever provide a group with a comfortable base to sit on, that is with a stable order worth living under. Ehrlich's image that it is difficult to sit on bayonets illustrates well that we do not gain a good understanding of the legal order by viewing it only through the lens of theories of coercion. Law is, after all, an order which frequently provides for relatively comfortable seating, at least for most of its subjects at most times. Focusing on coercion, Manfred Rehbinder notes, only provides us with a narrow view of the merits of law as it focuses exclusively on the *exceptions*, namely breaches of law, whilst leaving out the *rule*, namely everyday life.[52] Whilst the coercive side of law reveals itself in certain situations—in exceptional cases—, the legal subjects' everyday experience of law is not the experience of permanent coercion. In Sect. 3.1 I will deal with this topic, namely that legal subjects are not even really "aware" of law in their everyday lives most of the time, as the law

---

[48] See Gurvitch (1960, p. 129).

[49] Möllers (2020, p. 54).

[50] Möllers (2020, p. 245).

[51] Ehrlich (1936, pp. 373–374).

[52] See Rehbinder (2014, pp. 38–39).

constitutes a largely invisible basis for our social interactions. At this point in my study, it is sufficient to observe that defining law by coercion does not accurately reflect the phenomenon of law in its full sense. This is because coercion theories fail to sufficiently acknowledge the typical quality of the law as an invisible order which structures the legal subjects' everyday lives at most times without applying or even claiming coercion.

2.1.7 Low-Level Coercion of Canon Law

The view that it is imprecise to define law based on its coercive character is of considerable significance for canon law. This is because the law of the church is only partially coercive. In the context of modernity, observes dogmatic theologian Georg Essen, the ecclesiastical cultures no longer represent themselves as cultures of coercion.[53] The church is accordingly no longer in a position whereby it can depend upon coercion to enforce most of its norms. And it must get by for the most part without Weber's coercive apparatus. Whilst canon law possesses an adjudication system, it has no body to perform policing functions to exercise the sovereign enforcement of canonical claims on ecclesiastical legal subjects. Nevertheless, some canonists such as Peter Krämer view the enforceability of law as a self-evident characteristic of law—and therefore also of canon law.[54] Similarly, Antonio Rouco Varela sees an essentially coercive mechanism in the penal options available to canon law.[55] However, the critical question remains as to whether canon law possesses the institutional preconditions to make its character as law dependent on the enforceability of its legal norms. In fact, as things stand, the church has only limited options available to coerce its members into acting in accordance with canon law, and it has likewise only limited options to effectively sanction errant behaviour. In addition, canon law can no longer rely upon coercion as it could in the premodern period, by relying on the *brachium saeculare* whereby the state lent the church its coercive mechanisms.[56]

In addition to these practical failures to attribute canon law with coercive power, there are also *theological* reasons for being sceptical about defining canon law through coercion. Nowadays, the church largely uses theological arguments to justify its law. The church views its law as legitimate because it serves the faith and the community of the faithful on their path to salvation. Canon law is therefore essentially a normative order in the service of the faith. However, as canon law is only legitimised by its service to the faith and the community of the faithful, it cannot therefore exist apart from the principle of freedom which is integral to the act of faith.

---

[53] See Essen (2013, p. 217).
[54] See Krämer (1979, pp. 14–15).
[55] See Rouco Varela and Corecco (1998, p. 73).
[56] See Hecke (2017, p. 50).

Faith is inseparable from freedom. "The act of faith is of its very nature a free act",[57] states the Second Vatican Council in the Declaration on Religious Freedom *Dignitatis humanae*. As faith is essentially reliant on human freedom, there is no faith apart from individual autonomy as the human beings' capacity and right to govern themselves.[58] This makes faith and coercion fundamentally incompatible. In canon 748 §2 CIC/1983 we discover the following rule, "It is never lawful for anyone to force others to embrace the Catholic faith against their conscience." This prohibition is not only a command to refrain from the use of coercion in matters of faith, but offers the deeper anthropological insight that faith actually cannot be imposed through coercion because it rests upon the individual's free inner affirmation of the gift of faith. Consequently, a legal order that exists to serve the faith must by necessity sit rather uncomfortably with the idea of coercion for theological reasons, as canonist Peter Huizing observes. Huizing maintains, "In church it is pointless to impose or enforce external compliance with or non-infringement of a provision without considering the church member's inner attitude towards it. All church members need to experience canon law as law, but not as enforceable law. Its validity is based on free consent given by the community of faith."[59] Canonist Ladislas Orsy argues along similar lines. If compliance with the law in church is related to the act of faith, he argues, then it must be subject to the appropriate conditions, namely that individual decision and conscience are key. Orsy insists, "It would be immoral to ask an intelligent and free person to perform an act, even in obedience to a law, if he had not reached a personal judgment that the act was in pursuance of a true value and if he had not decided freely to do it."[60] Canon law and coercion therefore do not go together well—neither practically nor theoretically. Adherents of Weber's understanding of legal orders as coercive orders therefore find it hard to accept canon law as "law." Conversely, a sociology of canon law which conceives of canon law *as law* will have little room for coercion theories either.

2.1.8 Beyond Coercion Theories

So if it is not coercion that makes up the character of law, then this begs the question what does then in fact constitute law. In seeking to find an answer, it is quite

---

[57] No. 10. *Acta Apostolicae Sedis*, *58*, 936; English version: www.vatican.va/archive/hist_councils/ii_vatican_council/documents/vat-ii_decl_19651207_dignitatis-humanae_en.html. Accessed 19 June 2021.

[58] E.g. Striet (2014, p. 28).

[59] Original quote, "Das 'Auferlegen' und 'Erzwingen' des äußerlichen Haltens oder Nichtübertretens einer Vorschrift, ohne Berücksichtigung der inneren Haltung ihr gegenüber, ist in der Kirche sinnlos. Kirchenrecht muß von allen Gliedern als Recht erfahren werden, aber nicht als erzwingbares Recht. Seine Geltung beruht auf seiner freien Bejahung durch die Gemeinschaft im Glauben", Huizing (1973, p. 170).

[60] Orsy (1980, pp. 42–43).

enlightening to look back at Weber's statements, insofar as these hint at the fact that law is an order "endowed with certain specific guarantees of the probability of its empirical validity".[61] However much one might criticise Weber's assessment that the probability of the empirical validity of law necessarily rests on coercion, we may agree that one characteristic of law is that it is valid and that this validity must be empirically viable, that is that law must have some legal effect. With this in mind, Paul Schiff Berman defines law as an instrument for shaping the future, the fulfilment of which is dependent on the legal subjects' abiding by the law. He states, "the essence of law is that it makes aspirational judgments about the future, the power of which depends on whether the judgments accurately reflect evolving norms of the communities that must choose to obey them."[62] But one may ask what the basis is underlying the prospect of abiding by the law, if it is not coercion. Socio-legal scholars who are averse to coercion theory have provided a number of different answers to this question. Eugen Ehrlich, for instance, saw many legal norms and their effectiveness based less on coercion and more on *suggestion*, as he explains, "The most important norms function only through suggestion. They come to man in the form of commands or of prohibitions; they are addressed to him without a statement of the reason on which they are based, and he obeys them without a moment's reflection."[63] Ehrlich found that humans tend to accept norms habitually when they are presented to them by their environment, noting, "it is not a matter of conscious thinking, but of unconsciously habituating themselves to the emotions and thoughts of their surroundings."[64] Echoing Weber's thoughts on *custom*, Ehrlich believes that law gains its effectiveness because people abide by it as a matter of routine or habit. Here, Ehrlich made no categorical difference between legal norms and non-legal norms. All social norms can be internalised in such a way that individuals abide by them without conscious thought. This view also makes a reappearance in the current sociology of law, namely in reflections about the way in which norms take effect. Legal sociologists Hubert Rottleuthner and Margret Rottleuthner-Lutter, for example, point out that we may not always understand legal norms instrumentally, that is as instruments for bringing about desired effects or suppressing undesired effects by pushing the legal subjects to behave in a certain way, but should also perceive the expressive, declarative, or symbolic functions of norms.[65] Scholar of environmental science Jens Newig explains the difference between instrumental and symbolic effects of laws with regard to his field of research, environmental legislation. He understands as instrumental those laws which serve an explicit purpose and operate directly to attain that end, while only indirectly and in the long run seeking to change certain social conditions. In contrast, he understands as symbolic those laws which also serve certain yet less explicit

---

[61] Weber (1978, p. 313).

[62] Schiff Berman (2005, p. 1110).

[63] Ehrlich (1936, p. 78).

[64] Ehrlich (1936, pp. 77–78).

[65] See Rottleuthner and Rottleuthner-Lutter (2010, p. 14).

purposes and aim at mostly political effects by conveying a certain political message to the legal subjects.[66] One might criticise this definition for several reasons, above all for its rather weak understanding of symbolic functioning. What Newig rightly emphasises though, is that laws might become effective by operating either through instrumental or symbolic means. Whilst instrumental laws directly push to achieve their ends, symbolic laws bring about the desired legal reality by using symbols which represent that reality. Instrumental laws forbid and criminalise the pollution of rivers to prevent water pollution. Symbolic laws introduce a recycling system. So whilst they do not criminalise those who refrain from recycling, they do create an awareness for environmental issues, using symbolic norms to represent an environmentally-friendly system for bringing about an environmentally-friendly reality in the long run. In any case, a symbolic functioning of the law should not be considered less effective. Rottleuthner and Rottleuthner-Lutter reference legal history to show that in the past, laws have frequently had significant effects on legal communities through symbolic functioning. In such cases, symbolic norms frequently achieved the greatest effect when they expressed vibrant ideas and values which were shared by the legal community of their time. Thomas Raiser echoes these observations. He speaks of symbolic effects of the law in those cases in which the legal subjects espouse a law openly and abide by it quite naturally.[67] The effects of symbolic norms result in such cases from a process of *adoption* and *internalisation*. Legal coercion, in contrast, has little role to play in this type of context. Eugen Ehrlich might agree with these observations on the effectiveness of symbolic laws. Moreover, he would no doubt also broaden the idea of laws being naturally effective based on internalisation to encompass many instrumental laws, too. Ehrlich made the general observation that individuals largely abide by the law "without a moment's reflection",[68] mostly on the basis of their normative childhood conditioning. Rather than abiding by the law because the law says so, they abide by the law guided by feelings such as their peers' approval or disapproval of a certain behaviour. Ehrlich understood social interaction as an ongoing process of legal education. The legal subjects, as Ehrlich saw it, are permanently imprinted with those feelings aroused in society or in a group when they act contrary to the law. Ehrlich even made explicit reference to canon law in his observations. He referred to ecclesiastical law as an example of a stable order which successfully integrates the legal community without the use of coercion, noting, "Both friend and foe admire the compact structure which is seen everywhere in the Catholic Church, in its legal order no less than in other respects. Nevertheless the ecclesiastical law is enforced only to a very small extent by the state; and where separation of church and state is in effect, not at all. It rests, as a whole, chiefly on a social basis."[69] It is a matter of debate whether Ehrlich's view of the effectiveness of canon law is still true today; I

---

[66] See Newig (2003, pp. 40–41).

[67] See Raiser (2007, p. 245).

[68] Ehrlich (1936, p. 78).

[69] Ehrlich (1936, p. 65).

will take up this problem of canon law rapidly losing its effectiveness again later in my study. At this point in my study, in the search for a viable socio-legal definition of law, it is not necessarily the issue of effectiveness that is key, but the question of whether Ehrlich's concept of a minimally coercive law is reliable and convincing in determining what law actually is under modern conditions. After all, Ehrlich's assumption that individuals tend to accept law as a self-evident fact—however much of a soft spot I have for this concept—is based on the idea that there is an essential *homogeneity* of legal communities, something which is increasingly hard to claim nowadays. The question arising from Ehrlich's proposition is what happens to "law" when legal communities become more diverse and therefore less inclined to accept legal norms more or less unquestioningly. In increasingly diverse societies or communities it is also becoming increasingly unlikely that breaches of law are consistently met with the group's disapproval. As the homogenous social foundation upon which Ehrlich places law and even canon law can no longer be taken for granted, it becomes increasingly difficult to understand as "law" those norms which individuals abide by to avoid the group's disapproval. However, if it is not coercion which constitutes law either, we might then ask what the binding forces which provide for the stability of norms we call "law" in plural groups actually are. Confronted with these questions, modern pluralist societies and with them the sociology of law face something of a quandary. This quandary includes canon law studies. The assumption that church members might be forced to abide by legal norms bears not much relation to modern ecclesiastical reality. However, the assumption that legal compliance in church is a result of the legal subjects' imprinted and natural reaction to canon law is likewise unrealistic. I will take up the debate about the effectiveness of law and of canon law in particular in the sixth section of this study. In the present context, however, I have to clarify which norms can be identified as law from a socio-legal perspective, if it is neither coercion nor natural compliance which serve as Weber's "certain specific guarantees of the probability of its empirical validity".[70]

2.1.9 Law as Behavioural Expectation

Niklas Luhmann provides us with an alternative definition of law. Luhmann's understanding of law draws on the concept of *expectation*. He conceives of law as a means of communication which operates using the codification "legal"/"illegal." This binary code serves to identify communications as legal. These communications constitute a social system as a structure of "congruently generalised normative behavioural expectations".[71] Law thus derives from the generalisation of behavioural expectations which can be identified by applying the code "legal"/

---

[70] Weber (1978, p. 313).

[71] Luhmann (2014, p. 77).

"illegal." Whilst the above-mentioned approaches to defining law rest primarily on the issue of behaviour and behavioural control by law, Luhmann ascribes a subordinate role to the legal subjects' actual behaviour. He states with respect to the law, "Its primary function does not lie in bringing about a certain type of behaviour, but in the reinforcement of certain expectations."[72] Whilst members of society can endure a considerable degree of uncertainty about the factual behaviour of others, they are less tolerant with regard to uncertainty in their expectations, as Luhmann notes, "Uncertainty of expectation is far harder to bear than surprises or disappointments."[73] This focus on the stability of expectations, and less on the stability of behaviour, has consequences for Luhmann's understanding of what constitutes the law. He maintains, "Law is only law if there is reason to expect that normative expectations can be expected normatively."[74] However, if expectations are what define law, it is still essential not to lose sight of legal subjects' behaviour. This is because law results in some behavioural control, as Luhmann notes, "expectations and behaviour stabilize each other"[75]. Nevertheless, it is expectation that first makes a certain type of behaviour legally relevant by turning it into legal or non-legal behaviour. Luhmann states, "Only the expectation of expectations ensures behavioural harmonization beyond purely random conformity."[76] At the same time this presupposes that expectations are not formulated instantaneously and at will, but are well structured as a stable source of expectation. This stable structuring of the law supports one of the primary achievements of law, namely that it serves as a major *reducer of complexity* in modern pluralist societies. Luhmann explains,

> If one also factors in that we are dealing with a multiplicity of people and a multiplicity of potential topics of experience and actions, it becomes clear that it would far exceed the individuals' abilities to know what to relate to if they had to concretely and completely evaluate these expectations of expectations, or even expectations of expectations of expectations, on a case-by-case basis. Instead, individuals form meaningful structures—that is general patterns of experience and behaviour—which allow them to preselect from a list of anticipated expectations and to reduce the complexity of the options to such a degree that they can make a quick decision about their behaviour based on the situation before them.[77]

---

[72] Original quote, "Seine primäre Funktion liegt nicht in der Bewirkung bestimmten Verhaltens, sondern in der Stärkung bestimmter Erwartungen", Luhmann (1970, pp. 179–180).

[73] Luhmann (2004, p. 163).

[74] Luhmann (2004, p. 158).

[75] Luhmann (2004, p. 163).

[76] Original quote, "Erst das Erwarten von Erwartungen sichert über die bloß zufällige Konformität hinaus eine Abstimmung des Verhaltens", Luhmann (1970, p. 177).

[77] Original quote, "Nimmt man hinzu, daß es um eine Vielheit von Menschen und eine Vielheit möglicher Themen des Erlebens und Handelns geht, wird deutlich, daß es die Orientierungsfähigkeit des Menschen weit überfordern würde, müßte er diese Erwartungserwartungen und gegebenenfalls noch Erwartungserwartungserwartungen sich fallweise konkret und vollständig vorstellen. Statt dessen bildet er sinnhafte Strukturen, das heißt allgemeine Muster des Erlebens und Verhaltens, die eine Vorselektion dessen leisten, was man erwarten kann, und die Komplexität der Möglichkeiten so weit reduzieren, daß eine rasche, situationsnahe Verhaltenswahl möglich wird", Luhmann (1970, p. 177).

However, if we understand law as relatively reliable expectation, this begs the question what consequences arise when the legal subjects do not meet the behavioural expectations of the law. As Luhmann notes, "norms produce a higher degree of certainty of expectation than is warranted by behaviour"[78]. Therefore, the question evidently arises about how to deal with the problem that expectations are frequently *disappointed*. Luhmann outlines two basic possibilities: one can either give up the expectation, or abide by it and instead classify the reality that diverges from the expectation as a disappointment.[79] With normative expectations—including legal ones—the regular reaction is frequently the latter one, according to Luhmann. If certain behaviour contradicts a norm, we frequently do not amend or surrender the norm, but classify the behaviour diverging from the norm as disappointing. Unlawful behaviour does not therefore pose a challenge to the law. Hence, the law does not stop being law because of unlawful behaviour. Luhmann refers to the concept of *counterfacticity* to underline his belief that the validity claim of the law continues to exist even when the normative expectations associated with it are not consistently fulfilled. He refers to legal norms as "counterfactually stabilised behavioural expectations"[80] insofar as they are expectations which individuals maintain even in cases in which they are disappointed.[81] It is worth mentioning though that Christoph Möllers recently contested this Luhmannian concept of normative counterfacticity. Möllers criticised that speaking of "counterfacticity" implies an unintended dualism between norms and facts, which would be misleading. He therefore suggests replacing the term with "afacticity," explaining,

> The prefix 'counter', however, it [sic] too strong an expression if one does not want to imply that normativity and facticity stand in an antagonistic relationship. ... Normativity does not direct itself in opposition to the world as it is per se; rather, it opens up space both for deviation and correspondence. ... For these reasons, it is more fitting to speak of the *afacticity* of norms, in order to express the difference to (but not competition with) facts.[82]

Hence, we may understand norms as afactual, insofar as they prove to be fairly resistant to facts. However, this quality is not absolute. The afacticity of norms reaches a limit in those cases in which norms fully fail to connect with facts, or as Luhmann might put it, where behaviour completely fails to justify any expectations. In Sect. 6.2.7 I will discuss pathological cases of variance between expectation and behaviour in church, in which consistently unlawful behaviour leads to the erosion of legal expectations and therefore, in the light of Luhmann's approach, also casts doubt on the legal character of the affected canonical norms.

---

[78] Luhmann (2004, p. 163).

[79] See Luhmann (1970, pp. 177–179).

[80] Luhmann (2014, p. 33).

[81] See Luhmann (1986, p. 22).

[82] Möllers (2020, p. 75).

2.1.10 Expectation, Coercion, Sanction

When studying Luhmann in comparison to Weber it is noteworthy that the principle of coercion is not fully absent from Luhmann's concept of law, but occupies a different role to that in Weber's approach. Luhmann explains,

> Law is in no way primarily a coercive order, but rather a facilitation of expectation. The facilitation depends on the availability of congruently generalised channels of expectation ... The constitutive coercive situation pertaining to law is the coercion applied to select expectations which can in turn motivate the enforcement of certain behaviour in a few, though important, cases.[83]

Due to the stable expectations of the law, the legal subjects view it as being a low-risk endeavour to submit themselves to their expectations, that is to expect the fulfilment of the expectations they associate with the law. In this light, coercion plays a role to the extent that law compels its subjects to differentiate between their expectations and to decide whether they are *legal* expectations. This is the case whenever the expectations may be expressed in terms of the code "legal"/"illegal." Whenever these expectations are indeed identified as *legal* expectations, the legal community might well take this as grounds for enforcing lawful behaviour and sanctioning unlawful behaviour. Yet this possibility of responding to legal and illegal behaviour with coercion does not render coercion an essential element of the law, according to Luhmann. Instead, law serves as an *occasion* in which to use coercion, if only in those "few, though important, cases",[84] as we may find when studying penal adjudication. Here, the law reacts to disappointed expectations with the imposition of *sanctions*. Luhmann describes sanctions in this context as the "successful realisation of expectation".[85] Nevertheless, in the majority of cases, the non-fulfilment of legal expectations is not met with coercion. Luhmann, therefore, in contrast to Weber, does not view coercion or sanctions as constitutive of law, stating "that the concept norm cannot be defined solely by reference to the threat of sanctions, let alone by reference to imposing sanctions."[86] However, it is due to the structure of law as expectation that there is still the possibility of applying sanctions upon the non-fulfilment of legal expectations. Hence, as Luhmann states, "the prospect of sanctions is part of the symbolic apparatus that allows one to identify whether or not one's expectations are in line with the law".[87] This renders sanction mechanisms part of the symbol politics of the law, as Christoph Möllers emphasises. Möllers refers to sanctions in a similar way to Luhmann, calling them "reminding posts"[88] of norms. He explains, "The sanctioning responding to a norm

---

[83] Luhmann (2014, p. 78).

[84] Luhmann (2004, p. 78).

[85] Luhmann (2004, p. 78).

[86] Luhmann (2004, p. 150).

[87] Luhmann (2004, p. 150).

[88] Möllers (2020, p. 102).

transgression highlights both said transgression and the existence of the norm. ...
More precisely, a sanction cannot (directly) serve to implement the norm, as it only
kicks in after the transgression. Primarily, it should remind the community of the
existence and value of the norm. It plays an assuring and expressive role".[89] Hence,
sanctions remind the community of norms, including legal norms, but do not
constitute them. In Luhmann's definition where norms are expectations, these
expectations include the expectation of sanctions. In Möllers's approach where
norms are possibilities, these possibilities include the possibility of sanctions, yet
in both cases without sanctions becoming an essential element of norms, not even of
legal ones. This observation is critical for the unfolding discussion; Sects. 3.2 and
6.2 below will address canonical sanctions in this respect.

Summing up the aforementioned thoughts briefly and with regard to their merit
for my study, Luhmann's theory proves to be well suited as a theoretical basis for a
sociology of canon law. Not only has his approach received widespread acknowledgement among scholars of the sociology of law. It is also an approach which
enables us to understand canon law *as law*, even though canon law is in fact and also
theologically a legal order with a low level of coercion. Adding to this, Luhmann's
approach makes it possible to understand canon law as law, even though time has
eroded its self-evident role in the everyday lives of the faithful, a role which Eugen
Ehrlich could still take for granted at the outset of the twentieth century. With
Luhmann we may understand canon law as a system of counterfactual (or in
Möllers's diction: afactual) behavioural expectations. The provisions of canon
law map out prearranged pathways of expectation which exist irrespective of whether the
ecclesiastical legal subjects abide by the law or disappoint legal expectations. At the
same time, the widespread non-compliance with many provisions of canon law begs
the question what happens when certain expectations of canon law become largely
void. Following Luhmann, one may ask if canon law continues to be "law" when it
loses its character of expectation. Adding to this, one has to consider that the
non-fulfilment of canon law as an expectation increasingly fails to disappoint.
Following Luhmann one may ask if canon law continues to be "law" when the
legal community or greater parts of it no longer find breaches of canon law
disappointing. I will address this problem in greater depth in Sect. 6.2.7.

2.1.11 Norms and Facts, Norms as Facts

A sociological concept of law which takes the legal expectations of a group as its
point of departure reveals that law has a normative level connected with social
reality, and at the same time has a factual level influenced by those norms. This
challenges us to define what we understand by "law"—the legal norms, or the reality
which is constituted by the normative order. Here, it is helpful to study Jean

---

[89] Möllers (2020, p. 102).

Carbonnier, who differentiates between primary and secondary legal phenomena. Carbonnier defines primary legal phenomena as forms of law, such as legislative texts, judicial verdicts, or the hand signals of traffic police.[90] These in turn generate secondary legal phenomena, legal content, such as statutes, convictions and acquittals, and the motorists' stopping at a crossing. In the sociology of law, law therefore frequently has a double meaning, indicating both legal prescriptions as well as the legal reality generated by them. Roger Cotterrell states,

> law consists of prescriptions—'ought propositions' specifying the way legal subjects ought to behave. Yet at the same time it constitutes a social phenomenon which only 'exists' if the prescriptions of conduct actually have some effect on the way people think or behave. Law is thus both prescriptive norm and descriptive fact. It is to be considered in terms of its validity and also its efficacy.[91]

Cotterrell's quote contains two insights which are important for socio-legal scholars and which are omnipresent throughout socio-legal studies: first, law consists of norms *and* facts, as speaking of "law" incorporates legal provisions as well as legal practice. Second, the sociology of law derives from this finding that issues of legal validity always go hand in hand with issues of the effectiveness of law. In contrast to approaches of legal theory, the sociology of law cannot turn its back on the question of legal effectiveness. I will discuss this issue in greater depth in the sixth section of this study.

Niklas Luhmann points out the theoretical impossibility of deriving norms from facts.[92] However, the sociology of law devotes itself to the dual study of norms *and* facts, while actually viewing norms *as* facts. This acknowledges the fact that norms maintain a consistent connection to reality, as Christoph Möllers points out, "Norms are not some form deficient in reality but rather a curious cultural achievement in which imagination and capacity for abstraction must come together with reality."[93] However, viewing norms as facts presents a methodological challenge for the sociology of law, as Luhmann observes. He believes a particular "theoretical achievement of the sociology of law lies in explaining how it treats norms as facts, meaning: what conceptuality does it use to generate the theoretical relevance and connectivity of the particular fact known as 'norm'."[94] A particular challenge is how to determine how norms as facts are different from *other* facts, especially from social facts which influence the development of norms. In consequence, we need to clarify how normative facts can be separated from social facts while at the same time acknowledging that they relate to each other. Connecting norms and facts is a dialectical endeavour. The normative world, as Möllers notes, "is a counter-world

---

[90] See Carbonnier (1974, p. 103).

[91] Cotterrell (1984, p. 9).

[92] See Luhmann (1986, p. 21).

[93] Möllers (2020, p. 287).

[94] Original quote, "Theorieleistung der Rechtssoziologie in der Frage, wie sie Normen als Fakten behandelt, das heißt: mit welcher Begrifflichkeit sie die theoretische Relevanz und Anschlußfähigkeit des besonderen Faktums 'Norm' herstellt", Luhmann (1986, p. 21).

that is part of the world."[95] Therefore "it is imperative to grasp the curious circumstance that norms can claim their autonomy from this world *while being* part of it."[96] Möllers examines the characteristics of norms from the viewpoint of norm theory. But his thoughts are also of use to sociology, insofar as they help to clarify how the curious facts we call "norms" exist in relation to other facts. In his theory, Möllers locates norms in close relation to other facts as a matter of necessity, but at the same time as facts detached from those other facts. He explains,

> Norms are to build up and maintain a distanced tension with the world. Norms that only codify what will inevitably happen gain no distance; they can ultimately not be distinguished from the world as it is. Conversely, norms that remain so distant from the circumstances of the world that there can hardly be any talk of their affirming a 'possibility' either remain meaningless, since that which is normed by them is so distant that it has no perspective for realization, or they aim for effects that no longer show any consideration for the state of social practice, thereby tearing apart the social fabric.[97]

To be identifiable as "norms," norms cannot therefore simply become indiscernible from facts on the one hand, nor may they exist at too great a distance from them on the other hand. This dialectic, in which Möllers proposes that norms exist in relation to the world but at the same time at a distance to it, resonates in the minds of Catholic theologians, inasmuch as the connection with and distance to the "world" rings an ecclesiological bell. The ecclesiological quest for a concept of "church" which comprehends the church as part of the world as well as part of a counter-world permeates through the texts of the Second Vatican Council and has been a matter of ecclesiological debate ever since.[98] This debate also serves as the point of departure for ecclesiastical legal theory and its considerations about how to conceive of the ecclesiastical legal order if we understand it as an order *of the church*, which has, in consequence, to adequately reflect this dialectic of identity and distance between the church and the world. Reading Möllers shows that this core issue, with which ecclesiology and canonical norm theory both grapple, is intimately connected with norm theory as such. The norm-world dialectic is an integral part of how normativity is constituted, as Möllers sees it. Hence, ecclesiology is grappling with a similar problem to norm theory. It must explain how it is conceivable to go about "simultaneously distinguishing and connecting the normative and the factual, treating both autonomously and in relationship to each other".[99] In ecclesiastical legal theory, this problem is duplicated. Here, the issue of intimacy and distance between norms and facts must be addressed both in relation to the church itself as well as in relation to ecclesiastical norms of a social, moral, or legal nature.

---

[95] Möllers (2020, p. 75).

[96] Möllers (2020, p. 73).

[97] Möllers (2020, p. 288).

[98] E.g. *Gaudium et spes*, no. 1. *Acta Apostolicae Sedis*, *58*, 1025; *Lumen gentium*, no. 31. *Acta Apostolicae Sedis*, *57*, 37.

[99] Möllers (2020, p. 59).

2.1.12   Law in Books, Law in Action

Inasmuch as norms maintain a distance to the "world" but are at the same time part of it, the question remains how to identify them. This challenge is particularly difficult when the distance of norms from the "world" is almost negligible. Christoph Möllers addresses this question. He seeks to identify norms and distinguish them from the "world" by looking out for elements of formalisation. Norms, as Möllers finds, possess formal characteristics to ensure that they are distinguishable from other facts, for instance by inserting a norm into a formalised rule.[100] By identifying these formalised features it is possible to assign phenomena to those facts which we call "norms." Norms are also norms without formalisation, as Möllers concedes. Yet as formal characteristics help to identify norms, we tend to rely on these formalities to disclose norms as norms. The sociology of law is in any case interested in *all* norms of the law. In consequence, it cannot restrict itself to the study of norms which we may formally identify as legal prescripts. Instead, the sociology of law must cast its net wider to include those norms that are in fact legal norms as they exert a de facto influence on legal practice. To distinguish between those formal and those rather informal norms of the law, sociologists of law today often refer to a differentiation which Roscoe Pound elaborated, distinguishing between "law in books" and "law in action."[101] Pound's distinction corresponds with Eugen Ehrlich's frequently quoted observation that legal norms do not arise from books but from social practice. Ehrlich devoted himself to the "study of the living law"[102] which he understood as law which "has not been posited in legal propositions",[103] and is therefore not imprisoned in statutes, rulings, or other official legal texts. In addition to those norms reified in legal texts, Ehrlich found legal norms to flow from conventions and customs. As sources of "living law" he relied on "the modern legal document; secondly, direct observation of life, of commerce, of customs and usages, and of all associations, not only of those that the law has recognized but also of those it has overlooked and passed by, indeed even of those that it has disapproved".[104] According to Ehrlich, we should not understand it as a weakness of "law in books" that "living law" is much more than those norms laid down by official legislation, adjudication, and administration. It is rather a natural phenomenon, as Ehrlich states. As "law in books" is always a product of the past and therefore only able to regulate the present to a certain degree, it is a natural matter that "our codes are uniformly adapted to a time much earlier than their own, and all the juristic technique in the world would be unable to extract the actual law of the present from it, for the simple reason that it is not contained therein."[105] Hence, as Ehrlich adds, it

---

[100] See Möllers (2020, pp. 167–168).

[101] See Pound (1910, pp. 12–36).

[102] Ehrlich (1936, p. 486).

[103] Ehrlich (1936, p. 493).

[104] Ehrlich (1936, p. 487).

[105] Ehrlich (1936, p. 487).

is not only that legal codes do not contain the "living law" by chance, but that they are essentially incapable of containing it as "the legal relations with which they deal are so incomparably richer, more varied, more subject to change … that the mere idea of making a complete presentation in a code would be monstrous."[106] Sociologies of law cannot therefore limit themselves to the study of "law in books," but must also address how "law in action" augments, amends, or even contradicts the written rules of law. In this light, the sociology of canon law must also address how "living" ecclesiastical law augments, modifies, or supplants positive canon law.

One authorised example of ecclesiastical "law in action" is customary law, formed from a local practice of legal customs. Customs may go beyond positive law—generating authorities, duties, rights, and sanctions which positive law does not cover—or are contrary to it—introducing authorities, duties, rights, and sanctions which contradict those of positive law. Canon law only explicitly rules out the formation of customary law in cases in which customs are incompatible with "divine law" (see canon 24 §1 CIC/1983). Other customs which go beyond the law or are unlawful become customary law after having been practiced for a full and uninterrupted span of thirty years (see canon 26 CIC/1983). A shorter period applies when the legislator gives special approbation to a custom. However, one also has to note the restrictive conditions for the emergence of customary law in canon law (see canons 23–28 CIC/1983). First, for customs to become customary law it requires a community of the faithful to take up a custom with the *intention* of introducing it *as law* (see c. 25 CIC/1983). In addition, a custom only regularly obtains legal force upon receiving the legislator's approval (see canon 23 CIC/1983). Ecclesiastical customary law therefore derives from a twofold dynamic. It grows from the bottom up insofar as a group in church establishes a customary practice. But it also requires top-down acknowledgment, as customs do not grow into customary law without the legislator's consent. A custom without the legislator's approval can acquire the quality of a law, but only after it has been practiced for many years and has remained unchallenged by the legislator, which one might understand as the legislator's tacit consent (see canons 26, 28 CIC/1983). Customary law in church therefore requires either the active involvement of the legislator in its formation, or his passive tolerance of its existence. This restriction has consequences for customs as ecclesiastical "law in action." On a practical level one may observe with Ladislas Orsy that canon law easily allows ecclesiastical authorities to suppress the emergence of customary law, which is also what happens in fact.[107] In terms of the sociology of law, the situation in church is therefore that "law in books" strictly controls customary "law in action" and, as a result, largely prevents its formation.

This gives rise to the further question to what extent positive canon law exerts a restrictive effect on ecclesiastical "law in action" in general. This question is difficult to answer: it would require a targeted in-depth study on the relationship between statutory and living law in the church. However, the first impression one gains when

---

[106] Ehrlich (1936, pp. 487–488).

[107] See Orsy (1984, pp. 67–68; 1992, p. 116).

examining statutory canon law is that the ecclesiastical legislator seeks to control the formation of "law in action" in general and deals with it restrictively as a matter of principle. One example may be found in the canonical regulations on associations where the law provides church authorities with manifold reservations allowing them to control the emergence and the content of the ecclesiastical associations' law to a great degree (see canons 299 §3, 314, 587 §2, 595 §1 CIC/1983). This overall top-down dynamic in church makes it difficult for "living law" to grow and flourish.

The insistent inclusion of church authorities in the formation of customary law and the emergence of other bottom-up law is also interesting in the light of the sociology of law, for a reason discussed by Brian Tamanaha. Tamanaha points out that the involvement of official agents in the development of customary law decreases the probability of customary law being real "living law." He observes that customary law tends to lose its reference to the de facto customs of a local group as soon as representatives of the official legal system become involved in its formation or are relevant for its continued existence. Tamanaha notes, "'customary law' recognised by official legal systems does not necessarily match actual lived customs."[108] For ecclesiastical customary law, this means that the involvement of the church authorities in the emergence of customary law as required by canon law can lead to customary law becoming detached from genuine local customs. This in turn threatens to deprive customary law of its character as true "law in action." This issue merits a study of its own which could examine in greater depth the degree to which the ecclesiastical authorities' approach to controlling the formation and existence of "living law" affects the character of the ecclesiastical legal system as an order composed of "law in books" and "law in action." Previous studies have identified a tendency in canon law to prefer "law in books." However, in light of the effectiveness of law, this also means that canon law is at risk of becoming a mere "law on paper"[109] which exists in written texts, but is largely ineffective in real life. I will continue to examine this problem in Sect. 6.2.7.

2.1.13 Institutionally Bound Doctrine

Having discovered legal norms in "law in books" and "law in action," the sociology of law must take a further step and clarify which of the norms influencing social practice are truly *legal* norms. My study has already referred to the temptation to succumb to the "panjurism" inherent within pluralist approaches to the law, to consider all social norms legal, and to run the risk of becoming arbitrary in distinguishing diverse normativities from one another as a consequence. We therefore need a criteriology which permits the identification of norms as legal norms. One first step towards solving this challenge, as I find, is provided by approaches

---

[108] Tamanaha (2008, p. 410).
[109] Original quote, "Papierrecht", Rehbinder (2014, p. 2).

which only recognise social norms as "law" when these derive from and are embedded in legal *institutions* as systems of legal norms. Brian Tamanaha, for instance, in critically scrutinising pluralist approaches to the law, states that legal pluralism tends to identify two phenomena as law, namely institutionally embedded social norms and their enforcement, and de facto social structures ordering the social.[110] However, as Tamanaha finds, the only candidates that really qualify as "law" are norms embedded in legal institutions. However, clarification is needed about what exactly it is that constitutes a *legal* institution. For the purposes of differentiation, Tamanaha finds it helpful to speak of "law" only when institutional structures are in place to allow for the *application* of norms. Hence, we may find institutions to be legal institutions when they also provide for the application of norms which they provide and embed. Harold Berman labelled this approach, which defines law as norms based on and connected with legal institutions—which are largely autonomous in comparison to other institutions—, a characteristic of western legal thought.[111] Berman wonders whether this approach would find acceptance in non-western legal cultures. Nevertheless, in the search for a definition of ecclesiastical law it is certainly of value. The institutional foundation of law can—in accordance with the western understanding of law, upon which canon law is also based—serve as a reliable legal attribute. Taking Roger Cotterrell's lead, we may understand the contribution of institutions to defining "law" to exist in their capacity to merge doctrine and practice. Cotterrell describes law as a doctrinal system in an institutionalised framework. In doing so, he points to the importance of doctrine as an attribute of law and to the significance of institutions which create and shape the doctrine. Cotterrell notes,

> Law thus consists, like many other normative systems, of rules, concepts, and principles and is distinguished from them in degree rather than in kind by the existence of an institutional structure for the development and organisation of doctrine. ... Law appears as doctrine produced in, embodied in and legitimating institutional practices.[112]

Jürgen Habermas expressed a similar thought when he referred to law as a doctrine-based system of knowledge and as an institutionalised system of action. He stated, "It is equally possible to understand law as a text, composed of legal propositions and their interpretations, and to view it as an institution, that is, as a complex of normatively regulated action."[113] In order to distinguish between law and other regulatory systems which are also doctrine-based, Habermas introduces two distinguishing criteria: first, law as an action system differs from other normativities such as morality insofar as "legal norms have an immediate effect on action".[114] With respect to doctrine, Habermas refers to the high level of rationalisation in law when he notes that "the comparatively high degree of rationality connected with

---

[110] See Tamanaha (1993, p. 211).

[111] See Berman (1983, pp. 7–8).

[112] Cotterrell (1983, p. 251).

[113] Habermas (1996, p. 79).

[114] Habermas (1996, p. 80).

legal institutions distinguishes these from quasi-natural institutional orders, for the former incorporate doctrinal knowledge, that is, knowledge that has been articulated and systematized, brought to a scholarly level, and interwoven with a principled morality".[115] Following Habermas, it is neither the institutionalisation nor the doctrinal structure of the law in itself that makes the law, but it is the effect of law on action and its rationality which marks out legal doctrine as belonging to an elaborate knowledge system. The significance of this latter characteristic for identifying law as law is of such importance to the criminologists Karl-Ludwig Kunz and Martino Mona that they define law as a three-dimensional phenomenon consisting of normativity, facticity, and logical systematicity.[116] So whilst all forms of social normativity work with abstract principles—and therefore possess doctrinal features—it is a particular characteristic of legal norms that they are institutionally embedded in an established regulatory system that not only contributes to the production of concrete rules but also to the production of a consistent doctrine. Accordingly, legislation, adjudication, and administration not only create legal norms but also contribute to the formation and development of legal doctrine. They produce doctrine via their institutional practices, insofar as they contribute to the development of doctrine by applying the legal norms to concrete facts. These contexts of applying the law merit additional scrutiny to understand what law is. Jean Carbonnier has contributed to understanding the connection between law and its application by defining law as norms and contexts of a *questioning* and *challenging* nature. For Carbonnier the essence of law does not lie in coercion but in the potential of the law to question facts and to challenge them. Carbonnier speaks of an "interrogative nature" of the law, which he understands as typical for the law.[117] The specificity of this interrogative structure of the law, in any case, is that the law allows us to challenge facts not merely privately, but in *institutional* form. By applying legal norms to concrete cases, the law creates procedures and verdicts as "institutions of contestation." These institutions, as Carbonnier finds, are so uniquely legal that they allow us to identify them as characteristics of law. One might sum up his approach and generalise his observation by identifying *justiciability* as an essential characteristic of the law. Law is a doctrine within an institutional framework. This institutional embedding ensures the justiciability of law. However, understanding law as justiciable norms and judicial practices does not in fact require law to essentially involve procedures and institutional contestation. "Law" is rather about the *possibility* of turning to institutional contestation, as Carbonnier understands it. In a similar vein and with regard to canon law, Ludger Müller speaks of justiciability as the possibility of relying on organised procedures to receive a verdict about what is legal and what is illegal.[118] Following these approaches, the key characteristic of law is therefore not its enforceability in a Weberian sense, but the

---

[115] Habermas (1996, p. 80).

[116] See Kunz and Mona (2006, pp. 6–8).

[117] See Carbonnier (1974, p. 125).

[118] See Müller (1991, p. 79).

opportunity to turn to legal institutions to receive their decision about what is legal and what is illegal. However, the much-cited Eugen Ehrlich refused to accept this kind of approach. Ehrlich considered law to be a factual phenomenon, and not necessarily a justiciable one. He wrote, "The order of human society is based upon the fact that, in general, legal duties are being performed, not upon the fact that failure to perform gives rise to a cause of action."[119] In light of the reality of the law, Ehrlich might well be right: social orders largely function tolerably well without legal adjudication. Nevertheless, adjudication and other forms of institutional contestation, as I want to argue here, remain part of the concept of the law as a possibility. A norm that cannot be reified in legal procedures and comes without the possibility of being applied to a concrete case in a concrete legal setting is not a legal norm. If we follow this definition and apply it to canon law, it becomes most obvious that canon law formally identifies a number of norms as legal norms, although they are, strictly speaking, nothing of the kind. The current Code of Canon Law, for instance, contains a number of doctrinal statements which are formally posed as legal norms by inserting them into the Code, yet without giving them a justiciable quality. Sacramental law in particular contains these kinds of non-legal norms which present some fundamental propositions about the sacraments of a theological nature without carrying any legal meaning (eg canon 834 §1 CIC/1983). As these norms defy the option of institutional contestation, we may hardly understand them as legal norms. I will deal with this problem from a sociological perspective in Sect. 5.2.1. At this point in the discussion, it suffices to say that if we follow the concept of law which I rely upon, then we must note that not all norms which bear the formal appearance of legal norms possess genuine legal character.

2.1.14   State Law and Sub-state Laws

If we take law to mean a rationally structured knowledge system which offers us justiciable norms endowed with the option of institutional contestation, then the problem of panjurism, which declares all social norms to be law, is largely contained. The concept of law begins to take shape. However, Brian Tamanaha believes that this definition still needs some fleshing out. He says that it should be borne in mind that the modern concept of "law" is primarily concerned with *state* law.[120] Whilst non-state entities are indisputably able to generate quasi-legal social norms, the primary characteristic associated with the law in modernity is that it originates from the state. It comes as something of a surprise to find that the father of legal pluralism, Eugen Ehrlich, argues in much the same way. Ehrlich cites four reasons why the focus of attention is on the state when we speak of modern law, observing,

---

[119] Ehrlich (1936, p. 23).

[120] See Tamanaha (1993, pp. 192–217).

First its participation in lawmaking through legislation; secondly, its participation in the administration of law through the state courts and in parts through other tribunals; thirdly, its power and control over the state tribunals, by which it is enabled to give effect to its statutes; lastly, the idea that the preservation of a factual situation corresponding to the law can be effected primarily, or at least ultimately, through the state's power of compulsion.[121]

Whilst the primary focus of Ehrlich's sociology of law is on the diverse origins of the law, he also points out that the state is the predominant influence on law in modernity. However, as Ehrlich also emphasises, whilst state law accordingly occupies a position of primacy in socio-legal debates, this is certainly not the result of its exclusive status as law and more an indication of its *dominant* position in modern societies.

Similar considerations about the dominance of certain legal agents play a role in the current debates about the globalisation of law. Studies on the development of law as it adapts to the conditions of increased global unboundedness are currently recognising the limitations of statehood as the basis for forming global regulatory systems. The approaches acknowledge the state as the contingent source of law which has made a significant contribution to the field of modern law over the centuries, but note that the nation states are now reaching the limit of their capacity in a global order. These studies consequently document a certain ebbing away of state dominance in the field of law. Paul Schiff Berman points out, for example, that the traditional link between law and the national *territoriality* of states is an idea rooted in the seventeenth and eighteenth centuries. In the debates about the theory and sociology of law, this link has resulted in the close association between the concept of law and the sovereignty of the state, binding it in to the positive law of the nation states. But law and territoriality are not necessarily connected. Especially in the modern era, transnational law is increasingly demonstrating that the formation of legally relevant groups may occur based on criteria other than the territorial boundaries of nation states. It no longer seems necessary for a group to share a common geography or history in order to constitute a legal community. As a consequence, when discussing the constitutive elements of law, limiting one's perspective to nation states and their law is not justifiable. As Schiff Berman observes, different types of groups can invoke their status as a legal community and their own law, "if communities are based not on fixed attributes like geographical proximity, shared history, or face-to-face interaction, but instead on symbolic identification and social psychology, then there is not intrinsic reason to privilege nation-state communities over other possible community identifications that people might share."[122] Supranational, transnational, and subnational law, such as the law of religious groups, are therefore currently gaining in importance in the debates on law in the context of globalisation, questioning the traditional dominant position of modern state law to some degree.

---

[121] Ehrlich (1936, p. 139).
[122] Schiff Berman (2005, pp. 1109–1110).

With respect to the concept of law, these observations support my study's proposition that "law" is not identical with state law. As far as legal theory is concerned, there is no reason for the primacy of state law over the law of other legal groups. From a sociological viewpoint, however, we should not overlook that state law is accorded a position of primary importance due to its key social significance, even if globalisation is currently auguring a shift in this equation. Hence, state law cannot claim a monopoly of influence in the field of the law, neither theoretically nor practically, but still is, in any case, the dominant legal presence in the field of the social. This should always be borne in mind in socio-legal studies. The question arising from this finding is how it is possible to acknowledge the central role of state law sociologically without relapsing into a form of monism that is blind to non-state law. Roger Cotterrell argues against a narrow monistic understanding of law (as well as against the indefinable boundaries of law inherent in pluralist approaches) by arguing in favour of an intermediary position which acknowledges the state as the preeminent producer of law—and therefore acknowledges that the sociology of law must be particularly attentive to state law—but which is also alert to other groups as sources of law.[123] Nevertheless, the crux of Cotterrell's intermediary position is not that it avoids the monistic exclusion of non-state law and indiscriminate panjurism, but that it draws its understanding of the law from the interactions between state and non-state law. Cotterrell attempts to come to an understanding of what defines the law in a sociological sense by studying the relation between state and non-state law and subjecting it to comparative examination. From an historical perspective, this approach is supported by studies which point to the common origins of different legal traditions. Eugen Ehrlich points to the history of state law to show that many state norms have their roots in social, and often religious norms. Ehrlich even presumed that "we shall have to call the part played by the state in the creation of law a very limited one."[124] It is difficult to speculate about quantity, though. Max Weber, for instance, stressed the contribution canon law had made to the development of modern state law.[125] Whilst Harold Berman's thesis regarding the canonical roots of western law has not gone unchallenged in the historical debates, it demonstrates plausibly that we should not overlook the church's legal tradition in the formative history of state law in the western world.[126] It is a matter of debate whether the broad brush of Berman's theory is really tenable. But it is convincing in connection with certain individual legal matters. For example, numerous individual studies trace the religious roots of certain institutions of state law. Political scientist Tine Stein, to mention one example, mapped out the relations between Christian anthropology and modern constitutional law, by analysing especially the religious heritage of the principle of human

---

[123] See Cotterrell (1984, p. 304).

[124] Ehrlich (1936, p. 389).

[125] E.g. Weber (1978, pp. 828–831).

[126] See Berman (1983).

dignity.[127] These and other studies underline the importance of taking an intermediary approach to improving our understanding of law from a diachronic perspective, as they examine the common roots and historical links between legal systems. Adding to their insights are *synchronic* approaches, which examine the way in which legal systems interact in the present. We find these approaches in numerous studies that seek to understand law by comparing different legal systems. It is first and foremost scholars of the sociology of law who argue in favour of the state's preeminent position with respect to the law in modernity and who largely approach non-state law by comparing it with state law. One such scholar is Brian Tamanaha, who advocates for comparison as a preferred method which can prove helpful in understanding plural legal phenomena by identifying similarities and differences between them. Tamanaha is forthright in his argumentation. He believes in the necessity of comparison with state law in order to clarify whether normativities of non-state provenance are actually law, "the main test we apply to determine whether the proposed definition captures what we mean by law is to measure it against our intuitions about the essential characteristics of state law, sans the state."[128] Whilst this approach does not seem applicable to legal theories which maintain that the concept of law is not identical with state law, Tamanaha's method is certainly applicable with regard to the sociology of law. There is much to learn about non-state law from a comparison with state law, as Klaus Röhl explains. Röhl finds, for instance, that it is only interesting to analyse the mafia, the Palestine Liberation Organization, or General Motors as so-called "states within a state" insofar as all of these organisations compete with and challenge the state and its monopoly on the law.[129] The examples Röhl cites show plausibly that, from a sociological perspective, there seems to be an obvious difference between state law and non-state legal systems. It is for this reason that Jean Carbonnier avoids speaking of "plural laws" in the first place, preferring instead to speak of *infra*legal phenomena[130] or "sub-law".[131] This problematic reduction in status that Carbonnier's term implies can be avoided by making use of a distinction applied by other socio-legal scholars. They differentiate between horizontal and vertical legal pluralism, depending on whether plural legal orders exist side by side or relate to each other in hierarchical schemes of sub- and superordination.[132] Similarly, Paul Schiff Berman speaks of the law of "subnational communities"[133] in relation to the law of religious communities and other non-state groups. This classification is

---

[127] See Stein (2007).

[128] Tamanaha (1993, p. 201).

[129] See Röhl (1987, p. 221). For an in-depth analysis of how criminal organisations and their norms challenge state law while building "illegal legal" orders see Diana Villegas's book on the "mafia law" of organised crime in Columbia, see Villegas (2018).

[130] See Carbonnier (1974, pp. 32–33).

[131] Original quote, "Unterrecht", Carbonnier (1974, p. 137).

[132] E.g. Raiser (2007, p. 316).

[133] Schiff Berman (2005, p. 1111).

conceptually helpful and appropriate for a sociology of canon law, too. It accommodates the central position of state law in modern societies without relapsing into legal monism, and also permits the accurate description of the various kinds of different connections between national entities such as the states and subnational groups producing non-state law such as canon law.

2.2 A Sociological Look at Canon Law

The differences between legal theory and the sociology of law outlined above must also be given due consideration as the discussion turns to canon law. As we have already noted, it is not necessary to involve the state to understand canon law *as law*. From a sociological viewpoint, however, much can be learned about current canon law by studying it in comparison with state law, the dominant law of modernity. However, we have to consider the consequences of doing this on the sociology of canon law. This includes asking if we can conceive of canon law either as a source, a support, or a rival to state law—three qualifications which Klaus Röhl proposes to describe the relationship between state law and non-state law.[134] There are a number of possible objections to studying canon law in comparison with state law. From an historical perspective, one might object that Roman Catholic canon law had already been established as law when modern state law emerged. Granted, arguments of seniority are of limited sociological value and historical arguments pointing out the reliance of secular law on canon law are also only of limited use in trying to comprehend the nature of law in modern society. Many historical roots of modern state law lie in religious law. Yet modern law does not depend upon a religious foundation for its validity in modern society. Nowadays, state law stands rather alone as the dominant law in society. However, it is closely connected with legal systems deriving from sub-state groups such as canon law and relates to them—at times constructively, at times in conflict. For a contemporary sociology of canon law, comparison of state law and canon law therefore promises to provide an insight into the status of canon law in our present times.

2.2.1 Sovereign Law of the Church

This comparison can only succeed, however, if we sufficiently account for the above-mentioned differences between legal theory and the sociology of law. Canonical legal theory assumes that canon law exists in its own right. Like the state, the modern church asserts a claim to autonomy, which imbues its law with authority. In

---

[134] See Röhl (1987, pp. 220–221).

consequence, the legal system of the church draws its validity from within the church itself, and is a result of the sovereignty of the church as its inherent power to govern its own affairs. The power of the church to produce its own law is also plausible from a sociological point of view. Georges Gurvitch, for example, also applies the concept of sovereignty to explain why non-state groups are legally productive. He understands the fact that groups emerge and develop the capacity to stand for themselves and assert themselves as the result of them developing sovereignty.[135] His argument rests on the phenomenon of emergence, which equips a group with abilities above and beyond the collective abilities of the group's individual members, allowing the group *as a group* to stand alone and to act as a sovereign entity. One inherent outcome of the sovereignty of groups is their ability to create law. Following Gurvitch, non-state agents can therefore also lay claim to the sovereign capacity to create law. Gurvitch also addresses the open question of the effectiveness of this law. He is aware of the problem that, even though we might understand non-state law as law produced by sovereign agents, this does not explain how this law can take effect in parallel to state law, bearing in mind that modern state law tends to sideline any other law. Gurvitch concedes that this is a challenge. However, he is adamant that this does not preclude understanding non-state law such as canon law as the sovereign product of a non-state legal community. According to his theory, we may understand canon law as rooted in the sovereignty of the church. This idea resurfaces as a self-conception in canon law itself. We may find it, for instance, in ecclesiastical penal law, in which the church claims "its own inherent right" for itself, "to constrain with penal sanctions Christ's faithful who commit offences" (canon 1311 §1 CIC/1983). This norm introduces punishment and sanctions as instruments that the church has at its own sovereign disposal to defend the public good of the church and the salvation of souls. The reference to the "*nativum et proprium Ecclesiae ius*" serves three functions: First, it stresses the natural foundations of ecclesiastical penal law as rooted in the sovereignty of the church. Second, it establishes an analogy between the church and the state insofar as it indirectly hints at the state as the primary institution of modernity which claims sovereign rights to sanction and punish. Third, by indirectly confronting state law with canon law and its own proper claim to sanction and punish, the norm serves to demarcate canon law from state law. We may detect similar lines of thought in other canons of the Code of Canon Law. Canon 362 CIC/1983 of ecclesiastical constitutional law attributes to the pope "the innate and independent right to appoint, send, transfer, and recall his own legates either to particular churches in various nations or regions or to states and public authorities." Canon 1260 CIC/1983 of ecclesiastical property law claims the "innate right" of the church "to require from the Christian faithful those things which are necessary for the purposes proper to it." Canon 1254 §1 CIC/1983 confronts the state with the ecclesiastical claim of sovereignty in property matters, by emphasising the "innate right" of the church "to acquire, retain, administer, and alienate temporal goods independently from civil power." The norm explicitly qualifies the claim of

---

[135] See Gurvitch (1960, p. 173).

the church to act independently and sovereignly with regard to its property in demarcation to any potentially conflicting claims by the state. In property matters, as the law underlines, the church acts independently of the state based on its own sovereign property law.

We have to note though that this claim to sovereignty in canon law does have a rather anachronistic side to it, in reality but also with regard to its theory. From the perspective of legal theory, the church can plausibly claim the sovereign roots of its law and therefore position itself in parallel to state law by claiming that its law is comparably genuine. However, the papal magisterium has tied this idea, since the nineteenth century, to the contestable claim that canon law and state law have a comparable *social* standing. In the nineteenth century, ecclesiastical social theory began to conceive of church and state and their legal systems as complementary agents shaping society. The papal theory described church and state as two perfect societies ("*societates perfectae*") whose task it is to provide society with a secular and a spiritual order respectively. This theory was outlined succinctly by Leo XIII in the Encyclical *Immortale Dei* on the Christian Constitution of States. In this encyclical, Leo elevates the dualistic structure of the social order by two perfect societies, church and state, to the central principle of ecclesiastical ecclesiology and state theory. He admits that the state is an autonomous power, but argues that God in fact "has given the charge of the human race to two powers, the ecclesiastical and the civil, the one being set over divine, and the other over human, things."[136] Both of these powers are rooted in the same source, as Leo states, namely in God's desire to order the social with regard to its spiritual and temporal needs. This gives rise to two distinctly separate domains, the church and the state, which are nevertheless complementary domains in the organisation of all socially relevant matters. Matters spiritual, the *causae spirituales* and the *causae spiritualibus adnexae*, are the responsibility of ecclesiastical legislation, adjudication, and administration, while secular powers are responsible for settling legal matters of a worldly nature, *causae temporales*. Within each of their domains, church and state enjoy not only exclusive power and authority, but are equipped with all instruments of governance necessary to create and exercise their power. The reference to church and state as "*societates perfectae*" is based on this idea of a *perfect* equipping of both authorities with all of the instruments of power and control they need for their respective temporal and spiritual dominion.

2.2.2 Canon Law as Sub-state Law

The theoretical conception of the church as a perfect society has continued to shape ecclesiastical legal thought beyond the nineteenth century and is still influential

---

[136]No. 13. *Acta Sanctae Sedis, 18*, 166; English version: www.vatican.va/content/leo-xiii/en/encyclicals/documents/hf_l-xiii_enc_01111885_immortale-dei.html. Accessed 19 June 2021.

today. However, it is not entirely compatible with the sociological observation that state law enjoys a predominant position in most current societies. Anyone who views the relation between church and state as a balance of power between two coequal and perfectly equipped societies will find it hard to accept the sociological verdict that canon law is the law of a sub-state group. Nonetheless, as I said, this qualification does not disregard the sovereign provenance of ecclesiastical norms. It rather acknowledges that sovereign canon law in modernity operates within a social framework largely defined by state law. Canonist Rik Torfs captured this status of the church in a rhetorical question, asking what social role the church and other religious groups seek to fulfil in the present day. There are two alternatives at hand, as Torfs suggests. The church might understand itself as part of civil society, albeit, as all religions, under the special protection of religious freedom as granted by the state. Alternatively, it might go on to understand itself as a society separate from civil society and as an autonomous power and even as a counterforce to civil society.[137] It is fairly evident which model Torfs finds realistic and convincing for a modern church. The idea that church and state are two coequal and complementary shapers of society is simply not reflected in today's reality. And it no longer enjoys widespread acceptance. Since the nineteenth century, society and politics has confronted Neo-Scholastic legal doctrine with growing opposition. Today, those faint echoes of the *Kulturkampf*, which aim at restoring the power of the Catholic Church in the social sphere, seem rather absurd, at least in the overwhelming majority of countries. In Europe, since the nineteenth century, ever fewer citizens have been willing to accept ecclesiastical attempts to subjugate society under ecclesiastical authority.[138] Attempts to stage the church as a social counterforce to the state already failed in the nineteenth century, and became fully obsolete in the twentieth century. The church therefore had and has to surrender its pretensions to quasi-statehood. It had to—and must still—learn to understand itself as part of civil society. This development had and has consequences for canon law. As the law of a sub-state agent in civil society, canon law can attain its social effectiveness in present-day society to no small degree only by constructively referencing state law. This becomes clear when studying the constitutional law on state and church relations of many western nations. The relation between church and state as set out in many secular constitutional systems does not reflect a balance between two coequal and independent authorities. On the contrary, the power of the church to act independently in plural societies is based to no small degree on constitutional commitments as granted by the states.[139] Otto von Gierke observed that the power of the church to shape society was already becoming increasingly dependent on the institutional guarantees provided by state law as early as the turn of the twentieth century. Gierke found that the state, by the end of the nineteenth century, had come to claim supreme sovereign power above all other powers and had come to

---

[137] See Torfs (2003, p. 42).

[138] See Hollerbach (1973, p. 29).

[139] See Carbonnier (1974, p. 138).

understand its law as supreme to all other legal orders. However, as the supreme source of law, the state also started to allow sub-state groups to benefit from state law whenever it found these groups served as public institutions.[140] In Germany, for example, the state grants religious communities under constitutional law the freedom to acquire the status of a public corporation (see article 140 of the German Basic Law in conjunction with article 137 section 5 of the Weimar Constitution). This status brings with it a number of legal benefits—such as the right to levy taxes (see article 140 of the German Basic Law in conjunction with article 137 section 6 of the Weimar Constitution). In addition, comprehensive institutional guarantees in the German legal system accord religious communities considerable freedom to participate in and contribute to society. Religious education in public schools, higher education in theological faculties at state universities, and pastoral care in the military or other state institutions are examples of the churches' involvement in society. Such contributions are certainly only possible because the state allows the churches and other religious groups to operate in these fields. Yet despite the state and its law enabling many of the activities undertaken by the religions in society today, we should also note that common state and church institutions such as religious education in German public schools are also partly based on religious law. Thus, they inter alia rely on canon law and hence on sovereign ecclesiastical legislation. Yet without the facilitation of the state these institutions would be inconceivable in the first place, both legally and practically. This finding does not diminish the authority of the church as sovereign in the generation of its law. But one has to observe that its institutional power to shape and influence modern society transpires in many ways to be an authority granted "on loan" by the states.[141] This imbalance of power is not always at the forefront of our minds. Jean Carbonnier calls it one of the great illusions created by legal pluralism that speaking of "legal pluralism" actually suggests cooperation and conflict between equal legal systems, whereas, as Carbonnier sees it, it is in fact rather a meeting of one true legal system and some rather poor imitation of it.[142] One might object to his rather stark polemic, but in many ways he describes the modern imbalance of power between state and sub-state law such as canon law with some accuracy.

---

[140] See Gierke (1902, p. 32).

[141] In light of this finding, Anglican canonist Norman Doe regards it as a major weakness of the sociology *of religion* that only very few studies analyse the relevance of state law for religious communities, see Doe (2004, pp. 68–92); see also Sandberg (2016, pp. 66–67, 76–77). Doe in particular suggests devoting more study of the sociology of religion to the state's law on religion as it is this law which fundamentally shapes the relationship between the state and religious communities.

[142] See Carbonnier (1974, p. 138).

2.2.3   Decreasing Social Significance

I have examined the difference between the law of the state and the law of non-state groups so far from the perspective of the social significance of the law. However, this difference also has an influence on sub-state law itself. This might become evident if we take the example of canon law. In this case, it is clear that canon law, despite the church self-confidently depicting itself as a "perfect society," was already losing much of its former social influence at the dawn of the twentieth century. The reduced social significance of canon law, which has been unfolding ever since, is reflected today in the limited extent of the church's legal reach. Simon Hecke explains how this development came about. He analyses the processes in which canon law changed from being an influential legal system in its own right with a major impact on society (Hecke speaks of former canon law as "*Gesellschaftsrecht*") to becoming a purely community-based "organisation law" ("*Organisationsrecht*") providing the church with a regulatory framework.[143] The processes of divergence between church and state in the modern era, which saw canon law sharpen its profile as the legal order of a sovereign church, also brought about the decline of its broader social relevance. Hecke describes this change in accordance with Luhmann as processes of functional social differentiation, pushing canon law out of the centre of society and confining it to the status of a law with relevance merely within the church. Hecke suggests that this development is unparalleled. He believes canon law to be the only example of a legal order which underwent this fundamental change from a broad *Gesellschaftsrecht* to a rather narrow *Organisationsrecht*.[144]

Canonical legal theory has now caught up with this change in the status of canon law. The Second Vatican Council, by attuning the definition of the church to speak more of "*communio*" than of "*societas*," not only liberated ecclesiology from ecclesiastical quasi-state ambitions, but also freed the legal foundations of the church from the grip of quasi-state approaches to canon law. In place of a quasi-state-like canon law which threatened to neglect the theological core of canon law, there appeared new theoretical approaches which saw canon law as emanating from the church as *communio* as the community of the faithful. Nowadays, legal theory is challenged with fleshing out the consequences of this ecclesiological shift. Its task is to continue to refine the theory of canon law to understand it more in terms of a law of the ecclesiastical community,[145] or as an "organisation law" in the Heckean sense. The Code of Canon Law of 1983 went some way towards achieving this goal, as the example of ecclesiastical penal law might help to illustrate. Whilst at the dawn of the twentieth century the church still conceived of itself as a quasi-state, generally criminalising all sorts of offences against Catholic morals, today's church makes do with a slimmed-down penal law. Compared to the old Code of 1917, the 1983 Code has a pro-liberal agenda and curbs some of the old regulatory frenzy to allow

---

[143] See Hecke (2017, particularly pp. 34–39).

[144] See Hecke (2017, p. 5).

[145] E.g. Hahn (2017a; b).

Catholics more freedom.[146] The reduced penal law now primarily focuses on preventing church members from engaging in behaviour which might endanger their salvation or damage the church. The significant streamlining of criminal offences in the current penal law of the Code reflects this reduced view. When revising the Code before 1983, the legislator followed the recommendation to dispense with those penal norms where non-legal means proved sufficient to protect ecclesiastical interests.[147] Whilst the old Code of Canon Law of 1917 still contained 101 canons with penal norms (see canons 2314–2414 CIC/1917), the current Code only contains 36 canons with penal prescripts (see canons 1364–1399 CIC/1983). The current law no longer includes the offences of desecrating a grave (see canon 2328–2329 CIC/1917), verbal abuse of a church dignitary (see canon 2344 CIC/1917), or attempted suicide (see canon 2350 §2 CIC/1917). Whilst all of these acts continue to be regarded as sinful according to Catholic morals, they have lost their status as crimes. This pro-liberal move coincides with Simon Hecke's sociological observation about canon law having to reduce its status and becoming more of an internal organisation law. And it answers to the theoretical need for a foundation of canon law which grounds the law less on ecclesiastical quasi-state ambitions and more on theological requirements. The church as a community of faith requires a law which acknowledges the freedom which is essential for the faith. The ecclesiastical legislator must therefore downsize canon law to a point at which it limits this freedom to the smallest possible degree and encourages religious freedom to the greatest possible degree. It is a matter of debate, however, whether this kind of canon law continues to be "law." A small number of canonists such as Peter Huizing are sceptical about whether the genuinely community-based character of canon law is adequately represented by understanding canon law as "law." For Huizing, speaking of "law" in the modern era always has a reference to state law. Huizing himself therefore suggests changing the wording and, instead of speaking of "canon law," suggests speaking of the "order of the church."[148] However, for a number of reasons his initiative to move canon law outside of "law" has met with a rather lukewarm response from most scholars of canon law.[149] Jan Vries, for example,

---

[146]E.g. Schmitz (1977, p. 382); Demel (2014, p. 50).

[147]See Pontifical Commission for the Revision of the Code of Canon Law (1969, p. 79).

[148]E.g. Huizing (1973, pp. 156–184). Following Huizing, Urs Brosi noted a couple of years ago that canon law might cease to be law in a stricter sense and become a mere "church order." In any case, Brosi thinks this change might be owed to canon law's loss of effectiveness. As canon law has increasingly come to lack enforceability, as Brosi argues, it will eventually cease to be law. Therefore it might be more adequate to speak of a "church order", in a similar vein to some Protestant churches, see Brosi (2013, p. 19). Whilst it seems necessary indeed to consider this terminological option, I am doubtful whether this is due to the reason mentioned by Brosi. I am doubtful, as mentioned, as I do not regard the concept of law to be essentially connected with the *enforceability* of norms. It is indeed evident that canon law is at present losing much of its former effectiveness. However, in my opinion, we neither capture that phenomenon adequately nor do we get a clearer understanding of the concepts of "law" and "order" by changing terminology from "canon law" to "church order."

[149]E.g. Krämer (1979, pp. 15–18); Vries (1998, pp. 137–149); Graulich (2006, pp. 304–305).

pointed out that understanding canon law as law does not inhibit the personal and free quality of the relationship between God and the faithful and among the faithful as a community,[150] concerns which Huizing had raised. Furthermore, as Vries found, calling canon law "church order" does not help to clarify what actually constitutes canon law. What speaks against referring to canon law as "law" is in fact that this wording in modernity inevitably evokes an analogy with the state, thereby concealing more and revealing less about what it is precisely that constitutes canon law. What does speak in favour of calling canon law "law" is not merely that "canon *law*" is an established term, but that this term actually denotes—in church as much as elsewhere—a doctrinal system of norms which derive from and are connected with institutions which guarantee their justiciability. Whilst state law and canon law pursue distinctly different aims, they are both guided by their purpose of establishing order, and are thus fairly comparable in some respects. As legal systems provide legal communities with structure, they share a number of similarities, as Ladislas Orsy observes,

> In all legal systems there is one common purpose: to bring balance into the life and operations of a human community. Now the church is a human community; therefore, to use the wisdom accumulated in legal tradition is obviously fitting for the church, although its use must be always selective and have due respect for the specific nature of a religious community.[151]

As I share Orsy's proposition, my study continues to speak of "canon *law*." However, it does this whilst acknowledging that Huizing is justified when he says that speaking of "law" in modernity casts a problematic quasi-state shadow over the church and its law.

2.2.4 State Law as a Frame of Reference

The above discussion shows that an intermediate theory which accounts for the central position of state law in modern societies has a role to play in the development of a sociology of canon law, as it helps to grasp the reality of canon law. This realisation led canonist John Huels to make the understandable statement, "canon law cannot be interpreted well without reference to a society's secular legal system or systems, whether formal or informal".[152] However much it is the task of canon law theory to locate the source of canon law inside the church itself, it is not currently possible to speak of canon law from a sociological perspective without considering it in terms of its relationship with other legal systems, with state law being foremost among them. One may accept this fact or regret it. However, one cannot and should not ignore it. To ignore the interrelationship between canon law and other legal

---

[150] See Vries (1998, pp. 154–158).

[151] Orsy (1992, p. 187).

[152] Huels (1987, p. 276).

systems would mean gravely misjudging its reality. One aspect of the reality of canon law in our present times is, among other things, that we tend to view it through the prism of state law. Not only have secular members of society chosen this rather comparative method of understanding religious law by comparing it with state law; Catholics, too, rely on this hermeneutical approach. Nowadays, the vast majority of citizens, including Catholic Christians, primarily associate "law" with state law. The legal culture of their own civil society creates the primary referential parameter for their experience of law and their expectations with regard to law. And they draw their knowledge of the law primarily from state law. My self-observation supports this thesis. As a canonist working with canon law on a daily basis, my first reaction when I hear the term "law" is intuitively to think of state law. I do not discern what canon law is or should be by examining canon law purely, but by comparing it with state law. So my familiarity with and knowledge of canon law are clearly epistemo-logically dependent: they are based on my more or less reliable pre-existing knowl-edge of state law. This prior knowledge also influences my attitude towards canon law and, as I want to suggest, most Catholics' attitudes towards it, too. John Huels already noted back in the 1980s, "The attitudes of people toward law and their experiences of it in society affect the way they view and approach canon law".[153] This is no different today. Individuals socialised in democratic states tend to judge ecclesiastical legislation based on their knowledge of democratic legislation. They evaluate ecclesiastical adjudication the light of state adjudication. And they assess the functioning of ecclesiastical administration in comparison to the modern bureau-cratic executive.

2.2.5 Simultaneous Non-synchronicity

Unsurprisingly, this comparative perspective is a source of conflict. This is because—in contrast to what we are familiar with in secular states and democratic orders—canon law does not come into being through democratic processes. And it proves to be less liberal than the law of modern constitutional states. Instead, the church still relies on an absolutist concept of governance. This collides with the democratic socialisation of many church members and impacts the way many Catholics perceive canon law. Historian Brian Tierney sees the roots of this conflict in history. It is the consequence, he believes, of an asynchronous modern develop-ment which has separated church members and in particular the laity from church leadership. Tierney senses an irony in the development that "vast Catholic populations became irrevocably committed to political democracy at a time when the Roman see had committed itself to the improbable task of governing a world-wide Church through the institutional apparatus of a petty baroque despotism."[154]

---

[153] Huels (1987, p. 276).
[154] Tierney (1966, p. 15).

Following Tierney, one has to understand canon law as the legal order expressing and securing the ecclesiastical authorities' absolutist ambitions. From the perspective of culture theory, this observation begs the question how we may conceive of this most peculiar coexistence of modern state law and premodern or rather early modern canon law. We have to understand how it is possible for canon law to feed elements of late medieval or early modern governance theory into current contexts. *Non-synchronicity* is a helpful concept to describe this phenomenon. To classify phenomena of this kind, the social sciences frequently use the theory of nonsynchronism, following the idea of the "non-simultaneity of the simultaneous," which Ernst Bloch formulated in the 1930s in order to explain the temporal coexistence of contrasting interpretations of the present in a society. Bloch stated, "Not all people exist in the same Now. They do so only externally, through the fact that they can be seen today. But they are thereby not yet living at the same time with the others. They rather carry an earlier element with them; this interferes."[155] In this light, we may also come to understand state law and canon law as existing at the same time. However, both laws deal with the same time in different ways. Following Bloch, one may find that canon law still includes many characteristics of earlier times. It brings a good many elements of premodern and early modern law with it into our present times. Notwithstanding these specific observations, we have to note that *all law* essentially contains asynchronous elements. This phenomenon is the focus of William Ogburn's theory of cultural lag, which describes the unavoidable cultural time delay in the development of law.[156] Law is always somewhat late, compared to the developments of society and its social and cultural evolution.[157] Legal norms are always a slightly delayed reflection of social norms. Consequently, one may detect phase shifts in the developments of society and law, as early socio-legal scholars such as Eugen Ehrlich already observed.[158] Émile Durkheim noted in a similar vein that situations occur in which "law no longer corresponds to the state of existing society".[159] Roscoe Pound likewise detected an "inevitable difference in rate of progress between law and public opinion."[160] After all, as Pound added, "law has always been dominated by ideas of the past long after they have ceased to be vital in other departments of learning."[161] This rather backwards-facing basic structure of law, which confronts each and every law with the allegation of being stagnant and conservative, as Klaus Röhl observes,[162] essentially applies to canon law, too. But it takes on an added significance in canon law, because canon law is not simply at one remove from the development of social norms like all law, but also lags behind the

---

[155] Bloch (1991, p. 97).

[156] See Ogburn (1964); in a similar vein already Gurvitch (1960, p. 215).

[157] See Röhl (1987, p. 244).

[158] E.g. Ehrlich (1936, p. 401).

[159] Durkheim (1960, p. 65).

[160] Pound (1910, p. 26).

[161] Pound (1910, p. 25).

[162] See Röhl (1987, p. 244).

achievements of modern law. This distance arises because the church intentionally adopts and sometimes must adopt a critical stance towards contemporary cultures in order to maintain its profile.[163] The church is a part of social culture, yet it also understands itself as countercultural. Distancing itself from society's mainstream culture, it adopts a position of conscious detachment. However, by doing so it increases the cultural deficits of canon law in relation to the cultural developments of society in general. Some of Catholic canon law is therefore—to borrow Bloch's phrase—located in a different "Now" to state law.

2.2.6 Dissonant Experiences of Law

However, because the *Now* of state law is what shapes the way church members experience the present, they tend to view canon law as an anachronistic legal order. Yet the solution to this problem does not lie in attacking the fact that their understanding of law is rooted in the modern state. First of all, it is sociologically unrealistic to expect church members to change their view of the law. Second, there is no theological basis or justification for expecting this to happen. This is because the influence of state law on the church members is not an accident of fate, but a perfectly normal development, as conciliar ecclesiology reminds us. This becomes clear when studying the teaching of the Second Vatican Council about the church. The Pastoral Constitution *Gaudium et spes* notes, "The joys and the hopes, the griefs and the anxieties of the men of this age ... these are the joys and hopes, the griefs and anxieties of the followers of Christ."[164] This statement is not only an expression of solidarity between Christians and the people of today—and hence with modern individuals living in plural societies and secular states—, but is also the acknowledgement that Christians are themselves members of plural societies and have therefore been socialised in their societies' cultures, including contemporary legal cultures. Pluralist societies are not therefore adversarial to the church and to its mission, but are adversarial to the space in which ecclesiastical life unfolds. This is not the result of an ecclesiastical "self-secularisation" (a catchword that has found increased usage in conservative circles within the church since Benedict XVI called for the church's "detachment from the world" in his controversial 2011 Freiburg speech),[165] but an acknowledgement that church and "world" are indivisible, both sociologically and theologically. It is therefore no accident that secular legal cultures shape the way in which Catholics understand the law. On the contrary, it is the natural way in which contemporary Catholics

---

[163] See Hecke (2017, pp. 92–93).

[164] No. 1. *Acta Apostolicae Sedis, 58,* 1025; English version: www.vatican.va/archive/hist_councils/ii_vatican_council/documents/vat-ii_const_19651207_gaudium-et-spes_en.html. Accessed 19 June 2021.

[165] See Benedict XVI (2011).

reflect their experiences in church in light of their other social experiences in the "world." When modern Catholics confront canon law with state law, this is neither provocation nor an error of category, but the natural consequence of understanding church as an entity which has its place in the "world" and among other agents influencing modern cultures.[166] However, sociologically and with respect to canon law, major tensions arise from this confrontation, particularly from many church members' disappointed expectations with respect to canon law. For Catholics socialised in democratic political and secular legal cultures, contact with canon law may be a sobering experience. Georg Essen describes this problem as follows,

> The fact that the modern world is the primary horizon of reference to Catholic Christians supports the finding of the sociology of law that a culture of transparency as called for by the plural public and a liberal culture of the law as is common in liberal democratic orders are formative for the liberal understanding of human beings to a degree that they cannot simply 'wipe it off' or relinquish it when they enter the inner realm of the church.[167]

Current canon law widely fails to fulfil many church members' expectations of law. Whilst state law grants freedom of speech, canon law restricts freedom of speech (see canon 212 §3 CIC/1983). Whilst state law grants freedom of science, canon law restricts freedom of science (see canon 218 CIC/1983). Whilst state law grants equality of women and men, canon law excludes women from ordination (see canon 1024 CIC/1983) and consequently from obtaining ecclesiastical offices endowed with the power to govern the church (see canon 274 §1 CIC/1983).

However, these divergent expectations are only one side of the story. In church, they meet with a dynamic which aggravates the problem. This is because canon law also confronts the church members with an additional expectation, namely with the expectation not only to abide by the law, as is the expectation of secular law, but also with the expectation to be obedient to church authorities and to *accept* the law as a consequence of this obedience. Hence, canon law not only expects the church members' compliance but expects them to embrace the law, including disappointing laws, as a result of their duty "to follow with Christian obedience those things which the sacred pastors, inasmuch as they represent Christ, declare as teachers of the faith or establish as rulers of the Church" (canon 212 §1 CIC/1983). Hence, Catholics are continuously called upon and expected to juggle the cognitive dissonances that arise out of colliding expectations deriving from state law and canon law. In consequence, being a Catholic nowadays means, to no small extent, experiencing and enduring cognitive dissonances. This reference to Leon Festinger's term "cognitive dissonance"[168] makes clear the socio-psychological predicament arising from the official

---

[166] See *Lumen gentium*, no. 31. *Acta Apostolicae Sedis, 57*, 37.

[167] Original quote, "Die Tatsache, dass die Welt der Moderne der primäre Referenzhorizont katholischer Christenmenschen ist, begründet den rechtssoziologischen Befund, dass die Kultur der Transparenz, die die plurale Öffentlichkeit einfordert, sowie die liberale Rechtskultur, wie sie freiheitlich demokratischen Rechtsordnungen eigentümlich ist, das Freiheitsbewusstsein von Menschen in einem Maße prägt, dass sie es nicht sozusagen abstreifen und hinter sich lassen können, wenn sie den Binnenraum der Kirche betreten", Essen (2013, p. 217).

[168] See Festinger (1957).

church's expectations of Catholics who have been socialised in democratic societies. This predicament also results in a problem of effectiveness for canon law, an issue that I will discuss in Sect. 6.2.

Bibliography

Baer, S. (2021). *Rechtssoziologie: Eine Einführung in die interdisziplinäre Rechtsforschung* (4th ed.). Nomos.

Bell, G. F. (2012). Religious legal pluralism revisited: The status of the Roman Catholic Church and Her Canon Law in Singapore. *Asian Journal of Comparative Law, 7,* 1–37.

Benda-Beckmann, F. v. (2002). Who's afraid of legal pluralism? *Journal of Legal Pluralism and Unofficial Law, 34,* 37–82.

Benedict XVI. (2011). Address during the meeting with Catholics engaged in the life of the church and society, 25 September 2011, Concert Hall, Freiburg im Breisgau. English version. Retrieved June 19, 2021, from www.vatican.va/content/benedict-xvi/en/speeches/2011/september/documents/hf_ben-xvi_spe_20110925_catholics-freiburg.html

Berman, H. J. (1983). *Law and revolution: The formation of the western legal tradition.* Harvard University Press.

Bloch, E. (1991). *Heritage of our times* (Neville & S. Plaice, Trans.). Polity Press.

Bottoni, R., Cristofori, R., & Ferrari, S. (Eds.). (2016). *Religious rules, state law, and normative pluralism—a comparative overview* (Ius Comparatum—Global studies in comparative law 18). Springer.

Brosi, U. (2013). *Recht, Strukturen, Freiräume: Kirchenrecht* (Studiengang Theologie 9, überarbeitet und mit einem Beitrag zum deutschen Staatskirchenrecht ergänzt von I. Kreusch). Theologischer Verlag Zürich.

Carbonnier, J. (1974). *Rechtssoziologie* (Schriftenreihe zur Rechtssoziologie und Rechtstatsachenforschung 31). Duncker & Humblot.

Carbonnier, J. (2001). *Flexible droit: Pour une sociologie du droit sans rigueur* (10th ed.). LGDJ.

Corecco, E. (1981). Erwägungen zum Problem der Grundrechte der Christen in Kirche und Gesellschaft. *Archiv für katholisches Kirchenrecht, 150,* 421–453.

Cotterrell, R. (1983). The sociological concept of law. *Journal of Law & Society, 10,* 241–255.

Cotterrell, R. (1984). *The sociology of law: An introduction.* Butterworths.

Demel, S. (2014). *Einführung in das Recht der katholischen Kirche: Grundlagen—Quellen—Beispiele* (Einführung Theologie). Wissenschaftliche Buchgesellschaft.

Doe, N. (2004). A sociology of law on religion—Towards a new discipline: Legal responses to religious pluralism in Europe. *Law & Justice—The Christian Law Review, 152,* 68–92.

Durkheim, É. (1960). *The division of labor in society* [1893] (G. Simpson, Trans.). The Free Press.

Ehrlich, E. (1936). *Fundamental principles of the sociology of law* (W. L. Moll, Trans., with an introduction by R. Pound). The Harvard University Press.

Essen, G. (2013). Nachholende Selbstmodernisierung? Katholische Kirche und politische Öffentlichkeit. *Theologie der Gegenwart, 56,* 208–220.

Ferrari, S. (2016). Religious rules and legal pluralism: An introduction. In R. Bottoni, R. Cristofori & S. Ferrari (Eds.), *Religious rules, state law, and normative pluralism—A comparative overview* (Ius Comparatum—Global Studies in Comparative Law 18, pp. 1–25). Springer.

Festinger, L. (1957). *A theory of cognitive dissonance.* Stanford University Press.

Gierke, O. v. (1902). *Das Wesen der menschlichen Verbände* (Rede bei Antritt des Rektorats am 15. Oktober 1902 gehalten). Duncker & Humblot.

Graulich, M. (2006). *Unterwegs zu einer Theologie des Kirchenrechts: Die Grundlegung des Rechts bei Gottlieb Söhngen (1892–1971) und die Konzepte der neueren Kirchenrechtswissenschaft.* Ferdinand Schöningh.

Gurvitch, G. (1960). *Grundzüge der Soziologie des Rechts* (Soziologische Texte 6, vom Verfasser autorisierte deutsche Ausgabe mit einer internationalen Bibliographie der Rechtssoziologie von P. Trappe). Luchterhand.

Habermas, J. (1996). *Between facts and norms: Contributions to a discourse theory of law and democracy* (W. Rehg, Trans.). The MIT Press.

Hahn, J. (2017a). Wieviel an Recht verträgt die Kirche? Eine theoretische und theologische Problemanzeige zur Reichweite des kirchlichen Regelungsanspruchs. In C. Ohly, W. Rees & L. Gerosa (Eds.), *Theologia Iuris Canonici: Festschrift für Ludger Müller zur Vollendung des 65. Lebensjahres* (pp. 81–97). Duncker & Humblot.

Hahn, J. (2017b). Regelungsarmut: Notwendigkeit und Herausforderung kirchlichen Rechts. In R. Althaus, J. Hahn & M. Pulte (Eds.), *Im Dienst der Gerechtigkeit und Einheit: Festschrift für Heinrich J. F. Reinhardt zur Vollendung seines 75. Lebensjahres* (Beihefte zum Münsterischen Kommentar 75, pp. 241–261). Wingen.

Hecke, S. (2017). *Kanonisches Recht: Zur Rechtsbildung und Rechtsstruktur des römisch-katholischen Kirchenrechts.* Springer.

Hollerbach, A. (1973). Das christliche Naturrecht im Zusammenhang des allgemeinen Naturrechtsdenkens. In F. Böckle & E.-W. Böckenförde (Eds.), *Naturrecht in der Kritik* (pp. 9–38). Grünewald.

Huels, J. M. (1987). Interpreting canon law in diverse cultures. *The Jurist, 47,* 249–293.

Huizing, P. J. M. (1973). Die Kirchenordnung. In J. Feiner & M. Löhrer (Eds.), *Mysterium Salutis: Grundriss heilsgeschichtlicher Dogmatik vol IV.2* (pp. 156–184). Benziger.

Krämer, P. (1979). *Warum und wozu kirchliches Recht? Zum Stand der Grundlagendiskussion in der katholischen Kirchenrechtswissenschaft* (Canonistica, Beiträge zum Kirchenrecht 3). Paulinus.

Kunz, K.-L., & Mona, M. (2006). *Rechtsphilosophie, Rechtstheorie, Rechtssoziologie: Eine Einführung in die theoretischen Grundlagen der Rechtswissenschaft.* UTB.

Leo XIII. (1885). Encyclical *Immortale Dei* on the Christian Constitution of States, 1 November 1885. *Acta Sanctae Sedis, 18,* 161–180.

Luhmann, N. (1970). Positivität des Rechts als Voraussetzung einer modernen Gesellschaft. *Jahrbuch für Rechtssoziologie und Rechtstheorie, 1,* 175–202.

Luhmann, N. (1986). *Die soziologische Beobachtung des Rechts.* Suhrkamp.

Luhmann, N. (1995). *Social systems* (J. Bednarz, Jr. & D. Baecker, Trans., foreword by E. M. Knodt). Stanford University Press.

Luhmann, N. (2004). *Law as a social system* (Oxford socio-legal studies, F. Kastner, R. Nobles, D. Schiff & R. Ziegert, Eds., K. A. Ziegert, Trans.). Oxford University Press.

Luhmann, N. (2014). *A sociological theory of law* (M. Albrow, Ed., E. King-Utz & M. Albrow, Trans.). Routledge.

Möllers, C. (2020). *The possibility of norms: Social practice beyond morals and causes.* Oxford University Press.

Müller, L. (1991). *Kirchenrecht—analoges Recht? Über den Rechtscharakter der kirchlichen Rechtsordnung* (Dissertationen, Kanonistische Reihe 6). EOS.

Newig, J. (2003). *Symbolische Umweltgesetzgebung: Rechtssoziologische Untersuchungen am Beispiel des Ozongesetzes, des Kreislaufwirtschafts- und Abfallgesetzes sowie der Großfeuerungsanlagenverordnung* (Schriftenreihe zur Rechtssoziologie und Rechtstatsachenforschung 84). Duncker & Humblot.

Ogburn, W. F. (1964). *On culture and social change: Selected papers* (O. D. Duncan, Ed., with an introduction by O. D. Duncan). The University of Chicago Press.

Orsy, L. M. (1980). The interpreter and his art. *The Jurist, 40,* 27–56.

Orsy, L. M. (1984). Reception and non-reception of law: A canonical and theological consideration. *Canon Law Society of America Proceedings, 46,* 66–70.

Orsy, L. M. (1992). *Theology and canon law: New horizons for legislation and interpretation.* Liturgical Press.

Pontifical Commission for the Revision of the Code of Canon Law. (1969). Principles guiding the revision of the code of canon law. *Communicationes, 1,* 77–85.

Pound, R. (1910). Law in books and law in action. *American Law Review, 44,* 12–36.

Raiser, T. (2007). *Grundlagen der Rechtssoziologie* (4th ed.). UTB.

Rehbinder, M. (2014). *Rechtssoziologie: Ein Studienbuch* (8th ed.). C. H. Beck.

Reuter, A. (2014). *Religion in der verrechtlichten Gesellschaft: Rechtskonflikte und öffentliche Kontroversen um Religion als Grenzarbeiten am religiösen Feld* (Critical studies in religion/ Religionswissenschaft 5). Vandenhoeck & Ruprecht.

Röhl, K. F. (1987). *Rechtssoziologie: Ein Lehrbuch.* Heymann.

Röhl, K. F. (2010). Die Macht der Symbole. In M. Cottier, J. Estermann & M. Wrase (Eds.), *Wie wirkt Recht? Ausgewählte Beiträge zum ersten gemeinsamen Kongress der deutschsprachigen Rechtssoziologie-Vereinigungen, Luzern 2008* (Recht und Gesellschaft/Law and Society 1, pp. 267–299). Nomos.

Rottleuthner, H., & Rottleuthner-Lutter, M. (2010). Effektivität von Recht: Der Beitrag der Rechtssoziologie. In G. Wagner (Ed.), *Kraft Gesetz: Beiträge zur rechtssoziologischen Effektivitätsforschung* (pp. 13–34). Springer.

Rouco Varela, A., & Corecco, E. (1998). *Sakrament und Recht—Antinomie in der Kirche?* (Kirchenrecht im Dialog 1). Ferdinand Schöningh.

Sandberg, R. (2016). A sociological theory of law and religion. In F. Cranmer, M. Hill, C. Kenny & R. Sandberg (Eds.), *The confluence of law and religion: Interdisciplinary reflections on the work of Norman Doe* (pp. 66–77). Cambridge University Press.

Schiff, D. N. (1976). Socio-legal theory: Social structure and law. *The Modern Law Review, 39,* 287–310.

Schiff Berman, P. (2005). Conflict of laws, globalization, and cosmopolitan pluralism. *The Wayne Law Review, 51,* 1105–1145.

Schmitz, H. (1977). Tendenzen nachkonziliarer Gesetzgebung. *Archiv für katholisches Kirchenrecht, 146,* 381–419.

Schuppert, G. F. (2017). *Governance of Diversity: Zum Umgang mit kultureller und religiöser Pluralität in säkularen Gesellschaften* (Religion und Moderne 10). Campus.

Searle, J. R. (2010). *Making the social world: The structure of human civilization.* Oxford University Press.

Second Vatican Council. (1965). Dogmatic Constitution *Lumen gentium* on the Church, 21 November 1964. *Acta Apostolicae Sedis, 57,* 5–75.

Second Vatican Council. (1966a). Declaration *Dignitatis humanae* on Religious Freedom, 7 December 1965. *Acta Apostolicae Sedis, 58,* 929–946.

Second Vatican Council. (1966b). Pastoral Constitution *Gaudium et spes* on the Church in the Modern World, 7 December 1965. *Acta Apostolicae Sedis, 58,* 1025–1120.

Sobański, R. (1986). Erwägungen zum Ort des Kirchenrechts in der Rechtskultur. *Archiv für katholisches Kirchenrecht, 155,* 3–15.

Stein, T. (2007). *Himmlische Quellen und irdisches Recht: Religiöse Voraussetzungen des freiheitlichen Verfassungsstaates.* Campus.

Striet, M. (2014). Sich selbst als geworden beschreiben wollen: Theologie und Soziologie. In M. Striet (Ed.), *"Nicht außerhalb der Welt": Theologie und Soziologie* (Katholizismus im Umbruch 1, pp. 13–32). Herder.

Tamanaha, B. Z. (1993). The folly of the 'social scientific' concept of legal pluralism. *Journal of Law & Society, 20,* 192–217.

Tamanaha, B. Z. (2008). Understanding legal pluralism: Past to present, local to global. *Sydney Law Review, 30,* 375–411.

Tamanaha, B. Z. (2017). *A realistic theory of law.* Cambridge University Press.

Teubner, G. (1996). Globale Bukowina: Zur Emergenz eines transnationalen Rechtspluralismus. *Rechtshistorisches Journal, 15,* 255–290.

Tierney, B. (1966). Medieval canon law and western constitutionalism. *Catholic Historical Review, 52,* 1–17.

Tönnies, F. (2001). *Community and civil society* [1887] (J. Harris, Ed., J. Harris & M. Hollis, Trans.). Cambridge University Press.

Torfs, R. (2003). Warum das EU-Recht für Kirchenjuristen immer wichtiger wird. *Österreichisches Archiv für Recht und Religion, 50,* 21–42.

Villegas, D. (2018). *L'ordre juridique mafieux: Étude à partir du cas de l'organisation criminelle colombienne des années 1980 et 1990* (Nouvelle Bibliothèque de Thèses 180, préface N. Molfessis). Dalloz.

Voigt, R. (1999/2000). *Globalisierung des Rechts* (Schriften zur Rechtspolitologie 9). Nomos.

Vries. J. (1998). *Kirchenrecht oder Kirchenordnung? Zum Kirchenrechtsverständnis bei Peter Huizing* (Dissertationen, Kanonistische Reihe 15). EOS.

Weber, M. (1978). *Economy and society: An outline of interpretive sociology* (G. Roth & C. Wittich, Eds.). University of California Press.

Wittreck, F. (2016). Religiöse Paralleljustiz im Rechtsstaat? In U. Willems, A. Reuter & D. Gerster (Eds.), *Ordnungen religiöser Pluralität: Wirklichkeit—Wahrnehmung—Gestaltung* (Religion und Moderne 3, pp. 439–493). Campus.

Chapter 3
Functions of the Law

Abstract In seeking to identify which function lies at the root of the law, some approaches of the sociology of law see the main function of the law in its contribution to ordering the social, whilst others primarily understand the law as avoiding and solving conflicts. Both functions might also be understood as complementing each other: law creates order—by anticipating, avoiding, and solving conflicts. The sociology of law and the sociology of canon law therefore need to shed some light on "law and conflict." This research area studies how the law deals with conflicts: by providing instruments of legal counselling and mediation, institutions for administering justice, and adjudication. Similar to secular law, canon law requires specialist knowledge and therefore provides legal counselling for "legal lays." However, institutions of law enforcement such as the police are absent in church. This finding begs the question in how far canon law can become effective without being supported by what Max Weber called a "coercive apparatus." Similar to secular law, canon law also revolves around a differentiated system of adjudication to deal with conflicts evolving in church.

Keywords Law as order · Social construction · Law as conflict resolution · Mediation · Administration of justice · Police · Adjudication · Class justice · Male justice · Clerical justice

3.1 Law and Social Order

Law is a unique type of social phenomenon, as it permeates throughout human societies and communities. Legal philosopher Ronald Dworkin described most famously in the preface to his book *Law's Empire* the largely undisputed omnipresence of law in virtually all areas of individuals' lives and group activities. Dworkin states that law is an ever-present reality that actually makes us into who we are,

> We live in and by the law. It makes us what we are: citizens and employees and doctors and spouses and people who own things. It is sword, shield, and menace: we insist on our wage, or refuse to pay our rent, or are forced to forfeit penalties, or are closed up in jail, all in the

© The Author(s) 2022

J. Hahn, *Foundations of a Sociology of Canon Law*,
https://doi.org/10.1007/978-3-031-01791-9_3

name of what our abstract and ethereal sovereign, the law, has decreed . . . We are subjects of law's empire.[1]

3.1.1 Law Creating the Social

Dworkin describes law as a phenomenon of *constructive* significance for human existence and social life that penetrates into even the most intimate nooks and crannies of our private lives. Its omnipresence is a precondition for the constitutive social power of law. The sociology of law often reflects this constitutive function of the law by resorting to vivid images and dense narratives to describe the way law influences human social relations in all areas of life.[2] In his 2017 book *A Realistic Theory of Law*, Brian Tamanaha provides one such description of how law influences life, noting,

> Rent an apartment, take out a mortgage, hook up gas and electricity, acquire a credit card, obtain a loan, open a bank account, sign with a phone carrier, download a computer program, enter an employment relationship, purchase goods, attend a sporting event or concert—for these and innumerable other daily transactions, while price can be haggled and quality and quantity decided, the legal arrangement is preset.[3]

In a similar vein, Klaus Röhl, in his textbook *Rechtssoziologie* [*Sociology of Law*], a classic survey of the sociology of law, states that law

> not only regulates the constitution of the state, the organisation of its subsystems, and the citizens' transactions. It also deals with medical malpractice and the performance of organ transplantations; it is at hand when a director opposes changes to his opera production, when soldiers complain about their superiors, when neighbours start a dispute, and when students take exams or protest against nuclear power plants.[4]

Law assigns authority and defines roles. Eugen Ehrlich describes it as "an organization, that is to say, a rule which assigns to each and every member of the association his position in the community, whether it be of domination or of subjection (*Überordnung, Unterordnung*), and his duties".[5] As an order which encompasses not only all members of the legal community but also their standing in the social fabric, law organises and legitimises power relations in societies, communities, and other groups. It constrains asymmetries of power to safeguard

---

[1] Dworkin (1998, p. VII).

[2] See also Luhmann (1995, p. 331; 2014, p. 1); Rottleuthner and Rottleuthner-Lutter (2010, p. 20).

[3] Tamanaha (2017, p. 140).

[4] Original quote, "regelt nicht nur die Verfassung des Staates, die Verwaltung seiner Untersysteme, es befaßt sich nicht nur mit dem Tauschverkehr der Bürger untereinander. Das Recht kümmert sich um ärztliche Kunstfehler und die Durchführung von Organtransplantationen; es ist zur Stelle, wenn ein Regisseur sich gegen die Veränderung seiner Operninszenierung wendet, Soldaten sich über ihre Vorgesetzten beschweren oder Nachbarn in Streit geraten, wenn Studenten Examen ablegen oder gegen Atomkraftwerke protestieren", Röhl (1987, p. 3).

[5] Ehrlich (1936, p. 24).

freedom—for example by guaranteeing individual liberties. It links social relations with legal expectations, and assigns rights and duties to the members of the legal community. As a stable and reliable system of rights and duties, law generates security of expectation. On the one hand, this benefits individuals and groups who find themselves confronted by law; for them, security of expectation means there is no doubt about what the law expects of them, thereby giving them the choice whether to abide by or break the law. On the other hand, as Manfred Rehbinder stresses, security of expectation also means that the legal subjects may expect that others, when engaged in a legal transaction, behave in a predictable and reliable way.[6] In this respect, law guides human behaviour. In addition, it also seeks to avoid conflicts of interest and conflicts of distribution to ensure a secure society. It stabilises exchange relationships and increases their prospect of success. Should they fail, the law possesses instruments to bring about the orderly settlement of conflicts. Brian Tamanaha notes,

> Law serves a fundamental role in coordinating social behaviour and responding to conflicts between actors (individuals and entities). Legal rules on property, personal injuries, binding agreements, labor, spousal relations, and offspring address the basic conditions of human social interaction. ... All societies have rules on these matters, though they vary greatly depending on cultural and religious values, the economic system, the political system, and the level of social complexity.[7]

Law provides clearly defined options for action and it embeds them in an ordered structure. In this vein, legal scholar Bernhard Losch understands the legal order as opening up a *realm of action* where individual and collective action may take place based on reliable rules.[8] This reveals that law not only has a constraining function, it also serves as an enabler, as Niklas Luhmann explains, noting, "Law is often understood as a *restriction* on behavioural choices. Equally well, however, law can be understood as *support* for behaviour, support which would not be possible without law."[9] But the constraining function of law is also important. It discounts certain actions and sanctions certain behaviour. To do this, the law frequently has it its disposal a range of punishment mechanisms.

3.1.2 Creating Social Order

The sociology of law deals with the fundamentally constructive value of law for human social life primarily by referring to *order theories* which are rooted in action theory or systems theory. In the words of Klaus Röhl, these theories define law as a "phenomenon of producing and protecting a certain degree of conformity and

---

[6] See Rehbinder (2014, p. 104).
[7] Tamanaha (2017, p. 127).
[8] See Losch (2006, p. 34).
[9] Luhmann (2004, p. 151).

integration which creates the fact of society".[10] The contribution of the law to creating society can be seen in a number of its functions. Manfred Rehbinder identifies five functions of the law for the construction of the social: an organisational function, insofar as the law by organising and directing a group initiates activities which integrate the group; an ordering function, insofar as the law guides human behaviour; a constitutional function insofar as the law organises and legitimises political governance; a supervisory function insofar as the law enforces its order through the administration of justice; and a reactive function insofar as the law seeks to settle disputes.[11] These functions enable the law to contribute to the success of human affairs on a number of different levels. Interestingly though, law seems to be particularly effective when it exerts an influence on society without being directly perceptible as a social regulator. Klaus Röhl, for instance, observes that individuals frequently do not view their legal relations—such as the relations between contracting parties—as *legal* relations but rather tend to view them as mere social relations.[12] It may be precisely this invisibility of the law that gives it its tremendous power to form the social. Legal scholar Naomi Mezey picks up on this thought by saying that law achieves its effectiveness by hiding its constitutive function for shaping reality behind other mechanisms, noting, "legal ground rules are all the more effective because they are not visible as law. Rather than think of legal permission as law, we tend to think of it as individual freedom, the market, or culture."[13] Law is most effective, as Mezey asserts, when its effect is not perceived as an effect *of law*, but as individual power, the market logic, or mere convention. Nevertheless, "all human action, from going to bed to going to work, is either implicitly or explicitly defined and structured by law, which operates all the more effectively for appearing not to be law."[14] The rather veiled significance of law makes it quite difficult for the sociology of law to research law in its function of constructing the social. It makes studying the law and its interaction with social reality particularly challenging. It is for this reason that Klaus Röhl labels the sociology of law as "a hyphen-sociology of a special kind".[15] Whilst other sociologies—such as medical sociology or the sociology of art—can focus on a distinct segment of social reality, the sociology of law is tasked with studying law as a whole and how it permeates the reality of all areas of human activity. With this in mind, it seems necessary to discuss whether we are in fact dealing with a "hyphen-sociology" at all when speaking of the sociology of law. Niklas Luhmann, for instance, describes his work on law as a sociology of law, albeit as an approach which is actually not exclusively or even primarily interested in law itself, but rather in its

---

[10]Original quote, "Phänomen der Herstellung und Wahrung eines bestimmten Grades von Konformität und Integration, der die Tatsache der Gesellschaft ausmacht", Röhl (1987, p. 129).

[11]See Rehbinder (2014, p. 112).

[12]See Röhl (1987, p. 464).

[13]Mezey (2001, p. 48).

[14]Mezey (2001, p. 51).

[15]Original quote, "eine Bindestrich-Soziologie besonderer Art", Röhl (1987, p. 3).

function in *society*. For this reason, as Luhmann argues, it is adequate to understand his sociology of law as part of his theory of society.[16] With a view to Luhmann's general theory of society, it therefore makes good sense either to call the sociology of law a "hyphen-sociology" (along with a host of other "hyphen-sociologies" that contribute to the theory of society) or to say that such hyphen-semantics are misleading in themselves, because we are not just studying a single segment of social reality, but by studying law are actually trying to come to an understanding of society itself. Roger Cotterrell reacts similarly when he says, "If we understand law as a social phenomenon we understand much about the society in which it exists."[17] This statement, as I find, is also very true for canon law and therefore applies to the sociology of canon law as well. Comprehending the reality of the ecclesiastical legal order is key to understanding the modern-day church. Examining the legal reality of the church helps us to identify the current state of the church.[18] Due to this, the sociology of canon *law* is, in its own way, a sociology of the Catholic Church.

3.1.3 Law Creating the Church

Law is also an omnipresent phenomenon in church, and serves as a socio-constructive force within the church. Canon law, writes Anglican canonist Norman Doe, "exists to facilitate order in the Church, it exists to make the Church more visible in society . . ., and it exists to distribute duties and to confer and protect the rights of its members."[19] As a system of behavioural and decisive norms, canon law creates order within the church. Furthermore, Doe's argument that canon law gives the church social visibility points to the capacity of the law to create order not only by acting as a cohesive force in groups, but also by giving those groups a discernible shape which marks them out from other groups and from society as a whole. This is true for all legal communities, the church being no exception. Correspondingly, Norbert Lüdecke and Georg Bier write in their introductory book on canon law that canon law is omnipresent in church.[20] No action which takes place in church is far from the law. Whoever operates within the church does so within the legal space of the church. This might astonish some readers at first, but upon reflection it makes good sense if we recall the degree to which ecclesiastical structures are founded on canon law: Law regulates who is a layperson or a cleric, what conditions must be

---

[16] See Luhmann (2004, p. VII).

[17] Cotterrell (1984, p. 2).

[18] At present, no canonist is clearer about this connection than Norbert Lüdecke, see Lüdecke (2021). Lüdecke emphasises that understanding the law is understanding the church, whilst ignoring the law—as many Catholics do—leads to a critical lack of understanding about why the hierarchy acts in the way it does and why the church, at present, is in the state we find it in.

[19] Doe (1992, p. 336).

[20] See Lüdecke and Bier (2012, p. 14).

fulfilled to become the latter, and how this takes place. Law determines which powers church officials have. Law settles who has access to the sacraments—and who does not. Of course, these issues are not genuinely legal and are not decided in the medium of law in the first place; instead they are primarily issues of ecclesiastical doctrine. Nonetheless, they have come to find their way into the law; and here they crystallise into rules and structures and become part of the organisational framework of the church. The above-mentioned examples also serve to illustrate that canon law—in addition to creating order as all law does—supports the church in providing religious functions. Norman Doe notes, "canon law has, what might be described as its end, a purpose formulated by theological doctrine. The canon law exists to serve the purposes for which Christ instituted the Church ..., it exists to enable and organise the constitutional, liturgical, sacramental, pastoral and proprietorial life of the Church".[21] Whenever the ecclesiastical constitution, the sacramental life of the church, pastoral issues, or financial matters are in dispute, canon law is never far away: it defines authority and roles; it specifies rights and duties; it organises ecclesiastical power structures; it seeks to avoid conflict and offers solutions which might defuse those conflicts that do arise. In doing these things, the law creates an arena of action, which enables the church to pursue its goals and within which the life of the church can unfold in an orderly manner. From the perspective of the sociology of law, it is therefore perfectly plausible to claim that one cannot operate within the church without finding oneself within the legal space of the church.

3.1.4   Ecclesiological Endorsement

Ecclesiastical legal theory supports this finding. The Second Vatican Council's ecclesiology supported a concept of church which encompasses the heavenly and spiritual church and the concrete and earthly church as an indivisible union. In the Dogmatic Constitution *Lumen gentium*, the council noted the church's view of itself as a single entity consisting of both a spiritual, salvific communion as well as of a hierarchical society,

> the society structured with hierarchical organs and the Mystical Body of Christ, are not to be considered as two realities, nor are the visible assembly and the spiritual community, nor the earthly Church and the Church enriched with heavenly things; rather they form one complex reality which coalesces from a divine and a human element.[22]

Seeking to explain how one might conceive of this, the text in *Lumen gentium* draws on a Christological analogy. The intimacy of the heavenly and earthly church makes the church itself a phenomenon of the incarnation. The text states, "For this reason,

---

[21] Doe (1992, p. 336).

[22] No. 8. *Acta Apostolicae Sedis, 57,* 11; English version: www.vatican.va/archive/hist_councils/ii_vatican_council/documents/vat-ii_const_19641121_lumen-gentium_en.html. Accessed 22 June 2021.

by no weak analogy, it is compared to the mystery of the incarnate Word. As the assumed nature inseparably united to Him, serves the divine Word as a living organ of salvation, so, in a similar way, does the visible social structure of the Church serve the Spirit of Christ, who vivifies it, in the building up of the body".[23] This passage parallels the intimacy of the earthly church and the spiritual church with the two natures of Christ. In the same way that Christ is fully human and fully divine, the church is both an earthly entity and a community of heaven. Its two natures are, as in the Christological confession of the Council of Chalcedon, "unconfused, unchangeably, indivisibly, inseparably".[24] Using this Christological paradigm, *Lumen gentium* succeeds in creating a twofold identity for the church in which the socio-logic of the church merges with its theo-logic, as systematic theologian Hans-Joachim Höhn describes, "Both dimensions, the sociological and the theological, are united in the church, 'unconfused' and 'undivided' (see LG 8). Therefore, this 'chalcedonensical signature' is the real reason why the social reality of the church may be interpreted sociologically as well as theologically."[25] One has to note though, that *Lumen gentium* does not mention the *law*. While the text accentuates the intrinsic connection between the church as a spiritual community and the church as a social entity, it does not qualify the earthly assembly explicitly as a legal community. However, the magisterium has traditionally considered the constitution of the concrete and earthly church to rest on law. *Lumen gentium* does not openly say so. Canonists, however, have read the magisterium's reference to the earthly church as a visible assembly and a hierarchical society as denoting the church as a social entity structured by law. In their understanding, they view canon law not as a merely facultative form of church organisation, but as an essential and indispensable characteristic of a church which exists in the world. In this light, trying to conceive of a church "without law" is impossible. Many canonists therefore argue that the church would and could not exist without its legal dimension. In fact, as they find, the spiritual church, when occupying a place in the world as a visible entity, always and by necessity becomes a legal entity.

In consequence, we may study the church as an earthly entity and as a legal institution by using the methodological approaches of the social sciences. And we may study its law by using the methodological approaches of the sociology of law. The law of the church is a human construct—and therefore open to academic endeavours to understand human institutions. Yet at the same time, due to the church not merely being an earthly but also a spiritual community, there is another side to its

---

[23] No. 8. *Acta Apostolicae Sedis*, 57, 11; English version: www.vatican.va/archive/hist_councils/ii_vatican_council/documents/vat-ii_const_19641121_lumen-gentium_en.html. Accessed 22 June 2021.

[24] Council of Chalcedon, Christological Confession. In Migne (1863, p. 514D).

[25] Original quote, "Beide Dimensionen, die soziologische und die theologische, vereint die Kirche in sich gleichwohl 'ungetrennt' und 'unvermischt' (See LG 8). Diese 'chalcedonensische Signatur' ist daher der eigentliche Grund, daß die gesellschaftliche Wirklichkeit der Kirche sowohl einer soziologischen wie einer theologischen Interpretation unterzogen werden kann", Höhn (1986, p. 353).

law. According to traditional teaching, the law serves salvation. This aspect touches upon issues which only theology can investigate and understand. Canonist Eugenio Corecco expresses this as follows,

> As actual historical facts, the ecclesiastical law and the canonical institutions bear some of the content that tangibly expresses the legally binding dimension of the mystery of the incarnation and the church. As an ecclesial reality, which is formed by legal institutions in which the legally binding dimension of the church is realised in history, canon law is one of the essential conditions in which the tradition of the church and, hence, the truth contained in the Word of God and the sacraments is expressed by implied facts.[26]

According to Corecco, the law of the church is an expression of the divine reality. It reifies the divine in a contingent form, however, in a form which humans may experience in the real world. Corecco expresses this in his statement, "the legal fact—whenever it comprehends the mystery of the church precisely—is in itself an expression of theological truth."[27] Seen in this way, canon law acts to some degree as the historical substantiation of the revelation, "As a reality in which the experience of the church ... is historically institutionalised, canon law—as an essential element in which tradition becomes real—carries with it at least part of the revealed truth, the meaning of which it attempts to understand using its own scientific instruments and its own way of thinking."[28] Such instruments must be theological. But whilst the theological dimension of canon law is admittedly quite alien to the social sciences, social science is most certainly still in a position to examine how and whether the law has a noticeable effect on legal practice and on the religious life of the church.

3.1.5 Concealed Canon Law

Similar to state law, which is most effective when hiding its constitutive function for the social behind other mechanisms, it also seems to be the case with canon law that it is most effective when it cannot be directly identified as law. Although canon law

---

[26]Original quote, "Als konkrete historische Fakten tragen das kirchliche Gesetz und die kanonischen Rechtsinstitute einen Teil des Inhalts in sich, indem sie die rechtsverbindliche Dimension des Mysteriums der Inkarnation und der Kirche greifbar zum Ausdruck bringen. Als kirchliche Wirklichkeit, die von Rechtsinstituten gebildet wird, in denen sich die rechtlich bindende Dimension der Kirche in der Geschichte konkretisiert, ist das kanonische Recht eine der wesentlichen Gegebenheiten, in denen sich die Tradition der Kirche und folglich die im Wort und Sakrament enthaltene Wahrheit durch konkludente Sachverhalte bekundet," Corecco (1994, p. 43).

[27]Original quote, "der rechtliche Sachverhalt—wenn er das Mysterium der Kirche genau erfaßt—in sich selbst Ausdruck der theologischen Wahrheit ist", Corecco (1994, p. 43).

[28]Original quote, "Als Wirklichkeit, in der sich die kirchliche Erfahrung ... geschichtlich institutionalisiert, trägt das kanonische Recht als wesentliches Element, in dem sich die Tradition verwirklicht, wenigstens einen Teil der geoffenbarten Wahrheit in sich, deren Sinn es mit seinem eigenen wissenschaftlichen Instrumentarium und in seiner eigenen Denkweise zu erfassen sucht," Corecco (1994, p. 53).

permeates all aspects of ecclesiastical life and is of fundamental significance for the church, many Catholics are either completely oblivious to it, or view it as some kind of peripheral phenomenon with an exclusively selective significance for some specific individuals in church, such as ecclesiastical officeholders. In the 1970s, Patricia Goler used the example of black Catholics in the USA to point out that canon law had virtually no significance for them, noting, "canon law or canon lawyers—they aren't real to the average black Catholic."[29] This is just as true for the average white Catholic nowadays. Canon law plays no obviously significant role in the everyday life of many Catholics, and only few see it as having any constitutive effect on their individual, social, or spiritual life. Here, it might be interesting to add a personal observation from the viewpoint of academic theology. It appears to me that of all theological disciplines, it is in particular the theological disciplines which study the reality of the church that frequently overlook or neglect the legal side of the church. For example, in current pastoral theology, which is clearly most concerned with the reality of the church, the legal dimension of the church plays virtually no role at all, or is cast aside by many pastoral theologians as an obstacle to church development.[30] Most remarkably, many pastoral theologians do not focus on the law, even though this might allow them to address the often disruptive influence of the law on the pastoral reality of the church; instead they mostly ignore the legal dimension of this pastoral reality as if all of the problems associated with canon law might vanish by ignoring the law altogether. An anecdote may help to illuminate this phenomenon. In 2017, canonist Norbert Lüdecke caused something of a sensation at a pastoral-theological congress organised by the Bochum Centre for Applied Pastoral Research (ZAP), when he adamantly expressed the key role of canon law in giving the present church its current shape.[31] The irritation with which many conference participants reacted to Lüdecke's insistence on the major significance of the law in shaping the church reveals that for many practical theologians and active Catholics it is obviously uncommon to examine the law and to reveal its constructive and sometimes destructive function in church. Attempts to identify the underlying causes for this bring to light a number of sociological questions. We may wonder if and why there is less theological interest in the legal dimension of the church than we might expect in light of *Lumen gentium*'s ecclesiology; after all, the document alludes to the theological relevance of the earthly church as a concrete social entity organised by human instruments of social structuring, which traditionally include the law. We may likewise wonder if the law as a constitutive feature of the church has fallen into such disrepute that it is no longer regarded as capable of constituting and integrating the church by creating order and mediating in conflicts. We may discuss if many Catholics perhaps no longer trust the legislator to adapt and develop current law, feeling instead that a life with canon law is only possible if one ignores the law or those parts of it which seem impossible to change. We may

---

[29] Goler (1972, p. 295).

[30] E.g. Bucher (2018, pp. 160–164).

[31] See Lüdecke (2017).

discuss whether the refusal of many practical and pastoral theologians to deal with the legal structure of the church is also a criticism of canonists and canon law studies. We may critically ask ourselves if we have disappointed the faith placed in us by other theologians by using our scholarly apparatus mainly to whitewash current canon law and to defend the legal status quo. We may also ask ourselves if we have given our colleagues reason to suspect that we are the legislator's extended arm and have no genuine interest in studying canon law critically. It is difficult to identify the motives underlying many Catholics' and theologians' impression that it makes better sense to ignore canon law than to subject it to sociological scrutiny. However, this myopic attitude of overlooking the law brings with it a number of problems. Canonist Werner Böckenförde has addressed some of them. Böckenförde himself was greatly interested in initiating a reform of the church and its law.[32] He placed his hopes in critical Catholics with a "clear-sighted" view of the law as the engines of reform. Böckenförde believed that reform requires knowledge, hence ecclesiastical legal reform requires a thorough knowledge of canon law. For Böckenförde, in consequence, neglecting canon law or underestimating its importance is tantamount to actually holding back reform. He felt that trivialising the law is in fact a strategy for stabilising the existing system. According to Böckenförde, anybody who fails to recognise the law or who views it as something of little practical relevance is inclined to leave it as it is—and therefore not question those structures of the church which require contestation. According to Böckenförde, the absence of an active critical debate on the law is therefore an implicit acceptance of the church's organisational structure. Böckenförde's thesis abuts against Naomi Mezey's observation that law is frequently at its most effective when it is perceived less *as law* and more as everyday normativity, as tradition, culture, custom, or moral imperative. In a similar vein, Böckenförde believes that canon law is more effective when Catholic individuals and groups are largely unaware of it. However, his argument becomes rather more piquant when he says that he does not believe that the church members' legal myopia has emerged out of nowhere, but posits that church authorities have actually *fostered* and encouraged it. Drawing attention to the need for reform is clearly not in the interest of groups within the church that are in fact benefitting from the law in its current form. Ecclesiastical authorities who play down the significance of canon law as a medium of church organisation should therefore ask themselves where their interest lies, as Böckenförde finds, noting, "Anybody who trivialises structural issues must be prepared to answer the question whether he might be a beneficiary of the status quo."[33] Böckenförde also finds that just as we should treat statements which trivialise structural issues with scepticism, we should also be suspicious of strategies which try to occlude the law within theology or push it aside in favour of ethics. This is observable particularly within theological approaches to canon law. In fact, theologising or spiritualising the law, in Böckenförde's eyes, might be an attempt

---

[32] See Böckenförde (2006, pp. 153–154).

[33] Original quote, "Wer Strukturprobleme bagatellisiert, muss sich fragen lassen, ob er möglicherweise Nutznießer des Status quo ist", Böckenförde (2006, p. 154).

to relativise the very few official instruments which protect the church members from the authorities' despotism and to take away from them those measures that they do actually possess to assert their rights within church. By emphasising "community" and downplaying "the law," church authorities tend to bring their legal subjects to heel by making them feel comfortable and at home in church, as Böckenförde suspects. It seems fair to assume that people who feel at home in church are not going to be the ones who feel inclined to seek legal redress. For the ecclesiastical authorities, who profit from this stasis, this guarantees the status quo. Böckenförde adopts a similarly critical stance to lines of argument that accord only secondary importance to complaints about canon law and ecclesiastical legal structures in contrast to the truly burning issues in church. Such arguments, as Böckenförde notes, work with false alternatives, for instance by setting third world issues or the question of God against structural issues, thereby disqualifying those Catholics who complain about the law as less focused on pressing moral issues. Böckenförde, at least, is convinced that contrasting legal issues with third world problems is a bogus argument, as he does not see why somebody with an interest in solving structural issues in church should be uninterested in social issues or the question of God. Irrespective of whether the tactic is one of simple concealment, theological cloaking, or moral disqualification, Böckenförde believes certain circles in the church are actively involved in maintaining the status quo and preventing change. This is a rather suspicious and distrustful view of things. Nevertheless, coming from an insider—Böckenförde was a canon at the cathedral chapter of the Diocese of Limburg and managed the legal department of the diocese for many years—we should certainly not underestimate the sociological value of his observations.

To these observations one may add a further observation which has taken shape in recent years, namely that church authorities tend to render ecclesiastical law unrecognisable by hiding it behind the notion of *culture*. Those in charge then blame a certain established male culture or the traditional image of women in Catholic circles for the fact that there are too few women in leading positions in the church—and brush aside the canonical norms on the power of governance and ecclesiastical offices which structurally exclude women from senior positions in church (see canons 129 §1, 274 §1 CIC/1983). Many voices also dismiss celibacy as part of clericalism, of a male cult of purity and elitism, or as an expression of the church's discomfort with sexuality. This might all be true; however it misses the point that celibacy is actually a legal obligation (see canon 277 §1 CIC/1983) and might be overcome fairly easily by changing the law. Saying this does not of course mean that I want to drive a wedge between law and culture. The connection between law and culture is rather obvious. Law is never established in a vacuum, but emerges from traditional beliefs, cultural values, and social practices. In this light, working on problematic aspects of ecclesiastical cultures may well result in changes to these cultures and, in the long term, to changes in ecclesiastical law as well. However, this path is an arduous one. It is slow and difficult to establish more female leaders in church as long as the ecclesiastical structures disadvantage women. And it is hard to fight clericalism as long as the ecclesiastical structures support celibacy and with it a cult of purity, elitism, and discomfort with sexuality. Approaching reform the other way around is much more effective. Whilst changing misogynist or clerical cultures is slow, changing the law disadvantaging women or banning married family men from entering clerical service might be done quickly, should the legislator perceive the need to change these norms of canon law. None of these norms are "divine law." They may be changed as soon as the legislator believes they should be changed. For church members afflicted by these and other laws, it is also much easier to target the law instead of initiating a cultural debate about what has to change in a particular ecclesiastical culture to make the church a place more welcoming to female leaders or to overcome a culture of clericalism. By veiling legal norms and hiding them well in the diffuse concept of culture, those who use this strategy make it difficult for others to identify the law and to criticise it. In this light, it is much harder for critical church members to target any resistance clearly and purposefully against specific norms of canon law. It is therefore apparent that dressing the law in the mantle of culture is also one way of protecting the law against change. Over the last couple of years it has become obvious how church authorities use this kind of cultural argumentation as an easy way of resisting reform. The key cultural argument used by the authorities pretends to be an expression of concern about the multiple cultures of the global world church. In the current reform debates, we often encounter the argument that western churches may be ready to accept women in leading roles in church, while many churches of the global South may not be ready to embrace female leaders. As the church is a unity, as many bishops argue, it is impossible to progress in the global North in those matters where the South disagrees.[34] In a similar vein, bishops ask their church members for patience with regard to blessing homosexual unions in church with the argument that they themselves would welcome that practice but that it would not find a positive reception in other parts of the global church and should therefore be rightfully sanctioned by Rome to protect the unity of the church.[35] It is rather astonishing that church representatives who usually shy away from culture and cultural arguments, suspecting them of promoting "relativist" positions, suddenly rediscover culture in this context and cultivate its function as a preserver of the status quo. We may understand both the strategies which Böckenförde discovered, as well as the protection of law by relying on the cultural argument, as diversionary tactics, which is what Böckenförde called them.[36] From the socio-legal perspective, they both reveal that some ecclesiastical authorities believe they can safeguard canon law and its effectiveness by concealing the law as a mechanism of control within the church. This concealment of its legal character means that canon law acquires its effectiveness in a unique way, namely by evading the deconstruction that would otherwise be possible if it were in fact clearly exposed

---

[34] Even liberal bishops argue that Catholics should be more patient with regard to women's ordination, as this decision applies not only to the western but to the global church, see Frank (2010). Instead of pointing at the justice problem connected with excluding women from ordination, they refer to *culture* as one impediment standing in the way of developing this issue in church.

[35] See Glenz (2019).

[36] See Böckenförde (2006, p. 154).

as law. Böckenförde identifies this finding as a call to action: active Catholics should always scrutinise structural aspects of the church carefully to excavate and reveal the legal structure of the church. My study, which as a sociology of canon law takes a largely descriptive approach, contributes to doing exactly this. Whilst I do insufficient justice to Böckenförde's normative concerns with church reform, I do wish, however, to lay the foundations of a sociology of canon law as an approach to the law within which Böckenförde stands as one of its pioneering minds.

3.2 Law and Conflict Resolution

The discussion thus far has been about law as a mechanism of order which serves to construct and integrate societies and communities. In the sociology of law, this perspective is at the forefront of approaches which we might subsume under the heading "order theories." These theories are supplemented—and occasionally criticised—by approaches which view law primarily as a mechanism of conflict resolution. Such conflict theories see the primary function of law in avoiding and pacifying conflicts. Most of these theories do not dispute that law is indeed a bringer of order, but they argue that this ordering function is secondary to the function of the law as a maker of peace. Thomas Raiser explains that sociological conflict theories see a threefold function of the law, of avoiding unnecessary conflict, of reacting to existing conflict, and of solving or containing conflict.[37] The sociology of law must not lose sight of the fact that legal conflicts can be highly complex. Vilhelm Aubert therefore divided them into conflicts of interest ("competing interests") and differences of opinion about norms or facts ("dissensus"); however, many conflicts are, as Aubert also admitted, a blend of both.[38] Conflict theories see the primal, founding moment of law in the social situations in which trust as the basis of all social relations diminishes to the degree that it is replaced by the law as "calculated mistrust",[39] as Klaus Röhl calls it. In this light, Aubert describes law as "a specific way of perceiving the participants in a conflict and the relationship between them."[40] According to conflict theories, the law arises from conflict or in anticipation of possible conflict. Nevertheless, this understanding of law reveals only part of the overall picture, as Niklas Luhmann observes when he states, "law develops its special instruments out of controversies about law."[41] Here, Luhmann stresses that law does indeed arise out of conflict, but he also makes clear that it arises out of conflicts about *what the law is*. Luhmann's observation ties in with the finding that law is not only concerned with settling conflicts, but is frequently actually the source

---

[37] See Raiser (2007, p. 274).

[38] See Aubert (1963, p. 26–42).

[39] Original quote, "kalkuliertes Misstrauen", Röhl (1987, p. 464).

[40] Aubert (1963, p. 26).

[41] Luhmann (2004, p. 153).

of conflict itself. His remark also indicates another characteristic of the law, namely that law precedes conflict about the law. If we read Luhmann's sentence in this way, order theory and conflict theory align. One might therefore conclude that the primary function of law is to bring order insofar as it is conflict about the ordering function of the law (among other things) that unleashes the potential of the law for conflict resolution. This observation also raises the point that law and its function as a bringer of order becomes *visible* primarily in conflictive situations. In this vein, Eugen Ehrlich points out that individuals only really see the law as law when they find themselves in critical situations. As members of a legal community frequently tend to understand their relations not as legal relations but as social relations characterised by mutual cooperation and trust, they tend to discover the legal nature of their relations only when conflict undermines their trust.[42] According to Ehrlich, conflicts therefore serve to reveal what was already the case: that many human social relations are rooted in law.

3.2.1 Subjective and Objective Conflicts

Even if my study examines the law primarily through the prism of order theory, the sociology of law must still provide answers which explain the most evident connection between law and conflict. Whether and how the law seeks to mitigate conflicts is an area of socio-legal research in itself. In the first place, as Klaus Röhl has pointed out, we should acknowledge that the understanding of "conflict" which is appropriate for describing the law's function as a responder to conflict is a limited one. The law is primarily interested in *subjective* conflicts; it consequently deals with conflict between individuals and between individuals and organisations, as Röhl observes.[43] Legal conflict resolution also does little more than end acute disputes, as Röhl states, noting, "From a juridical point of view conflict resolution has been successful when the acute conflict is over."[44] In doing so, the law in fact only touches the surface of conflicts. It frequently avoids addressing the structural roots of conflicts, such as justice problems which foster conflicts and afflict the social. This is at least the critical view put forward by *objective* conflict theories, as Röhl explains, as objective conflict theorists tend to trace legal conflicts back to more fundamental social conflicts. They tend to see the parties' fundamental social oppositions as lying at the root of many legal conflicts. Objective theories, for instance, tend to understand labour law cases as relying on the structural antagonism between employers and employees, tenant law suits as rooted in the fundamental disagreement between tenants and property owners, and many marriage cases as being rooted in the

---

[42] See Ehrlich (1936, pp. 23–24).

[43] See Röhl (1987, p. 515).

[44] Original quote, "Aus juristischer Sicht ist die Konfliktregelung gelungen, wenn der akute Streit beendet ist", Röhl (1987, p. 515).

structural discrimination against women.[45] Merely settling the legal disputes between the individual parties does not therefore contribute to resolving the actual social conflicts underlying the disputes. In consequence, law is not only relatively ineffective from an objective viewpoint, as Röhl emphasises; we may also actually view it critically as a form of suppression of the actual social conflicts or of the individualisation or personalisation of social conflicts.[46] This is virtually unavoidable from a legal standpoint, as Röhl contends. He acknowledges that there might be good reason to criticise the law's functional limitations in relating to the true conflicts underlying the individual disputes; however, he does not see an option for changing this problem.[47] In any case, from a socio-legal perspective we have to state that legal conflict resolution does little more than defuse the acute individual conflict itself. It is not within the power of the law to settle the objective conflicts; this is not the responsibility of lawyers but of politicians. It is up to legal politics to deal with objective conflicts, not up to the law itself.

This observation is likewise true with regard to canon law. From the perspective of the sociology of canon law we may therefore note the limited scope available to canon law for resolving conflicts in church. Whilst canon law can help to settle specific conflicts between ecclesiastical parties, we cannot realistically expect the law to resolve the structural problems which bring about many individual conflicts in church. In parallel to Röhl's observations with regard to the social foundation of secular legal conflicts, conflicts in church are also frequently rooted in objective problems which pit legal subjects of canon law against one another. Structural conflicts then come to a head in individual conflicts. I want to explain this by way of an example. One major source of structural conflict underlying individual conflicts in church is that magisterium and legislation use the division of church members into clergy and laity to ascribe fundamentally different rights and duties to these two groups. As already mentioned, under current law, only clerics can occupy leadership positions and can obtain offices attributed with the power to govern the church (see canons 129 §1, 274 §1 CIC/1983). In consequence, the law largely excludes lays from decision making in church. Not only do laypeople enjoy only limited rights within the church, they also have no access to the decision-making processes that might change this state of affairs. From these fundamental structural issues arise manifold individual conflicts in church. I would like to mention a concrete case to further elucidate my observation. It evolved between the diocesan bishop of the German Diocese of Regensburg and the lay organisations of his diocese in 2005–2006. The then-diocesan bishop of Regensburg, Gerhard Ludwig Müller (who later became the prefect of the Congregation for the Doctrine of the Faith), had fully reorganised the bodies of lay participation in his diocese in 2005, thereby considerably restricting the lays' rights to participate in diocesan decision making. One Catholic affected by this regulation, Johannes

---

[45] Examples given by Röhl (1987, p. 515).

[46] See Röhl (1987, p. 515).

[47] See Röhl (1987, p. 515).

Grabmeier, appealed to the Roman Curia against the bishop's reform by taking legal recourse (see canon 1737 CIC/1983). This recourse was unsuccessful. In 2006, the Congregation for the Clergy reaffirmed the bishop's decision formally and substantively.[48] Following these events, Grabmeier wrote a book on the case, revealing his major frustration with the curia's decision and its procedural standards.[49] Grabmeier voiced his displeasure particularly with his treatment as a plaintiff, above all with the congregation's refusal to talk to him personally. In his book he describes the curia as only protecting the members of the hierarchy, immunising them against laypeople's claims, whilst not even allowing individual Catholics a right to speak up and to explain their position in person. The events as Grabmeier retells them in his book describe an individual conflict. However, it is most obvious that there is a structural issue underlying it. This structural issue cannot be addressed adequately by relying on the law—ironically, it is the law itself that organises the ecclesiastical hierarchy and its rights in a way that is unfavourable for laypeople and their claims. Grabmeier's case would therefore not have changed the current hierarchical organisation of the church one iota even if he had been successful in winning his individual case—which he was not. The conflict resolution mechanisms available to law, including canon law, are not sufficiently effective to solve the structural issues underlying concrete conflicts. Instead, these issues need to be addressed at the political level. Yet this sphere of ecclesiastical legal politics is widely inaccessible to laypeople due to the hierarchical structure of ecclesiastical decision making, including legal politics. This creates something of a vicious circle. It is the law that brings about structural disadvantages for laypeople, including their exclusion from those political circles which could actually change the law. This state of affairs makes it very clear why canon law often fails to pacify even individual conflicts. As the mentioned example shows, the curia decided Grabmeier's individual legal case. However, this did not help to reconcile the parties and to settle their personal conflict, because it left Grabmeier seriously doubting whether the legal treatment he had received was truly fair.

3.2.2 Simple and Complex Structures

Law can only therefore function as a conflict resolution mechanism up to a point. To establish what law is actually capable of achieving in this respect, it helps to study the diverse applicable ways in which the law deals with conflict. In his work *The Division of Labor in Society* (1893), Durkheim examined which characteristics of legal conflict management are cross-cultural and what they indicate about the developmental state of a legal order. Richard Schwartz and James Miller used

---

[48] See Congregation for the Clergy (2006).

[49] See Grabmeier (2012).

Durkheim's findings as the basis for an empirical study of their own. In their study, Schwartz and Miller analysed the legal conflict resolution models of fifty-one peoples and tribal societies in the light of Durkheim's observations on societies with a low and high division of labour. They used three of the institutions of conflict management named by Durkheim by way of example: "mediation" as the participation of a neutral third party in settling conflicts; "police" or other agencies for the administration of justice equipped with the means of coercion to enforce the law; and "counsel" or advisory structures providing impartial and professional legal support for conflict parties. Schwartz's and Miller's empirical study of these three institutional approaches to conflict resolution found that even societies with a low division of labour contained restitution-orientated practices of mediation (Durkheim, on the contrary, had presumed they would only be found in societies with a high division of labour), whereas police or other agencies for the administration of justice were only evident in societies with a high division of labour (also contrary to Durkheim's assumption).[50] Legal counselling was also generally found only in societies with a high division of labour.[51] These findings are interesting in themselves—not least because they contradict some of Durkheim's assumptions. However, they tell us little about religious legal orders primarily because these do not fit neatly into Durkheim's system of societies with a high or low division of labour. Nevertheless, I believe it is possible to draw some tentative conclusions. Durkheim equates a high division of labour with complex modern societies; he equates a low division of labour with low levels of complexity. Certain parallels are therefore obvious insofar as it is possible to identify more or less complex groups among religious communities. Viewed through the lens of organisation theory, the Catholic Church is a fairly complex religious community. It exhibits a high level of functional differentiation, specialisation, and professionalisation—as can be seen in the highly differentiated structure of church ministries and offices. Parallels therefore exist to Durkheim's division of labour criterion. It therefore makes some sense to discuss Schwartz's and Miller's findings in the light of the sociology of canon law, too.

3.2.3 Counselling and Mediation

Schwartz and Miller found that virtually all societies had some kind of framework of *mediation* to settle social conflicts. This comes as no great surprise insofar as the sociology of law holds mediation to be the founding idea of adjudication across all cultures—Martin Shapiro commences his book *Courts* by calling mediation the "prototype of courts".[52] The core principle is that conflicting parties can call on the support of a third party in disputes they are unable to resolve themselves. The

---

[50] See Schwartz and Miller (1964, p. 166).

[51] See Schwartz and Miller (1964, p. 167).

[52] Shapiro (1981, p. 1).

roots of institutionalised conflict resolution therefore lie in the transition from the dyad of the conflicting parties to a *triad*, as legal sociologists such as Aubert and Shapiro state, drawing on the findings of philosopher and sociologist Georg Simmel.[53] Simmel stated that the triad was a fundamental prerequisite for the formation of certain types of social entity. He noted that some social structures require the "social constructing mediation of a third element".[54] The kind of third-party conflict management upon which the court system rests is one such social entity which can only be understood as a triad. Admittedly, it is not just the courts that are involved in conflict management. Nowadays, the sociology of law usually identifies four types of third-party involvement in conflict management: counselling, mediation, arbitration, and adjudication. Thomas Raiser explains the differences:[55] *Counselling*, as Raiser explains, means helping the conflicting parties to identify potential solutions, while letting them decide for themselves if and how they proceed with their issue. *Mediation* goes one step further. Here the mediator takes an active role in pointing out ways in which the conflicting parties might resolve their dispute. The mediator hence acts as a driving force in the conflict resolution process. However, the parties themselves must take the initial step of engaging in the mediation process. The result might then be an agreement between the parties, often in the form of a settlement. Canon law explicitly refers to agreements and reconciliations as ways of avoiding judicial contention in civil disputes (see canon 1713 CIC/1983). From the perspective of legal practice, mediation procedures such as conciliatory proceedings are of key importance for the administration of justice not just because successful mediation reduces the workload of the courts, but also because settlements are likely to enjoy the approval of both parties and often result in a greater level of pacification and satisfaction than court verdicts.[56] In church, the same motives are decisive in promoting mediation. However, as far as justice is concerned, not every case is suitable for mediation. Canon law therefore limits the possibility of resolving disputes through settlement to those cases in which only the parties' claims are in dispute, and which do not involve the interests of third parties. In matters about which the parties cannot make disposition freely or which affect the public good of the church, agreements or compromises are invalid (see canon 1715 §1 CIC/1983). Therefore, settlements are void when they pertain to matters related to the nullity of the sacrament of orders or of marriage, the separation of the spouses, or criminal matters. This is because the church holds that the primary aim of procedures in these cases is to establish the truth, it being only a secondary aim to bring about peace between the parties.

---

[53] See Aubert (1963, pp. 26, 33–42); Shapiro (1981, p. 1).

[54] Simmel (2009, p. 101).

[55] See Raiser (2007, pp. 286–287).

[56] See Raiser (2007, p. 288).

3.2.4 Arbitration and Adjudication

Arbitration is not dissimilar to mediation. It does however involve a greater degree of control. Arbitrators not only suggest a solution but truly settle the dispute, usually based on an arbitration agreement with the parties. Roger Cotterrell explains, "Between mediation and adjudication stands an intermediate process, arbitration, in which the third party's role can be seen as more explicitly directive and in which he is recognised as a decision-maker with responsibility for determining the rights and wrongs of the dispute rather than an honest broker for the disputants."[57] The arbitrators' decisions are frequently enforced by binding instruments such as the arbitration agreement; canon law refers to such instruments in canon 1714 CIC/1983. Even voluntary arbitration is more binding than mediation, as the parties bind themselves to the results of the arbitration by entering the arbitration agreement. However, there is also *compulsory* arbitration, in which the parties are not at liberty to choose whether or not to participate in the arbitration process. At the obligatory level, compulsory arbitration is similar to court verdicts. Hence, the degree to which arbitration and adjudication differ depends on whether the arbitration process is voluntary or compulsory and whether the result of the process is binding for the disputants or not. Nevertheless, arbitration, in contrast to adjudication, is usually less formal and more flexible.[58] This explains its widespread popularity as a method of conflict resolution in many legal areas, such as in international commercial disputes, even if arbitration remains somewhat ambivalent from the perspective of legal practice.[59] Whilst its flexibility can be seen as an advantage, arbitration often suffers from a lack of enforceability. This is because enforcing an arbitration award against the losing party requires the involvement of sovereign authorities with the power to enforce the decision. Yet most institutions of arbitration do not have access to authorities with a police function which could help them to enforce their decisions. A further serious disadvantage to arbitration is the lack of quality control, especially with respect to the arbitrators' qualifications and suitability. Hence, whilst arbitration has always been a more flexible and much-used alternative to adjudication throughout the history of institutionalised conflict resolution, it has never come to replace adjudication.

Arbitration also has an important function in church. Some local churches even provide fixed arbitration bodies to treat specific issues. In Germany, for instance, some dioceses have ecclesiastical arbitration boards that deal with disputes related to the pastoral life of the church or other local legal issues, such as conflicts arising from diocesan councils and committees. One arbitration board belonging to the German Conference of Superiors of Religious Orders deals with cases of hardship among former members of religious orders. In Germany, there are also ecclesiastical employment arbitration boards which deal with disputes about individual contracts

---

[57] Cotterrell (1984, p. 221).

[58] See Raiser (2007, p. 289).

[59] See Raiser (2007, p. 291).

of employment with the church and with conflicts arising from ecclesiastical employee participation law.[60] If ecclesiastical employers and their employees' representatives do not reach an agreement on matters in which the employees' representatives enjoy participation rights, it is mandatory according to ecclesiastical employee participation law to refer to the ecclesiastical arbitration bodies. The decisions of the arbitration bodies are binding. If the employer and the employees' representatives fail to come to an agreement, the arbitration board decides on their behalf.[61]

Adjudication is the most binding type of conflict management. A distinct feature of adjudication that sets it apart from less binding forms of institutionalised conflict resolution is that adjudication brings conflicts to a binding conclusion. We generally accept court decisions as final clarifications of legal disputes. Martin Shapiro notes, "one of the principal virtues of a trial is that it provides an official termination to conflict, relieving the disputants of the necessity of further reciprocal assertions or retributions."[62] While both adjudication and mediation aim at the common goal of resolving a conflict, courts differ from simple mediation agencies, particularly insofar as they are usually institutions of *sovereign* social control. Whilst mediation bodies focus on the interests of the parties, court decisions are based on the principle of sovereignty. While they decide single cases, their verdicts also have to keep the whole legal community in mind. In doing so, court decisions contribute to producing law, as Roger Cotterrell points out.[63] It is for this reason they are of decisive importance in the formation and ongoing development of legal doctrine. Court decisions address a specific case; however, in discussing this case in the light of the law and legal doctrine, courts also contribute to the shaping of doctrine.

As with all forms of institutionalised conflict resolution, adjudication is also originally rooted in the idea of managing conflict between two parties. However, of all the institutions of conflict resolution which share the triad as their point of departure, the court system has the most *complex* way of recreating the triadic structure common to all forms of conflict management. Contemporary societies in particular require elaborately structured judicial systems. Durkheim stated that initiating legal proceedings when social relations are disrupted is a characteristic reflex of complex societies. These require sophisticated *restitutive* mechanisms in order to generate social cohesion in the form of organic solidarity. Small, premodern societies, by contrast, according to Durkheim, are held together by mechanical solidarity. They can make do with the *repressive* subjugation of socially undesirable behaviour.[64] In this light, Martin Shapiro's hierarchy of courts from mediation agencies to modern adjudication correlates with Durkheim's observations on the development of societies from mechanical solidarity to organic solidarity.

---

[60] See §§40–47 Rahmen-MAVO.

[61] See §§40 sect. 3; 47 sect. 3 Rahmen-MAVO.

[62] Shapiro (1981, p. 39).

[63] See Cotterrell (1984, p. 218).

[64] See Durkheim (1960).

3.2.5   A Triad or Two Against One?

In complex organisations such as the church, there are frequently a number of judicial structures that work in the interests of conflict management. However, as the sociology of law observes, there are also significant obstacles in the way of transforming the initial structures of mediation into an elaborate court system. Vilhelm Aubert and Martin Shapiro point out convincingly that this kind of evolution has created a fundamental problem of legitimacy. They observe that it has often been rather difficult to identify the original idea of triadic conflict management as the basis for the concept of judicial systems. Particularly in complex judicial systems, it is now relatively hard to discern the simple and plausible idea of the triad. Whilst Simmel's triadic model is still easily identifiable in mediation processes, the triad seems to dissolve as soon as models of conflict management take on a formal judicial character. The regular-shaped triangle which balances the powers and interests of the parties and the mediator then seems to change profoundly, apparently becoming a "two against one" situation. It therefore becomes highly unlikely that the losing parties will view the verdicts against them as the result of an impartial triadic exchange. Instead, they often see themselves as having been outvoted by a majority—an understanding between the judge and the opposing party—, as Shapiro observes, noting, "To the loser there is no social logic in two against one. There is only the brute fact of being outnumbered."[65] This explains why courts enjoy only limited effectiveness in the resolution of individual conflicts between the parties. Thomas Raiser connects this problem with the tendency of judicial decisions to always look back, explaining, "The court has to establish a past fact and has to legally assess it. It is not its duty to help to build the parties' relationship for the future."[66] The courts therefore largely ignore the social afterlife of their decisions. Admittedly, there are a few exceptions such as custody disputes, where the judges understand their duty not only to settle the existing legal conflict, but also consider what might be a fruitful solution for children and their families. However, court verdicts are frequently less focused on the future and more on the past. As a consequence, law is regularly in no real position to rehabilitate social relations between the parties. Roger Cotterrell also takes up this idea, noting that court decisions are not designed to offer an acceptable solution to both parties, but to declare one party right—thereby declaring the position of the other to be wrong, "The dichotomous right/wrong judicial solution is likely to appear as an imposed two-against-one solution which may make continuing relations between the disputants difficult or impossible."[67] This is certainly a thorny problem for ecclesiastical adjudication in particular, because canon law is primarily concerned with the

---

[65] Shapiro (1981, p. 2); see also Aubert (1963, p. 35).

[66] Original quote, "Das Gericht hat in der Regel einen abgeschlossenen Sachverhalt festzustellen und rechtlich zu würdigen. Die Beziehungen zwischen den Parteien für die Zukunft zu gestalten ist nicht seine Aufgabe", Raiser (2007, p. 299).

[67] Cotterrell (1984, p. 222).

individual's salvation and the welfare of the church as a community. It is most evident, in any case, that a two-against-one solution is regularly not well-suited to contributing to spiritual perfection or the common good. Hence, it is unsurprising that the church traditionally relies more on mechanisms for reconciling the parties than on adjudication. In this respect, Jesus's words in the Sermon on the Mount—that it is key to make peace between disputants (see Matthew 5:21–26)—have proven to be highly influential regarding the Christian response to conflict. According to Christian teaching, peace is a prerequisite for salvation. Jesus's words "So if you are offering your gift at the altar, and there remember that your brother has something against you, leave your gift there before the altar and go; first be reconciled to your brother, and then come and offer your gift" (Matthew 5:23–24) reveal that reconciliation in the Christian community is not just seen as an option in the resolution of conflicts, but as a necessary precondition for living a godly life. Ecclesiastical law and adjudication are also a means to this end. Ecclesiastical adjudication theory and research must therefore seek to mitigate the conflictual effects of ecclesiastical adjudication with its limited effects on resolving individual and social conflicts, not only for the legitimacy reasons of reconnecting ecclesiastical tribunals with Simmel's triad, but also for theological reasons.

3.2.6 The Problem of Impartiality

Hence, adjudication as a whole, and ecclesiastical adjudication in particular, require strategies that avoid giving the impression that the basic triadic structure of conflict resolution turns into a "two against one" scenario when courts become involved. Judicial systems all over the globe have been more or less successful in accomplishing this, as Martin Shapiro observes. Ancient Roman law avoided these legitimacy issues by allowing the parties to freely choose their preferred judge and procedure, and by obliging them to accept the judge's decision before the verdict. Today, courts try to avoid giving the impression of "two against one" by emphasising the parties' equality of opportunity and the judges' neutrality as guaranteed by procedural law. Judicial independence plays an important legitimising function in most modern judicial systems. The parties tend to consider judicial decisions as acceptable on the premise that the courts making the decisions are independent and not governed by third-party interests. However, neither carefully compiled procedural law nor judicial independence can conclusively prevent the losing party from doubting a court's impartiality. Shapiro sees this as a perennial crisis of legitimacy for adjudication, owing to the fact that it fails to resemble the original triad. He notes, "Contemporary courts are involved in a permanent crisis because they have moved very far along the routes of law and office from the basic consensual triad that provides their essential social logic."[68] Moreover, as Shapiro

---

[68] Shapiro (1981, p. 8).

finds, the latent distrust of adjudication is by no means irrational, insofar as procedural law is always an expression of certain vested interests, namely the interests of
the state or the ruling class underlying the procedures, as Shapiro explains, stating,
"To the extent that the judge employs preexisting rules not shaped by the parties
themselves, he acts not independently but as a servant of the regime, imposing its
interests on the parties to the litigation."[69] This problem also affects ecclesiastical
adjudication. As the norms on the composition of ecclesiastical tribunals and the
procedural law directing the tribunals' actions originate in canon law, one may
suspect certain vested interests, in this case the ecclesiastical authorities' interests,
to underlie ecclesiastical procedures. The impression that hierarchical interests play a
role in the ecclesiastical adjudication system is therefore likely to undermine the
legitimacy of ecclesiastical adjudication in the eyes of the legal subjects. By way of
example, I want to recall the case of Johannes Grabmeier, to which I referred above
when speaking about the limited capacity of the law to solve objective social
conflicts.[70] This case is also a good example of the problems facing courts which
raise suspicion about their impartiality. In his book, Grabmeier above all revealed
that his frustration with the result of his case was rooted less in the fact that he
eventually lost it, and more in his impression that the decision regarding his case had
already been made before the congregation had even studied the facts. For
Grabmeier, the congregation's refusal to hear him and talk to him in person served
as proof that the decision about the bishop winning and him losing the case had
already been made before the procedure started. It is not up to me to decide whether
his impression was actually true. However, from a sociological perspective, we may
note that impressions such as Grabmeier's are liable to undermine the legitimacy of
adjudication in the eyes of the legal subjects.

3.2.7 Employing Elements of Mediation

The courts, hence, have a major interest in developing strategies which address their
legitimacy problem. Martin Shapiro provides some insights into *how* courts in fact
address this problem. He observes that the courts' primary approach is to invoke
Simmel's triad. To avoid giving the impression of "two against one," adjudication
must work to lend greater plausibility to its basic triadic structure. To do this, Shapiro
states, the courts still make considerable use of elements of mediation.[71] Shapiro
notes that, cross-culturally, a significant amount of the courts' business consists not
of actual judicial decision making, but of negotiation and mediation, by which the
courts fulfil their "original" role as mediators between two conflicting parties.
Manfred Rehbinder adopts a similar line, arguing that the work of the courts is

---

[69] Shapiro (1981, p. 26).

[70] See Grabmeier (2012).

[71] See Shapiro (1981, pp. 8–9).

actually often an incremental process of counselling, mediation, arbitration, and adjudication, so that in fact, in many cases, the work of the courts ends before it reaches an actual legal verdict.[72] We can also observe this strategy of adjudication as a further back reference to the mediation triad in ecclesiastical procedural law. The Code of Canon Law actually introduces its whole chapter on ecclesiastical tribunals and the discipline to be observed in tribunals (see canons 1446–1457 CIC/1983) with canon 1446 §1 CIC/1983, a norm that urges all Catholics "to strive diligently to avoid litigation among the people of God as much as possible, without prejudice to justice, and to resolve litigation peacefully as soon as possible." §2 adds the duty of ecclesiastical judges "not to neglect to encourage and assist the parties to collaborate in seeking an equitable solution to the controversy and to indicate to them suitable means to this end, even by using reputable persons for mediation." The legislator is even more explicit in §3 where he advises all judges in cases which concern the private good of the parties "to discern whether the controversy can be concluded advantageously by an agreement or the judgment of arbitrators" following the canons on ecclesiastical arbitration (see canons 1713–1716 CIC/1983). Hence, canon law emphasises the advantage of amicable out-of-court settlements and of the peaceful resolution of disputes. It strongly favours out-of-court solutions over litigation, in those cases where this seems possible without violating justice. This approach has a longstanding tradition in church which reaches back as far as the times of the early church. When Paul was dealing with conflicts in the early Christian community of Corinth, he recommended the benefits of consensual conflict resolution to the Corinthians (see 1 Corinthians 6:1–11). Instead of relying on heathen adjudication, which Paul referred to as the "court before the unrighteous" (1 Corinthians 6:1), the apostle urged the congregation to settle their disputes amicably or through arbitration by other members of the community. For Paul, however, this instruction is less a reflection of his understanding of the secular courts as illegitimate, and more indicative of his wish to prevent the disputants' spiritual aberration. Establishing peace between fellow Christians is a religious priority. As Paul seemed to have understood that adjudication may well settle a concrete legal conflict but seldom solves the social problem underlying the actual conflict, he found the amicable out-of-court settlement to be the Christian way of coming to a satisfactory solution which could bring lasting peace to the disputants and the community. In a similar vein, the *Syrian Didascalia* from the third century underscores that the early Christians' preference for mediation and arbitration was religiously motivated. The *Didascalia* suspects that initiating legal proceedings encourages sinfulness because going to the courts can inflame sinful feelings of anger and hatred towards the opposing party.[73] Hence, the *Didascalia* recommends arbitration over adjudication, with the aim of bringing about peace between the disputants. The text calls to mind Jesus's words from the Sermon on the Mount that peace among Christians must precede an offering at the altar, to emphasise that reconciliation with one's

---

[72] See Rehbinder (2014, p. 155).

[73] See chap. 11. In Gibson (1903, p. 63).

neighbour is of key importance for salvation. Whereas conflict provokes sinfulness and is harmful, peace is regarded as a prerequisite for leading a Christian life.

3.2.8 Penal Procedures as Social Control

Martin Shapiro observes that emphasising the legitimacy of judicial decisions by pointing at elements of mediation is a particularly effective strategy in civil proceedings. This notwithstanding, it is considerably more difficult to reconstruct the triad in criminal proceedings. In criminal cases, it is most evident that the courts are not acting as impartial third parties, but have a vested sovereign interest in maintaining social order.[74] Manfred Rehbinder attributes this to the simple fact that criminal procedures are not primarily about conflict resolution, but about social control.[75] In this sense, criminal proceedings depart from the triadic structure underlying the justice system to a noticeable degree. The courts can therefore only rarely cite the principle of conflict resolution to defend their legitimacy. In fact, they must justify their legitimacy by emphasising their essential service to the group by fulfilling the function of social control. However, this justification is significantly more difficult than referring to the triad. In light of this finding, it is surprising that canon law attempts to prioritise extrajudicial conflict resolution not merely in civil proceedings but also in penal cases; ecclesiastical penal law maintains that ordinaries are to initiate penal proceedings only if fraternal correction, warning, or other pastoral measures have proven ineffective for the purposes of sufficiently restoring justice, reforming the offender, and repairing the scandal (see canon 1341 CIC/1983). Hence, the church still relies on the biblical *correctio fraterna* (see Matthew 18:15) as a way of dealing with conflicts arising from criminal offences. If peace can be restored to the individuals affected and to the community without resorting to a judicial or an administrative procedure, the legislator considers this path to be preferable. This approach is remarkably in line with the triadic conception of conflict resolution. This observation is interesting from a sociological perspective, because it might enable the church more easily than other legal orders to legitimise its criminal proceedings by reconnecting them with the triadic conception underlying all institutionalised mechanisms of conflict resolution. However, from the perspective of the sociology of canon law, the actual effect on legitimacy brought about by linking punishment and triadic conflict resolution is at present more negative than positive, as it seems. As things stand, one may hardly state that ecclesiastical criminal proceedings possess a high level of legitimacy in the eyes of many Catholics. Quite the reverse; many Catholics are very sceptical of ecclesiastical penal procedures, particularly due to the way in which many ecclesiastical authorities have dealt with sexual abuse over the past decades. As recent investigations on

---

[74] See Shapiro (1981, pp. 26–28).

[75] See Rehbinder (2014, p. 151).

how the authorities have dealt with sexual allegations against clerics and church officials have revealed, they made widespread use of extrajudicial instruments to avoid legal proceedings, before both secular courts and ecclesiastical tribunals.[76] They often chose not to prosecute cases of abuse at all, but to cover up the crimes. Disguised as fraternal conflict management, the outcome was often more a form of "conflict procrastination." With regard to ecclesiastical penal adjudication and its legitimacy issue, the triadic structure aimed at balancing the interests of the parties is therefore only of little help. Indeed, it can be rather counterproductive. Instead, the church can only counter the legitimacy issue of its penal proceedings by placing the focus less on triadic mediation and more on the fact that penal adjudication relies on sovereign power to investigate crimes and punish those found guilty in order to maintain and protect the social order. Due to this, ecclesiastical penal judges share the very same problems as secular criminal courts. Because conflict resolution can only play a secondary role where criminal prosecution is concerned, it is difficult to detect the triadic model underlying criminal adjudication. It is certainly particularly challenging for the church, as social control is obviously a good protected by the state, and a good which, in modernity, is connected with the church to an ever-diminishing degree. It is evidently more difficult to argue why the church needs instruments for social control than it is to argue why states require these measures. It is therefore unsurprising that many voices in the public debates demand that the church refrain from punishing church members with penal sanctions and leave this task to the state. Most certainly, from the inside perspective of the church and of canon law, it makes sense to argue that the church as a community is also dependent on instruments of social control. However, it is a matter of continued debate as to whether these instruments must be legal or—more precisely—*penal* ones. From the inside perspective, one may question whether the church today still has any need for penal adjudication, in light of the alternative options for dealing with wrongdoing and transgression. Whilst the church needs instruments to protect itself against the actions of its members which violate the physical and spiritual wellbeing of individual members and the community, one may debate whether this finding is a reason for possessing its own system of ecclesiastical penal adjudication. An alternative is at hand, as I want to sketch briefly. As it is, secular penal adjudication punishes crimes which violate the physical and mental integrity of others, including crimes committed in church. Within the ecclesiastical legal system, a feasible disciplinary law could respond to crimes and other deeds which prove clerics and ecclesiastical officeholders unqualified to fulfil their positions and duties. Actions incompatible with the Catholic faith and morals may be subjected to penitence rather than punishment. So one might well argue that there are other—and maybe even more adequate—means for responding to crimes and other forms of wrongdoing in church than maintaining an ecclesiastical system of penal adjudication. I am not writing this to decide this case and not even to promote my personal opinion on this issue. I mention these considerations at this point because they show, from a sociological

---

[76] For Germany see Dreßing et al. (2018).

point of view, why the church has and will continue to have a hard time proving the legitimacy of its adjudication system particularly in penal matters, and why it is more difficult for the church to argue in favour of its legitimacy than it is for secular adjudication to do so.

3.2.9 Adjudication and Legal Politics

The legitimacy problems which agents of conflict resolution face when they depart from the triad address the courts particularly in their function as *producers* of law, as this is where the impartial application of law merges with partisan legal politics. Martin Shapiro views this problem as particularly acute in common law traditions where courts are key developers of law. Nevertheless, civil law—with its stronger focus on statute law and the legislators as producers of the law—is also showing an increasing tendency to embrace judge-made law: in the German legal system, for example, the decisions of the Federal Constitutional Court are highly influential and shape the legal order profoundly; in a similar vein, European case law is leaving its mark on the ongoing development of the national laws of member states of the European Union. Hence, the courts not only make use of the law as they find it in statutes, they also contribute to creating the law. They are not operating exclusively within a framework of traditional legal doctrine, but are also pursuing political goals with their decisions. In doing so, they are shaping legal doctrine. On this point, however, Martin Shapiro and Roger Cotterrell agree that it is exactly this function of the courts as producers of law and shapers of legal doctrine which raises issues of legitimacy.[77] This is the case because the losing parties in a case might feel they have not lost their case for legal reasons but that they have become the victims of political expediency. This danger is comparatively low in the ecclesiastical legal system, not because ecclesiastical tribunals are more impartial or apolitical than state courts, but because they have only a small role to play in the development of canon law. As a civil law legal system deciding its cases based on codified law, canon law has, since 1917, used statutory law as its main source of law. Ecclesiastical tribunals lack independent authority as lawmakers as they do not create precedent law. The legislator explicitly states that the tribunals' verdicts do not have the force of law and only bind those persons for whom they are given (see canon 16 §3 CIC/1983). Yet the lawmaking capacity of ecclesiastical tribunals is even narrower than that of most other courts in civil law systems. The tribunals' task is limited to interpreting and applying statute law within the narrow system of interpretation rules which are also codified (see canons 17, 18 CIC/1983). By restricting even the tribunals' interpretation with the help of statutory law, the legislator ensures the tribunals have a minimal impact on the development of canon law. Admittedly, some exceptions apply to the Roman tribunals, such as the Roman Rota, the verdicts of which

---

[77] See Shapiro (1981, p. 36); Cotterrell (1984, pp. 260–261).

have some exemplary function for the lower tribunals and also have a political impact on the legislator and his development of the law.[78] However, even these tribunals have no direct impact on the legal development of the church in terms of a precedential function. Canonist Gerhard Neudecker examines this issue in his dissertation entitled *Ius sequitur vitam*.[79] In his book, Neudecker emphasises that the ecclesiastical tribunals' contribution to the development of canon law is largely limited to filling in the gaps in the law (see canon 19 CIC/1983). At this point in my study I will not examine what this restriction of the tribunals means for canon law itself—for its restricted ability to renew itself through legal change or its hampered ability to relate to the everyday life of the church. In this context, it is more important to note that ecclesiastical tribunals, insofar as they play virtually no role as active producers of canon law precedents, are not as far removed from the original idea of impartial triadic conflict resolution as are the courts in judicial systems in which they play a more important role in the ongoing development of law. At least in this respect, the legitimacy problem of canonical adjudication is less significant than that of judicial systems which rely more heavily on judge-made law.

3.2.10   Appeals as Approval

Martin Shapiro suggests one further remedy to address the legitimacy problem of courts, namely the losing parties' option to appeal judicial decisions. Shapiro speaks of the possibility of an appeal as "a psychological outlet and a social cover for the loser at trial. For appeal allows the loser to continue to assert his rightness in the abstract without attacking the legitimacy of the legal system or refusing to obey the trial court."[80] By launching an appeal, the losing parties are explicitly stating that they *accept* the legitimacy of the legal system, because "[a]ppealing to a higher court entails the acknowledgment of its legitimacy".[81] Legal scholar Piero Calamandrei makes a similar observation, namely that proceedings support the state's claim to legitimacy because going to court in fact means that the plaintiff believes in the state and in its legal system.[82] A similar effect applies to the courts and their legitimacy: trials and appellate proceedings benefit the courts, because they reflect the litigants' belief that, in the end, they will receive an impartial and just verdict. At the same time, as Shapiro emphasises, appellate courts also represent sovereign interests and are therefore not entirely free of third-party interests.[83] Here, too, the inevitable ambivalence of the way judicial structures have developed is apparent, as they

---

[78] See Heidl (2012/2013).

[79] See Neudecker (2013).

[80] Shapiro (1981, p. 49).

[81] Shapiro (1981, p. 49).

[82] See Calamandrei (1956, p. 96).

[83] See Shapiro (1981, p. 56).

clearly diverge from the original triad of conflict resolution. Hence, it is particularly dangerous with regard to their legitimacy if appellate courts and their decisions give the impression they are guided by political interests. This problem likewise applies to ecclesiastical adjudication. I want to refer once more to the example of Johannes Grabmeier, the Catholic who was very active in diocesan committees of lay partic-ipation in his Diocese of Regensburg, who published his experiences about his unsuccessful attempt to win a lawsuit in the ecclesiastical appeals process.[84] In his book, Grabmeier describes the impression he gained that the ecclesiastical instances were acting in the interests of the official church, namely to immunise church officials against the legal concerns of church members, particularly of laypeople, by rejecting the lays' judicial claims. Whether Grabmeier's view is just the one-sided opinion of a defeated plaintiff or provides an accurate insight into the interests that guide decisions in ecclesiastical proceedings is a matter for others to judge. Never-theless, it is problematic enough in itself if ecclesiastical tribunals give the impres-sion that they are not deciding impartially in the appeals process, but are guided by sovereign interests. Moreover, the fact that canon law did not establish channels of appeal for *all* types of proceedings—in church, adjudication deals with criminal cases, civil cases, and declaratory cases (see canon 1400 §1 CIC/1983) but has not yet established a thorough system of administrative procedure which allows to contest administrative acts on the diocesan level—reduces, from a sociological point of view, the chance of mitigating the legitimacy problem facing ecclesiastical tribunals. This is because the tribunals cannot always direct legal subjects burdened by an ecclesiastical decision towards a respective channel of appeal if there simply is none. If we accept Piero Calamandrei's remark as correct that active litigation is also a statement about the confidence the litigants have in the authorities, then the church, by lacking administrative procedures against administrative decisions taken at the diocesan level, is not only jeopardising the legitimacy of its adjudication system but is also foregoing an opportunity to engage in confidence building among the church members.

Irrespective of whether we are talking about state courts or ecclesiastical tri-bunals, the observations compiled in this section show that we must view the legitimacy of modern judicial systems critically, as contemporary adjudication is consistently at the edge of its capacity to manage conflicts. In light of this finding, Roger Cotterrell asks the obvious question why adjudication has nevertheless been able to establish itself so pervasively in our societies, wondering, "Why are such 'unstable' legal institutions nevertheless seemingly essential to developed legal systems?"[85] We may probably only answer this question by noting the contribution adjudication has made to reducing complexity in society. In complex modern legal communities and societies, an elaborate adjudication system makes it possible to manage conflicts in an orderly manner, including those cases which overburden the mediation triad. However, this observation does not explain how adjudication has

---

[84] See Grabmeier (2012).

[85] Cotterrell (1984, p. 221).

been able to overcome its persistent legitimacy problems throughout the course of history. It is probably impossible to answer this question conclusively. In Cotterrell's view, the state, or rather the political framework in which a court system exists, appears to be a significant factor in offsetting the legitimacy problems posed by the structure of adjudication. The state contributes to the stability of adjudication "by maintaining the integrity of the legal order itself—the ideological conditions upon which legal domination depends."[86] This assumption reflects Calamandrei's view, which sees adjudication as supporting the legitimacy of the state. It is therefore fair to assume that the state and trust in the political order lend support to the legitimacy of adjudication in return. Ideally, the same interdependency should also apply in church. Trust in the ecclesiastical authorities strengthens trust in ecclesiastical adjudication, while distrust in the ecclesiastical authorities weakens it. At present, many Catholics probably do not expect too much from either.

3.2.11 Sanctions and Police Function

Summing up the findings of the previous sections, we may observe that almost all societies and many larger groups contain agencies and bodies which work in a more or less triadic way towards the resolution of social conflicts; we may also find similar bodies in the church. Yet Richard Schwartz and James Miller observed that only societies with a high division of labour entrust official police forces or comparable agencies with the sovereign administration of justice. This finding is interesting from the point of view of the sociology of law, because it indicates that while institutionalised conflict management seems to be essential to every society and larger community, this does not likewise apply to the need to enforce conflict solutions. Schwartz and Miller therefore note that "mediation is not inevitably accompanied by the systematic enforcement of decisions."[87] Their observation contradicts the assumption that sovereign control and sanctions are of crucial importance for social coexistence. This finding merits further discussion, especially from a criminological perspective. Criminology usually alludes to three benefits of sovereign sanctions:[88] in their repressive function of specific or general prevention, sanctions have the effect of encouraging future compliance with non-observed norms; in their restitutive retributive function, they provide redress for the victims of crime; in their socio-psychological function, they endeavour to overcome the cognitive dissonance in the legal community, bridging the perceived variance between what is and what ought to be that has arisen as the result of a breach of law.[89] In view of this record, Schwartz and Miller's observation on the lack of a

---

[86] Cotterrell (1984, p. 247).

[87] Schwartz and Miller (1964, p. 166).

[88] E.g. Rehbinder (2014, p. 102).

[89] On the concept of cognitive dissonance, see Festinger (1957).

police function in many societies with a low division of labour begs the question how these societies engage in prevention, respond to retaliatory needs, and resolve the cognitive dissonance that a breach of law may cause among members of society. At first glance, one may find that this problem is not a pressing issue for the sociology of canon law, as the elaborate ecclesiastical adjudication system includes a sophisticated penal system, similar to those identified by Schwartz and Miller in complex communities. Although the church has significantly slimmed down in this field and—as I already explained in Sect. 2.2.3—cut back its massive former penal law to some degree, it has not fully renounced its fundamental right to impose punishments on its members (see canon 1311 §1 CIC/ 1983). Instead, in line with Schwartz and Miller's observations, the church proves to be an institution that manages its complexity—its high degree of functional differentiation, specialisation, and professionalisation—by relying on a system of sanctions. I did note in Sect. 3.2.8 though that it is open to debate whether this sanctioning function, which helps to control the social in church, must by necessity be a penal system. There are good reasons to debate whether it might be adequate to replace the ecclesiastical penal system by leaving criminal sanctioning to secular penal adjudication, while endowing the church with a robust disciplinary law and leaving all those actions incompatible with Catholic faith and morals to penitence rather than to ecclesiastical punishment. However, at this point in my study, I do not wish to discuss the pros and cons of the ecclesiastical penal system, but merely take the existence of this system as proof that the church concords with Schwartz and Miller's complex communities which provide elaborate penal systems. However, in light of Schwartz and Miller's results, the situation in church paints an ambivalent picture. This is because the church is completely devoid of a police force or alternative executive bodies that can enforce judicial decisions. In modernity, the church has been unable to establish a policing function over its own members, neither has it been able to cooperate with the modern nation states to establish any secular support to serve this purpose, as was common in mediaeval times. I already touched upon this point in the discussion about whether law requires coercion. Yet again, this lack of executive policing power in church raises questions in this context too—even if we dismiss Max Weber's idea that the law essentially requires a coercive apparatus that enforces legal claims in the legal community by sovereign means.[90] As I discussed in Sect. 2.1, I do not share Weber's view of the law as a coercive order by necessity. But we nevertheless need to think about the consequences deriving from the fact that the church is not even remotely likely to operate a policing function, as it does not have a police force at its disposal. This fact does not touch upon the issue of whether canon law is law, as the concept of law, as I argued, is not essentially connected with coercion. But it does touch upon the issue of effectiveness, insofar as a law without a police function may face challenges with regard to its very functioning as law. We must therefore discuss whether a penal system that has to manage without a police force has any chance of being effective at

---

[90] See Weber (1978, p. 313).

all and if and how verdicts and administrative decisions under canon law stand any chance of being heeded if there is no one to police their compliance. These questions are of particular interest to the sociology of canon law as a sociology studying a legal order with an exceptionally low level of coercion. I will return to these questions again in the sixth section of this study.

3.2.12 Coping with Complexity

In their study, Schwartz and Miller also found that we discover legal counselling predominantly in societies with a high division of labour, along with a police force or alternative executive bodies of legal enforcement.[91] The existence of legal counselling in these complex societies is understandable, says Roger Cotterrell, insofar as these societies often also have a complex legal doctrine and elaborate legal procedures whose rules are familiar only to the legal professions. In order to legally defuse conflicts under these complex conditions, it is therefore necessary "to call upon people with special knowledge of such matters for advice and aid."[92] Complex contemporary law requires experts particularly because legal conflict resolution necessitates successful legal communications. Hence it requires experts who speak "Legalese." The problem posed by legal language therefore plays a major role in the sociology of law, especially in sociological studies of adjudication and administration.[93] In his empirical research on the German adjudication system, Rüdiger Lautmann stressed the importance of legal language as a key factor separating professional and non-professional actors in the courtroom, observing, "The language of judicial trials is so specific that only professional parties (such as business people or lawyers) understand it and speak it; at best an educated individual from the upper middle class may follow and join in from time to time."[94] Lautmann views this as a social problem because it implies that making one's voice heard in courts, and in legal disputes in general, depends on the social status of those involved. For most disputants, it is virtually impossible to participate in their own cases, as Lautmann observes, "Those directly concerned are isolated and kept away from participating in solving the problem. Many of those who actually carry the [essential] information cannot take part and cannot intervene to correct the process of abstraction."[95] These observations also apply to the law of the church. Ecclesiastical law is also highly

---

[91] See Schwartz and Miller (1964, p. 167).

[92] Cotterrell (1984, p. 188).

[93] See Bourdieu (1987, pp. 819–821).

[94] Original quote, "Die Sprache einer Gerichtsverhandlung ist so spezifisch, daß nur professionell Beteiligte (etwa Kaufleute und Juristen) verstehen und reden können; allenfalls ein Gebildeter aus der oberen Mittelschicht kann hier folgen und gelegentlich sich einschalten", Lautmann (2011, p. 84).

[95] Original quote, "Die unmittelbar Betroffenen werden damit isoliert und von einer Teilnahme an der Problemlösung ferngehalten. Viele der eigentlichen Informationsträger können nicht mitreden und in den Abstraktionsprozeß korrigierend eingreifen", Lautmann (2011, p. 84).

specialised, and understanding it requires specialist canonical knowledge. If potential litigants wish to successfully contest a case under canon law, they require the expertise of legal professionals with a profound knowledge of canon law and the skill to speak ecclesiastical "Legalese." "Counsel"—one of the three categories examined by Schwartz and Miller—is one characteristic which clearly shows how complex ecclesiastical law is as a legal system.

3.2.13   Perplexing Selectivity of the Law

In addition to the problem of understanding legal language, as Klaus Röhl finds, successful legal communications also require expert knowledge to adapt people's general everyday understanding of the world to the *selectivity* of the law. Röhl illustrates this using the example of oral hearings in court proceedings. He notes that it is less a matter of language comprehension which creates the greatest difficulty for legal lays, and more the problem of differentiating between information that is legally relevant and that which is not.[96] In functionally differentiated societies, legal communications are only concerned with those selected aspects of the social that pertain to the law. It is hard for legal lays to tell this legally relevant information apart from other information pertaining to other social facts and social relationships. At the same time, non-experts are often confused or even irritated by the obvious disinterest of the law in the non-legal aspects of the social. Judges who trammel party or witness statements to restrict them to legally relevant information, for instance, are often criticised for not demonstrating an interest in learning the *whole* truth. It is hard to understand for legal lays that the law is indeed not interested in the "whole truth," but only in legal truth, that is in those facets of social reality which clearly pertain to the legal facts of a concrete case. This selectivity of the law may in fact raise fundamental criticism among legal subjects, especially in church. While many legal lays perceive the disinterest of secular courts in extra-legal realities as an irritant, they may still tolerate it. Church members, however, often expect church authorities to act more "holistically." This expectation includes ecclesiastical adjudication and administration, even in those cases in which ecclesiastical institutions, in a functionally differentiated church, act as agents of the law and therefore restrict their focus to legally relevant information. Yet as the church is not merely a legal system but a religious community, it is difficult to explain why church authorities act differently when fulfilling different functions in church. It is difficult to understand why the authorities present themselves as being interested in the full truth of human life, with all its personal and social facets when acting as religious leaders, while only showing an interest in fragments of the very same reality when acting as legal authorities. My belief that this twofold approach to dealing with reality in church is a source of specific tensions is based on my observations of many church members' reactions to

---

[96] See Röhl (1987, p. 507).

the legal handling of abuse cases by church officials. While many church members welcome the fact that ecclesiastical authorities now frequently address abuse cases legally, they often tend to receive the authorities' actions and decisions as insufficient. Some examples might help to illustrate these tensions. Many investigations answering to allegations end without a conviction or do not even go to trial in the first place, often due to the statute of limitations (see canon 1362 §1 no. 2 CIC/1983), sometimes despite obvious guilt. Whilst the statute of limitations, with its protection of legal certainty, is a plausible impediment to legal proceedings from a legal perspective, it is not easy to convey this restriction to the church members— particularly as many of them experience the church as a community that prioritises individual and communal salvation and well-being elsewhere. In those cases in which proceedings do lead to a conviction, church members often criticise ecclesiastical sentencing as inappropriate, even in those cases in which the authorities make full use of the penalties available under ecclesiastical penal law. It perplexes many church members to learn that the maximum penalty for clerical sex offenders is dismissal from the clerical state (see canon 1398 §1 CIC/1983). Many are also critical of the fact that the bishops or tribunals, when investigating accusations, limit their interests to the legal aspects of the cases, without examining the effects that abuse has on the victims and on the community, such as on parishes which have to deal with accusations against parish priests. In this light, many Catholics criticise the restricted legal view of abuse and the narrow view of penal procedures and verdicts as insufficient, one-sided, and of little benefit to the victims and the local communities. I do not refer to this common lack of understanding for the limitations of the law in order to complain about it. Nor do I want to express surprise that many church members do not seem to accept the selectivity of social subsystems that goes along with functional differentiation in the church as an organisation which transects various subsystems such as the law, the economy, politics, science, and art. Instead, I suggest that this common lack of understanding for the limitations of the law might have a specific edge in church. From the point of view of the sociology of law, one may indeed argue that a lack of understanding for the limitations of the law is rather common. However, as I want to argue, one may also find that a common misapprehension about how courts operate and what they can and cannot do is more troubling in religious legal communities, such as the church, than in secular legal systems. As religious communities promise to act in the interests of their members' salvation and well-being, it seems to disappoint many church members all the more whenever ecclesiastical authorities view a conflict merely through a legal lens. It is clear that there is not much alternative for a professional legal system. However, it is understandable that church members find it confusing that representatives of the official church at times act as agents of a professional legal system and at other times as leaders of a religious community, particularly as in church these positions are frequently filled by the very same individuals. Further study seems necessary to identify if and how it is possible to reconcile these two competing concepts of authority, legal and religious, without causing massive discord among the church members.

3.2.14 Ecclesiastical Adjudication Research

My study is not a sociology of canonical institutions. I therefore refrain from engaging in an in-depth study of ecclesiastical adjudication and forego developing an institutional sociology of the ecclesiastical tribunal system. Both approaches are of interest to the sociology of canon law, but a basic overview such as my book can do sufficient justice to neither. Nevertheless, I want to make some suggestions where further research might prove to be insightful to the sociology of canon law, by identifying topics discussed in socio-legal research on adjudication which potentially resonate with a sociology of ecclesiastical adjudication. First, I find it necessary to discuss which existing theories are suitable for providing a theoretical foundation for research on ecclesiastical adjudication. Rüdiger Lautmann stresses that research on adjudication does not make it easy for the sociology of law to choose one theoretical approach, given the plurality of theoretical approaches suitable for studying adjudication. There are several approaches to choose from, as Lautmann suggests,

> adjudication as professional action of professional judges; verdicts as outputs of the judicial system as an organisation; as an exercise of power; as an act of social control; as sanctioning of [unwanted] behaviour; as a solution of social conflicts; adjudication as a group process; as interaction or as role behaviour of those involved in the procedure; as communication between them; as evaluation; and as decision making.[97]

Lautmann's assemblage of approaches relating to legal institutions and organisations, to power issues, legal roles and professions, legal communications, and decision making, reveals how complex the field of adjudication and of court systems is. It is no less complex within the church, and therefore merits a study of its own.

3.2.15 Class Justice, Clerical Justice

One research question of major interest with regard to research on ecclesiastical adjudication is connected with the class issue, even though the class question is slightly different when raised with regard to ecclesiastical adjudication compared to secular adjudication. In the sociology of law, the class issue has repeatedly been at the centre of post-war sociological justice research. In the 1960s, German-British sociologist Ralf Dahrendorf, on the basis of data on the social origins of German judges, made the oft-cited statement "that in our courts one half of society is

---

[97] Original quote, "Rechtsprechen als Berufshandeln der Richterprofession; Urteile als Output der Organisation Justiz, als Ausübung von Macht, als Akt sozialer Kontrolle, als Sanktionierung von Verhalten, als Lösung sozialer Konflikte; Rechtsprechen als Gruppenprozeß, als Interaktion oder als Rollenverhalten der am Verfahren Beteiligten, als Kommunikation zwischen ihnen, als Bewertung und als Entscheiden", Lautmann (2011, p. 30).

authorised to judge over the unknown other half of society."[98] However, nowadays, there is little talk of "class justice" any more. The debates of the 1960s and 1970s surrounding this topic have cooled noticeably, particularly because empirical justice research was unable to prove that class and social status were decisive in court verdicts.[99] This does not mean, however, that the class issue in adjudication has been resolved across the board, just because it looks somewhat different today to the way it appeared in the 1960s.[100] In the 1990s, for example, Kai-Detlef Bussmann and Christian Lüdemann argued that adjudication touches upon class issues when studying criminal proceedings for certain types of offence. Criminal proceedings for white-collar crimes, which were brought against disproportionately large numbers of socially better-off defendants, regularly ended more favourably for the defendants than common criminal proceedings.[101] In many cases this was due to so-called "deals." This finding is not "class justice" in the conventional sense for several reasons: the phenomenon is neither the result of inequality in the conduct of the trials; nor due to the one-sided interpretation of the trial material; nor a result of a discriminatory reading of the law; nor of unequal sentencing. Nevertheless, Bussmann and Lüdemann observed an obvious imbalance between economic and other crimes which results in an inequality of opportunity for the defendants. In another study, sociologist Jochen Dreher found that parts of the German public perceived the verdicts in the 2005 Volkswagen corruption affair as class justice because they considered the different social status of the defendants as having been influential in the proceedings and their outcome.[102] Whilst defendants representing the employer Volkswagen entered deals to reduce their punishment, there was no deal with the former employee representative. Dreher does not propose that the Volkswagen verdicts were indeed examples of class justice. But he shows that there is a certain sensitivity in the public mind about the courts' different treatment of defendants in patterns of class justice.

One gap in research on ecclesiastical adjudication is the dearth of knowledge about the social background of ecclesiastical judges. It is equally unclear whether social criteria and class issues play a role in their decision making. What is clear, however, is that ecclesiastical adjudication is, in the main, clerical justice. It is therefore also male justice, since according to current ecclesiastical doctrine and law only men can become members of the clergy (see canon 1024 CIC/1983). The gender issue also plays a role in secular law and, consequently, in the secular sociology of adjudication. Ulrike Schultz and Gisela Shaw have made significant progress in this field by surveying the representation and underrepresentation of

---

[98] Original quote, "daß in unseren Gerichten die eine Hälfte der Gesellschaft über die ihr unbekannte andere zu urteilen befugt ist", Dahrendorf (1960, p. 275).

[99] For further references see Raiser (2007, pp. 301–302); Rehbinder (2014, pp. 137–139).

[100] See Gephart (2006, p. 19); Struck (2011, pp. 98–100).

[101] See Bussmann and Lüdemann (1995, pp. 151–154).

[102] See Dreher (2010, pp. 336–343).

women in the legal professions of individual countries.[103] In the church, however, the low proportion of female judges is particularly problematic, since the underrepresentation of women is not merely a consequence of the common social conditions in church, but is a direct consequence of legal regulation. This is because canon law prescribes the recruitment of ecclesiastical judges predominantly from the clergy, thus ensuring that ecclesiastical tribunals mostly consist of men. Ecclesiastical single judges must always be clerics, according to current canon law (see canons 1421 §1, 1673 §4 CIC/1983). In collegiate tribunals consisting of three judges, one lay judge can be included if the bishops' conference votes in favour of this arrangement (see canon 1421 §2 CIC/1983). So far, the bishops' conferences in only a handful of countries (for example, the German Bishops' Conference) have done so. However, in his *Motu proprio Mitis Iudex Dominus Iesus*, Francis paved the way for *two* lay women or lay men to act as judges in collegiate tribunals, even without a vote of approval by the bishops' conferences (see canon 1673 §3 CIC/1983).[104] In doing so, Francis also created the basis for ecclesiastical tribunals to become—or potentially become—more female. This also depends on the one hand on whether women choose to take the path of canonical qualification—despite the misogynous work setting—and, on the other hand, on whether the bishops do actually appoint more women to the relevant positions. So whilst one may argue that Francis has opened up ecclesiastical adjudication to make it more of a common workplace for laypeople, there are still regulations which make one wonder how welcome lay canonists truly are on the ecclesiastical benches. Lays may not decide as single judges. And they are systematically excluded from certain ecclesiastical proceedings, such as from penal proceedings against clerics. In these proceedings, only priests may be called upon as judges, promotors of justice, notaries, and chancellors.[105] The Congregation for the Doctrine of the Faith can grant a dispensation from this requirement for the aforementioned offices.[106] However, church authorities rarely rely on this option. After all, the regular restriction of the offices to priests testifies to the congregation's and the church authorities' reluctance to include laypeople as well as deacons in proceedings against clerics.

Bibliography

Association of German Dioceses. (2019). Rahmenordnung für eine Mitarbeitervertretungsordnung (Rahmen-MAVO), 19 June 2017, Retrieved April 3, 2018, from www.bag-mav.de/wp-content/uploads/2015/06/SHMAVO-Flie%C3%9Ftext-_05.07.2017-%C3%84nderungen.pdf

Aubert, V. (1963). Competition and dissensus: Two types of conflict and of conflict resolution. *The Journal of Conflict Resolution, 7*, 26–42.

---

[103] E.g. Schultz and Shaw (2003).

[104] *Acta Apostolicae Sedis, 107*, 961.

[105] See Congregation for the Doctrine of the Faith (2021, articles 13 and 20).

[106] See Congregation for the Doctrine of the Faith (2021, articles 14 and 21).

Böckenförde, W. (2006). Zur gegenwärtigen Lage in der römisch-katholischen Kirche: Kirchenrechtliche Anmerkungen. In N. Lüdecke & G. Bier (Eds.), *Freiheit und Gerechtigkeit in der Kirche: Gedenkschrift für Werner Böckenförde* (Forschungen zur Kirchenrechtswissenschaft 37, pp. 143–158). Echter.

Bourdieu, P. (1987). The force of law: Toward a sociology of the juridical field. *The Hastings Law Journal, 38*, 814–853.

Bucher, R. (2018). Einige pastoraltheologische Probleme des Kirchenrechts. *Lebendige Seelsorge, 69*, 160–164.

Bussmann, K.-D., & Lüdemann, C. (1995). *Klassenjustiz oder Verfahrensökonomie? Aushandlungsprozesse in Wirtschafts- und allgemeinen Strafverfahren* (Bremer soziologische Texte 6). Centaurus.

Calamandrei, P. (1956). *Lob der Richter: Gesungen von einem Advokaten.* Piper.

Congregation for the Clergy. (2006). Dekret über die Änderung der Mitwirkungsorgane in der Diözese Regensburg [Decree on the Changes made with respect to the Bodies of Lay Participation of the Diocese of Regensburg], 10 March 2006, Prot. no. 2006/0224. *Archiv für katholisches Kirchenrecht, 175*, 156–158.

Congregation for the Doctrine of the Faith. (2021). Norms on delicts reserved to the Congregation for the Doctrine of the Faith, 11 October 2021. Retrieved May 17, 2022, from www.vatican.va/roman_curia/congregations/cfaith/documents/rc_con_cfaith_doc_20211011_norme-delittiriservaticfaithen.html

Corecco, E. (1994). Handlung „contra legem" und Rechtssicherheit im kanonischen Recht. In L. Gerosa & L. Müller (Eds.), *Ordinatio fidei: Schriften zum kanonischen Recht* (pp. 36–54). Ferdinand Schöningh.

Cotterrell, R. (1984). *The sociology of law: An introduction.* Butterworths.

Dahrendorf, R. (1960). Bemerkungen zur sozialen Stellung und Herkunft der Richter an Oberlandesgerichten: Ein Beitrag zur Soziologie der deutschen Oberschicht. *Hamburger Jahrbuch für Wirtschafts- und Gesellschaftspolitik, 5*, 260–275.

Doe, N. (1992). Toward a critique of the role of theology in English ecclesiastical and canon law. *Ecclesiastical Law Journal, 2*, 328–346.

Dreher, J. (2010). Zur Wirkungsweise von Kollektivsymbolik im Recht: Symbolische Macht und "Klassenjustiz". In M. Cottier, J. Estermann & M. Wrase (Eds.), *Wie wirkt Recht? Ausgewählte Beiträge zum ersten gemeinsamen Kongress der deutschsprachigen Rechtssoziologie-Vereinigungen, Luzern 2008* (Recht und Gesellschaft/Law and Society 1, pp. 323–345). Nomos.

Dreßing, H., Salize, H. J., Dölling, D., Hermann, D., Kruse, A., Schmitt, E., & Bannenberg, B. (2018). Sexueller Missbrauch an Minderjährigen durch katholische Priester, Diakone und männliche Ordensangehörige im Bereich der Deutschen Bischofskonferenz, Mannheim/Heidelberg/Gießen, 24 September 2018. Retrieved October 25, 2020, from www.dbk.de/fileadmin/redaktion/diverse_downloads/dossiers_2018/MHG-Studie-gesamt.pdf

Durkheim, É. (1960). *The division of labor in society* [1893] (G. Simpson, Trans.). The Free Press.

Dworkin, R. (1998). *Law's empire.* Hart Publishing.

Ehrlich, E. (1936). *Fundamental principles of the sociology of law* (W. L. Moll, Trans., with an introduction by R. Pound). The Harvard University Press.

Festinger, L. (1957). *A theory of cognitive dissonance.* Stanford University Press.

Francis. (2015). Apostolic letter issued *Motu proprio Mitis Iudex Dominus Jesus* by which the canons of the code of canon law pertaining to cases regarding the nullity of marriage are reformed, 15 August 2015. *Acta Apostolicae Sedis, 107*, 958–970.

Frank, J. (2010). Streitgespräch unter Katholiken "Macht in der katholischen Kirche. . ." . . .aber wie lange wollen die Männer sie den Frauen noch vorenthalten? Der Osnabrücker Bischof Franz-Josef Bode im Streitgespräch mit der Theologin Marianne Heimbach-Steins, 20 July 2010. Retrieved June 22, 2021, from www.fr.de/politik/streitgespraech-unter-katholiken-macht-in-derkatholischen-kirche-a-1013611

Gephart, W. (2006). *Recht als Kultur: Zur kultursoziologischen Analyse des Rechts* (Studien zur europäischen Rechtsgeschichte 209). Klostermann.

Gibson, M. D. (Ed.). (1903). *The Didascalia Apostolorum in English: Translated from the Syriac* (Horae Semiticae 2). C. J. Clay and Sons.

Glenz, T. (2019). Limburger Bischof fürchtet Spaltung: Bätzing: Segensfeiern für Homosexuelle "im Moment" nicht möglich, 23 August 2019. Retrieved July 27, 2021, from www.katholisch. de/artikel/22717-baetzing-segensfeiern-fuer-homosexuelle-immoment-nicht-moeglich

Goler, P. A. (1972). Must canon law be color blind? *Catholic Lawyer, 18*, 293–299.

Grabmeier, J. (2012). *Kirchlicher Rechtsweg—vatikanische Sackgasse! Kirchliches Rechtssystem in der römisch-katholischen Kirche endgültig gescheitert—dargestellt am konkreten Fall eines hierarchischen Rekurses von Regensburg bis Rom zur Mitwirkung der Laien in der Kirche* (mit einem Vorwort von H. Geißler). Animus.

Heidl, S. (2012/2013). Die Leitbildfunktion der Römischen Rota. *De Processibus Matrimonialibus, 19/20*, 87–109.

Höhn, H.-J. (1986). Gnade vor Recht? Sozialtheoretische Überlegungen zu Ansatz und Aufbau einer Theologie des Kirchenrechts. *Freiburger Zeitschrift für Philosophie und Theologie, 33*, 345–390.

Lautmann, R. (2011). *Justiz—die stille Gewalt: Teilnehmende Beobachtung und entscheidungssoziologische Analyse* (2nd ed.). Springer.

Losch, B. (2006). *Kulturfaktor Recht: Grundwerte—Leitbilder—Normen.* Böhlau.

Lüdecke, N. (2017). Die Übermacht definitiver Festlegungen: Partizipation nach Stand und Geschlecht, Speech, 13 February 2017. Retrieved June 22, 2021, from http://theosalon. blogspot.de/2017/02/loben-statt-weihen.html

Lüdecke, N. (2021). *Die Täuschung: Haben Katholiken die Kirche, die sie verdienen?* Wissenschaftliche Buchgesellschaft.

Lüdecke, N., & Bier, G. (2012). *Das römisch-katholische Kirchenrecht: Eine Einführung* (unter Mitarbeit von B. S. Anuth). Stuttgart.

Luhmann, N. (1995). *Social systems* (J. Bednarz, Jr. & D. Baecker, Trans., Foreword by E. M. Knodt). Stanford University Press.

Luhmann, N. (2004). *Law as a social system* (Oxford socio-legal studies, F. Kastner, R. Nobles, D. Schiff & R. Ziegert, Eds., K. A. Ziegert, Trans.). Oxford University Press.

Luhmann, N. (2014). A sociological theory of law (E. King-Utz, M. Albrow, Trans.). M. Albrow (Ed.). Routledge.

Machura, S. (2010). Rechtssoziologie. In G. Kneer & M. Schroer (Eds.), *Handbuch Spezielle Soziologien* (pp. 379–392). Springer.

Mezey, N. (2001). Law as culture. *Yale Journal of Law & the Humanities, 13*, 35–67.

Migne, J. P. (Ed.). (1863). *Patrologiae cursus completes: Series Latina, vol 62: Eugyppii, africani abbatis, opera omnia.* Excudebat Sirou.

Neudecker, G. (2013). *Ius sequitur vitam—Der Dienst der Kirchengerichte an der Lebendigkeit des Rechts: Zugleich ein Beitrag zur Vergleichung des kanonischen und staatlichen Rechtssystems* (Tübinger Kirchenrechtliche Studien 13). LIT.

Raiser, T. (2007). *Grundlagen der Rechtssoziologie* (4th ed.). UTB.

Rehbinder, M. (2014). *Rechtssoziologie: Ein Studienbuch* (8th ed.). C. H. Beck.

Röhl, K. F. (1987). *Rechtssoziologie: Ein Lehrbuch.* Heymann.

Rottleuthner, H., & Rottleuthner-Lutter, M. (2010). Effektivität von Recht: Der Beitrag der Rechtssoziologie. In G. Wagner (Ed.), *Kraft Gesetz: Beiträge zur rechtssoziologischen Effektivitätsforschung* (pp. 13–34). Springer.

Schultz, U., & Shaw, G. (Eds.). (2003). *Women in the world's legal profession* (Oñati International Series in Law and Society). Hart Publishing.

Schwartz, R. D., & Miller, J. C. (1964). Legal evolution and societal complexity. *American Journal of Sociology, 70*, 159–169.

Second Vatican Council. (1965). Dogmatic Constitution *Lumen gentium* on the Church, 21 November 1964. *Acta Apostolicae Sedis, 57*, 5–75.

Shapiro, M. (1981). *Courts: A comparative and political analysis.* The University of Chicago Press.

Simmel, G. (2009). *Sociology: Inquiries into the construction of social forms vol 1* (A. J. Blasi, A. K. Jacobs & M. Kanjirathinkal, Ed. & Trans., introduction by H. J. Helle). Brill.
Struck, G. (2011). *Rechtssoziologie: Grundlagen und Strukturen*. Nomos.
Tamanaha, B. Z. (2017). *A realistic theory of law*. Cambridge University Press.
Weber, M. (1978). *Economy and society: An outline of interpretive sociology* (G. Roth & C. Wittich, Eds.). University of California Press.

Chapter 4
Law and Legal Validity

Abstract Modern law is positive law. It gains its validity through the respective authority's decision. The issue of power is therefore key for the sociology of law, from two perspectives: as the question of how the law contributes to generating and distributing power, and as the question of how power and authorities with power contribute to making the law. That positive law is based on decision-making, however, points at the fact that positive laws are changeable. Positive law, including canon law, is open to change. Occasions encouraging legal change are phenomena of recurrent non-compliance. Constant non-compliance with the law may trigger legal learning. This is a fragile process, however, as processes of legal learning may also destabilise legal orders. Legislators therefore face the challenge of reforming their laws by aligning the members of the legal community to the new laws without losing their trust in the stability of the order. In a similar vein, the church risks destabilisation should the legislator decide to reform the law rapidly and thoroughly. However, from the perspective of a sociology of law, it is also crucial to note that avoiding reform may cause destabilisation, too, insofar as premodern and outdated laws may raise concerns of legitimacy.

Keywords Divine law · Legal development · Non-compliance · Positive law · Power · Validity of the law

To explain why law is valid in a legal sense, proponents of positivism need only point to the *legality* of the law. Norms become legal norms if a competent authority with legislative power promulgates them, and they remain legal norms if no competent authority derogates them and as long as they prove to be compatible with higher ranking law.[1] I will devote this section to a close examination of the legal validity of law, and in particular of canon law. However, in discussing the legitimacy of law, proponents of prepositive legal theories point out that legality is a first but not a conclusive step towards discussing the validity of law. Law may never fully align with justice, yet one may argue that justice is its goal. For the validity of law it is

---

[1] See Raiser (2007, p. 237).

© The Author(s) 2022
J. Hahn, *Foundations of a Sociology of Canon Law*,
https://doi.org/10.1007/978-3-031-01791-9_4

therefore also essential that law finds recognition in a legal community because the community members find it acceptable as a more or less just order. I will discuss this connection between law and its legitimacy in the fifth section of this study. In addition, sociology also posits that the validity of law is indivisible from its facticity. Any debate about the validity of law must also include the factual validity of law as the actual effect that law has in a legal community. The issues are intertwined. The legitimacy of the law has an influence on the factual validity of the law, insofar as the actual effectiveness of the law depends in part on the legal subjects' acknowledgment of the law. Whether the de facto validity of the law also has an effect on legal validity is open to debate. With these connections in mind, Manfred Rehbinder describes "living law" as "valid law which is effective. Normativity without facticity is dead law . . ., and facticity opposed to normativity is injustice."[2] Hence, there are three separate levels of validity, which are set out below. I will talk about mere legal validity in this, the fourth section. I will then address validity as legitimacy in the fifth section, and effectiveness of the law as its factual validity in the sixth section of my study.

4.1   Law Born of Power, Power Born of Law

Modern law is positive law. Defining law in this relatively strict way is a response to the complexity of modern societies.[3] Instead of looking at the legal community's full gamut of normative beliefs, modern society restricts "law" to norms that result from a sovereign act of legislation or adjudication. Niklas Luhmann expresses this in a tautology that is often cited as a way of explaining the meaning of legal positivity, "Law is what law deems to be law."[4] Or, to rephrase Luhmann's sentence, law is what the authorities empowered by law declare law to be, in the manner provided by the law for doing so. Elsewhere, Luhmann also states, "Law is called positive when it is established and when its validity is based on decision."[5] Whenever modern positive law is concerned, the focus of attention is on those authorities empowered to create law. In civil law traditions the focus of attention is mainly on legislation and the legislative procedures; in common law traditions the focus is also on adjudication and the courts which are involved in developing the law according to the principle of precedent. Understanding law as positive law consequently means focusing on the

---

[2]Original quote, "lebendes Recht"; "geltendes Recht, das wirksam ist. Denn Normativität ohne Faktizität ist totes Recht . . ., und Faktizität im Gegensatz zur Normativität ist Unrecht", Rehbinder (2014, p. 2).

[3]See Luhmann (1970, pp. 176–202); Kunz and Mona (2006, p. 26).

[4]Luhmann (2004, p. 157).

[5]Original quote, "Als positiv wird Recht bezeichnet, das gesetzt worden ist und kraft Entscheidung gilt", Luhmann (1970, p. 182).

agents with the authority to make law, and examining the processes in which law comes into being.

The question of who is competent to create law shifts the focus towards *power*, or the ability to use the law to influence the expectations and behaviour of those who are subject to it. Power plays a dual role with respect to the law. The sociology of law, insofar as it examines not only the influence of social realities on law, but also the influence of law on the social realities of groups such as communities or societies, conceives of power in a twofold sense: as the generation of power through the law, and as the generation of law through power.[6] The connection between law and power is thus reflected in the power of law because law controls social realities. It is also reflected in the power of the political agents who influence and develop the law. We might call to mind Jean Carbonnier's differentiation between the primary and secondary manifestations of law: form and content. Carbonnier sees the primary manifestations of law, such as statute law, judicial verdicts, and the hand signals of traffic police in particular as being closely tied to power and as phenomena of power.[7] At the same time, the secondary manifestations of law generated by primary law—such as the rules of the law, the conviction, or the road users stopping at the traffic signals—have a powerful effect on social reality. Daniel Witte and Christian Striebel defined the duality of the power issue with regard to the law to the effect "that the validity of eventually contingent positive law necessarily (also) points at the underlying power structures and that its enforcement per definition requires power"[8]. However, it should also be borne in mind "that social balances of power do not merely condense into legal structures accidentally, but do so rather systematically and totally."[9] Similarly, Roger Cotterrell stated, "law can be seen as both the *expression* of power relations and an important mechanism for *formalising* and *regularising* such relations."[10] Both aspects are closely interwoven because law not only generates and legitimises power relations, but in turn derives its own power from them,

> It protects and legitimises power, for example by guaranteeing economic power through the development of concepts of property and maintenance of rules to protect property. Further, it derives its own power partly from the political power which it expresses—whether of a permanent power elite or the result of a struggle between power centres—and partly from the benefits which regularisation and formalisation of power, in themselves, are seen to offer.[11]

---

[6]See also Hahn (2020).

[7]See Carbonnier (1974, pp. 103–105).

[8]Original quote, "dass die Geltung von letztlich kontingentem, positiv gesatztem Recht notwendig (immer auch) auf dahinter liegende Machtstrukturen verweist und dass zudem für seine Durchsetzung geradezu qua Definition Macht vonnöten ist", Witte and Striebel (2015, p. 162).

[9]Original quote, "dass sich gesellschaftliche Machtbalancen nicht lediglich akzidentiell, sondern vielmehr systematisch und umfassend in rechtlichen Strukturen niederschlagen", Witte and Striebel (2015, p. 162).

[10]Cotterrell (1984, p. 119).

[11]Cotterrell (1984, pp. 119–120).

Hence, contrary to what much scholarly literature states, law not only serves to control and constrain power; and contrary to the findings of critical legal studies, law is not exclusively an instrument for exercising power. Instead, as Cotterrell notes, "law controls and expresses power at the same time, as two sides of the same process."[12] This duality prompts Thomas Raiser to speak of a dialectical relationship between law and power.[13] In a similar vein, Pierre Bourdieu places law in a "juridical field"[14] which arises out of the social practice of law. This field is defined by "specific power relations", which provide it and its inherent conflicts of authority with structure and order. Bourdieu focuses first and foremost on the state, which he understands as the primary power to use both physical and also symbolic power to construct social reality, to create groups, to differentiate groups from each other, and to establish institutions.[15] In modernity, this power and the state enjoy a close, almost—albeit only almost—exclusive relationship. However, the power of the state, as Thomas Raiser points out, takes on different forms in the various fields of law. While criminal law is concerned with the exercise of the penal power of states, constitutional law and administrative law regulate the power which states exercise over their citizens in order to ensure a convivial social order for their citizens to live in. One field which is more problematic regarding power, as Raiser points out, is civil law. This field was originally thought to be largely free of state control—at the core of civil law lies the idea of the *contract*, and thus the idea of private legal relationships between free and equal citizens organised largely without the intervention of states.[16] However, civil law has increasingly fallen under the influence of the state as well. We may observe this when studying labour law, commercial law, and corporate law. Here, states are encroaching into private autonomy and restricting civil freedom of contract to a noticeable degree. This indicates that the states are advancing into areas of law in which state influence has hitherto been largely limited. However, it also indicates that the states possess differentiated degrees of power in the various legal fields, thus revealing at the same time that the states are not the only origin of law, even in modern times. In civil law arrangements, for example, other agents besides the state are legally powerful, such as contracting partners. And we cannot conceive of state and church law without the contribution of the churches and religious communities. Hence, legal power is also in the hands of these non-state agents. They rely on the power of the law to shape social reality through legal practice. With reference to the church, where canon law determines ecclesiastical reality to a great degree, it is necessary to discuss the power of canon law and the power of the ecclesiastical authorities which create and shape canon law. It is rather apparent, from a socio-legal perspective, that canon law confers power by granting certain agents the power to organise the church and its law. Most interesting,

---

[12] Cotterrell (1984, p. 120).

[13] See Raiser (2007, p. 269).

[14] Bourdieu (1987, p. 816).

[15] See also Witte and Striebel (2015, p. 171).

[16] See Raiser (2007, p. 272).

however, is the conspicuous reticence in church to interpret the law through the prism of "power." One might even speak of an obvious reluctance to openly discuss the issue of power. Instead, ecclesiastical authorities frequently discuss "power" in the umbra of other concepts, cloaked for example in the terminology of "service." We may find one example for this in Francis's address at the conclusion of the III General Assembly of the Extraordinary Synod of Bishops in 2014, when he pointed out that it is the primary task of the pope "to remind everyone that authority in the Church is a service"[17]. Equating "power" and "authority" with "service" in this way might be theologically plausible. And yet it leaves a bad aftertaste as it is an obvious attempt to cover up the issue of power. From a sociological perspective, the occlusion of factual power by dressing it as "service" leaves the impression that this strategy is less about emphasising "service" and more about hiding "power." This "theologising" or "spiritualising" of power calls to mind Werner Böckenförde's observation that canon law is particularly powerful when it is concealed, as the law and ecclesiastical structures based on the law are immune to being challenged by reform when the law is well hidden. Böckenförde staunchly criticised this strategy of trivialising structural issues in order to preclude structural reforms.[18] In a similar vein, those who seek to "theologise away" power structures make them harder for church members to identify, and make it increasingly difficult to criticise the structural asymmetries of power. After all, as the papal equation suggests, if power is "service," then those with more power are rendering greater service to the church. This is a questionable equation, nevertheless one which makes it difficult for the church members to criticise the power of the ecclesiastical authorities. At the same time, as we will see in in Sect. 5.2.8, by hiding power and thereby preventing it from being identified and questioned, the church creates a major problem of legitimacy that also affects the legitimacy of canon law.

4.2 Characteristics of Positive Law

The fact that contemporary law is positive law points to two distinct characteristics of the law, which Jürgen Habermas describes as follows, "the positivity of law means that a consciously enacted framework of norms gives rise to an artificial layer of social reality that exists only so long as it is not repealed, since each of its individual components can be changed or rendered null and void."[19] On the one hand, positivising law means producing legal norms and thereby creating a social reality. The positivity of law therefore affects the validity and the facticity of law. As a consciously built normative structure, however, positive law is only one layer of social normativity. This layer consists of those norms created in positivising acts of

---

[17] Francis (2014).

[18] See Böckenförde (2006, p. 154).

[19] Habermas (1996, p. 38).

norm production, such as legislation or adjudication. One has to note though, that normativities that do not fulfil this criterion of positivity are frequently no less influential for society. Customary and conventional norms, for instance, are powerful norms with a major influence on the social, even though they are not what modernity calls "law." On the other hand, Habermas emphasises that understanding law as positive norms points at the changeability of law. Habermas observes, "In light of this aspect of changeability, the validity of positive law appears as the sheer expression of a will that, in the face of the ever-present possibility of repeal, grants specific norms continuance until further notice."[20] Statute law, for instance, is based on the legislator's will. Consequently, it is a decision and as such it is changeable. Niklas Luhmann considers this to be a key characteristic of positive law, too. Indeed, one way we experience the law is to understand it as the result of decisions that can be revised, according to Luhmann, who observes, "Law is only positive when its decidability and changeability becomes a permanent presence and may be tolerated as such."[21] These two aspects—the restriction of the contemporary concept of law to the legally positive and the fact that law as the result of decision is changeable—are equally important for the sociology of canon law. If canon law wishes to lay claim to being modern law, then as characteristics of positive law, both of these aspects must also apply to the law of the church.

4.2.1 Law as the Result of Decision

By understanding positive law as norms born out of decision, sociology characterises the law as a choice between several possibilities, as Luhmann notes, "It is part of positivity to consider that the law which is valid 'in any specific context' is a selection made from a variety of other options and that it is valid based on this selection."[22] Creating positive law is therefore a process of selection which takes certain norms from a group of norms and attributes them with the force of law. This also applies to canon law. Ecclesiastical legal norms are the result of legislative decisions—and are therefore simultaneously decisions *against* any alternative regulatory choices. And judicial and executive decisions as their interpretations are decisions against alternative interpretations of the norms. However, as some canonists have pointed out, it is a matter of debate whether the ecclesiastical concept of "law" can truly be limited to positive law as legal norms which result from decisions. This doubt arises from the close connection between canon law and prepositive

---

[20] Habermas (1996, p. 57).

[21] Original quote, "Erst dann gilt Recht positiv, wenn die Entscheidbarkeit und damit die Änderbarkeit des Rechts permanente Gegenwart wird und als solche ertragen werden kann", Luhmann (1970, p. 184).

[22] Original quote, "Zur Positivität gehört, daß das 'jeweils' geltende Recht als Selektion aus anderen Möglichkeiten bewußt wird und kraft dieser Selektion gilt", Luhmann (1970, p. 184).

norms of so-called "divine law." Some voices consequently argue that "canon law" must also include prepositive norms.[23] After all, the church teaches that the matter of canon law is divided into two parts, namely purely human law ("*ius mere ecclesiasticum*") and divine law ("*ius divinum*"). It is uncontroversial that purely human canon law, which has its basis in human decision, is positive law. More problematic is the classification of *ius divinum*, which denotes norms that are based on the divine will as expressed in revelation ("*ius divinum positivum*") and in nature ("*ius divinum naturale*"). Therefore we may ask if the resultant "law of revelation" and "natural law" are actually part of positive canon law. This is undoubtedly the case for those norms derived from the divine will which the ecclesiastical legislator formally put into force as law. The norms of the Code of Canon Law that draw on divine law (see, for instance, canons 113 §1, 129 §1, 145 §1, 207 §1, 375 §1, 748 §1, 1008, 1249 CIC/1983) became positive canon law when the pope promulgated the Code of Canon Law, in the same way as those norms of the Code of purely human origin. However, canon law theory also speaks of "divine law" when referring to prepositive norms of a divine origin which have not—yet—been promulgated to become positive canon law. In a broader sense, therefore, "law" in church refers not only to positive law but also to its prepositive validity sources. Some canonists even go a step further, assuming that this prepositive divine law may also penetrate directly into the positive ecclesiastical legal order. Representatives of the so-called canon law School of Navarre, for example, consider the prepositive divine will to be effective "law" and, consequently, emphasise that the *ius divinum* is valid *as law* for ecclesiastical legal subjects, even if an act of human decision has not taken place. Javier Hervada and Pedro Lombardía argue that a norm recognised as an expression of divine law by the magisterium or the faithful's sense of faith has immediate juridical effects in church without a preceding act of promulgation.[24] A similar position is held by the so-called Munich School of canonists. Winfried Aymans and Klaus Mörsdorf's famous canon law textbook states in this respect, "All of divine law is directly applicable canon law even when it is not embedded in an ecclesiastical statute."[25] However, one may ask whether we may truly regard an ecclesiastical norm as law without an act of human decision. Surprisingly, even sociologist Simon Hecke seems inclined to agree with this view, insofar as Hecke concedes that limiting the definition of "law" to positive law might represent an unacceptable act of self-secularisation for the church.[26] Yet, as I want to argue, there is also good reason to view this critically. "Law," as stated above, in its modern sense, is always based on decision, and, from a sociological point of view, there is no possible alternative. And this restriction of what we understand as "law" in a modern

---

[23] Eg Aymans and Mörsdorf (1991, p. 26); Demel (2010, p. 341); Brosi (2013, pp. 20–27); Lüdecke and Bier (2012, pp. 17–18).

[24] See Hervada and Lombardía (2002, pp. 52–53).

[25] Original quote, "Alles göttliche Recht ist unmittelbar anwendbares Kirchenrecht, auch wenn es nicht in kirchliche Satzung eingekleidet ist", Aymans and Mörsdorf (1991, p. 26).

[26] See Hecke (2017, p. 98).

sense, as I want to argue, does not pose a significant problem for canon law. Besides sociological reasons, there are even good theological reasons to share this view, since the validity theory of canon law understands the law of the church as an expression of the divine will *in human history*. In this way, we may understand canon law, in line with the Chalcedonensical paradigm, as having an incarnational structure, as I already discussed in Sect. 3.1.4. Hence, the divine will must "incarnate" itself, in order to become "law." It must take the form of human legal norms and become part of positive canon law in order to be regarded as "law" in the strict sense of the term. As such, prepositive norms of a divine origin go through processes of human decision making, in which the legislator turns them into legal norms and promulgates them as such. Instead of speaking of "divine law" with regard to all norms deriving from the divine will, positive and prepositive norms, it would therefore make better sense for canon law theory to adopt a more granular semantics that makes a clear conceptual distinction between prepositive divine norms and positive law. Since the concept of law in contemporary legal systems inevitably refers to positive law, it makes sense to limit the use of the term "law" to positivised norms. "Divine law" would then exclusively denote the positive legal norms that can be traced back to the divine will. We may discuss elsewhere whether canon law can live with this break with its semantic tradition—after all, "*ius divinum*" traditionally includes prepositive norms. But I have come to find that a terminological readjustment of this kind helps to make a clear distinction between prepositive and positive norms. Jürgen Habermas explains best why it is indeed necessary to draw this line. He is critical of the "duplication of the concept of law," which is still sometimes apparent in contemporary law, as a "burden of debt from traditional natural law." For Habermas, this blurred boundary between prepositive and positive norms is a burden for the reason that it "is sociologically implausible and has normatively awkward consequences"[27]. The lack of differentiation between positive and prepositive norms, he argues, is not only conceptually imprecise, but also contentually misguided, since it blends together law and morality in a way that is intolerable for modern thought.

4.2.2 Legal and Moral Norms

Studying canon 1399 CIC/1983 reveals the problems this blend of law and morality might give rise to for canon law. This last canon framing the Code's ecclesiastical penal law sees the legislator cross the border between law and morality. The canon contains a threat of punishment that allows ecclesiastical penal law to respond to "the external violation of divine or canon law" by imposing punishments even when punishment has not been prescribed by ecclesiastical penal norms, in cases in which "the special gravity of the violation requires it and necessity demands that scandals

---

[27] Habermas (1996, p. 105).

be prevented or repaired." Hence the ecclesiastical legislator makes it possible to punish an act that breaks ecclesiastical law, but which should in fact not be punishable as there is no punishment attached to the prohibition. The legislator likewise permits the prosecution of an act that the authorities understand to be the transgression of a divine norm—and thus a *sin*—even when there is not only no relevant penal norm, but also when the divine norm itself has no positive expression in ecclesiastical law and is therefore not part of positive canon law. The prescription of canon 1399 CIC/1983 most evidently breaks the legal principle of "no penalty without a law" ("*nulla poena sine lege*"), which states that a punishment is only permissible on the basis of a penal norm that was already in existence when the breach of law occurred. Hence, by making the breach of a *moral* norm the basis of a *legal* punishment, canon 1399 CIC/1983 breaches the borders of modern law. One may be highly critical of this step, as canon law disregards the autonomy of morals by appropriating morality in this way. It also damages the law by enabling the arbitrary imposition of punishments, and by overriding equality and legal certainty as basic principles of legal justice. However, a law that is open to arbitrariness is not simply a bad law, it also undermines its character *as law*. Taking a sociological perspective, Roger Cotterrell points out that arbitrariness in law constitutes an attack on the rule of *generality* as constitutive of law.[28] This is because arbitrariness compromises the general and abstract effect of the law. Cotterrell inter alia refers to indeterminate legal concepts and general clauses in laws that serve as gateways for arbitrary decisions as examples of arbitrary elements in positive law.[29] A law that works with indeterminate legal concepts and general clauses opens the way for decisionism in the application of the law. Law, then, ceases to be "law" in the strictest sense and becomes moral tyranny or mere power politics. The fact that the current Code of Canon Law, unlike the former 1917 Code of Canon Law, contains few definitions and often relies on general clauses and indeterminate legal terms indicates once again that it is open to interventions of a moral or political nature. Ecclesiastical legal norms, for example, often refer to a "just cause"[30] as a reason for action or inaction, which gives ecclesiastical authorities considerable leeway in their decision making. Criminal law often makes reference to "just punishment",[31] thereby threatening unspecified and unquantified punishments for certain acts. This presents problems with regard to certainty as a key principle of penal law. Moreover, from a sociological point of view, this lack of clear boundaries between law and morality may inflict serious damage on the law, because arbitrariness in law

---

[28] See Cotterrell (1984, p. 177).

[29] See Cotterrell (1984, p. 172).

[30] Eg canons 56, 72, 90 §1, 98 §2, 104, 187, 189 §2, 193 §3, 270, 271 §2, 308, 318 §2, 527 §2, 533 §1, 538 §1, 550 §1, 552, 554 §3, 563, 657 §3, 665 §1, 667 §4, 668 §2, 689 §1, 726 §1, 831 §1, 857 §2, 874 §1 n. 2, 881, 905 §2, 906, 918, 920 §2, 933, 936, 963, 964 §3, 1015 §2, 1125, 1142, 1143 §2, 1146 n. 2, 1196, 1245, 1267 §2, 1293 §1 n. 1, 1308 §1, 1310 §1, 1335 §2, 1342 §1, 1429, 1465 §2, 1469 §2, 1482 §2, 1555, 1650 §2, 1668 §2, 1698 §1, 1704 §1 CIC/1983.

[31] Eg canons 1328 §2, 1367, 1368, 1369, 1370 §3, 1371 §§3 and 5, 1373, 1374, 1375 §1, 1377 §1, 1379 §5, 1381, 1386 §2, 1389, 1390 §2, 1395 §2, 1396, 1398 §1, 1399 CIC/1983.

and in particular in penal law casts doubt on the character of law *as law*. It is therefore imperative for all modern legal systems including canon law to differentiate between positive and prepositive norms, both terminologically and with regard to their content. This principle of making an essential distinction does not seek to diminish either the obligatory nature of moral norms or the significance of morality for law. It is undisputed that prepositive norms expressing a divine will exert a binding force on church members, but they do so in a *different* way to legal norms. Moral norms are no less binding in church than legal norms, but they are binding in a different, namely *moral* sense. It is also undisputed that prepositive norms which express a divine will, once they are recognised as such, can have legal implications and therefore require the ecclesiastical legislator to include them in positive law. Doing so means the legislator makes these moral norms legally binding by turning them into legal norms. And even subsequently, morality retains its significance for the law. This becomes apparent with respect to the legitimacy of law. Jürgen Habermas notes, "In virtue of the legitimacy components of legal validity, positive law has a reference to morality inscribed within it."[32] I will discuss this reference of the law to morality in detail in the fifth section of my study. Hence, the relation between law and morality is maintained, albeit without blurring the boundaries between moral and legal norms. Law must safeguard the autonomy of morality— and do this even when the *same matter* is in dispute. This is essential because even in cases where law and morality both relate to the same matter, they do so differently, as Habermas points out,

> To be sure, moral and legal questions refer to the same problems: how interpersonal relationships can be legitimately ordered and actions coordinated with one another through justified norms, how action conflicts can be consensually resolved against the background of intersubjectively recognized normative principles and rules. But they refer to these same problems in different ways. Despite the common reference point, morality and law differ prima facie inasmuch as posttraditional morality represents only a form of cultural *knowledge*, whereas law has, in addition to this, a binding character at the institutional level. Law is not only a symbolic system but an action system as well.[33]

This transformation from the symbolic level to the action level occurs in law through the act of decision which, in some cases, even turns formerly moral norms into positive law. However, this act transforms the moral norm, as Habermas explains, "inasmuch as moral contents, once *translated* into the legal code, undergo a change in meaning that is specific to the legal form."[34] If canon law wants to be "law" in a way that sounds convincing to contemporary thinkers, the church cannot therefore ignore the act of decision which transforms norms of a conventional, moral, or religious nature into positive law.

---

[32] Habermas (1996, p. 106).

[33] Habermas (1996, pp. 106–107).

[34] Habermas (1996, p. 204).

4.2.3 The Changeability of Law

That positive law is based on decision corresponds with the finding that positive law is changeable. Niklas Luhmann explains this connection between positive norms and change. As law is based on decision—that is on the selection of certain legal norms from a range of possible alternatives—these alternatives remain plausible options and could thus still potentially become law if the law were to change. Luhmann elucidates, "Valid positive law in any given case excludes other options but it does not eliminate them from the horizon of legal experience. Instead, it keeps them present and ready as possible topics of the law for such a time when a change of positive law seems apposite."[35] The same applies to canon law. Positive canon law is essentially mutable. It represents the legislator's choice of legal norms from a range of possible alternative norms. However, these norms are not eliminated by the act of legislation. Consequently, they might still replace those norms in force to become positive canon law themselves. From a sociological point of view, changes in the law are therefore possible. Not only are they possible, however, they are also necessary. This is because law, in order to stay in touch with the reality of the legal subjects' lives, must remain in a state of constant change. It must evolve in line with the social order to which it refers. It is the inherent changeability of positive law which helps to maintain a connection between law and social reality. The changeability of positive law therefore also benefits ecclesiastical legislation, as it must maintain the balance between ecclesiastical law and ecclesiastical reality. As positive law, canon law can be adapted to the regulatory needs of any given time. And this happens not only with respect to the norms of purely human origin, but also with norms that the church sees as being rooted in the divine will. In this light, Simon Hecke states that throughout the history of canon law, norms which were formerly regarded as being sacred were frequently changed, added to, or omitted from the body of ecclesiastical law.[36] Indeed, the ecclesiastical legislator has often gone to considerable lengths to conceal this process of legal reform from view throughout the history of canon law, as Christoph Möllers observes, noting,

> Thus, long into modernity, law was rarely understood as an object one could shape or as an instrument of change. It is not by chance that one of the earliest examples of a normative order oriented towards alterability and change was the canonical law of the Catholic church of the late Middle Ages; that is, a normative order that itself is not transcendent but traces its validity to a transcendent order.[37]

Here, Möllers makes two points: Whilst the rootedness of ecclesiastical law in a transcendent prepositive source has inhibited, and still inhibits, many individuals'

---

[35] Original quote, "Das jeweils geltende positive Recht schließt diese anderen Möglichkeiten zwar aus, eliminiert sie aber nicht aus dem Horizont des Rechtserlebens, sondern hält sie als mögliche Themen des Rechts präsent und verfügbar für den Fall, daß eine Änderung des geltenden Rechts opportun erscheint", Luhmann (1970, p. 184).

[36] See Hecke (2017, p. 104).

[37] Möllers (2020, p. 259).

understanding of the changeability of law, canon law is unquestionably a legal order that was and is profoundly changeable. Difficulties in conceiving *how* law founded on transcendent norms can change do not alter the fact *that* law is capable of change and has changed significantly over the course of history. Scholars of canon law also make the very same observation. Canonist Joseph Koury noted in connection with the 1983 reform of the Code of Canon Law that some legal norms no longer appear in the new version of the Code even though the 1917 Code had claimed they were based on divine law, and that some norms had been transferred from the 1917 Code to the 1983 Code but without retaining their previous reference to divine law. For example, canon 727 of the old Code differentiated between a mere simony "by ecclesiastical law" (§2) and simony "by divine law" (§1). Hence, the old law understood the offence of trading in spiritual goods under certain conditions as having been proscribed by God himself. This differentiation no longer appears in the current Code. While simony is still forbidden and is still punished in some cases (see canon 1380 CIC/1983), it is no longer associated with divine law.[38] Another example which Koury discusses is the norm in the old Code which prohibited inter-confessional marriages (see canon 1060 CIC/1917). It designated a mixed-denomination marriage as being forbidden by divine law if this marriage might potentially tempt the Catholic partner and the couple's common offspring to commit apostasy. The issue of mixed marriages as a threat to the faith reappears in the 1983 Code (see canon 1125 no. 1 CIC/1983), but the reference to divine law has been removed. In both cases, and in many others, Koury concludes that there has been a change in the qualification of the respective legal norms. According to Koury, this legislative decision to drop the connection between these regulatory matters and divine law is proof of the legislator's acknowledgement that the respective regula-tions are actually purely human canon law.[39] However, how to explain such a change is open to debate. For Koury, *interpretation* is key to understanding the development of divine law, "To answer the question of how it is possible that something that was (or was claimed to be) of divine law can be suppressed, some would hold that these were references to interpretations of divine law, and that what has been suppressed are only interpretations."[40] Silvio Ferrari follows the same line of thought. He starts with the problem of identifying the divine will. Since the human capacity to grasp the divine will is naturally incomplete, human beings must concede that they can always only partially understand God's will when making law, "Human capacity to understand the divine law is limited: therefore it is always possible to improve understanding of what God really meant."[41] This means that it is always possible and even necessary to revise earlier insights and to amend law which is rooted in the divine will in order to account for new insights about what God truly wants. There is some merit in these epistemological explanations, which see the

---

[38] See Koury (1993, pp. 111–112).

[39] See Koury (1993, p. 114).

[40] Koury (1993, p. 118).

[41] Ferrari (2002, p. 51).

constraints of human knowledge as the reason why divine will and human norms are not congruent and why humans can change and amend the latter. However, these epistemological approaches, at least if they restrict themselves to the epistemological problem, exclude the *ontological* dimension of the relation between God's will and human norms. The ontological perspective focuses more on the necessity of giving God's will an earthly embodiment in the form of human norms. This incarnatorial approach may, at the same time, explain how changes to norms with a divine origin can come about. Silvio Ferrari clarifies, "most Canon law scholars affirm that divine law cannot be directly operative unless it is not embedded in a human rule: a law in itself is something connected to history, divine law can be known and become binding only through a historical, human medium."[42] Hence, we must redefine the blanket claim made by some scholars of canon law that a change in divine law is unthinkable, as Ferrari proposes, "divine law is immutable in itself but it is apprehended by men through instruments which are subject to change."[43] Moral theologian Karl-Wilhelm Merks states in a similar vein that the divine does not appear as an additional quality of human reality but *within* human reality itself. Consequently, for Merks it is clear that divine law can only express itself within human reality and within human norms and human law.[44] We may reformulate this finding for canon law to take into account the incarnation paradigm mentioned above: The divine will is expressed in human—and therefore positive—law. As it becomes concrete law, the *ius divinum* becomes thoroughly human as soon as it is incorporated into human norms. And it requires translation into human norms in order to acquire legal validity in church. Consequently, the legislator can reform legal norms, including those which are rooted in the divine will, and adapt them to current regulatory needs of the church. However, the legislator cannot act arbitrarily when pursuing reform, but has to act in accordance with the current state of theological knowledge about what constitutes God's will and how this will may be expressed best in human norms. It is the task of the ecclesiastical legislator to determine a theologically responsible way in which the divine will can be expressed in human norms in such a way that it corresponds to the ecclesiastical need for regulation in the respective here and now. It is the task of scholars of canon law to critically study if and in what sense the legislator is successful in creating a law that truly responds to the need of the church and to the current state of theological research.

---

[42]Ferrari (2002, p. 51).

[43]Ferrari (2002, p. 52).

[44]See Merks (2014, p. 12).

4.2.4   Change as a Learning Process

While the sociology of law acknowledges that changes to positive law are possible and necessary, it nevertheless struggles to explain *how* legal change occurs. In order to help understand legal change sociologically, Niklas Luhmann constructs a model in which he interprets the development of law as a process of legal *learning*. Luhmann in fact reconstructs legal change as a learning process in which the legislator reacts to breaches of law. To explain his approach, Luhmann first divides legal decision making into *two* categories, the legislator's *programming* decisions and the courts' *programmed* decisions.[45] While the legislator's decisions create programmes, it is the task of the courts to apply these programmes. According to Luhmann, it is an indispensable aspect of modern complexity reduction to differentiate between these two types of decision making. At the same time, the differentiation has "a crucial function of implementing learning possibilities into the law."[46] Explaining this, Luhmann returns to his definition of law as counterfactual behavioural expectation. Legal norms are counterfactual insofar as they represent expectations which we uphold even after experiencing disappointment.[47] However, there are two possible types of reaction to the disappointment produced by a breach of law. Some legal actors "process disappointments while holding on to their normative expectations"[48]. These include the courts. As programmed decision-makers, they react to breaches of law not by learning, but by remaining disappointed, as Luhmann explains, "Programmed decision making, and in particular adjudication, are wont to the representation of positive law, the keeping up and sanctioning of normative expectations, the expression of determination not to learn from the lawbreaker. The judge must act in a disappointed and not in a learning way whenever normative expectations are disappointed."[49] On the other hand, there are legal agents that are not actually disappointed by breaches of law. A *programming* decision-maker such as a legislator is regularly not disappointed but rather interested in learning about the reality of legal norms. This includes learning about the effectiveness of the law, but also about its ineffectiveness and dysfunctionalities, about the conflicts arising from legal expectations, and also about the alternative behaviour

---

[45]Luhmann, as he states, derives his terminology from computer technology to introduce it into systems theory, see Luhmann (1970, p. 190 fn 49).

[46]Original quote, "eine wesentliche Funktion für den Einbau von Lernmöglichkeiten in das Recht", Luhmann (1970, p. 191).

[47]See Luhmann (1986, p. 22).

[48]Original quote, "unter Festhalten normierter Erwägungen Enttäuschungen verarbeiten", Luhmann (1970, p. 191).

[49]Original quote, "Die Darstellung des geltenden Rechts, das Durchhalten und Sanktionieren normativer Erwartungen, der Ausdruck der Entschlossenheit, vom Rechtsbrecher nicht zu lernen, wird im Bereich des programmierten Entscheidens, vor allem in der Justiz gepflegt. Der Richter hat sich, soweit normierte Erwartungen verletzt werden, enttäuscht, nicht lernend zu verhalten", Luhmann (1970, p. 191).

which the legal subjects engage in when breaking the law.[50] Instead of expressing disappointment, says Luhmann, the legislator can receive breaches of law as an impulse to learn. In doing so the legislator "may show a readiness to change his expectations. He is the addressee of change requests, the instance of institutionalised learning within the law."[51] In order to learn from breaches of the law, it is therefore necessary for programming decision-makers *not* to react to breaches of law with disappointment, but with interest and a willingness to receive the aberrations. Of course, a legislator cannot respond to every breach of law by changing the law. But if there is broad non-compliance with certain legal norms, the legislator might react by amending the norms. If the legislator concludes that certain norms have become predominantly dysfunctional, then an obvious solution might be to revise them. However, in order to fulfil their function of learning from unlawful behaviour to amend the law, programming decision-makers must resist the temptation to respond to breaches of law with disappointment, because they will otherwise miss the opportunity to learn. Luhmann warns that it is actually possible for legal systems to become immune to legal innovation through disappointment, stating that it is "evident that institutions which reward abiding with normative expectations and a concordant approach to dealing with disappointments block learning opportunities."[52] I want to suggest that this tendency exists in church. Observations suggest that ecclesiastical legislators, the decision-makers who programme canon law, tend to react to breaches of canon law with disappointment—thereby squandering much of the innovative potential of legal non-compliance. First of all, it should be noted that the church differentiates between programming and programmed decisions far less decisively than secular political orders. Simon Hecke even suggests that the Catholic Church completely lacks any differentiation between programming and programmed legal decision making.[53] Although this diagnosis is slightly exaggerated, it is not entirely wrong. What is accurate is that the church does not uphold the strict separation of powers commonly upheld in contemporary democratic political orders. This is because ecclesiastical power theory does not rank the separation of powers among the principles underlying the legitimate exercise of power in church. On the contrary, it traces back all power in church to one "sacred power." The unity of ecclesiastical power is justified Christologically. All power in church is derived from Christ.[54] And it is Christ who endows the ordained ministers with all power required to govern the church. This theory of the unity of ecclesiastical power with

---

[50] See Luhmann (1970, p. 191).

[51] Original quote, "Er darf die Bereitschaft zeigen, seine Erwartungen zu korrigieren. Er ist der Adressat für Änderungswünsche, die Instanz für institutionalisiertes Lernen im Recht", Luhmann (1970, p. 191).

[52] Original quote, "offensichtlich, daß Institutionen, die das Festhalten normativer Erwartungen und eine entsprechende Technik des Umgehens mit Enttäuschungen prämieren, die Lernmöglichkeiten blockieren", Luhmann (1970, p. 191).

[53] See Hecke (2017, p. 111).

[54] Klaus Mörsdorf was one canonist who particularly elaborated upon the consequences resulting from this idea for ecclesiastical power theory, eg Mörsdorf (1989a; 1989b).

its origin in Christ places power in church firmly in the hands of the clergy. The power to govern the church is administered by the clergy alone (see canons 129 §1, 274 §1 CIC/1983). Ecclesiastical power of governance, which includes the capacity of ecclesiastical legislation, adjudication, and administration, is in the hands of the pope and the college of bishops as far as the global church is concerned (see canons 331, 336 CIC/1983), and in the hands of the diocesan bishops with regard to their local churches (see canons 381, 391 CIC/1983). These authorities' powers are not separated according to the democratic principle of the separation of powers. Instead, the power attributed to the pope, the college of bishops, and the diocesan bishops is concentrated in accordance with the absolutist model of governance. Nevertheless, the power to govern the church is functionally divided into legislative, judicial, and executive power (see canon 391 §1 CIC/1983). Whilst the church does not therefore have a separation of powers, it does have a division of powers at the functional level. However, this differentiation is for purely pragmatic reasons. It allows for the division of the organisational work involved in governing the church (see canons 360, 391 §2 CIC/1983). While the task of ecclesiastical legislation always remains with the pope and the college of bishops with regard to the global church, and with the diocesan bishops for their local churches, these authorities can carry out adjudication and administration themselves, but may also entrust these tasks to other clerics, such as the vicars general who exercise executive power and the judicial vicars who exercise judicial power on behalf of the diocesan bishops. The Roman Curia and the episcopal curias carry out administrative tasks on the level of the global and on the level of the local churches, while the papal and episcopal tribunals carry out the adjudication. So whilst there is a functional separation between programming and programmed decisions in church, their separation of powers is not understood as being necessary with regard to the legitimate exercise of power in church. This is why the church sees no need to draw a clear distinction between the powers as one might expect to find in contemporary secular orders. As for the question of whether ecclesiastical legislators succeed in *learning* from their legal subjects' breaches of law, this finding suggests that the relevant authorities might find it hard *not* to react to breaches of law with disappointment and instead with interest and curiosity, which allows for legal learning. Since the pope, the college of bishops, and the diocesan bishops have the authority to make programming *and* programmed decisions, each authority would have to succeed in a strict internal separation of roles in order to react differently to breaches of law. While the authorities have to respond with disappointment to breaches of law in their role as programmed decision-makers, they have to explicitly not react with disappointment in their role as programming decision-makers; instead, they must react with an openness to learning. However, as I want to suggest, it is rather unlikely that ecclesiastical decision-makers can constantly switch roles in this way. This observation might explain, from a sociological point of view, why canon law often seems slow to learn and why there are obvious difficulties in increasing legal learning and development in church. The deficiency of legal learning in church might therefore be—at least in part—the consequence of a lack of distinction between programming and programmed ecclesiastical decision making. This observation in fact supports the thesis that the absence of a clear separation of powers in church is hostile to innovation in canon law.

4.2.5 How to Procure Legal Change

A clear separation of programming and programmed decision making enables programming decision-makers to recognise the innovative potential of breaches of law. Yet from a sociological point of view, the actual process of changing and developing positive law is by no means as easy as Luhmann's learning model suggests. Quite simply, it is not enough if only those who develop the law learn from breaches of law. They must also succeed in *communicating* legal changes to the legal subjects. The legal community, however, associates certain behavioural expectations with the legal norms it is familiar with, even if breaches of law have repeatedly disappointed these expectations. Changes in the law therefore present legislation with the challenge of effectively converting the legal subjects' expectations "to adapt expectations and actions to other norms."[55] Luhmann states that legislation can with relative ease replace norms when there is a political need to do so with norms which are widely unknown to the legal community. Whenever the legal subjects fail to notice legal change, development of the law does not arouse much critical interest, as Luhmann observes, "This facilitates an almost unnoticeable exchange of norms according to the extent of the interest of particular minorities, without having to tear essential meanings away from hearts and minds."[56] This virtually invisible method of reforming the law represents an enormous benefit to legislative work, as it frees the legislators from constantly having to provide detailed justifications for their actions. From the viewpoint of political science, with its associated empirical perspective, Klaus Röhl adds the observation that political institutions rely to some extent on the apathy and ignorance of the public, insofar as an informed and critical public tends to inhibit their smooth functioning, including the functioning of legislation.[57] Without diminishing the value of a critical public, especially for key legal issues such as legitimacy, we may perceive public criticism—from a sociological point of view—primarily as an obstacle to the activities of political institutions. This obstacle is frequently lacking in the development of rather insignificant legal norms about which the legal subjects have only a rudimentary knowledge. In such cases, Niklas Luhmann speaks of "trivial law," citing by way of example regulations on "premiums for the destruction of apples in a particular harvest"[58] about which, in contrast to norms about murder, marriage, or property, the legal community knows relatively little. According to Luhmann, we should not

---

[55]Luhmann (2014, p. 243).

[56]Luhmann (2014, p. 196).

[57]See Röhl (1987, p. 271).

[58]Luhmann (2014, p. 196).

regret most legal subjects' lack of knowledge in this regard, but rather understand it as a necessary coping strategy for dealing with the sheer complexity of sophisticated and elaborate laws. Their ignorance, in any case, is also a prerequisite for the constant development of the legal system, because it allows the legislator to undertake any necessary adjustments to the law in circumstances of enormous social complexity without having to anticipate any major resistance. While the legislator can adapt trivial law to changing regulatory needs without attracting much attention, the development of key legal matters—such as socially significant and prominent norms—proves much more difficult. The silent and seamless exchange of legal norms in this field is unrealistic, insofar as the general public has at least a rudimentary knowledge of them and their revision frequently triggers a critical response. Moreover, changing norms without the community noticing would make little sense with respect to compliance, since it would inevitably lead to the legal subjects involuntarily breaking the new law, due to their being uninformed about the change. When changing relatively prominent norms, the legislators must therefore seek to align the legal subjects' expectations and actions with the new norms, without fundamentally disappointing the legal subjects. This is only possible, as sociologist of law Stefan Machura explains, if the legislator refrains from making too many changes at once. Whilst it might be true that all legal norms are replaceable in principle, they cannot be changed at will and at any time.[59] Gradual change is likely to find greatest social acceptance, Machura argues, because it allows for the legal subjects' expectations of the law to evolve slowly over time.

4.2.6 Destabilisation Through Change

We should not underestimate the difficulty of reforming key legal norms under the watchful eyes of a critical legal community, not even in church. Simon Hecke points out that while canon law, including norms grounded in divine law, has been renewed constantly and sometimes erratically throughout history, the contemporary context makes it far more difficult to amend norms, not because of the challenges posed by making legal changes per se, but because of the public perception and appraisal of such changes. As is the case with state law, it is virtually inconceivable that any amendments to key canonical norms might go unnoticed today. Public interest is simply too great. The ecclesiastical legislator is therefore also tasked with ensuring he amends legal norms in a way that allows the legal subjects to adjust their expectations to the new norms and to experience as little disappointment as possible. A very recent example serves to illustrate this difficulty. When Francis, with the help of the papal law *Traditionis custodes*, abrogated his predecessor's regulations on the old Latin Tridentine liturgy a couple of months ago,[60] this legal change affecting the

---

[59] See Machura (2010, p. 385).

[60] See Francis (2021).

liturgy as a public action of the church did not go unnoticed. Many traditional Catholics were outraged. Some groups are at present calling for resistance to the law and even considering a schism following their huge disappointment in this piece of papal legislation. From a sociological point of view, this example shows that legal reform may have serious repercussions in a legal community, even legal reforms undertaken with the express intention of avoiding further division among antagonistic groups within a legal community, such as liberal and conservative Catholics in the Catholic Church, as was intended with *Traditionis custodes*. However, whilst the recent papal legal reform of the liturgy deeply disappointed some legal subjects, others have embraced the very same reform as an urgent and necessary step towards reforming the church. Many Catholics would also welcome further reform measures. Most German Catholics, for instance, would welcome any move by the legislator towards abrogating the obligation of celibacy for the clergy (see canon 277 §1 CIC/1983). Whilst there are certainly church members, even in Germany, who consider celibacy meaningful for the clergy, an overwhelming number of German Catholics would welcome its abolition.[61] In a similarly way, they would welcome amendments to the law on ordination with respect to gender equality (see 1024 canon CIC/1983),[62] and an opening of offices with the power to govern the church to lay women and men (see canon 274 §1 CIC/1983). Consequently, these and similar key legal changes, which would affect ecclesiastical organisation profoundly, would not disappoint many Catholics—at least from the churches of the northern hemisphere—too greatly on the whole. However, despite low levels of disappointment, the transition from the old to the new law might still prove difficult, as Simon Hecke assumes, due to the challenge of keeping the ecclesiastical legal system stable during the transition process. As a legislator who is willing to surrender important legal provisions gives the impression that other norms are also susceptible to change, radical change might undermine the stability and permanence of the law, as Hecke points out. Changing key regulations can therefore have a destabilising effect on a legal order as a whole or on major sections of the law. And it might affect the legal community greatly, as change also touches upon associated issues of *identity*, as the example of *Traditionis custodes* demonstrates. A community that suspects the law and the structures built upon the law of instability might lose its belief not only in the law itself but also in the community as a source of identity. In this light, it is rather unsurprising, from a sociological point of view, that church authorities currently tend to prefer a strategy of immunisation and resistance to reforming canon law. Hecke explains, "'Whatever I touch falls apart' Franz Kafka once noted in one of his *Oktavhefte* ... The Catholic Church therefore refrains from 'touching' canon law

---

[61] A survey conducted in 2013 already showed that an overwhelming majority of 84% of German Catholics were against the church imposing the duty of celibacy on clerics, in comparison to 12% who supported clerical celibacy, see Forschungsgruppe Wahlen (2013).

[62] The 2013 survey showed that 75% of German Catholics supported women's ordination, compared to 22% who opposed it, see Forschungsgruppe Wahlen (2013).

with reformist intentions of all sorts."[63] And even when the church touches the law, as happened just recently with the reform of canonical penal law, the changes tend to be rather minimal. While the reform of canonical penal law, published in June 2021, was presented to the ecclesiastical public with much ado, it was actually much ado about—not much, to put it mildly. The fact that "touching" individual norms can trigger processes of disintegration that affect the entire order or individual sections of it is an insight that the sociology of law has inherited from general sociology. It coincides with the principle of the *domino effect* or the so-called *broken window theory*, as elaborated by sociologists James Wilson and George Kelling in the 1980s.[64] Even a small impulse, such as one broken window, is often enough to initiate a destructive chain reaction; this principle is as established in organisational sociology as it is in criminology. The broken window theory also pertains to changes in the law, especially when the legal system or a legal matter in question is already under pressure. Removing sections of an order that is already under attack might lead to its partial or total collapse. A thought experiment might help to illustrate this phenomenon with regard to ecclesiastical law. In the foreseeable future, the ecclesiastical regulation excluding women from ordination might serve as an example of how changing one legal norm might create a domino effect which brings down other norms as well. Canon 1024 CIC/1983, which restricts ordination to men is, after all, a legal provision which has come under considerable pressure in church—as described above. Should the diaconate for women become a reality, as is currently being discussed (again), this "touching" of a single provision could have far-reaching consequences for the whole regulation on women's ordination. This is because reforming the law on the diaconate would most probably, in the long run, have a knock-on effect on women's access to the priesthood and the episcopate. Although the magisterium and the legislator have been seeking dogmatic and legal clarifications that make a clear distinction between the diaconate on the one hand and the priesthood and the episcopate on the other,[65] one may strongly assume that reform on the entry requirements of the diaconate will eventually lead to a call for further legal changes with regard to the priesthood and the episcopate, too. If the highest authority of the church agrees to review the law of the diaconate, it seems inconceivable that he will be able to do so whilst perpetually excluding the female priesthood and episcopacy from the debate. I do not write this as an appeal, but simply as a plausible description of a possible reality. However, that I am obviously not alone in making these assessments is clear to judge by the already cautious reactions by many members of the hierarchy to the diaconate for women. Their hesitance can be interpreted as factual doubt. However, it might also be motivated by

---

[63] Original quote, "'Was ich berühre, zerfällt' hat Franz Kafka in einem seiner Oktavhefte einmal notiert . . . Die katholische Kirche scheut daher heute 'Berührungen' mit dem kanonischen Recht in reformistischen Absichten aller Art", Hecke (2017, p. 105); in a similar vein already Kaufmann (1974, p. 32).

[64] See Wilson and Kelling (1982, pp. 29–38).

[65] See Benedict XVI (2010). *Motu proprio Omnium in mentem*, 26 October 2009. *Acta Apostolicae Sedis, 102*, 10; canon 1009 §3 CIC/1983.

the desire to avoid initiating processes of disintegration unleashed by change, which would affect the laws on ordination and the clergy more generally. Just as New York Police Commissioner William Bratton—reacting to Wilson and Kelling's study on the effects of broken windows—pursued a strategy of zero tolerance in the 1990s to save certain New York neighbourhoods from decline, so today many members of church hierarchy are seeking to prevent the entry of women into the clergy by adopting a policy of "zero tolerance." Whilst the recent reform of canonical penal law has not changed much about the law, the legislator has been at pains to integrate the offence of attempting to confer ordination on women, sanctionable by the serious punishment of a *latae sententiae* excommunication, into the Code of Canon Law (see canon 1379 §3 CIC/1983). While the penal norm itself is not new,[66] it has now found a prominent place among the canonical list of offences against the sacraments. Here it stands as a reminder to all Catholics that the official church does not tolerate women breaking and entering into the hierarchy, by punishing women who try and take this step and by punishing men who support them in their attempt to do so. One may either wonder about the harshness of the regulation, or one may read it in the light of the broken window theory as a policy of zero tolerance. Concealed behind the formula of the "unity of the sacrament of Holy Orders"[67] there seem to be concerns that are less about theology and more about the fear that "touching" one legal provision could trigger an unstoppable momentum for reform with consequences for the whole legal order. The ecclesiastical authorities' strategy of immunisation therefore serves to protect the stability of canonical constitutional law in its present shape. Nevertheless, we should not forget that immunisation is also a risky strategy, because it diminishes many legal subjects' willingness to acknowledge a law which is widely resistant to change. Simon Hecke outlined in this respect that the critical dearth of reform with regard to canon law has led many church members to withdraw their support for canon law.[68] This precarious balancing act between the need for change and maintaining stability is not unique to the church, but applies to all law. In his theory of norms, Christoph Möllers states, "The question of where exactly to draw the line between identity affirmation and problem-solving remains a fundamental challenge for every normative order."[69] In church, this problem certainly needs to be addressed rather urgently, because canon law is facing massive problems of legitimacy. I will revisit this observation in the following section in my discussion on how the validity of law connects with its legitimacy.

---

[66] See Congregation for the Doctrine of the Faith (2007); Congregation for the Doctrine of the Faith (2010, article 5). *Acta Apostolicae Sedis, 102,* 423–424.

[67] International Theological Commission (2002, chap. 7 sect. 3.1).

[68] See Hecke (2017, p. 105).

[69] Möllers (2020, p. 288).

Bibliography

Aymans, W., & Mörsdorf, K. (1991). *Kanonisches Recht: Lehrbuch aufgrund des Codex Iuris Canonici, vol 1: Einleitende Grundfragen und Allgemeine Normen*. Ferdinand Schöningh.

Benedict XVI. (2010). Apostolic Letter issued *Motu proprio Omnium in mentem*, on Several Amendments to the Code of Canon Law, 26 October 2009. *Acta Apostolicae Sedis, 102*, 8–10.

Böckenförde, W. (2006). Zur gegenwärtigen Lage in der römisch-katholischen Kirche: Kirchenrechtliche Anmerkungen. In N. Lüdecke & G. Bier (Eds.), *Freiheit und Gerechtigkeit in der Kirche: Gedenkschrift für Werner Böckenförde* (Forschungen zur Kirchenrechtswissenschaft 37, pp. 143–158). Echter.

Bourdieu, P. (1987). The Force of Law: Toward a Sociology of the Juridical Field. *The Hastings Law Journal, 38*, 814–853.

Brosi, U. (2013). *Recht, Strukturen, Freiräume: Kirchenrecht* (Studiengang Theologie 9, überarbeitet und mit einem Beitrag zum deutschen Staatskirchenrecht ergänzt von I. Kreusch). Theologischer Verlag Zürich.

Carbonnier, J. (1974). *Rechtssoziologie* (Schriftenreihe zur Rechtssoziologie und Rechtstatsachenforschung 31). Duncker & Humblot.

Congregation for the Doctrine of the Faith. (2007). General Decree regarding the Delict of Attempted Sacred Ordination of a Woman, 19 December 2007. *Acta Apostolicae Sedis, 100*, 403.

Congregation for the Doctrine of the Faith. (2010). Norms regarding Offences reserved to the Congregation for the Doctrine of the Faith or Norms against the Faith and More Serious Offences, 21 May 2010. *Acta Apostolicae Sedis, 102*, 419–430.

Cotterrell, R. (1984). *The sociology of law: An introduction*. Butterworths.

Demel, S. (2010). *Handbuch Kirchenrecht: Grundbegriffe für Studium und Praxis*. Herder.

Ferrari, S. (2002). Canon Law as a Religious Legal System. In A. Huxley (Ed.), *Religion, Law and Tradition: Comparative Studies in Religious Law* (pp. 49–60). Routledge.

Forschungsgruppe Wahlen. (2013). Umfrage Politbarometer, 19 February 2013. Retrieved April 13, 2018, from www.forschungsgruppe.de/Umfragen/Politbarometer/Archiv/Politbarometer-Extra/PB-Extra_Kirche_und_Papst

Francis. (2014). Address for the Conclusion of the Third Extraordinary General Assembly of the Synod of Bishops, Synod Hall, 18 October 2014. Retrieved June 21, 2021, from www.vatican.va/content/francesco/en/speeches/2014/october/documents/papa-francesco_20141018_conclusione-sinodo-dei-vescovi.html

Francis. (2021). Apostolic Letter issued *Motu proprio Traditionis custodes* on the Use of the Roman Liturgy prior to the Reform of 1970, 16 July 2021. Retrieved August 5, 2021, from www.vatican.va/content/francesco/en/motu_proprio/documents/20210716-motu-proprio-traditionis-custodes.html

Habermas, J. (1996). *Between facts and norms: Contributions to a discourse theory of law and democracy* (W. Rehg, Trans.). The MIT Press.

Hahn, J. (2020). The Power of the Law—The Law of Power: On the significance of Canon Law for Issues of Power in the Church. *Concilium*, issue 3, 52–62.

Hecke, S. (2017). *Kanonisches Recht: Zur Rechtsbildung und Rechtsstruktur des römisch-katholischen Kirchenrechts*. Springer.

Hervada, J., & Lombardía, P. (2002). Prolegómenos I: Introduccion al Derecho Canónico. In Á. Marzoa, J. M. Miras & R. Rodríguez-Ocaña (Eds.), *Comentario Exegético al Código de Derecho Canónico vol 1* (3rd ed., pp. 33–155). Ediciones Universidad De Navarra.

International Theological Commission. (2002). From the Diakonia of Christ to the Diakonia of the Apostles. Retrieved June 20, 2021, from www.vatican.va/roman_curia/congregations/cfaith/cti_documents/rc_con_cfaith_pro_05072004_diaconate_en.html

Kaufmann, F.-X. (1974). Kirche als religiöse Organisation. *Concilium, 10*, 30–36.

Koury, J. J. (1993). Ius Divinum as a Canonical Problem: On the Interaction of Divine and Ecclesiastical Laws. *The Jurist, 53*, 104–131.

Kunz, K.-L., & Mona, M. (2006). *Rechtsphilosophie, Rechtstheorie, Rechtssoziologie: Eine Einführung in die theoretischen Grundlagen der Rechtswissenschaft.* UTB.

Lüdecke, N., & Bier, G. (2012). *Das römisch-katholische Kirchenrecht: Eine Einführung* (unter Mitarbeit von B. S. Anuth). Kohlhammer.

Luhmann, N. (1970). Positivität des Rechts als Voraussetzung einer modernen Gesellschaft. *Jahrbuch für Rechtssoziologie und Rechtstheorie, 1,* 175–202.

Luhmann, N. (1986). *Die soziologische Beobachtung des Rechts.* Suhrkamp.

Luhmann, N. (2004). *Law as a social system* (Oxford socio-legal studies, F. Kastner, R. Nobles, D. Schiff & R. Ziegert, Eds., K. A. Ziegert, Trans.). Oxford University Press.

Luhmann, N. (2014). *A sociological theory of law* (M. Albrow, Ed., E. King-Utz, M. Albrow, Trans.). Routledge.

Machura, S. (2010). Rechtssoziologie. In G. Kneer & M. Schroer (Eds.), *Handbuch Spezielle Soziologien* (pp. 379–392). Springer.

Merks, K.-W. (2014). Göttliches Recht, menschliches Recht, Menschenrechte: Die Menschlichkeit des *ius divinum.* In S. Goertz & M. Striet (Eds.), *Nach dem Gesetz Gottes: Autonomie als christliches Prinzip* (pp. 9–46). Herder.

Möllers, C. (2020). *The possibility of norms: Social practice beyond Morals and Causes.* Oxford University Press.

Mörsdorf, K. (1989a). Munus regendi et potestas iurisdictionis (1970). In W. Aymans, K.-T. Geringer & H. Schmitz (Eds.), *Klaus Mörsdorf: Schriften zum Kanonischen Recht* (pp. 216–228). Ferdinand Schöningh.

Mörsdorf, K. (1989b). Heilige Gewalt (1968). In W. Aymans, K.-T. Geringer & H. Schmitz (Eds.), *Klaus Mörsdorf: Schriften zum Kanonischen Recht* (pp. 203–215). Ferdinand Schöningh.

Raiser, T. (2007). *Grundlagen der Rechtssoziologie* (4th ed.). UTB.

Rehbinder, M. (2014). *Rechtssoziologie: Ein Studienbuch* (8th ed.). C. H. Beck.

Röhl, K. F. (1987). *Rechtssoziologie: Ein Lehrbuch.* Heymann.

Wilson, J. Q., & Kelling, G. L. (1982). Broken Windows: The Police and Neighborhood Safety. *The Atlantic Monthly, 249,* 29–38.

Witte, D., & Striebel, C. (2015). Recht und Macht bei Bourdieu und Foucault, oder: Wie selbst aufgeklärte Machtanalysen des Rechts dessen Kulturalität ausblenden. *Sociologia Internationalis, 53,* 161–198.

Chapter 5
Validity and Legitimacy

Abstract The sociology of law deals with the legitimacy of the law in asking why and how laws receive recognition and acceptance. Canon law, in that respect, is currently facing some major difficulties. Thus far, the ecclesiastical legislators have widely excluded the Catholic laypeople from participating in legislation. Their non-participation has weakened their belief in the legitimacy of the law. Furthermore, canon law does not consistently follow the rule of law. The law of the church grants its authorities maximum power without providing for those checks and balances which control power according to a modern democratic understanding. Neither does canon law fully provide nor protect those fundamental rights of church members which modern individuals indulge according to the law of modern democratic states. That many church members at present show a rather anti-juridical attitude towards the law may be due to their verdict that canon law is a result of illegitimate power, and power in church a result of illegitimate law.

Keywords Legitimacy · Validity of the law · Recognition of the law · Consensus theory · Jürgen Habermas · Procedures · Rule of law · Legal protection · Fundamental rights

In the previous section I discussed the validity of law with the aim of identifying the legal norms which constitute positive law. This section now returns to the validity issue, this time to examine what makes law legitimate. This part of the validity debate takes up the problem that the mere legal validity of the law does not suffice to fully understand what makes the law valid, as many contemporary thinkers find, and that validity also always entails the question of legitimacy. Jürgen Habermas observed, "Law borrows its binding force, rather, from the alliance that the facticity of law forms with the claim to legitimacy."[1] Habermas therefore concludes, "positive law, too, must be legitimate."[2] As my study is not first and foremost about the foundation of law, I mostly forego determining the validity reasons which justify the

---

[1] Habermas (1996, pp. 38–39).
[2] Habermas (1996, p. 31).

© The Author(s) 2022
J. Hahn, *Foundations of a Sociology of Canon Law*,
https://doi.org/10.1007/978-3-031-01791-9_5

legitimacy of canon law.[3] Instead, I adopt a sociological approach which seeks to identify the conditions under which individuals and groups, including Catholics and groups in church, tend to perceive the law as legitimate nowadays. In this light, Niklas Luhmann speaks of legitimacy as "the purely factual and widespread belief of the validity of the law, of the binding force of certain norms or decisions, or of the value of principles which justify them".[4] In this context, it is the task of the sociology of law to address whether validity theories have any chance of convincing contemporary legal subjects of the legitimacy of the law. Consequently, the sociology of law studies legitimacy issues in a descriptive light. Frequently it does not bother with the question of whether the law deserves the legal subjects' acceptance, and is more concerned with studying whether legal subjects accept the law in fact, whatever their reasons. Stefan Machura observes that, in the past, legal scholars and philosophers have sometimes struggled to accept this narrow sociological focus on the factual acceptance of the law.[5] However, sociology and the sociology of law have largely fallen into line behind Luhmann, who repeatedly argued that sociology should adopt the position of a mere observer if it sought to study whether and why individuals or groups accept the law. As Luhmann's approach has been highly influential for the sociology of law, I will also follow his approach in my study.

Sociology and the sociology of law, when speaking of individuals or groups who deem the law to be legitimate, frequently rely on terms such as "recognition," "acknowledgement," or "acceptance."[6] These terms express that individuals or groups perceive of the law in an affirmative way. However, their essential affirmation does not necessarily lead to their compliance. John Searle provides an example to show that accepting the law does not necessarily mean abiding by it. On the contrary, even breaches of law might be a way of acknowledging the law, as Searle explains, using theft as an example,

> Even if I am a thief, I recognize that I am violating your rights when I appropriate your property. Indeed, the profession of being a thief would be meaningless without the belief in the institution of private property, because what the thief hopes to do is to take somebody else's private property and make it his own, thus reinforcing his commitment and the society's commitment to the institution of private property.[7]

It might seem paradoxical to view a crime such as theft as an act acknowledging the institution of property and of property law. However, Searle's example helps to show how abiding by the law as well as breaking the law might both be acts which demonstrate a recognition of the law and of the institutions created by the law. This twofold perspective is particularly interesting for my study, as my fifth section

---

[3] For considerations on the foundation of canon law see Hahn (2012a; 2012b; 2019).

[4] Original quote, "die rein faktisch verbreitete Überzeugung von der Gültigkeit des Rechts, von der Verbindlichkeit bestimmter Normen oder Entscheidungen oder von dem Wert der Prinzipien, an denen sie sich rechtfertigen", Luhmann (1969, p. 27).

[5] See Machura (2010, p. 386).

[6] See Röhl (1987, p. 177).

[7] Searle (2010, p. 9).

examines the ways in which individuals and groups respond to the law, and in particular how church members and ecclesiastical groups react to canon law. For the sociology of canon law, in any case, it is particularly relevant to examine the consequences of the legal subjects' *failure* to acknowledge canon law, as the non-acceptance of some legal matters of canon law is a widespread phenomenon. Analysing the phenomena of acceptance and non-acceptance, however, also makes it necessary to study the reasons why individuals and groups tend to accept or reject the law. As Manfred Rehbinder notes, there is frequently a reason why legal subjects accept the law, as they tend to accept the law only when it seems plausible to them.[8] His remark alludes to one major reason for acknowledging the law which lies in the legal subjects' belief about what constitutes legitimate law. One may assume that rejecting a law is often based on the very same reason too, namely that legal subjects find the law implausible in light of their beliefs about what makes law legitimate. The sociology of law is therefore not only interested in identifying cases in which law is accepted and cases in which it is not, but also seeks to understand the reasons underlying the legal subjects' acceptance or rejection of the law. As a result, a sociology of canon law has to analyse the conditions under which church members accept canon law or reject it. It is of key interest to ask why ecclesiastical legal subjects are increasingly tending to disregard canon law as the legitimate order of the church.

5.1   A Sociological View of Validity Reasons

As I stated above, the sociology of law is not concerned with identifying viable validity reasons for the law with the aim of justifying the law. Nevertheless, validity reasons do play a role in the acceptance or non-acceptance of law. They are of interest for the sociology of law insofar as validity reasons may actually be reasons why the legal subjects find the law legitimate or not, and, in consequence, accept or reject it. Studying what fosters the acceptance or rejection of law, one may find that not all validity reasons which were suitable for grounding legitimate law in the past are acceptable for contemporary legal subjects. Some further explanation might help to illustrate this. In plural and secular legal orders, for instance, it is impossible to ground law in revelation, even though some members of the legal community might believe in the revelation and might be open to accepting it as a reason of law. However, as there is no common agreement on the revelation as fact across the entire legal community, we may not refer to the revelation as a validity reason of law which is relevant to the whole community. A similar problem applies to nature as a validity reason of law in plural societies. This is because society, to allow for law to be grounded in natural law, would also have to agree on overarching normative ideas

---

[8] See Rehbinder (2014, p. 93).

about what is naturally just, something which is equally unlikely in plural societies.[9] Revelation and nature have therefore lost their traditional influence in the current secular justification of law, which is most evident in the European debates. Insofar as norms founded in this way are not based on a common understanding which all or most legal subjects share, they also have little chance of finding acceptance in pluralist societies. Remnants of revelation and nature which we might still find here and there in contemporary law—article 6 section 2 of the German Basic Law speaks, for instance, of the parents' right to care for their children as their "natural right"— are frequently relics left over from older law which have found their way into the language of present-day political communities. Whilst these validity reasons were persuasive in the more homogeneous societies that predated the mid-twentieth century, today they stand little chance of convincing secular individuals and plural groups of the validity of the law. It should be noted though that this rejection of the viability of natural law as a justification of law is a rather Eurocentric argument. In Anglo-American legal theory, natural law arguments are far more widely accepted and continue to play a role in the justification of law—at least on a small scale. However, they are likewise not uncontested for the precise reason mentioned, namely that it is becoming ever more difficult to ground the law of increasingly pluralist societies on a shared belief of what is naturally right.

5.1.1 Validity Derived from Power

Admittedly, it is not completely out of the question, even in plural societies, to base law on revelation and nature. However, this is only genuinely an option if one abandons any attempt to gain the legal subjects' acceptance, and resorts to the power argument instead. By using power, the authorities might simply override the differing beliefs of plural groups by declaring a specific belief about what is normatively binding according to the revelation or nature to be the norm, and by directing individuals and groups to abide by it. Natural law arguments in particular tend to resort to the power argument to assert one specific belief about what is naturally right over other competing views. In this light, legal theorist Bernd Rüthers notes that natural law arguments, when confronted with pluralism, tend to turn questions of fact into questions of power. Rüthers points out that the epistemological problem of identifying which norms accord to nature immediately becomes an authority issue about who defines what "natural law" is. Since plural conceptions about what is good and just make it virtually impossible for the members of heterogeneous groups to agree on what is naturally right, the issue of power is never far away. This in turn means that whoever relies on natural law as the foundation of law must also name an authority that is empowered to provide a binding definition of what is naturally right. Rüthers maintains, "Whoever claims the existence of binding natural law must also

---

[9] See Hahn (2019).

name a defining authority, a 'magisterium' of natural law, for the cases in which no consensus about its content can be found".[10] However, this strategy of preserving nature and likewise revelation as validity reasons for contemporary law by having them morph into the validity reason of power does not solve the problem of legitimacy. This is because at present, revelation and nature are not alone in losing influence as validity reasons of law. In addition, legal subjects of today have developed equally serious reservations about the validity reason of power. This has little to do with power as such, which, as I explained in Sect. 4.1, is always closely associated with law. Yet power, in order to serve as a legitimate force behind the law, requires legitimation. Legal subjects only tend to recognise law as legitimate law when they find the power from which the law derives to be legitimate power. Following Max Weber, we may expect this whenever power takes on a form of legitimate domination which Weber calls "authority." A short study of Weber's definitions may help to understand this. Weber defines "power" as all available options for enforcing an actor's will, even if this requires violence. He describes power as "the probability that one actor within a social relationship will be in a position to carry out his own will despite resistance, regardless of the basis on which this probability rests."[11] Weber uses the term "domination" to describe those power relations under which those exercising power may expect their commands to meet with obedience. Weber states, "'Domination' (Herrschaft) is the probability that a command with a given specific content will be obeyed by a given group of persons."[12] According to Weber, "authority" is a particular way of exercising "domination." It describes legitimate forms of domination as those acts of domination whereby those with power do not require force to implement their will, as those under their power respond to their commands with obedience because they accept the authorities' domination for reasons such as charisma, tradition, or law.[13] According to Weber, individuals or groups accept their charismatic leaders' domination insofar as the leaders' charisma justifies their rule. Group members accept traditional authorities—such as those authorities "founded upon the sacredness of tradition, i.e., of that which is customary and has always been so"[14]—due to their domination "resting on an established belief in the sanctity of immemorial traditions and the legitimacy of those exercising authority under them".[15] So individuals and groups accept the authority of a certain person as long as this person or the group to which this person belongs is traditionally endowed with a certain authority. Finally, in the case of domination legitimised by law, those subjected to domination tend to

---

[10] Original quote, "Wer die Existenz von verbindlichem Naturrecht behauptet, muß, für den Fall des fehlenden Konsenses über dessen Inhalt, zugleich eine Definitionsautorität, ein verbindliches 'Lehramt' für Naturrecht, angeben können", Rüthers (2005, no. 443).

[11] Weber (1978, p. 53).

[12] Weber (1978, p. 53).

[13] See Weber (1978, p. 215).

[14] Weber (1978, p. 954).

[15] Weber (1978, p. 215).

accept the authorities' power over them because their power is legitimised by law. The authorities are legitimate rulers as their power is not unlimited and is circumscribed by the law in the form of rules governing authority and procedure. Legal subjects, hence, tend to accept decisions made by administration or adjudication precisely because their power is not arbitrary but is constrained and controlled by the law.

5.1.2 Social Contract and Consensus

According to Weber, in modernity authority based on law largely eclipses charismatic and traditional authority, although it never does so entirely.[16] Individuals and groups tend to accept authority based on law primarily because law provides them with a rational framework for pursuing their own interests. Weber considers economic interests to be of primary albeit not exclusive importance in modern capitalist societies.[17] The law itself creates the conditions by which it may be accepted, namely by providing a rational and logical system of rules that creates a reliable and resilient framework for capitalist exchange relations. Whilst we need not share Weber's focus on economic matters, it does seem expedient to make the interests of individuals and groups the starting point for discussing why they accept the law. In this light, Thomas Raiser suggests that accepting authority based on law is in the legal subjects' own interests insofar as they find the existence of the law and of authority based on the law to be beneficial as a means of curbing individual egoism and group interests to the end of protecting common interests and the well-being of all members of society.[18] The idea that legal subjects agree to the limitation of their individual aspirations because it is in their long-term interests to do so points clearly to the social contract as a source of legal validity and thus to the validity reason which the legal theorists of the Enlightenment mobilised in response to the forces of pluralisation in early modernity. Modern legal theories no longer accept that the content of common belief serves as the basis of law; instead they base the law on a common agreement that it is good for all to submit to a common order. Above and beyond any religious and ideological beliefs, these theories assume that legal subjects consent to the law because doing so facilitates social life in general. One contemporary variant of social contract theory that has been the subject of extensive debate in recent decades is consensus theory, which is foremost the work of Jürgen Habermas. Consensus theory posits that the cohesion of modern societies is built upon consensus and that, consequently, the law, which is supposed to contribute to the integration of modern societies, is also subject to the principle of consensus. Consensus, in consequence, becomes the validity reason of law. It is achieved

---

[16] See Weber (1978, pp. 219–220).

[17] See Weber (1978, p. 212).

[18] See Raiser (2007, p. 267).

through discourse, as Habermas writes, "Just those action norms are valid to which all possibly affected persons could agree as participants in rational discourses".[19] Habermas bases his argument in favour of consensus as a validity reason of law on the principle of human autonomy. In order to do justice to their individual freedom, modern human beings may only be bound by self-legislation. This makes it necessary to understand individuals themselves as the producers of the norms to which they are subject, as Habermas explains, "The idea of self-legislation by citizens, that is, requires that those subject to law as its addressees can at the same time understand themselves as authors of law."[20] This authorship develops through rational discourse as a process of negotiation in which the legal subjects identify the legal norms which are deserving of their acceptance. Discourses are rational if they offer the conditions under which a rational will can come into being. For Habermas, these conditions include first and foremost the freedom from hierarchical domination to create an ideal speech situation undistorted by asymmetrical power relations. Only relations which are free from non-egalitarian domination can ensure that discourses "remain porous, sensitive, and receptive to the suggestions, issues and contributions, information and arguments that flow in from a discursively structured public sphere, that is, one that is pluralistic, close to the grass roots, and relatively undisturbed by the effects of power."[21] If these conditions are guaranteed, we may assume that the legal norms resulting from discourse may be considered legitimate insofar as they can obtain the consent of all those they concern.

5.1.3   Improbable Consensus

Consensus theory has met with broad approval, but it has also attracted criticism. One of the main points of criticism relates to doubts about whether consensus building, as Habermas seems to suggest it, is actually practicable. The question is whether ideal speech situations in the Habermasian sense are a realistic prospect. Even if they are, it remains unclear whether one can realistically expect discourse to end in consensus, as we might also expect discourse to end in ultimate dissent.[22] It is also doubtful whether discourse can be constructed in such a boundless way that it includes all those potentially affected by its results. Sociologists of law in particular have been at pains to point out the limits of the consensus model. They stress that in complex contemporary societies it is impossible to achieve a consensus on the law, either with respect to substantive law or with respect to procedural law.[23] To expect consensus is illusory, as Luhmann states, "No society can found its law on consensus

---

[19] Habermas (1996, p. 107).

[20] Habermas (1996, p. 120).

[21] Habermas (1996, p. 182).

[22] See Beckermann (2012, p. 11 fn 2).

[23] Eg Cotterrell (1984, pp. 105–106 with further references); Röhl (1987, p. 271).

if one means by that that all of the people will agree to all of the norms all of the time."[24] Luhmann considers such a consensus both ontologically unrealistic because society can never achieve it, and epistemologically unlikely insofar as we could never prove consensus, even if it existed. Luhmann therefore states that "such a criterion for the distinction between validity/invalidity cannot be tested in court. It is not justiciable, and thus it cannot be practiced in the legal system itself."[25] Consequently, as Luhmann finds, "A system-wide universal test of validity/invalidity for each legal norm apparently is not convertible into practical programs."[26] Habermas himself also responded to these comments on his theory. He agrees that it is unrealistic to expect a discourse in which all those affected by a norm can actually participate. But, as he suggests, this does not render the idea of discourse redundant. Indeed, as Habermas argues, it is important to remember the fictitious value of the ideal speech situation. This functions best when the actual participants in norm-finding or norm-debating processes not only exclusively pursue their own interests, but also consider the concerns of those who are not present. Habermas states, "as participants in rational discourses, consociates under law must be able to examine whether a contested norm meets with, or could meet with the agreement of all those possibly affected."[27] His remark offers two possible approaches to the justification of norms: either to involve all those concerned in a rational discourse, or to consider the views of those who are not present. Habermas considers the latter approach to be workable when it comes to evaluating the legitimacy of concrete and thus pre-existing law, "the legitimacy of statutes is measured against the discursive redeemability of their normative validity claim—in the final analysis, according to whether they have come about through a rational legislative process, or at least could have been justified from pragmatic, ethical, and moral points of view."[28] Habermas does not therefore see the crux of consensus theory in whether a consensus exists or arises in fact, but in whether a consensus is conceivable. The law cannot continually insist on the legal subjects' factual recognition. Instead, the aim is to secure conditions under which law can come into being which in principle allows for the recognition of the emergent law. Habermas describes as one key condition "that the legal order must always make it possible to obey its rules out of respect for the law."[29] Thus, law does not always draw its legitimacy from its legal subjects' actual consent. However, it may be considered legitimate if this consent might be obtained in principle. The legal subjects' potential consensus is then the validity reason of law. However, we may also ask whether it is realistic to expect consensus to be even potentially possible. From the perspective of legal theory, Christoph Möllers and others doubt this is the case, noting that consensus theories overestimate the power

---

[24] Luhmann (2004, p. 247).

[25] Luhmann (2004, p. 123).

[26] Luhmann (2004, p. 123).

[27] Habermas (1996, p. 104).

[28] Habermas (1996, p. 30).

[29] Habermas (1996, p. 31).

of consensus in this respect. Möllers does not argue against consensus per se, but against the idea that it can serve as the foundation of a whole normative order. He elucidates,

> We can think of consensus as a goal that cannot be achieved yet nevertheless guides our thought process, but not as an existing foundation that is ingrained in a norm such as the guarantee of human dignity. The claim would be that consensus practically and continuously arises from solving small and concrete questions, not in great formulas. Questions of war and peace or basic standards of human rights, by contrast, are not capable of consensus if one takes consensus to mean more than the agreement to a compromise formula.[30]

While Möllers does not banish consensus from the validity debate of legal norms, he is sceptical of overarching theories that use consensus as a conclusive answer to the validity problem of law. The sociology of law has similar critical voices that cast doubt on the power of consensus to justify legal norms. Doris Mathilde Lucke, for instance, stresses that consent to the law is not only frequently absent throughout the onward march of modernity, but is becoming increasingly unlikely.[31] This is because law is losing its capacity to gain the legal subjects' recognition as a consequence of its ongoing rationalisation, as Lucke maintains. This process of progressively rationalising the law by standardisation, abstraction, subsumption, the definition of typical facts, and the creation of case groups is broadening the gap between social and legal reality. Accordingly, the intersection between social reality and legal reality where one might expect consensus on the capacity of the law to support the community and to serve justice is becoming ever smaller. As law becomes ever more detached from the legal subjects' everyday life and everyday knowledge, its chance to generate consensus decreases; in fact, law is becoming the exclusive preserve of legal experts, detached from everyday reality and with only sporadic connections to it. As a result, it becomes unrealistic to hope that the legal subjects might embrace it. In fact, it seems fair to expect the opposite, as Lucke explains. The tendency is for law to become increasingly unacceptable to its legal subjects and is, in consequence, losing much of its effectiveness. We may identify a number of contemporary signs of anomie which point at this problem. Lucke's observations raise genuine doubts about whether the law may expect much support in present societies, as legal rationalisation takes its course. Her objection is certainly worthy of further consideration. Whilst it does not contradict Habermas's approach, it does raise some fundamental questions about it. From the perspective of validity theory, Habermas relies on consensus as a legitimacy reason for law; from the point of view of the sociology of law, Lucke observes that current law is in fact increasingly incapable of forging this consensus. While it seems necessary to have at least a potential consensus to establish the legitimacy of law, the steady rationalisation of law is depriving the law of any chance of achieving a de facto consensus. Hence, consensus becomes unlikely, yet there seems to be no alternative to it as a validity reason of law. This impasse suggests that legal systems will increasingly struggle to

---

[30]Möllers (2020, p. 264).

[31]See Lucke (2010, pp. 84–85).

achieve recognition. From the perspective of the sociology of law, it remains unclear if there is a way to address this fundamental problem, and how to go about it in the future.

5.1.4 Procedural Legitimation

Roger Cotterrell's deliberations on this subject may be of help. In view of the fragility of any consensus and the necessity of achieving one, Cotterrell considers it to be an important symbolic achievement of the law that it successfully conceals the fact that it cannot rely on a genuine consensus in the legal community or on the legal subjects' consent. The law succeeds in hiding any lack of consensus by employing a rhetoric of consensus that actually conceals grave and irreconcilable differences in the expectations placed upon it. Cotterrell speaks of "conflicting interests disguised by the consensus rhetoric of the law".[32] Since true consensus is becoming increasingly improbable in contemporary pluralist societies, the law falls back on the rhetorical invocation of consensus to evoke a presumption or fiction of consensus. In a similar vein, Niklas Luhmann believes that law must assert that it expresses consensus, if only probably, provisionally, and temporarily.[33] Claims of this kind remain convincing as long as nobody deconstructs them. Klaus Röhl clarifies this point by emphasising that it is not the actual experience of consensus that is essential for the presumption of consensus, but the absence of profound dissent. The problem that a general consensus is not at hand is unimportant as long as there is no fundamental dissent that proves consensus to be fully delusive.[34] While dissent might expose that consensus is merely fictitious, the law—most of the time—profits from the fact that nobody voices major dissent. However, this begs the question why we might expect legal subjects to be content with a fictitious consensus. Luhmann responds by referring to the institutionalisation of law which suggests consensus. In modern societies, he says, the behavioural expectations associated with law are institutionalised, so that seeking a real factual consensus is not consistently necessary, as institutions come with a presumed consensus.[35] For the most part this illusion is largely sustainable. It is sufficient, Luhmann explains, that

> the 'general societal consensus' needs only to be matched in certain respects and moments by the actual experience of some people. The function of institutions depends, therefore, less on the creation than on the economy of consensus. The saving is achieved mainly by anticipated consensus in the expectation of expectations, acting as a presumption and not normally even requiring a concrete text.[36]

---

[32] Cotterrell (1984, p. 109).

[33] See Luhmann (1969, p. 196).

[34] See Röhl (1987, p. 271).

[35] See Luhmann (1970, p. 188).

[36] Luhmann (2014, p. 51).

Clearly, we may not expect institutionalisation to consistently succeed in generating the presumption of consensus. This is because institutionalisation itself is contested and raises questions of recognition;[37] in this respect, Luhmann concedes that sociology struggles to explain how institutions, burdened with their own problems of recognition, support the recognition of other norms, such as legal norms. Nevertheless, institutionalisation seems to support a fiction of consensus based on a generalisation of consensus.[38] Luhmann notes that a generalisation of consensus consists of two strategies. First, it is important to support the fictitious consensus so that the legal subjects gain the impression that there is actually a consensus about the law; second, it is necessary to ostracise those who openly undermine the idea of consensus.[39] Hence, those who dissent must expect the imposition of negative sanctions. Both strategies for the generalisation of consensus—the generation of the fictitious consensus as well as the suppression of dissent—take place in the context of institutionalised procedures in which the legal subjects participate, directly or indirectly, such as elections, parliamentary debates, and court proceedings.[40] By generating a presumed consensus and stifling dissenting voices, institutionalised procedures in which the law is generated and applied contribute to creating an aura of legitimacy around the law. Stefan Machura uses court proceedings by way of illustration. If a court makes a procedurally correct decision, the losing party has no other socially adequate option but to conclusively accept the decision. This is because a losing party who continues to reject the decision would run the risk of being ostracised and being regarded as a social pariah.[41] Following Luhmann, one can therefore assume that law can claim to be consensual if it originates from procedures which adhere to the rule of law and is applied in procedures under the rule of law.[42] The results of these legislative and judicial procedures, such as laws and judicial decisions, are thus endowed with the presumption of legitimacy.[43] Jürgen Habermas agrees with this from the perspective of validity theory, noting, "In the demanding conditions of fair procedure and the presuppositions of communication that undergird legitimate lawmaking, the reason that posits and tests norms has assumed a procedural form."[44] Habermas emphasises that modern legislation is therefore accompanied by high expectations. This is because legislation must live up to the promise to produce laws rationally deserving of recognition, as Habermas explains, "The positivity of law is bound up with the promise that democratic processes of lawmaking justify the presumption that

---

[37] See Luhmann (1970, p. 188).

[38] See Luhmann (1970, p. 188).

[39] See Luhmann (1970, p. 189).

[40] See Luhmann (1970, p. 189).

[41] See Machura (2010, p. 386).

[42] See Luhmann (2004, p. 123).

[43] See Luhmann (2014, pp. 203–204).

[44] Habermas (1996, p. 287).

enacted norms are rationally acceptable."[45] In contrast to premodern legal norms, modern law cannot simply be the expression of an individual ruler's will, but must express the citizens' will and give due expression to their self-legislation, either factually or fictitiously. Habermas explicates, "Rather than displaying the facticity of an arbitrary, absolutely contingent choice, the positivity of law expresses the legitimate will that stems from a presumptively rational self-legislation of politically autonomous citizens."[46] However, as Habermas also notes, contemporary law arises from political procedures that we cannot simply interpret as the politically autonomous self-legislation of rational citizens. Hence, the connection between autonomous self-legislation and concrete legislation is only plausible if the rule of law controls legislative procedures. Habermas observes, "legitimate law reproduces itself only in the forms of a constitutionally regulated circulation of power, which should be nourished by the communications of an unsubverted public sphere rooted in the core private spheres of an undisturbed lifeworld via the networks of civil society."[47] Legislative authorities prove to be legitimate only if they are constrained by the rule of law, including the authorities' subjection to the law, the separation of powers, the election of public officeholders, and limited time periods for public offices. Law therefore proves to be legitimate only if it derives from legitimate authorities and flows from procedures controlled by the rule of law. Yet Habermas is not entirely convinced by a purely proceduralist ratio. In his view, the formal rule of law as represented by constitutional procedures must be supplemented by substantive elements which qualify the legal order as a framework of procedures which are worthy of recognition. The rule of law must therefore justify itself formally and substantively. Among the relevant substantive criteria of the rule of law from a socio-legal point of view are the state's guarantee of fundamental rights, such as equality before the law, freedom of speech, and freedom of assembly, which allow for the public criticism of officeholders, and their subjection to control by a free press and public discourse.[48]

5.1.5 Accepting Majority Decisions

But even when the law follows the rule of law, the question arises as to why modern-day individuals consider law to be particularly worthy of recognition if it is the result of constitutional procedures. After all, there are often reasons to doubt the results of concrete legislative procedures. As their results are frequently based on majority decisions, they are undeniably contingent. Majorities have only a limited legitimising effect. Compared to consensus, we can only consider them to be stopgap

---

[45] Habermas (1996, p. 33).

[46] Habermas (1996, p. 33).

[47] Habermas (1996, p. 408).

[48] See Raiser (2007, pp. 269–270).

solutions, as Luhmann emphasises.[49] Philosopher John Dewey remarked in a similar vein, "Majority rule, just as majority rule, is as foolish as its critics charge it with being."[50] Majorities are therefore merely of an interim nature, as Habermas observes from the perspective of legal theory, "Majority rule retains an internal relation to the search for truth inasmuch as the decision reached by the majority only represents a caesura in an ongoing discussion; the decision records, so to speak, the interim result of a discursive opinion-forming process."[51] Yet at the same time, majorities also prove to be helpful and even essential for taking decisions. When consensus-based "ideal procedures"[52] fail, majorities might achieve the desired result, "as a rule of an actual—not imagined—procedure",[53] as Christoph Möllers emphasises. Möllers therefore argues against any attempts to devalue majority rule, as is common in some approaches to legal theory. He criticises these theories as guided by

> idealization ... which views every form of practical implementation as deficient. For example, if majority rule only represents an incomplete representation of an idealized public use of reason, which builds on the generalization of arguments, then rightness and reality are played out against each other in a way that misses a social practice that aims for realization.[54]

Hence, we must accept that majority decisions are contingent and may be reversed, but without devaluing majority rule as such. Instead, we must come to a differentiated view of majority rule, as Habermas argues, stating that a majority must "be viewed as the rationally motivated yet fallible result of a process of argumentation that has been interrupted in view of institutional pressures to decide, but is in principle resumable".[55] However, one may ask what consequences ensue from this sociologically. From the perspective of sociology, the key question is whether majority decisions, as obviously fallible as they are, stand a chance of being accepted as legitimate decisions. Hence, the sociological debate is not concerned with the normative dimension of the majority issue but with the empirical question of whether majorities may expect to find widespread acceptance among those whom their results concern. We have to discuss whether it is plausible that majorities may find acceptance and, if so, for what particular reasons. Luhmann expects them to find acceptance due to the proceduralist ratio of majority rule which helps us cope with the highly complex conditions of modernity. According to Luhmann, procedures serve to absorb the shock effect of social development. Procedures present developments as decisions and, thus, as purposeful progress. And they provide individuals and groups with opportunities to participate in decision making. Consequently, as Luhmann notes, "A decision does not fall upon the individual as an unexpectable surprise, as luck or bad luck, which one may only expect helplessly without having a

---

[49] See Luhmann (1969, p. 196).
[50] Dewey (1946, p. 207).
[51] Habermas (1996, p. 179).
[52] Möllers (2020, p. 16).
[53] Möllers (2020, p. 17).
[54] Möllers (2020, p. 253).
[55] Habermas (1996, p. 179).

chance to prepare for it, but as the result of a decision-making process which one may prepare for by witnessing it and acting according to it."[56] Accordingly, Luhmann finds expectability and participation to be the two major criteria which provide procedures with legitimacy. These criteria motivate legal subjects to accept the law resulting from these procedures even though the law proves to be the result of a contingent and fragile majority decision. Procedures, thus, are an "existential complement of positivising the law. They minimise and absorb the moment of shock which is connected with decision."[57] Despite a complex present and uncertain future, they hold out the promise of security without seeming to be fully arbitrary, as Luhmann explains,

> In light of an uncertain future and the sense of overload resulting from the immense complexity of options of variable law, procedures help to create security and allow for significant, expressive, meaningful, and dutiful behaviour in the present time. In this way, the individuals may experience the present time as meaningful and may act according to it, even though their lives are moving towards an uncertain future.[58]

By providing individuals with opportunities for participation, procedures also help to absorb protest, as Luhmann notes.[59] Susanne Baer agrees, citing empirical evidence that opportunities for participation in legislation, adjudication, and administration actually help to reduce conflicts in these fields.[60] John Dewey links this idea to the majority principle. As limited as the majority principle is, it is not exclusively about finding a majority result which serves as a decision, but also about the procedural logic revolving around "antecedent debates, modification of views to meet the opinions of minorities, the relative satisfaction given the latter by the fact that it has had a chance and that next time it may be successful in becoming a majority."[61] In this light, opportunities prove particularly suitable for increasing the tolerability of any acute deficits arising from concrete decisions. Opportunities increase the acceptability of a decision even when there are justified doubts about its correctness, as Luhmann notes. We may witness this, for example, in decisions that promote rather

---

[56] Original quote, "Die Entscheidung fällt nicht als eine unerwartbare Überraschung auf ihn zu, als Glück oder Unglück, dem man ratlos entgegensieht, ohne sich darauf einstellen zu können, sondern als Ergebnis eines Entscheidungsprozesses, in dem man sich miterlebend und mithandelnd auf sie vorbereiten kann", Luhmann (1969, p. 232).

[57] Original quote, "ein existentielles Komplement der Positivierung des Rechts. Sie verkleinern und entschärfen das Moment der Überraschung, das mit der Entscheidung verbunden ist", Luhmann (1969, p. 232).

[58] Original quote, "Verfahren verhelfen dazu, angesichts einer ungewissen Zukunft und vornehmlich angesichts einer Überforderung durch eine unübersehbare Komplexität von Möglichkeiten des variablen Rechts gegenwärtige Sicherheit zu schaffen und ein darstellendes, expressives, sinnerfülltes, verpflichtendes Verhalten in der Gegenwart zu ermöglichen. So kann der Betroffene in einer laufend aktuellen Gegenwart sinnvoll miterleben und mithandeln, obwohl er auf eine ungewisse Zukunft zulebt", Luhmann (1969, p. 232).

[59] See Luhmann (1970, p. 189).

[60] See Baer (2021, p. 125).

[61] Dewey (1946, pp. 207–208).

questionable inequalities. In light of the principle of equality, all inequalities require justification to become tolerable. According to Luhmann, procedures render precisely this service. He observes, "It must be possible to present all differences and all inequalities as the result of a procedure and to justify them as such."[62] If unequal rights arise from a decision in which everyone can potentially participate, it is more likely that those to whom they pertain will accept them. These decisions become tolerable because the procedures offer a fair chance to everyone and also because future procedures hold out the prospect of further opportunities. This renders these decisions more than just fate, and at least gives the impression that those affected by them may influence their outcome. However, this scenario also presupposes a certain culture of decision making. Obviously contingent decisions, for instance, may find acceptance only if the majority continues to treat the minority with respect, as Luhmann emphasises. Democratic systems respond to this need by providing dissenting individuals and minority groups with subjective rights and procedural rules which protect them from the majority.[63] The conditions under which majority decisions are taken also play a role. In order to be able to assert the legitimacy of their results, decision-making processes must ensure that conditions prevail under which one might at least conceive of a general consensus. Whilst a general consensus rarely occurs, it must remain possible. This means that processes must refrain from excluding certain individuals or groups from the process of will formation in advance. Not all members of society can be members of every decision-making body. However, this is unproblematic as long as participation at least remains an option, as Luhmann finds,

> It is more important . . . that the procedural form in which we strive for consensus shows a certain attitude towards the consent of others and determines that every voice counts. Each individual's consent (in an election, each voter's consent; in legislation: each parliamentarian's consent) is relevant in principle—not in the sense that everyone in fact needs to agree with each decision, but in the sense that nobody's opinion is a priori declared irrelevant.[64]

5.1.6 Representative Participation

Luhmann's observations on the legitimacy of majority decisions coincide with other sociological findings. Hanna Pitkin's ground-breaking work on political

---

[62] Original quote, "Alle Unterschiede und alle Ungleichheiten müssen als Ergebnis eines Verfahrens dargestellt und begründet werden können", Luhmann (1969, p. 197).

[63] See Luhmann (1969, p. 196).

[64] Original quote, "Wichtiger ist . . ., daß die verfahrensmäßige Form, in der um Konsens geworben wird, eine bestimmte Einstellung zum Konsens anderer impliziert und festlegt: Jede Stimme zählt. Der Konsens eines jeden einzelnen (bei der Wahl: des Wählers; im Gesetzgebungsverfahren: des Abgeordneten) ist prinzipiell relevant – zwar nicht in dem Sinne, daß zu jeder Entscheidung alle faktisch zustimmen müßten, wohl aber in dem Sinne, daß niemandes Meinung a priori für irrelevant erklärt werden könnte", Luhmann (1969, pp. 196–197).

representation (1967) comes to mind. In her reflections, Pitkin refers to complex political decision making in which not all members of society are able to participate themselves, but in which participation takes place through representation, by agents representing the members of society. In modernity, formal representation—such as the "Leviathan," the absolutist ruler of the premodern era representing his people—is no longer acceptable. To achieve legitimacy in this day and age, representation must consist of a substantive link between those who represent and those who are represented. Jürgen Habermas stresses this point in reference to decisions made through elections, which "must provide for a fair representation and aggregation of the given interests and preferences."[65] This includes representation of the outer fringes of the spectrum of opinion to be found in a society, as Habermas observes, "Here representation can only mean that the selection of members of parliament should provide for the broadest possible spectrum of interpretive perspectives, including the views and voices of marginal groups."[66] The question arises how to ensure the adequate representation of this spectrum. Practically speaking, it is unrealistic to expect to assemble a perfect selection of representatives to represent the diverse opinions that exist in a plural society. Hanna Pitkin does not deem this necessary. Instead, for reasons of acceptance, it is more important that the represented may be regarded as represented adequately in the procedures, even if the representatives do not represent their precise interests. Pitkin refers, for example, to representation based on "standing for",[67] in which the representatives stand for the key characteristics of those they represent, without having to ensure that every view that exists in society is actually represented in decision making. She observes that successful representation by the representatives "depends on the representative's characteristics, on what he is or is *like*, on being something rather than doing something. The representative does not act for others; he 'stands for' them, by virtue of a correspondence or connection between them, a resemblance or reflection."[68] It is therefore necessary to ensure in the formation of political bodies that their composition reflects the represented individuals and groups in this sense of "standing for." Pitkin consequently notes, "In political terms, what seems important is less what the legislature does than how it is composed."[69] Yet, as Pitkin also observes, it does not seem necessary for the represented individuals and groups to be represented with respect to *all* of their distinct features and qualities, which would in itself be practically inconceivable due to the limited size of decision-making bodies. In order to be able to speak of representation, however, it is imperative not to deliberately exclude any individuals or groups to whom decisions pertain. The ideal selection of representatives must achieve the representation of society as a whole or rather not exclude the possibility of full representation, as Pitkin finds, "What is

---

[65] Habermas (1996, p. 183).

[66] Habermas (1996, p. 183).

[67] Pitkin (1967, p. 60).

[68] Pitkin (1967, p. 61).

[69] Pitkin (1967, p. 61).

necessary to make a representation is not accuracy of depiction of something visible, but simply depiction of something visible, the intention to depict."[70] Selecting representatives by the drawing of lots, for example, does not ensure that the whole community is substantively represented. Nevertheless, one may consider this selection legitimate because it is open to and does not preclude the representation of any members of a group.[71] On the other hand, a process of selection that intentionally excludes certain individuals or groups from being represented creates a problem of legitimacy. With regard to the question posed here about how majority decisions may find acceptance even though their results are obviously contingent, it follows from these considerations that majority decisions tend to appear acceptable whenever we may regard the decision-making bodies as legitimate representative bodies for those for whom they make their decisions. If no one's opinion is declared irrelevant a priori and all those affected are at least potentially represented in the decision-making process, decisions have a good chance of being accepted, even if they do not correspond to the will of all. In addition, majority decisions may particularly hope for approval from the defeated minority if the minority has the reasonable expectation of becoming a majority in a future decision.

5.2   The Recognition of Canon Law

In light of the foregoing discussion, I want to use the following section to analyse what the situation is with respect to canon law. Particularly in a community such as the church, which is at its core based on a shared faith, it seems reasonable at first glance to assume that the legal subjects share a wide-ranging consensus on many issues. But contrary to expectations, the reality of canon law is rather different. Recognition of canon law is often a matter of dispute, as theologians and canonists can confirm.[72] Above all, many church members accuse canon law of oppressively juridifying church life. The result is disenchantment with the law among many legal subjects and a weariness in church with many institutional issues. Noting a new phenomenon in the history of canon law, Ladislas Orsy describes how the law struggled to achieve recognition after the Second Vatican Council, which was followed by what Orsy describes as an increase of anomie in church, noting, "A new phenomenon arose: canon law was acquiring an increasingly bad reputation among God's people."[73]

---

[70] Pitkin (1967, p. 67).

[71] See Pitkin (1967, p. 73).

[72] Eg Müller (1978, pp. 3–4); Coughlin (2011, pp. 3–4, 65–67); Bucher (2018, pp. 160–164); Hahn (2018, pp. 154–159).

[73] Orsy (1992, p. 97).

5.2.1 Juridification and Trivialisation

Canon law itself has contributed in no small measure to its own poor reputation. The fact that many church members experience the encroachment of the law into the various spheres of ecclesiastical life as oppressive rather than empowering has much to do with the intrusive nature of canon law and its failure to accept certain boundaries of law. Canon law is more expansive and in some respects more invasive than modern individuals are accustomed to from the majority of secular law. It extends to or includes extra-legal spheres, as discussed in Sect. 4.2.2, without consistently respecting its own boundaries and thus the difference between law, morality, and theology. In official texts, the boundaries between magisterial theology and law are often so fluid they are virtually invisible to the legally untrained eye. Individual papal laws frequently start off with a lavish introductory section containing doctrinal or moral content preceding the legal norms. Although the threshold where doctrine passes into law is evident to most canonists, it is not always so clear that others can easily distinguish the legally binding part of a papal law from statements of a non-legal nature.[74] Moreover, in some cases canonical norms in themselves do not exclusively contain legal content. The current Code of Canon Law, for example, contains statements of a doctrinal nature that were formally transformed into positive law without there being any obvious need for them within a legal document. Sacramental law, in particular, contains official sacramental doctrine in the form of positive legal norms that one might expect to find in the catechism, liturgical books, or papal letters rather than in a legal code. These norms describe the meaning of sacramental acts in a descriptive and theological manner (eg canon 834 §1 CIC/1983) without drawing a link to legal consequences, or include legal norms in theological statements (see canons 840, 849 CIC/1983) without the doctrinal elements contributing anything to the legal content. According to the definition of law as given in Sect. 2.1.13, these statements are not legal norms in terms of their content, because they are not justiciable. Instead, ecclesiastical doctrine takes on the formal appearance of law, albeit without any legal consequence. One wonders what the underlying idea is behind this practice. The legislator undoubtedly intended the formal legalisation of doctrine to be an instrument for highlighting the specifically religious character of canon law and for emphasising the relevance of theological knowledge in the application of the law. However, these doctrinal norms predominantly serve to create an altogether different impression among the legal subjects. Those Catholics who are positively disposed towards the law may see in this practice a premodern category error in the mixing of theology, morality, and law. Others might find the juridification of the non-legal a strategy by the legislator which has highly problematic implications, such as submitting doctrine to law, and thus also constraining the freedom of faith through the law. Whilst it is hard to verify whether this accusation is true or not, it should be noted from a

---

[74] Eg Benedict XVI (2010). *Motu proprio Omnium in mentem*, 26 October 2009. *Acta Apostolicae Sedis, 102*, 8–10.

sociological standpoint that the lack of clear boundaries between ecclesiastical doctrine and law, as shown in the formal juridification of official sacramental theology, feeds accusations of juridism.

Contributing to this impression of juridism are also certain legal particularisations that are not infrequently found in canon law. I use the term "particularisation" to refer to legal regulations that undermine the generality of the law. Particularised law includes legal norms that get lost in the minutiae of regulations without their level of detail yielding any recognisable benefit for the legal community. Critics of European law, for example, often criticise European regulations for their minute concern with the degree of cucumber curvature to the detriment of general regulatory concerns. This once again brings to mind Niklas Luhmann's example of "trivial law," namely "claims of premiums for the destruction of apples in a particular harvest".[75] The legal subjects commonly react to this type of trivial law by developing "strategies of defence",[76] as Luhmann observes. Particularisations are therefore intimately connected with the issue of recognition, as Roger Cotterrell states.[77] They frequently have a negative effect on the legal subjects' acceptance of the law. Canon law also contains evident particularisations that tend to undermine the legal subjects' acceptance of canon law, as we may assume. One example is the recent controversy over Eucharistic matter, which culminated in a discussion about how much gluten hosts should contain in order to be considered valid Eucharistic matter.[78] Whilst the discussion of the Eucharistic matter should be approached with sensitivity due to the importance of the Eucharist as a core sacramental rite of the church, it is doubtful whether a naturalistic debate about the nature of "real bread" that revolves around its gluten content does justice to the subject. These kinds of arguments might reinforce the impression among many Catholics that canonical regulations tend to be about trivial issues and thus do not deserve any serious attention. In the concrete case, this impression not only damages the debate about the Eucharist, it also damages the law, which, as a medium for such particularising regulations, leads the legal subjects to wonder whether it truly deserves their attention and their acceptance.

5.2.2 Constitutional Challenges

The above examples show that canon law itself contributes in no small way to weakening its chance of achieving a consensus among its legal subjects. But while consensus on the law is unlikely and becoming ever more unlikely in any complex legal community, as argued in Sect. 5.1.3, the situation in church is even more dramatic, as Simon Hecke posits. This is because, with regard to canon law, not only

---

[75] Luhmann (2014, p. 196).

[76] Luhmann (2014, p. 196).

[77] See Cotterrell (1984, pp. 176–177).

[78] See Congregation for Divine Worship and the Discipline of the Sacraments (2017, no. 4).

is any attempt to reach a consensus destined to fail—a problem which, as discussed, applies to consensus on the law in general—, but there is also significant *dissent* on the law in church, as Hecke observes, noting, "Research and survey findings as well as protest movements within the Catholic Church have been proving for a long time that there is less common consensus and more common dissent with canon law among the ordinary church members."[79] Anyone currently studying the level of acceptance of canon law will soon discover a range of phenomena which not only reveal a lack of acceptance of the law among the legal subjects, but demonstrate their open dissent. Hecke sees the main causes of this dissent in those much-disputed regulations of canon law, such as the ban on the ordination of women, the papal primacy of jurisdiction, and in the essential distinction between the clergy and laity and its legal consequences.[80] Whilst these examples prove to be particularly contested among the Catholics of the northern hemisphere, other legal norms are the source of similar conflicts in other parts of the Catholic world church. The obligation of celibacy for clerics, for instance, is received rather critically among African Catholics who place great store by marriage and parenthood.[81] Voices from Latin America have criticised the canonical norms on parishes, as these norms widely obstruct a fruitful organisation of parish life seeking to respond to the pastoral needs of large Latin American dioceses, such as Andean communities.[82] Criticism includes the canons on ecclesiastical administration for their obvious European understanding of dioceses as urban organisations with a huge and professional apparatus of modern bureaucracy, a view which is not borne out by reality in many dioceses across the globe.[83] These examples certainly show that dissent about the law is neither a uniform phenomenon across the local churches all over the globe nor a phenomenon triggered by the whole body of law, but that it is triggered by certain selective issues, often of ecclesiastical constitutional law. Hecke also notices this, observing that there are many canonical norms which church members neither dispute nor challenge. Indeed, only a small number of legal norms provoke fundamental dissent. Yet this does not help to solve the problem which canon law has with regard to its recognition. Hecke puts forward two pieces of evidence for this. First, many of the legal norms which provoke dissent are so dominant that they overshadow the recognition of other legal norms. This assessment is understandable in the examples Hecke discusses, which mostly relate to constitutional law. If key constitutional issues provoke fundamental dissent, we may hardly expect the legal subjects to acknowledge less central matters of law as worthy

---

[79] Original quote, "Ergebnisse von Untersuchungen und Umfragen sowie Protestbewegungen innerhalb der katholischen Kirche zeugen bereits seit langem weniger von einem allgemeinen Konsens als vielmehr von einem allgemeinen Dissens des einfachen Kirchenvolks mit dem Kirchenrecht", Hecke (2017, p. 44).

[80] See Hecke (2017, pp. 103–104).

[81] Eg Schreiter (1985, p. 2).

[82] Eg Dammert Bellido (1986, pp. 115–116).

[83] See Dammert Bellido (1986, pp. 113–114).

of their approval. And it is even less likely that the legal subjects' potential recognition of these minor regulations might solve the recognition problem of the ecclesiastical legal system as a whole. Hecke therefore suggests that only serious changes in the ecclesiastical constitution and in constitutional law might help to increase the legal subjects' approval of canon law. The legislator would have to radically reform the legal norms which are currently most controversial to achieve this. Second, Hecke suggests that the uncontested norms of canon law may seldom help with the recognition of canon law as such, as the legal subjects' approval of these norms is often not a conscious decision in favour of canon law and consequently not an explicit act of recognition. In reality, church members primarily accept those canonical norms which are also norms which are common in other social contexts or in state law. Hence, they need not identify and accept those norms explicitly as canonical norms if they have already accepted them as norms in other contexts.[84] A few examples serve to support Hecke's point. Canon law, for instance, regulates that an election is invalid if the number of ballots in the ballot box exceeds the number of voters (see canon 173 §3 CIC/1983). This regulation does not call for an explicit recognition in church, as it applies to elections in the same way elsewhere. Hence, there is also little reason to give the ecclesiastical legislator credit for that piece of regulation. The same applies to the legal norm in the computation of time that the first day is regularly not computed in the total of a time limit (see canon 203 §1 CIC/1983). Church members probably also take it for granted that a sermon should be preached in a contemporary form, "in a manner adapted to the needs of the times" (canon 769 CIC/1983), even if their experience has often proven different—further proof of Luhmann's thesis of the counterfacticity of law. This regulation on sermons regulates what is self-evident. Adding to this, it has virtually no justiciable content. The legal subjects' potential approval does not therefore provide these legal norms with any recognition which might be of help in supporting the wider acceptance of canon law. The above-mentioned examples and many others might help to illustrate, on the one hand, that most canonical norms are not in question. On the other hand, however, they show that canon law cannot, or cannot consistently, bank on this fact to solve its problem of recognition. If the recognition of legal norms is not based on their explicit approval, then it is poorly suited to stabilising the legitimacy of the entire legal order, particularly when this order increasingly finds itself under attack as is the case with canon law. And if core regulations, such as constitutional law, which help to structure the church, fail to find approval, then the approval of minor regulations is only of minor value for the issue of recognition. Canon law, in many of the local churches around the globe, has a problem of recognition that is centred in one way or another on the structure of the church as constituted by its constitutional law. It is here that doubts start to crystallise about whether the ecclesiastical legal order is worthy of recognition.

---

[84] See Hecke (2017, p. 46).

5.2.3 Revelation and Nature

The power issue also comes into play here. Modern legal subjects are suspicious of law based on mere power. Most individuals receive law that is too obviously based on power alone with scepticism. In this respect, it is particularly problematic that the official church tends to justify canon law with the help of validity reasons which in modernity test the sociological limits of legitimacy. Official legal theory differentiates canon law into the law of revelation ("*ius divinum positivum*"), natural law ("*ius divinum naturale*"), and mere ecclesiastical law ("*ius mere ecclesiasticum*"). This is challenging because all of the validity reasons behind these laws can be interpreted as well-concealed power arguments. The acceptance of law based on revelation and nature is called into question because neither revelation nor nature provides norms that are equally convincing to all members of contemporary legal communities. Whoever invokes revelation and nature in plural societies is ultimately destined to use a power argument to provide an overarching standard doctrine which accommodates what is ordered by revelation and what is naturally just. Thus, from a pluralist point of view, revelation and nature frequently serve as a veil for power as a validity argument of the law. Admittedly, the question arises whether this problem affects the church to the same degree. Just because revelation and nature are unsuitable as validity grounds for the law of plural groups does not mean they are equally unsuitable for more homogeneous and uniform groups, such as faith communities. If a group reaches a consensus about what is divinely ordained or can accept natural law on the basis of common conceptions of nature, then any law founded in this way may indeed have significant persuasive power for this group. Taking Ferdinand Tönnies's differentiation between societies and communities,[85] we can argue that whilst basing the validity of law on revelation and nature might not be relevant for modern societies, communities might remain open to them. Hence, a community might not merely produce law based on a shared belief in what accords to revelation or nature, but might also expect this law to find the group members' wide acknowledgement. If we follow this train of thought, it seems fair to assume that in church revelation and nature might indeed serve as convincing grounds for canon law insofar as they derive from a shared faith and a shared understanding of the naturally just. Canonical laws based on a shared understanding of revelation and nature therefore have an excellent chance of finding the church members' recognition. Yet contrary to what one might expect, we may perceive that many ecclesiastical norms based on revelation and nature are at present struggling with problems of recognition, such as norms on the role of the hierarchy or the role of women in church. This indicates that official concepts of revelation and nature which serve as the foundation of ecclesiastical norms are not based on concepts of faith and morals shared by the whole community. Recognition problems therefore imply that the church is actually more plural than one might believe it to be. The church members, it seems, have rather different understandings of what constitutes revelation and

---

[85] See Tönnies (2001).

nature and what accords with them in a normative sense. This phenomenon is currently playing out within many local churches. It is becoming ever more difficult to argue that society is diverse, but that the church is a homogeneous and uniform group. In fact, local churches are directly affected by the dynamics of pluralisation issuing from contemporary societies. Their members are members of a pluralist society, too, and are of course not immune to its influence. They bring pluralist ideas of the social and divergent normative ideas into the church. As a consequence, the local churches are increasingly becoming communities in which, despite the unifying bond of a shared faith, plural concepts exist about what accords with God's will for the church and for humanity. This growing presence of plural opinions about the normative meaning of revelation and nature in the churches is increasing pressure on the official church to justify those of its laws which are based on revelation and nature. Many church members are increasingly doubting the plausibility of the magisterium's and the legislator's interpretation of revelation and nature as reflected in the current law of revelation and in natural law. With regard to the law of revelation, they have come to doubt whether those norms which the magisterium and the legislator derive from revelation truly concord with God's will for God's church. For the church as a community based on revelation and a shared faith derived from revelation, this is in fact a dangerous situation. Fundamental disagreement on matters of the revelation is no minor issue. It may undermine the community and damage the integrity of the church. It is therefore particularly serious if dissent on law based on revelation turns out not to be a momentary difference of opinion, but an irreversible divergence between the legislator and many legal subjects. If fully irreconcilable, fundamental differences in matters of the revelation and of the law of revelation may divide the church. It is therefore no coincidence that some canonists have gone to considerable lengths *not* to interpret the statement contained in the Apostolic Exhortation *Ordinatio Sacerdotalis*,[86] which once and for all rejects the possibility of women's ordination, as part of the law of revelation.[87] Interpreting it as such would be evidence of an insurmountable gulf between the magisterium's teachings about revelation as positivised in canon law (see canon 1024 CIC/1983) and the view of many church members, particularly in the churches of the global North. However, the Congregation for the Doctrine of the Faith's 1995 "Response to a Posed Doubt concerning the Teaching Contained in 'Ordinatio Sacerdotalis'" supports the position that excluding women from ordination is indeed closely connected with the revelation and has to be considered as part of the deposit of faith. Not long ago, the Prefect of the Congregation for the Doctrine of the Faith reaffirmed this view.[88] This shows that there is major disagreement about core constitutional norms of the church which the magisterium derives from revelation. The validity of norms based on revelation is therefore in dispute, which likewise affects doctrinal and legal norms.

---

[86] *Acta Apostolicae Sedis, 86*, 545–548.

[87] On this debate see Lüdecke (1996), 161–211; Bier and Demel (2017), 4–5.

[88] See Ladaria (2018).

Similarly, many Catholics are no longer taking rulings by the magisterium about what is right according to nature at face value. The magisterium has in no small measure contributed to this state of affairs. The view presented by the papal magisterium in 1968 in the Encyclical *Humanae vitae*[89] on the immorality of artificial contraception marked for the churches of the northern hemisphere a turning point in the process of alienation between the magisterium and many church members. It sowed fundamental doubts, especially in Central Europe and North America, about the magisterium's narrow and Neo-Scholastic understanding of nature.[90] Today, many church members of the northern hemisphere no longer accept many of those ecclesiastical norms which are grounded in natural law. 2010 and 2021 surveys of German Catholics found that 85% (in 2010) or 82% (in 2021) of respondents rejected the official ecclesiastical teaching on contraception (only 9% or 10% approved of the official position), 79% or 77% were critical of the official teaching on sexual ethics (only 13% in both years found it acceptable), and 68% or 75% rejected the church's official position on homosexuality (17% or 15% approved).[91] In 2005, William D'Antonio, James Davidson, Dean Hoge, and Mary Gautier conducted a survey of Catholics in the United States called *American Catholics Today*, which yielded the following results:[92] 42% of Catholics questioned believed that each individual should decide for themselves whether to remarry after divorce; 22% considered the official ecclesiastical position relevant; 35% considered both positions—their individual belief and the official teaching—to be significant. In the case of artificial contraception, 13% considered the magisterium's position to be more important, while 61% considered their own opinion more important; here too, 27% considered both positions as relevant. 25% felt the magisterium's position had a role to play in deciding to have an abortion or not, while 44% believed this issue to be an individual decision; 30% considered a combination of the personal and magisterial positions to be correct. Practiced homosexuality was seen by 46% as a personal decision; 24% followed the magisterial opinion; 28% were open to both views. Extra-marital sex was seen by 47% as a private matter; 22% viewed it as a matter in which the magisterium's teaching was key; 30% considered both positions significant. As these findings refer to moral norms one may argue that they reveal little about the acceptance of law. Nevertheless, widespread doubts about the magisterium's teaching on natural law have obvious consequences for positive law based on natural law, too. Accordingly, we may assume that laws cannot hope for much acceptance on the part of the legal subjects if they are based on a magisterial interpretation of nature that the church members find unconvincing.

---

[89] *Acta Apostolicae Sedis*, *60*, 481–503.

[90] Eg Ebertz (2010, p. 327).

[91] See MDG-Trendmonitor (2010, p. 65; 2021, p. 51).

[92] See D'Antonio et al. (2007, p. 96).

Hence, today, we can no longer expect the church members to accept canonical laws merely because the legislator connects them with divine law. Grounding law in revelation and nature is therefore evidently as problematic in church as it is in plural societies. As the church becomes an increasingly plural community, it faces similar challenges to plural societies in how to justify its law. In essence, there is no unanimity among church members about what is naturally right or what derives from revelation normatively. So it should come as no surprise when church members' suspicions are aroused when ecclesiastical authorities, in the absence of any consensus on what is right and just according to revelation and nature, issue sovereign decrees about how to understand revelation and nature and binding norms based on their findings. The church members might come to suspect that these norms are not actually based on revelation and nature at all, but on power. The result is that the very norms of canon law which should in fact integrate the church, as they are supposed to express a shared normative understanding among church members about what is right according to revelation and nature, will end up doing the very opposite. Many church members contest them as absolutist expressions of power and refuse to acknowledge them as legitimate law of the church.

5.2.4 Lacking a Consistent Rule of Law

Certainly, it is not a problem per se to base the validity of legal norms on power. As shown in Sect. 5.1, modern individuals do not object to power as a validity reason of law in itself. However, they do tend to object to power that has not been legitimised. Applying Max Weber's criteriology to canon law, one may assume that power is considered legitimate in church if it is justified by charisma, tradition, or the law. To this day, power in church is indeed sometimes legitimised by charisma. Many Catholics view the current pope as a charismatic leader and recognise his power because they feel an emotional attachment to him. Thus, they tend to observe norms posed by him because they identify with him. We may likewise discover elements of traditional authority in church. The offices of the pope and of the bishops, with their patriarchal and patrimonial structure, encourage church members to find power in church legitimate for reasons of tradition. However, many present-day church members are no longer convinced by power justified by mere tradition because they, just as other members of plural societies, have developed a modern distrust of mere traditional justifications of power. The idea that tradition is sufficient justification for power to become legitimate authority has been widely replaced by the expectation that power be limited by law and bound by legal procedures. The rule of law as an instrument for curbing power and thus creating legitimate authority through the restriction of pure power has widely replaced charismatic and traditional approaches for legitimating power. We may therefore expect many church members to connect their recognition of ecclesiastical authority with the demand that power in church is subject to the law and to legal control. Legitimising power by subjecting it to the law, in any case, requires more than merely restricting power somehow with the help of law. According to an understanding which is common in democratic societies, the legal limitations of power must substantively accord with the rule of law. Certainly, the church is not a state. One might therefore object that it is necessary to restrict power exercised in church to the same extent as power exercised in secular legislation, adjudication, and administration. However, such objections to introducing a substantive rule of law to the church are in fact of little practical help. From a sociological point of view, which studies the conditions under which church members are factually inclined to recognise authority in church, these interventions are of limited value. Catholics who as citizens of modern democratic states have learned to assess the legitimacy of political power according to the rule of law go on to use these criteria to evaluate power in church. Ecclesiastical authorities may criticise them for doing this,[93] but they can do little to stop them. Hence, factually speaking, power in church must submit to standards which accord with common standards of the rule of law to have a chance of being recognised by many church members as legitimate authority. The rule of law in church is therefore subject to similar principles to the rule of law of constitutional states. Many Catholics' expectations with regard to the law and its ability to control power in church are virtually identical to those they have of the constitutional state. They demand to see the protection of fundamental rights, especially equality in and before the law, as well as fundamental rights that challenge power, such as freedom of speech and freedom of assembly; they demand that the law limits the exercise of power, for instance through the separation of powers, through elections, and limited terms of office; and they request that the law is constrained by procedures, such as control mechanisms and conditional decision-making programmes;[94] unsurprisingly, we may discover all of these demands when studying the documents of the current so-called "Synodal Path" which the church has taken in Germany to reform the German churches.[95] A church which follows these principles increases the chance of its members, who have been socialised under the democratic rule of law, accepting power in church as legitimate authority. In the following section I will analyse whether and to what extent these principles are already present in current canon law.

5.2.5   Protection of Fundamental Rights

The rule of law is based first and foremost on the principle of equality and on guaranteed fundamental rights. This is also the case in the legal order of the church. Canon law relies on equality in and before the law. In addition to certain basic obligations, it also provides basic rights which the church members may invoke. The protection of fundamental rights is an element of the canonical rule of law which the

---

[93] Eg Facius et al. (2011).

[94] See Raiser (2007, pp. 269–270).

[95] See www.synodalerweg.de/dokumente-reden-und-beitraege#c6239. Accessed 3 October 2021.

ecclesiastical legislator guarantees. Nevertheless, it is evident that the degree of protection the church can offer falls short of what citizens are accustomed to in democratic constitutional states. This becomes visible if we examine a complex of fundamental rights that is important for limiting power under the rule of law, namely freedom of opinion and freedom of speech. Canon law defines both freedom of opinion as well as freedom of expression more narrowly than state law; we may make parallel observations with regard to freedom of religion (see canons 209 §1, 748 §1 CIC/1983) and with regard to freedom of scientific research (see canon 218 CIC/1983). First, freedom of opinion in church is not completely free, but is restricted by legal norms on the teaching function of the church. Catholics for instance are legally obliged to believe doctrines that are part of the deposit of faith (see canon 750 §1 CIC/1983). They are obliged to adhere to doctrines that are marked by the magisterium as being part of definite teaching, but moreover also obliged to firmly embrace and retain them (see canon 750 §2 CIC/1983). In these matters, the church demands an attitude of assent from its members, which legally restricts the free formation of opinion. With regard to the freedom of expression, Catholics are free to express their opinion in an appropriate manner to the ecclesiastical authorities (see canon 212 §3 CIC/1983), but not without restriction and conditional on their knowledge, their competence, and their position in church. Addressing the ecclesiastical public is lawful only if a public utterance does not attack Catholic faith and morals, is made with due reverence towards the church authorities, and preserves the personal dignity of others. Moreover, speakers must assess the general utility of their statement in advance. The law permits academic theologians to publicly share their expertise. Yet it obliges them to ensure when doing so that they are "observing due submission to the magisterium of the church" (canon 218 CIC/1983). Thus, freedom of opinion and expression in church do not stand alone; instead, the law ties them to the obedience which Catholics owe to the church authorities. However, since it is freedom of expression that enables the public to criticise the exercise of power and the authorities in possession of that power— which is highly relevant from the point of view of the rule of law—this restriction is problematic for the legitimation of ecclesiastical power. If the law bars public criticism and widely restricts the right of church members to criticise ecclesiastical authorities, it deprives free speech and public debate of much of its potential to legitimise the authorities' power. Ladislas Orsy's complaint that the ecclesiastical legislator does not even solicit the church members' consent to the law, and instead relies on a premodern structure of command and obedience,[96] is also of relevance in the light of the legitimation of power. This strategy of limiting freedom of opinion and expression by commanding obedience is widely unsuccessful. But it is also counterproductive with regard to the legitimation of ecclesiastical power. By suppressing dissenting voices, command and obedience feeds the church members' suspicion that ecclesiastical power could in fact be illegitimate insofar as it seeks to evade public scrutiny. With regard to the protection of fundamental rights and its

---

[96] See Orsy (1980, p. 42; 1992, pp. 49, 100).

legitimising significance for the rule of law in church, one may therefore conclude: such protection exists, but to a lesser extent than in state law. This is not only a problem in itself; it is also problematic primarily because restricting fundamental rights in church as in the case of freedom of expression undermines precisely those processes of legitimation that church authorities need in order to be recognised as legitimate.

5.2.6   Abundant Ecclesiastical Power

Ecclesiastical authorities are at present subject to only a few of the typical instruments which the rule of law applies to limit power. Limited terms of office are virtually non-existent. The office of the pope is a life-long position, even if Benedict XVI recently made it clear that, in practice, relinquishing office is an option. Diocesan bishops are required to offer their resignation upon reaching the age of 75 (see canon 401 §1 CIC/1983). Nevertheless, this does not equate to the limitation of tenure in office in the constitutional sense, which regularly limits time in office to a predetermined period. Similar observations apply to the principle of election. Certainly, election plays a role in the attainment of high-ranking ecclesiastical offices, foremost in the case of the pope and also in some regions where the diocesan bishops obtain their office by election—and not in the regular way of free papal appointment (see canon 377 §1 CIC/1983). However, it is not the ordinary church members who participate in these elections, as one might expect in a democracy, but selected representatives of the church hierarchy. The cardinals are responsible for electing the pope; in Germany the cathedral chapters elect the bishops. It would therefore be erroneous to speak of elections in a democratic sense in church. The church is not a democracy. I do not want to address this observation in light of its associated institutional legitimacy issues. However, it is important to note the sociological consequences deriving from the non-democratic constitution of the church with regard to the legitimation of the officeholders' power. As elections in church do not accord with the rule of law with regard to democratic standards, the election of church officials cannot claim to produce the same presumption of legitimacy as democratic elections. We may not therefore expect them to fully convince church members who have been socialised in the rule of law.

Another important aspect of the rule of law is that legislation, adjudication, and administration are bound by the law. This is a widely accepted principle of constitutional theory. In this light, the absolutist conception of hierarchical government in church raises a number of questions. After all, the structure of the church is still based on models of governance from the early modern period, as Norbert Lüdecke and Georg Bier remind us, "The law of the church is phenomenologically and structurally understood in analogy to the law of the state, although not of the contemporary democratic constitutional state, but of the modern absolutist authoritarian state."[97] Accordingly, the diocesan bishops have considerable power, including powers of legislation, adjudication, and administration for their dioceses. Nevertheless their power is also limited, as the Code states, "A diocesan bishop in the diocese entrusted to him has all ordinary, proper, and immediate power which is required for the exercise of his pastoral function except for cases which the law or a decree of the Supreme Pontiff reserves to the supreme authority or to another ecclesiastical authority" (canon 381 §1 CIC/1983). Episcopal power is abundant but restricted in two respects. On the one hand it is functionally limited to the power necessary to exercise the episcopal ministry; on the other hand, it is restricted with regard to competing authorities, insofar as episcopal power is limited by universal canon law and the authority which the law accords to other authorities. Therefore, diocesan bishops are in fact bound by general canon law. The case of the pope is somewhat different. He is a monarch at the head of the church who is bound by morals only and acts autonomously without being bound or restricted by the law.[98] The pope has at his disposal "supreme, full, immediate, and universal ordinary power in the church, which he is always able to exercise freely" (canon 331 CIC/1983). This indicates that the pope's power is largely unlimited, something which is also evident in ecclesiastical procedural law, which exempts papal acts from judicial review, following the ancient maxim "The First See is judged by no one" (canon 1404 CIC/1983). Due to this, the question arises as to whether and to what extent the pope is bound by general canon law. He is certainly limited in his official conduct by divine law—canonists agree on this. But I have also already pointed out that divine law only takes on a justiciable form through the exercise of official power. In this respect, divine law proves, on closer inspection, to restrict the pope's power to a significantly lesser degree than one might initially assume. After all, the pope himself is entitled to define what constitutes divine law. Purely ecclesiastical laws bind him to an even lesser extent. Norbert Lüdecke and Georg Bier provide a lucid explanation of the issue. They believe that the pope is not bound by purely human canon law as he is *dominus canonum*. As a master of canon law he is above the law. He is therefore free to override the law whenever he deems it necessary.[99] However, canonist Hubert Socha objected to this reading of the pope's power.[100] He interposed that the pope's wide-ranging powers do not give him the option of wielding his power arbitrarily. The pope, as Socha states, is bound by canonical procedural law when acting as a judge, in a form of self-commitment. Nevertheless, this does not alter the fact that it is up to the pope whether to abrogate and reformulate laws he himself or one of his predecessors has made. Lüdecke and Bier, however, reject Socha's defence of papal arbitrariness. They admit that

---

[97] Original quote, "Das kirchliche Recht wird phänomenologisch und strukturell analog zum Recht im Staat verstanden, gleichwohl nicht dem des modernen demokratischen Rechtsstaates, sondern dem des neuzeitlichen absolutistischen Obrigkeitsstaates", Lüdecke and Bier (2012, p. 26).

[98] See Lüdecke and Bier (2012, p. 26).

[99] See Lüdecke and Bier (2012, p. 118); see also Bier (2015, p. 244); Beal (2011, p. 149).

[100] See Socha (1991, p. 5 no. 13).

arbitrariness and pure self-interest should not determine a papacy, insofar as the office of the pope obliges the pope to act consistently in accordance with the rules of his office. The pope is therefore morally bound by the duties of his office, as well as by the revelation and the tradition of the church.[101] However, as Lüdecke and Bier also slyly remark, "What is required by the papal office is decided by the pope himself in his responsibility before God."[102] This includes the pope's freedom to decide how and in what way to limit his own freedom to act. Georg Bier consequently speaks of a papal "Kompetenz-Kompetenz" ("competence-competence") as the pope's authority to determine which authority actually derives from the papal power.[103] From a sociological perspective we may therefore note that the pope is not bound by general canon law. Regardless of whether canonists agree on this issue or not—there is no legal authority that can prevent the pope from disregarding existing law. The pope may be morally bound to observe the law of the church, but if he chooses not to, he will face no legal consequences for breaking the law. If we recall Max Weber's theory of the legitimation of power by law, this raises major questions with regard to the legitimation of power in church. Insofar as the highest ecclesiastical authority is not bound by law, it cannot base its legitimacy on the rule of law. The legitimacy of papal power vis-à-vis the members of the church thus succeeds either through charisma, as seems to be the case with Francis for many Catholics, or through tradition—or it does not succeed at all. Inasmuch as modernity relies first and foremost on the rule of law, it is therefore unsurprising that many church members doubt the legitimacy of papal power when a less charismatic pope is at the head of the church than the current officeholder.

5.2.7   Controlling Decision Making

If we examine the decision-making programmes of the church, we may find that decision-making power in church is limited only by a few procedural rules. This is most evident with regard to legislation. In secular law, and particularly in civil law traditions with their strong focus on statute law, constitutional legislative procedures play a key role. Insofar as canon law is civil law and attaches key importance to statute law, one might actually expect highly formalised legislative procedures in church as well. Contrary to expectation, however, sophisticated procedural regulations are largely absent, as Simon Hecke has noted.[104] Although the Code contains some procedural rules for legislation, such as the need for the legislator's promulgation of ecclesiastical laws in order for them to come into force (see canons 7, 8

---

[101] See Lüdecke and Bier (2012, p. 118).

[102] Original quote, "Was vom Amt des Papstes her gefordert ist, entscheidet der Papst in Verantwortung vor Gott", Lüdecke and Bier (2012, p. 118).

[103] See Bier (2015, p. 245).

[104] See Hecke (2017, pp. 110–111).

CIC/1983), or the regulation that diocesan bishops when acting as legislators for their particular churches have to exercise legislative power themselves—hence, have to issue a law themselves and cannot entrust other officeholders with the duty of legislation (see canon 391 §2 CIC/1983)—, the law does not set out a comprehensive, predefined legislative process. This does not mean, of course, that legislation comes into being informally, as the Code's provisions on promulgation make clear. However, the fact that canon law does not prescribe a formal legislative procedure and leaves it up to the ecclesiastical legislators to decide how to draft a law and whom to involve in the process of its creation is an obvious deficit from the perspective of the rule of law. It points once again to the problem mentioned above, namely that to this day an absolutist form of governance has been cultivated in church which sits uncomfortably with many legal subjects' understanding of democratic rule, and is therefore plagued by a deficit of legitimacy. Because canon law is largely silent on procedural formalities, it does little to support the recognition of ecclesiastical legislation. This has a negative knock-on effect for the recognition of canon law as the result of ecclesiastical legislation. It is helpful to refer to Niklas Luhmann's considerations on programming and programmed decisions once more to better understand why the lack of formal procedures and the insufficient separation of powers are problematic in church. Luhmann argues that programming and programmed decisions differ insofar as they are dissimilarly open to control. Assessing the correctness of programmed decisions is comparatively easy because their correctness is judged on the basis of the existing programmes. One may assume the correctness of a decision if it proves to be the correct result of a programme. This poses a problem in church, insofar as sophisticated programmes are largely absent, as I have stated. However, even if these programmes existed, doubt may still be cast on the correctness of the programmes themselves. Assessing the correctness of programmes is in any case virtually impossible, as Luhmann finds. They are the result of programming decisions, and these are extremely hard to control, as Luhmann observes, noting, "Programming the law takes place ... under so much complexity that this in fact excludes adequate information and control of the correctness of decision making."[105] It is not even possible to use existing norms to prove the rationality of programming decisions, because this would require pre-existing programming. As a consequence, as Luhmann finds, it is only possible to prove the correctness of programming decisions hypothetically. And it remains essential to allow for a change of programming decisions whenever they transpire to require adjustment.[106] This possibility of keeping programming decisions open to change depends, however, on several factors. It depends inter alia on the precondition that a legal community may deal with political conflicts in an institutionally regulated way in order to prevent these conflicts from becoming sclerotic. Luhmann

---

[105] Original quote, "Die Programmierung von Recht erfolgt ... unter so hoher Komplexität, daß zureichende Information und kontrollierbare Richtigkeit des Entscheidens praktisch ausgeschlossen sind", Luhmann (1970, p. 190).

[106] See Luhmann (1970, p. 190).

speaks of the "institutionalisation of political conflict as a permissible, system-compatible, and regulated normal process".[107] This is particularly problematic with regard to the church, which has hardly any predefined structures for political conflict management at all. One might find that ecclesiastical decision-makers are putting the presumption of correctness of their programming decisions at stake insofar as they neither grant the ecclesiastical legal community an insight into these procedures nor provide them with institutional procedures to process political conflicts in church in cases of doubt about these procedures.

5.2.8 Excluding the Laypeople

A further complicating factor confronting the church is how it deals with representation in its function of legitimising decisions. I have already referred to Luhmann's observation that modern-day individuals tend to accept decisions only if the structures of decision making in principle allow for a consensus and do not exclude anyone in advance. This presupposes that every rational perspective has its legitimate share in the debates and that therefore no point of view may be declared a priori as irrelevant for the decision. Hanna Pitkin's studies on political representation accommodate this principle by stating that those who are affected by a decision must be represented by the decision-making body in an appropriate manner, which first of all entails that those who compose the decision-making bodies do not omit social groups deliberately from the composition of those bodies whose decisions pertain to them. If decision making fulfils these conditions, decisions stand a fair chance of finding widespread acceptance. However, this finding poses a problem for decisions in church, insofar as it is mostly clerics who serve as members of ecclesiastical decision-making bodies. This is most obvious with regard to legislation. In the 1983 reform of the Code of Canon Law, the last comprehensive legislative project to affect the whole church, the preparatory bodies, the so-called *coetus*, were mainly composed of clerics, while the decision-making body, the Reform Commission of the Code, was composed exclusively of clerics, namely cardinals and bishops. Lays were given no or next to no say at all—as usual in high-level decision making in church. This is no coincidence, but is ensured by canon law, which reserves the exercise of ecclesiastical power to the clergy first and foremost by reserving offices endowed with the power of governance to clerics (see canon 274 §1 CIC/1983), allowing clerics alone to obtain offices responsible for legislation, adjudication, and administration in church. As a consequence, ecclesiastical decision-making bodies frequently do not represent the laity in the sense of Pitkin's "standing for",[108] in which the representatives stand for the key

---

[107] Original quote, "Institutionalisierung des politischen Konflikts als eines zulässigen, systemgerechten und regulierten Normalvorgangs", Luhmann (1970, p. 190).

[108] Pitkin (1967, p. 60).

characteristics of those they represent. In the last reform of the Code, all church members were formally represented by the episcopal members of the reform commission. However, as being a layperson may count as an essential characteristic of church members, this formal representation is not representation in the substantial sense of Pitkin's "standing for." It is therefore fair to say that the lays are either underrepresented or not represented at all in ecclesiastical decision making. This is a major disadvantage of ecclesiastical decisions with regard to their chances of finding the lays' acceptance.

One may make a similar observation with regard to adjudication when studying the staffing of ecclesiastical tribunals. According to current canon law, ecclesiastical single judges must always be clerics (see canons 1421 §1, 1673 §4 CIC/1983), even though the bishops' conference may give permission for collegiate tribunals to consist of two clerics and one lay person (see canon 1421 §2 CIC/1983). This evidently does not give blanket permission to tribunals to rely on lay judges. Their participation is dependent on the vote of the bishops' conferences, and only in a handful of countries have the bishops' conferences seen fit to entrust laypeople with such responsibilities. Moreover, it remains essential that a cleric presides over a collegiate tribunal (see canon 1426 §2 CIC/1983). However, as I mentioned in Sect. 3.2.15, in his *Motu proprio Mitis Iudex Dominus Iesus* Francis introduced the option of appointing two lays to act as judges in matrimonial matters in three-member collegiate tribunals which are presided over by a cleric even without a vote of approval by the bishops' conference (see canon 1673 §3 CIC/1983).[109] This demonstrates that co-decision making by the laity in ecclesiastical adjudication is being extended slowly but surely. Despite this progress, the law systematically excludes lays from penal proceedings against clerics dealing with allegations of sexual abuse, in which only priests may serve as judges, promotors of justice, and notaries.[110] Hence, we cannot consider the current situation as a fair representation of the lays in Pitkin's sense of representation as "standing for," as long as judges are selected based on their ecclesiastical status. This practice intentionally underrepresents laypeople in ecclesiastical adjudication and systematically prevents them from presiding over tribunals. From a sociological point of view, this kind of targeted marginalisation of a group may have a counterproductive effect on the acceptance of adjudication and the decisions made by ecclesiastical tribunals. From a sociological perspective, it is unrealistic to expect the laity to support decisions in which they are only marginally or not at all involved, while their participation in the decision-making process was already largely or completely excluded from the outset. The a priori exclusion of the numerically largest group of church members means that canon law does not support presumptions of consensus in the Luhmannian sense. As a consequence, Simon Hecke understandably notes that it is now virtually impossible to claim the existence of a fictitious consensus among the church members with

---

[109] *Acta Apostolicae Sedis, 107,* 961.

[110] See Congregation for the Doctrine of the Faith (2021, articles 13 and 20).

regard to current canon law.[111] At best, there might be a consensus in selected sections of the church, perhaps among some members of the clergy, but there is no longer even a presumed consensus on the law throughout the church as a whole.

In light of these findings, the strategy used by some church officials of hiding issues of power behind the language of "service" seems rather expedient. It is currently virtually impossible to respond to questions about the legitimacy of ecclesiastical power and the law that springs from it in a way that most legal subjects with a democratic upbringing and from liberal constitutional states might find acceptable. Theologian and sociologist Karl Gabriel notes that the church at present still falls below the minimum of legal certainty and participation which modern-day individuals expect of organisations seeking to recruit and retain their dedicated members.[112] At present, the dual relation between power and the law—the generation of power through the law and the generation of law through power—creates a self-sustaining vicious circle in church which proves to be immune to strategies of legitimation which follow the rule of law. The growth of anti-juridism and the crisis of leadership in church are therefore not two separate challenges facing the church in contemporary times, but are actually two facets of the same problem. They result from the view held by many ecclesiastical legal subjects that in the church illegitimate power produces law and illegitimate law recreates power. One may therefore frequently understand criticism of canon law as a criticism of power. Church members refuse to recognise a legal system that, in the view of many, arises from the illegitimate exercise of power. And they refuse to accept power which is recreated and established by that legal system.

Bibliography

Baer, S. (2021). *Rechtssoziologie: Eine Einführung in die interdisziplinäre Rechtsforschung* (4th ed.). Nomos.

Beal, J. P. (2011). Something there is that Doesn't love a law: Canon law and its discontents. In M. J. Lacey & F. Oakley (Eds.), *The crisis of authority in Catholic modernity* (pp. 135–154). Oxford University Press.

Beckermann, A. (2012). Die realistischen Voraussetzungen der Konsenstheorie von J. Habermas (1972). In A. Beckermann (Ed.), *Aufsätze, vol 2: Erkenntnistheorie, Philosophie und Wissenschaft, Willensfreiheit* (pp. 9–28). Universitätsbibliothek Bielefeld.

Benedict XVI. (2010). Apostolic letter issued *Motu proprio omnium in mentem*, on several amendments to the Code of Canon Law, 26 October 2009. *Acta Apostolicae Sedis, 102*, 8–10.

Bier, G. (2015). Einsame Spitze: Die innerkirchliche Rechtsstellung des Papstes. In R. Heinzmann (Ed.), *Kirche—Idee und Wirklichkeit: Für eine Erneuerung aus dem Ursprung* (pp. 229–250). Herder.

Bier, G., & Demel, S. (2017). Priesterweihe für Frauen: Ist die Tür endgültig zu? *Kirchenbote: Wochenzeitung für das Bistum Osnabrück, 39*, 4–5.

---

[111] See Hecke (2017, p. 105).

[112] See Gabriel (2013, p. 13).

Bucher, R. (2018). Einige pastoraltheologische Probleme des Kirchenrechts. *Lebendige Seelsorge, 69*, 160–164.

Congregation for Divine Worship and the Discipline of the Sacraments. (2017). Circular letter to Bishops on the bread and wine for the Eucharist, 15 June 2017. Retrieved June 21, 2021, from www.vatican.va/roman_curia/congregations/ccdds/documents/rc_con_ccdds_doc_20170615_lettera-su-pane-vinoeucaristia_en.html

Congregation for the Doctrine of the Faith. (1995). Response to a Posed Doubt concerning the Teaching Contained in "Ordinatio Sacerdotalis", 18 October 1995. Retrieved June 21, 2021, from www.vatican.va/roman_curia/congregations/cfaith/documents/rc_con_cfaith_doc_1 9951028_dubium-ordinatio-sac_en.html

Congregation for the Doctrine of the Faith. (2021). Norms on delicts reserved to the Congregation for the Doctrine of the Faith, 11 October 2021. Retrieved May 17, 2022, from www.vatican.va/roman_curia/congregations/cfaith/documents/rc_con_cfaith_doc_20211011_norme-delittiriservaticfaith_en.html

Cotterrell, R. (1984). *The sociology of law: An introduction*. Butterworths.

Coughlin, J. J. (2011). *Canon law: A comparative study with Anglo-American legal theory*. Oxford University Press.

Dammert Bellido, J. (1986). The new Code in an Andean diocese. In J. H. Provost & K. Walf (Eds.), *Canon law—Church reality* (Concilium 185, pp. 110–117). T. & T. Clark.

D'Antonio, W. V., Davidson, J. D., Hoge, D. R., & Gautier, M. L. (2007). *American Catholics today: New realities of their faith and their church*. Rowman and Littlefield.

Dewey, J. (1946). *The public and its problems: An essay in political inquiry*. Gateway Books.

Ebertz, M. N. (2010). Gesellschaftlicher Wandel und Kirche. *Theologie und Glaube, 100*, 319–343.

Facius, G., Kamann, M., & Schmiemann, B. (2011). Erzbischof Woelki: "Die katholische Kirche ist keine Demokratie", 20 August 2011. Retrieved October 16, 2018, from www.welt.de/politik/deutschland/article13554783/Die-katholische-Kirche-istkeine-Demokratie.html

Francis. (2015). Apostolic letter issued *Motu proprio mitis Iudex Dominus Jesus* by which the canons of the Code of Canon Law pertaining to cases regarding the nullity of marriage are reformed, 15 August 2015. *Acta Apostolicae Sedis, 107*, 958–970.

Gabriel, K. (2013). Die Religion der Stunde? Anmerkungen zur Soziologie des gegenwärtigen Katholizismus. *Theologisch-Praktische Quartalsschrift, 161*, 12–19.

Habermas, J. (1996). *Between facts and norms: Contributions to a discourse theory of law and democracy* (W. Rehg, Trans.) The MIT Press.

Hahn, J. (2012a). "Gesetz der Wahrheit": Rechtstheoretische Überlegungen im Anschluss an aktuelle päpstliche Äußerungen zur Rechtsbegründung. Archiv für katholisches Kirchenrecht, 181, 106–128.

Hahn, J. (2012b). Die Ansprache des Papstes im Deutschen Bundestag: Gedankenanstoß für Überlegungen zur Kirchenrechtsbegründung. In G. Essen (Ed.), *Verfassung ohne Grund? Die Rede des Papstes im Bundestag* (Theologie kontrovers, pp. 91–105). Herder.

Hahn, J. (2018). Recht und Realität: Warum sie nicht mit- und nicht ohneinander auskommen. *Lebendige Seelsorge, 69*, 154–159.

Hahn, J. (2019). *Church law in modernity: Toward a theory of canon law between nature and culture* (Cambridge law and Christianity). Cambridge University Press.

Hecke, S. (2017). *Kanonisches Recht: Zur Rechtsbildung und Rechtsstruktur des römisch-katholischen Kirchenrechts*. Springer.

John Paul II. (1994). Apostolic letter *Ordinatio sacerdotalis* on reserving priestly ordination to men alone, 22 May 1994. *Acta Apostolicae Sedis, 86*, 545–548.

Ladaria, L. (2018). Il carattere definitivo della dottrina di "Ordinatio Sacerdotalis", 22 May 2018. Retrieved June 2, 2018, from www.osservatoreromano.va/it/news/il-carattere-definitivo-della-dottrina-di-ordinati

Lucke, D. M. (2010). "Unwissenheit schützt vor Strafe nicht:" Wissen und Wirkung im Recht. In G. Wagner (Ed.), *Kraft Gesetz: Beiträge zur rechtssoziologischen Effektivitätsforschung* (pp. 65–90). Springer.

Lüdecke, N. (1996). Also doch ein Dogma? Fragen zum Verbindlichkeitsanspruch der Lehre über die Unmöglichkeit der Priesterweihe für Frauen aus kanonistischer Perspektive. *Trierer Theologische Zeitschrift, 105*, 161–211.

Lüdecke, N., & Bier, G. (2012). *Das römisch-katholische Kirchenrecht: Eine Einführung* (unter Mitarbeit von B. S. Anuth). Kohlhammer.

Luhmann, N. (1969). *Legitimation durch Verfahren* (Soziologische Texte 66). Luchterhand.

Luhmann, N. (1970). Positivität des Rechts als Voraussetzung einer modernen Gesellschaft. *Jahrbuch für Rechtssoziologie und Rechtstheorie, 1*, 175–202.

Luhmann, N. (2004). *Law as a social system* (Oxford socio-legal studies, F. Kastner, R. Nobles, D. Schiff & R. Ziegert, Eds., K. A. Ziegert, Trans.). Oxford University Press.

Luhmann, N. (2014). *A sociological theory of law* (M. Albrow, Ed., E. King-Utz & M. Albrow, Trans.). Routledge.

Machura, S. (2010). Rechtssoziologie. In G. Kneer & M. Schroer (Eds.), *Handbuch Spezielle Soziologien* (pp. 379–392). Springer.

MDG-Trendmonitor. (2010). *Religiöse Kommunikation 2010, Kommentarband I: Erkenntnisse zur Situation von Kirche und Glaube sowie zur Nutzung medialer und personaler Informations- und Kommunikationsangebote der Kirche im Überblick. Ergebnisse repräsentativer Befragungen unter Katholiken sowie der Gesamtbevölkerung* (im Auftrag der MDG Medien-Dienstleistung GmbH durchgeführt vom Institut für Demoskopie Allensbach in Zusammenarbeit mit Sinus Sociovision, Heidelberg). MDG Medien-Dienstleistung GmbH.

MDG-Trendmonitor. (2021). *Religiöse Kommunikation 2020/21. Einstellungen, Zielgruppen, Botschaften und Kommunikationskanäle* (im Auftrag der MDG Medien-Dienstleistung GmbH durchgeführt vom Institut für Demoskopie Allensbach, Sinus Markt- und Sozialforschung GmbH). Herder.

Möllers, C. (2020). *The possibility of norms: Social practice beyond morals and causes*. Oxford University Press.

Müller, H. (1978). *Das Gesetz in der Kirche "zwischen" amtlichem Anspruch und konkretem Vollzug: Annahme und Ablehnung universalkirchlicher Gesetze als Anfrage an die Kirchenrechtswissenschaft*. Minerva.

Orsy, L. M. (1980). The interpreter and his art. *The Jurist, 40*, 27–56.

Orsy, L. M. (1992). *Theology and canon law: New horizons for legislation and interpretation*. Liturgical Press.

Paul VI. (1968). Encyclical *Humanae vitae* on the regulation of birth, 25 July 1968. *Acta Apostolicae Sedis, 60*, 481–503.

Pitkin, H. F. (1967). *The concept of representation*. University of California Press.

Raiser, T. (2007). *Grundlagen der Rechtssoziologie* (4th ed.). UTB.

Rehbinder, M. (2014). *Rechtssoziologie: Ein Studienbuch* (8th ed.). C. H. Beck.

Röhl, K. F. (1987). *Rechtssoziologie: Ein Lehrbuch*. Heymann.

Rüthers, B. (2005). *Rechtstheorie: Begriff, Geltung und Anwendung des Rechts* (Grundrisse des Rechts, 2nd ed.). C. H. Beck.

Schreiter, R. J. (1985). *Constructing local theologies* (Foreword by Edward Schillebeeckx). Orbis Books.

Searle, J. R. (2010). *Making the social world: The structure of human civilization*. Oxford University Press.

Socha, H. (1991). Commentary on canon 135. In *Münsterischer Kommentar zum Codex Iuris Canonici unter besonderer Berücksichtigung der Rechtslage in Deutschland, Österreich und der Schweiz* (K. Lüdicke, Ed., loose-leaf collection, 15th supplementary sheets). Wingen.

Tönnies, F. (2001). *Community and civil society* [1887] (J. Harris, Ed., J. Harris & M. Hollis, Trans.). Cambridge University Press.

Weber, M. (1978). *Economy and society: An outline of interpretive sociology* (G. Roth & C. Wittich, Eds.). University of California Press.

Chapter 6
The Effectiveness of the Law

Abstract Laws are effective when individuals abide by them or, alternatively, when they do not, but have to face legal sanctions for their non-compliance. The effectiveness of canon law in that respect is partially weak. Whilst the constitutional norms of the church are rather effective for structuring the church, laws tend to be ignored whenever abiding by them depends on the church members' individual decision. Church members tend to ignore their legal duties; the authorities, however, sanction non-compliance only very rarely. Church members also tend to neglect opportunities provided by canon law. To understand the underlying causes of this, it is necessary to study the reasons which motivate individuals to abide by the law in general. The sociology of law particularly relates to the knowledge of the law among members of the legal community, their expectations of sanctions, and their idea of legitimacy. Many canonical laws are rather unknown to church members. The church has no police to coerce offending members to follow the law and rather weak penal authorities to punish them with sanctions. Adding to this is that the degree of normative variance (that is the degree to which the normative ideas of church members differ from the normative ideas expressed in canon law) is exceptionally high with respect to many issues, as canon law does not provide the same legal standard as secular liberal states with regard to individuals' rights and freedom, and is regarded as culturally insensitive and theologically deficient by many church members. They respond to their finding by refusing to abide by the law.

Keywords Effectiveness of the law · Sanctions · Expectations · Legal knowledge · Normative variance

Studying canon law reveals that the sociology of law cannot content itself with simply studying the validity of law, and that it must also examine the conditions which make law effective. Whilst valid law may be mere law on paper, it is the effectiveness of law which brings it to life and allows it to shape the social. When we speak of "effective" law, what we mean is the power of the law to influence individuals and groups. Law is effective when it is powerful enough to impact the social. Accordingly, sociologist Gerhard Wagner describes law as a normativity that is "in force." Law, as he states, is about the enactment of norms, their coming into

© The Author(s) 2022
J. Hahn, *Foundations of a Sociology of Canon Law*,
https://doi.org/10.1007/978-3-031-01791-9_6

force, their being in force as well as their ceasing to be in force. Wagner interprets this "force" metaphor as expressing the power of the law to influence social interaction. He observes that the law, in a similar vein as physical nature, seems to bring about causal effects, as it impels individuals or groups to conform to its norms.[1] Discussing the effectiveness of the law, as Wagner finds, is a response to this quasi-physical experience of legal force. Examining the reality of law sociologically therefore means perceiving law as an effective medium of human social formation. However, as one may also find, law is in fact not always successful in shaping the social. Naomi Mezey observes, echoing Ronald Dworkin's observations in *Law's Empire*, "law is a colony in culture's empire, and sometimes a rather powerless one."[2] Manfred Rehbinder's comment that norms fully detached from facts are in fact dead law points to the same phenomenon.[3] The fact that law aims to shape the social but is not necessarily successful in doing so means it falls to the sociology of law to investigate the conditions, mechanisms, and limits of legal effectiveness. In the following section. I will therefore seek to identify the conditions which make canon law effective, how it achieves its effectiveness, and what causes its effectiveness to fail.

6.1 Effectiveness as Compliance

Law is effective when it affects the legal community. The sociology of law therefore often equates effectiveness with legal compliance: the law shapes reality because its legal subjects adjust their behaviour to comply with it. However, legal subjects regularly fail to comply with the law. This does not pose a significant problem for the effectiveness of the law, as most sociologists find. Nevertheless, at least some compliance is essential for the law to be effective, as Eugen Ehrlich emphasises, "The order of the social machine is continually being interfered with. And though it does its work with much creaking and groaning, the important thing is that it shall continue to function."[4] Yet it is important to note that breaches of law may also contribute to the effectiveness of law, namely in cases in which a legal community sanctions those breaches of law. Hence, we may consider law as effective when it has an effect on the legal community's social reality—be it that the law effectuates some legal subjects' lawful behaviour, or be it that the law effectuates the legal community to sanction breaches of law. Summing up, one may find that legal norms are effective when they are observed at least by some legal subjects or when their violation is sanctioned; and they are ineffective when they are not observed and

---

[1] See Wagner (2010, p. 145).

[2] Mezey (2001, p. 52).

[3] See Rehbinder (2014, p. 2).

[4] Ehrlich (1936, p. 58).

when their non-observance has no consequences, insofar as no one sanctions breaches of law.

6.1.1 Non-Compliance and Causality

Compliance with the law means that the law induces its legal subjects to act in accordance with legal norms. If they comply with a law, this law takes effect, albeit only in cases where the legal norm and their behaviour are causally linked. Sociologist Theodor Geiger points out that it is therefore incorrect to conclude that a legal norm is effective based on the legal subjects' behaviour according with the norm. This is because a certain behaviour can occur independently of a legal norm. Due to this, one can only consider a legal norm to be effective if the legal subjects' compliance actually occurs *because of* the norm.[5] Consequently, sociologist Andreas Diekmann only speaks of the effectiveness of a law in cases where compliance with the law is actually a direct consequence of the law.[6] This is also the case when legal subjects regularly fail to abide by a law, but comply with it occasionally. Infrequent compliance also contributes to the effectiveness of a law, as Diekmann argues, as a law which legal subjects follow occasionally is more effective than laws which completely lack compliance.[7] A legal norm is therefore effective, as Diekmann maintains, if it increases the level of a certain behaviour as mandated by the law, even if only to a small extent. Following on from his observation, we may also find that the legal subjects' behaviour may fully correspond with a legal norm, but the norm is nevertheless ineffective, because it does not in fact cause the lawful behaviour. On the contrary, legal norms which individuals rarely observe are effective because they have an effect on at least some legal subjects' behaviour. The sociology of law therefore broadly shares a gradual perception of the effectiveness of legal norms. Theodor Geiger introduced this idea in his *Vorstudien zu einer Soziologie des Rechts* [*Preliminary Studies on the Sociology of Law*], by noting, "A norm is not per se valid or invalid, but it is valid to a greater or lesser degree. Certain norms are more strictly, others are less strictly followed and enforced."[8] Applying this idea to elucidate the effectiveness of law, Andreas Diekmann proposes, "We may say that a law is effective to the degree by which

---

[5] See Geiger (1964, p. 87).

[6] See Diekmann (1980, p. 23).

[7] See Diekmann (1980, p. 23).

[8] Original quote, "Eine Norm ist nicht schlechthin gültig oder geltungslos, sondern verbindlich in höherem oder geringerem Grad. Gewisse Normen werden strenger, andere minder konsequent befolgt und durchgesetzt", Geiger (1964, p. 72).

the legal measures influence legal subjects' behaviour with respect to the norm stipulated by the law."[9]

6.1.2   Abiding by Legal Norms

Examining the effectiveness of legal norms on the basis of compliance yields a very heterogeneous picture, depending on the type of legal norms involved. There is an obvious difference in what compliance with legal norms means depending on whether these norms are commands, prohibitions, permissions, exemptions, authorisation rules, or procedural norms. With regard to procedural law, a further differentiation may be made by distinguishing between norms which allow for direct state action and norms for decision, as Eugen Ehrlich noted.[10] Many legal norms also simply provide legal subjects with invitations for the legal regulation of their affairs, insofar as they offer institutional frameworks for organising social relationships. They regulate social relations by offering the legal subjects rules and legal institutions which allow them to organise their relations in legal terms. Sociologist Stefanie Eifler illustrates this by citing a number of different examples: property law which provides legal subjects with rules regarding the acquisition of property; marriage law which provides legal subjects with access to the institution of marriage; or inheritance law which provides legal subjects with a reliable procedure for arranging how their inheritance is passed on to their heirs.[11] Abiding by a prohibition by refraining from acting in the prohibited way or complying with a penal norm by not committing a crime is markedly different from accepting such a regulatory mechanism, for example, by entering into a marriage or making a will. Eifler therefore differentiates between compliance with criminal and regulatory laws on the one hand, and compliance with private laws on the other. In the case of criminal and regulatory norms, abiding by the law frequently entails the failure to act in a forbidden or criminal way, be it by acting lawfully or by preventing criminal action. Abiding by private law, on the contrary, frequently means that legal subjects accept the invitation of the law to legally organise their social relationships. When Catholics enter into an ecclesiastical marriage, for example, they are complying with canon law insofar as they are accepting the church's invitation to give their relationship a legal form. Hence, as abiding by the law describes different forms of the legal subjects' behaviour, it comes as no surprise that legal subjects tend to exhibit a different degree of inclination to abide by these norms. Eugen Ehrlich was among the first sociologists of law to point out that it is unrealistic to expect the legal subjects to

---

[9] Original quote, "Wir können sagen, ein Gesetz ist in dem Grade wirksam, in dem die gesetzlichen Maßnahmen das Verhalten gegenüber der vom Gesetz vorgeschriebenen Norm beeinflussen", Diekmann (1980, p. 23).

[10] See Ehrlich (1936, pp. 371–372).

[11] See Eifler (2010, p. 96).

show the same readiness to comply with different types of norms. Ehrlich found prohibitions to be particularly effective in this respect, as he observed, "The commands of the state are most effective when they are exclusively negative, when it is not a matter of compelling people to act but of constraining them to refrain from action".[12] Compulsions to act, on the contrary, often come to nothing. Either people do what the law tells them to do anyway—because a certain instruction of behaviour corresponds with social custom—or they tend not to abide by the commands at all. We may observe a similar effect in church. This is partly due to the fact that canon law does not consistently draw a clear connection between breaches of laws and sanctions. Whilst canon law commands many things, it often does not bother either to invalidate the result of illegal actions or to criminalise the non-compliance with its commands. Canon law thus contains many legal norms which are so-called "imperfect laws" ("*leges imperfectae*") as they forbid or command a certain action but neither render illegal actions invalid nor threaten offenders with sanctions. Canon law, for instance, prohibits suspended clerics from exercising their power of orders (see canon 1333 §1 no. 1 CIC/1983); however, a suspended priest who breaks that law to celebrate the Eucharist does so validly. The law also obliges all Catholics to confess their grave sins at least annually (see canon 989 CIC/1983); yet it does not provide for a penal norm punishing those Catholics who do not abide by that obligation. In these cases where the law fails to sanction non-compliance with its norms either through invalidation of illegal actions or with punishments threatening the offenders, we should not be too surprised if many legal subjects do not follow these norms too closely or do not even abide by them at all. Saying this, I do not want to imply that most suspended priests tend to go on to exercise their power of orders. And neither do I want to suggest that no Catholics go to confession regularly. Most suspended priests cease to administer the sacraments and many Catholics go to confession, yet hardly anybody acts in the way prescribed by the law *because the law tells them so*. Priests who leave the pastoral ministry usually do so after having decided to leave the priesthood to work in other fields. Those Catholics who go to confession regularly or at least once a year tend to do so for spiritual reasons or because they have the habitual practice of going to confession yearly, for example before Easter. Here we may observe the phenomenon to which Andreas Diekmann alluded, namely that behaviour that accords with a legal norm does not necessarily result from that norm. Hence, those suspended priests who refrain from exercising their power of orders and those Catholics who go to confession regularly behave lawfully but they do not contribute much to the effectiveness of canons 1333 §1 no. 1 and 989 CIC/1983.

With regard to civil law, there are two main reasons why legal subjects are inclined to accept institutional invitations made by the law, as Stefanie Eifler observes, namely to prevent or to solve conflict. Eifler elucidates that laws either serve to avoid conflicts before they arise, for example by making a marriage contract

---

[12] Ehrlich (1936, p. 375).

or a will, or to solve existing conflicts.[13] One might add that the creation of order might serve as a similar motive encouraging individuals to use institutions provided by the law to organise their personal affairs. However, the legal subjects' inclination to abide by civil law is naturally less strong than abiding by criminal and regulatory laws. In church we may observe pretty much the same effect. It is interesting, in any case, to take note of the legal subjects' declining inclination to make use of the opportunities provided to them by canon law, particularly in local churches of the northern hemisphere. Evidence for instance shows that the reception of sacraments as institutions to which canon law provides Catholics with regular access has declined significantly in the northern churches since the middle of the twentieth century. The church members are for example less inclined to marry in church today than they were in the 1960s.[14] They are now clearly far less inclined to rely on an ecclesiastical institution to bring order to their private affairs. Bearing in mind Stefanie Eifler's observation that making use of legal opportunities often connects with the wish to avoid conflict, one might also presume that legal subjects in many churches of the global North perceive of the opportunities provided to them by canon law as being ever less capable of preventing or solving any of their conflicts. In Germany a few decades ago, Catholic couples who wanted to live together were expected to marry in church to legitimise their relationship; however, among German Catholics today, even among staunch Catholics, it hardly raises an eyebrow anymore if couples refrain from entering a canonical marriage. In other local churches, in contrast, where fellow Catholics expect couples to live in Christian marriages, the numbers of Catholic marriages are naturally higher, hence ecclesiastical marriage law is more effective.

Norms which allow for direct state action should in principle be very effective, as Eugen Ehrlich maintains.[15] However, as he finds, a lack of "measures taken by the state for supervision and enforcement"[16] frequently compromise their effectiveness too. Ehrlich also points to "the unwillingness, the weakness, or the incapacity of the authorities"[17] to take action. Christoph Möllers observes the same phenomenon, but interprets it in a slightly different light. He challenges the notion that the state is in fact either unable or unwilling to abide by its own laws, by saying that state authorities frequently remain intentionally inactive in order to save economic and normative costs which would occur from attempting to prosecute each and every offence.[18] Ehrlich observes that, in contrast to legal norms which allow for direct state action, compliance with procedural law is generally lower. While procedural law stipulates the authorities' path of decision making, its application does not merely depend on the authorities but, in civil cases, also on the private parties. Yet

---

[13] See Eifler (2010, p. 96).

[14] For the United States see D'Antonio et al. (2007, pp. 57–58).

[15] See Ehrlich (1936, p. 371).

[16] Ehrlich (1936, p. 372).

[17] Ehrlich (1936, p. 372).

[18] See Möllers (2020, p. 245).

private parties are less likely to initiate legal action and only occasionally make use of the judicial or administrative channels made available to them by the state or another authority.[19] The issue of compliance with procedural law is thus completely different with regard to penal procedural law in comparison to civil procedural law. As civil procedures always require legal subjects to avail themselves voluntarily of the possibilities made available to them by the law, civil procedural norms are always less effective than penal procedural norms. The church also presents a differentiated picture in this regard. Canon law empowers ecclesiastical authorities to intervene directly in some matters. In penal cases or other cases which are related to the public good of the church or the salvation of souls, for instance, ecclesiastical tribunals proceed with the investigation of these matters *ex officio* after proceedings have been initiated (see canon 1452 §1 CIC/1983). However, one party must first undertake the initiation of the proceedings in accordance with the principle of party operation. In civil disputes, this must be done by a litigant. In criminal proceedings, a local ordinary initiates the proceedings and hands them over to the promoter of justice who is then to present a *libellus* of accusation to the tribunal and who acts as the prosecuting party *ex officio* in the proceedings (see canon 1721 CIC/1983). Yet, as I said, this only happens if the local ordinary decides, after the conclusion of the preliminary enquiry, to initiate a judicial procedure (see canon 1718 CIC/1983). Undoubtedly, it is at least partly due to this procedural hurdle that the prosecution of penal cases in church often fails to take place even though canonical norms exist which allow the authority direct action. Particularly with regard to the sex abuse cases, many church members and the general public have criticised the fact that the church had widely failed for decades to prosecute abuse cases even though the law allowed for it to do so.[20] Most certainly, whilst this should not be blamed merely on the procedural hurdle of local ordinaries who have to initiate procedures, it did not help with efficiently prosecuting these cases either. In recent years, it is worth noting, the church has made some changes in this regard which attempt to stimulate the prosecution of abuse cases. Since 2016, the legislator has threatened to remove diocesan bishops and others who preside over other ecclesiastical communities from office if they fail to exercise due diligence in the prosecution of abuse cases.[21] It would require empirical clarification to examine whether this new law increases the effectiveness of ecclesiastical penal procedural law in the abuse cases. However, it is not out of the question that this threat has in fact improved the effectiveness of ecclesiastical procedural law and has encouraged bishops and other ecclesiastical authorities to take action whenever they become cognisant of an abuse case, as canon law prescribes (see canon 1717 §1 CIC/1983).

Apart from cases of sexual abuse, ecclesiastical prosecution is rather reluctant to take action with regard to other offences according to canonical penal law and to

---

[19] See Ehrlich (1936, p. 368).

[20] See D'Antonio et al. (2007, pp. 68–75); Hahn et al. (2013, pp. 127–135).

[21] See Francis (2016, article 1 §3). *Acta Apostolicae Sedis, 108*, 716.

initiate ecclesiastical procedures. Whilst ecclesiastical penal law criminalises manifold offences in church, prosecution is nowadays a rarity. Penal proceedings often fail in the first instance because the ordinaries lack the knowledge of a legal violation to initiate legal action. Here, the lack of an obligation to report one's knowledge of a criminal offence, which used to be influential in canon law in former times (see canon 1935 CIC/1917), becomes apparent. This obligation was dropped from the Code in order to accommodate the conciliar desire to decriminalise ecclesiastical life. In addition, the relationship between church and state is probably a contributory factor in the widespread withdrawal of the church from penal prosecution, insofar as the church in most countries may rely upon the state with regard to running a functioning penal system that defends order, peace, and freedom in society, and therefore, unlike in the premodern era, no longer views these functions as its own task. With regard to procedural law, however, this gives rise to the rather peculiar situation that whilst there is a sophisticated ecclesiastical penal law and concomitant penal procedural law, this law is for the most part gradually becoming mere law on paper due to its lack of use. Examining what consequences this peculiar fact—that large chunks of canon law, namely penal law and penal procedural law, are becoming mere law in books—are likely to have for the whole body of canon law would merit a study of its own. I will not follow up on this question in my book, but find it well worth examining what it does to a whole body of law when a significant part of the law becomes dead letter.

In church, the general reluctance to take civil matters to court is even more pronounced than in secular legal life. Party litigation over civil disputes is extremely rare.[22] One reason for this seems to be that legal subjects are largely oblivious to the fact that they can refer civil matters to ecclesiastical tribunals. Adding to this is certainly that ecclesiastical litigation is relatively unpragmatic nowadays. Ecclesiastical tribunals lack the coercive power to oblige the opposing party to participate in the proceedings. If the opposing party does not participate voluntarily, the chances for judicial fact-finding are not good. Moreover, ecclesiastical tribunals lack coercive power to enforce their rulings over reluctant defeated parties, whereas secular courts are more likely to succeed in obtaining justice for the successful party where necessary despite the resistance of the defeated party. Due to this, it seems reasonable for Catholic parties to prefer secular civil courts for the resolution of private disputes. However, in a similar vein—as I stated with regard to penal procedural law which is not fully dead due to the cases of sexual abuse of minors prosecuted by ecclesiastical tribunals—we also have to find that the ordinary contentious trial as the regular procedure for ecclesiastical civil litigations is still law in action (see canons 1501–1655 CIC/1983). This is due to the fact that canonical procedural law also applies the ecclesiastical norms on the ordinary contentious trial in marriage annulment procedures (see canon 1691 §3 CIC/1983). Today, ecclesiastical tribunals deal almost exclusively with marriage annulment proceedings. This has the peculiar

---

[22] Statistics of matters heard before the Roman Rota are provided by Neudecker (2013, pp. 292–293, 623–626).

effect that the norms on the ordinary contentious trial are living procedural law in the annulment proceedings, whilst they are law on paper for the most part in the practically extinct canonical civil procedures. In the churches of the northern hemisphere, the numbers of marriage annulment cases are also in decline. This is no doubt because their marital affairs, if they live in a canonically valid or invalid marriage, are no longer as important to Catholics as they once were. In Germany, marital affairs have retained some importance for church employees due to the continuing threat of dismissal if Catholics remarry after divorce. The current situation, in any case, has become less tense for employees than it used to be. However, even at present, the basic law of ecclesiastical employment in Germany, the so-called "Grundordnung   des   kirchlichen   Dienstes   im   Rahmen   kirchlicher Arbeitsverhältnisse"—which one might roughly translate as "Basic Order of Ecclesiastical Ministry by Employment Contracts"—still states that entering a mere civil marriage without also entering a valid canonical marriage is grounds for dismissal for Catholic employees (see article 5 sect. 2 no. 2 lit. c and d). The usual situations which the legislator has in mind are church employees' civil remarriage after divorce as well as gay marriage. These result in the dismissal of personnel in pastoral and catechetical ministry and others who require for their work an episcopal admission to preach and teach. For the majority of church employees dismissal is only a realistic threat if their remarriage after divorce or their gay marriage may cause scandal in the workplace or potentially damage the reputation of the church. Some divorced church employees therefore take it upon themselves to undergo marriage nullity procedures. The numbers are dwindling though, at least in the northern local churches.

6.1.3   Ratios of Effectiveness

Discussing the effectiveness of legal norms—for example based on levels of compliance, as above—is a complex task. So far, I have merely stated that legal norms usually have some kind of effect, without citing any unit of measurement, a scale, so to speak, which makes it possible to measure the actual effectiveness of legal norms. Whether it is possible and meaningful to draw up a scale of effectiveness for legal norms in any case remains a controversial question in the sociology of law. One approach the empirical sociology of law uses to measure the effectiveness of legal norms is to calculate a ratio of their effectiveness and ineffectiveness. How one may do this and what it tells us is, however, a matter of critical debate. After all, assessing the effectiveness of commands, for instance, means not only quantifying the number of cases in which breaches of law occur, which might be somehow measurable or at least projectable with the help of the numbers of detected breaches of law, but also quantifying the number of cases in which the legal subjects abide by a legal norm. Hubert Rottleuthner and Margret Rottleuthner-Lutter point out the difficulty of attempting this kind of quantification by asking, "how many times was I tempted today to (refrain from) murdering someone?"[23] Sociologist Karl-Dieter Opp observes that compliance and non-compliance with a law is also a matter of opportunity insofar as the frequency of occasions on which individuals may actually abide by a law is also influential for the quantification of compliance.[24] Determining the ineffectiveness of a command, on the other hand, requires recording the number of times legal subjects break a law. While there are usually statistics on how often legal subjects are caught acting unlawfully, the actual number of breaches of law remains shrouded in darkness. Quantifying the effectiveness and ineffectiveness of legal norms is therefore often infeasible. The question also arises as to what information any such quantification provides about the effectiveness of law. Rottleuthner and Rottleuthner-Lutter cite two reasons why quantifying the effectiveness and ineffectiveness of legal norms may prove to be of little relevance for assessing legal practice and the capacity of the law to shape the social. First of all, they doubt that compliance with a legal norm can be equated with its effectiveness. After all, laws are not simply about compliance, they are also about the goals associated with their compliance. Rottleuthner and Rottleuthner-Lutter understand a legal norm to be effective when the legal subjects' compliance serves to fulfil the purposes which the legislator pursues with a law.[25] In some cases, the legal subjects fulfil the purpose of a law by abiding by a legal norm and—as in the case of the prohibition of murder—by not murdering anyone. Similarly, in the case of the canonical obligation to confess grave sins at least annually (see canon 989 CIC/1983), the purpose of the legal norm is directly achieved when church members receive the sacrament of confession at least once a year. However, as this example might also help to show, many legal norms pursue goals which they do not contain in themselves. It is evident that the obligation to confess grave sins at least annually is less about shoving Catholics into the confessional every twelve months and more about encouraging them to establish a spiritual practice of seeking reconciliation with God and the church on a regular basis. Admittedly, it is a matter of discussion whether a legal obligation is the right method for accomplishing this, a query, in any case, which I will not pursue at this point. Nevertheless, the example might help to show that legal norms often aim at goals or pursue purposes which reach far beyond what the law can actually command. The ecclesiastical legislator, who legislated that marriages are not valid in cases of abduction (see canon 1089 CIC/1983) was not so much seeking to reduce the number of abductions for the purpose of marriage, but was rather striving to promote the inner freedom of the spouses, which legislation itself cannot enjoin. In a similar vein, Rottleuthner and Rottleuthner-Lutter emphasise that the legislator cannot direct individuals to improve the situation in the labour market, as a direct obligation would only be

---

[23] Original quote, "wie häufig war ich heute in der Situation, jemanden (nicht) zu ermorden?", Rottleuthner and Rottleuthner-Lutter (2010, p. 22).

[24] See Opp (2010, p. 58).

[25] See Rottleuthner and Rottleuthner-Lutter (2010, p. 23).

appellative.[26] Yet the legislator can create laws which indirectly support an improvement, for instance by issuing laws on protection against unlawful dismissal. According to Rottleuthner and Rottleuthner-Lutter, it follows from this that determining the effectiveness of a particular legal norm is less about its ratio of compliance, and more about the ratio in which this legal norm, directly or indirectly, has an actual influence on the social reality.[27] However, this kind of effectiveness is difficult to nigh on impossible to measure empirically. It is virtually impossible to measure whether the ecclesiastical legislator has succeeded in any way in increasing the number of valid ecclesiastical marriages through the many norms of marriage law that are aimed at ensuring the inner freedom of those entering into marriage. While this has undoubtedly helped to increase the number of marriages that can in principle be annulled, it remains unclear whether the legislator can in fact influence the actual goal at all, namely that spouses contract a marriage based on their free decision to do so.

A second reason why Rottleuthner and Rottleuthner-Lutter are sceptical about whether quantification is helpful in determining the effectiveness of legal norms is that quantity does not seem to be the right measure of effectiveness for all types of legal norms. While it is of interest how often legal subjects obey prohibitions or abide by legal commands, this approach seems strangely misguided with respect to those norms which offer the legal subjects institutional frames for organising their social affairs. It is first of all difficult to measure these actions in terms of quantity. To quantify the effectiveness of norms which allow legal subjects a legal organisation of their affairs, it is necessary to quantify the degree to which legal subjects make use of the possibilities presented to them by the law. Klaus Röhl observes accordingly that the effectiveness of law is not merely about many abiding by the law but also about many taking advantage of the possibilities which the law offers to them.[28] Determining the ineffectiveness of these norms, on the contrary, means determining the extent to which legal subjects do *not* make use of their legal options.[29] In most cases, this is a considerably more complex undertaking. Whilst it might be possible to determine how often church members request the sacrament of the anointing of the sick in accordance with sacramental law (see canon 1006 CIC/1983),[30] it is impossible to determine the extent to which they do not do so, even though canon law offers them this possibility. Moreover, even if this kind of quantification were to succeed, Rottleuthner and Rottleuthner-Lutter believe it would not constitute a reliable basis for drawing conclusions about the true effectiveness of the law. After all, law which presents opportunities is not usually

---

[26] See Rottleuthner and Rottleuthner-Lutter (2010, p. 23).

[27] See Rottleuthner and Rottleuthner-Lutter (2010, pp. 24–25).

[28] See Röhl, Rechtssoziologie (1987, p. 250).

[29] See Rottleuthner and Rottleuthner-Lutter (2010, pp. 20).

[30] However, these data are not reflected in many church statistics, as William D'Antonio, James Davidson, Dean Hoge, and Mary Gautier lament in their study *American Catholics Today*: see D'Antonio et al. (2007, p. 55).

designed to maximise the use of the legal options it provides. Rottleuthner and Rottleuthner-Lutter explain this by referring to examples such as contracts or last wills to note that it is not the intention of the legislator to maximise the number of contracts or last wills. Instead of providing for a maximum quantity, the legislator is more concerned about providing the legal subjects with potential structures for ordering the social which they are free to use or not.[31] So while it is significant for the effectiveness of these laws that some individuals indeed make use of the opportunities provided by them, the aim is not to attain some kind of maximum use. For canon law, this observation is of interest in a number of ways, not least with regard to the norms of sacramental law, which provide the church members with rights to receive the sacraments. In assessing the effectiveness of these norms, it is certainly relevant that there are Catholics who do receive the sacraments and thus take advantage of the legal options that the law offers to them. However, measuring the effectiveness of these norms by the frequency with which Catholics receive the anointing of the sick or enter into a canonical marriage seems rather pointless. Nevertheless, when musing about numbers it is still of interest to study the rise or decline of quantities, such as of Catholics receiving the sacraments over a certain period of time, in order to draw conclusions from comparative observations. For instance, evidence shows that the reception of the sacrament of penance in the churches of the northern hemisphere has declined significantly since the middle of the twentieth century. Likewise, empirical evidence shows that Catholics from these churches are less inclined to enter into canonical marriages today than they were in the 1960s.[32] Whilst this decline in sacramental practice does not fundamentally inhibit the effectiveness of sacramental law, as sacramental law continues to influence sacramental life even in the churches where its options are realised to a lesser extent, it is evident that the effectiveness of the law has declined. Hence, as noted by Rottleuthner and Rottleuthner-Lutter, quantification is not always an appropriate benchmark for measuring legal effectiveness per se. However, quantitative observations may nevertheless be a useful stimulus for sociological consideration, as changing numbers may point at the fact that legal communities are undergoing a process of change.

6.1.4   Cultural Idiosyncrasies

The above example shows that the intensity with which legal subjects make use of legal opportunities also depends on social and cultural factors.[33] It is evident that the Catholic reality in many churches is changing, and with it the readiness to use legal options provided by canon law. The sociology of law examines this and similar

---

[31] See Rottleuthner and Rottleuthner-Lutter (2010, p. 28).

[32] For the USA see D'Antonio et al. (2007, pp. 57–58).

[33] Eg Shapiro (1981, pp. 14–15); Röhl (1987, pp. 491–492); Rehbinder (2014, p. 145).

observations by studying the connection between legal effectiveness and culture. Klaus Röhl, for instance, observes that culture influences whether people tend to use the law to settle conflicts or not. He assumes that legal subjects' readiness to turn to the law and take legal action is rooted in their local approaches to dealing with conflicts.[34] Röhl finds that individuals raised in individualistic and less community-orientated cultures and in competitive societies are more likely to take legal action. He also assumes that more bureaucratised societies foster this effect as a more depersonalised adjudication decreases the legal subjects' reluctance to go public with their legal cases.[35] Thomas Raiser points to the Germans' litigiousness.[36] He ascribes this phenomenon to the fact that access to the judicial system in Germany is relatively uncomplicated and inexpensive, and that the courts work professionally and effectively. However, Raiser also understands the Germans' inclination to take legal action to be a result of their mentality. In his fellow Germans he identifies a mentality that understands conflict resolution primarily as the duty of the state. Therefore it seems quite natural to take individual conflicts to court. Yet whilst going to court seems relatively easy in Germany and many other countries, and can even have a playful and competitive character, legal subjects elsewhere may frown upon this practice. Many Asian cultures, especially those influenced by Confucianism, prefer extra-judicial mediation to settle disputes peacefully and without disturbing social harmony in the long term. In Japan, as Röhl notes, society would find it questionable to turn to the courts. Individuals who do so would prove themselves to be incapable of resolving conflicts by other means. This has consequences not only for the effectiveness of procedural norms, but also for the fundamental status of law in Japanese society. As law is not a preferred medium for solving conflicts and is held in lower esteem than in most occidental countries, many conflicts which the occidental mentality typically identifies as legal conflicts, as Röhl notes, are not even recognised as potential legal conflicts in Japan, but are instead treated as social conflicts to be solved extra-judicially by social means.[37] Most interestingly, we may discover similar phenomena in church. There seems to be little inclination among Catholics to settle ecclesiastical matters with the help of canonical procedures. This also applies to churches in those countries which have a strong affinity for the law and are traditionally open to litigation, such as Germany. However, this litigiousness evidently does not generally carry over to the church and its law. German Catholics show no particular tendency to engage ecclesiastical tribunals in conflicts arising in church. This might result from the particular Christian tradition. After all, the church can look back on a longstanding and even biblical tradition of extra-judicial conflict resolution, to which I have already referred in sect. 3.2.7. In dealing with conflicts in the early Christian churches, Paul recommended extra-judicial dispute settlement to the Christian community of Corinth as the

---

[34] See Röhl (1987, p. 491).

[35] See Röhl (1987, p. 492).

[36] See Raiser (2007, p. 340).

[37] See Röhl (1987, pp. 491–492).

Christian model of conflict resolution. Rather than relying on pagan adjudication, the "court before the unrighteous" (1 Corinthians 6:1), Paul encouraged the Corinthians to settle conflicts amicably or to submit them to the judgment of other community members. It is conceivable that this tendency to favour extra-legal and extra-judicial solutions has influenced the church's culture of conflict resolution to the present day.[38] However, this non-inclination to turn to the law to settle conflicts may also have other and less Christian reasons. I have already referred in sect. 3.2 to Johannes Grabmeier's attempt to contest a decision of his then-diocesan bishop by taking legal recourse to the Roman Curia. With Grabmeier's example in mind, one might suspect that many German Catholics avoid bringing their cases before ecclesiastical tribunals to avoid frustration, as they do not expect much of ecclesiastical procedures. For Grabmeier, the congregation's refusal to even hear him supported his view that the decision about the bishop winning and him losing the case had already been made before the procedure started. If many Catholics likewise perceive of ecclesiastical procedures as partial and do not expect them to work professionally and effectively, this might explain why even Catholics who tend towards litigiousness for cultural reasons hesitate to take legal action in church. This assumption certainly requires further empirical study. Yet if it proves to be true, this finding, from the perspective of the sociology of canon law, alludes to the fact that legal norms which depend on the legal subjects' decision to become effective tend to lose their effectiveness whenever the legal subjects have reason to suspect that the law does not serve their purposes, as it is in fact ineffective for changing their social reality. While some canonical norms reproduce their effectiveness quasi-automatically, such as constitutional norms which automatically reproduce the hierarchical structure of the church independently of most legal subjects' individual decision, others do not. Their effectiveness depends on the legal subjects' decision to abide by them and to make use of the opportunities provided by them. However, when the legal subjects do not trust these laws to actually help them to realise opportunities and tend instead to anticipate disappointment, they will be inclined to refrain from relying on that law. Laws which the legal subjects suspect of being ineffective eventually also become ineffective whenever their effectiveness depends on the legal subjects' decision to make use of legal opportunities.

6.1.5 Intercultural Challenges

One pressing question, especially in the sociology of canon law, is the degree to which intercultural differences in understanding law influence globally applicable canon law. As a law that spans the entire Catholic world, universal canon law must accommodate the fact that its legal subjects have different attitudes towards the law based on their various cultural backgrounds. Globalisation has exacerbated this

---

[38] See Hahn (2017, pp. 473–479).

problem. While canonical conflicts of a cultural nature were largely inner-European controversies in the premodern era, today's tensions and differences have taken on a truly global character. Surprisingly, there are but few voices in the church and among canonists that seem truly aware of this problem. One exception is John Huels, who points out that the European cultural thumbprint of canon law is problematic for non-European Catholics and hard to digest in non-European local churches.[39] In the non-European churches, canon law confronts legal subjects with Central European legal thought which is in many respects foreign to them or even irritating. For example, the common law traditions of the Anglo-American legal sphere frequently struggle with the statutory character of law in the European civil law tradition, to which canon law belongs, as Huels observes, "Catholics living in a society with a common law tradition and a literalistic attitude towards interpretation and observance of law often have difficulty comprehending the canonical system and sometimes experience canon law more as a source of conflict rather than as a source of unity in the community."[40] These issues which make communication between common and civil law traditions difficult are all the more serious when western law collides with non-western legal cultures. These cultural differences can even result in a negative attitude towards the law itself, something demonstrated by the example of Asian cultures mentioned above. In cultures impacted by Confucianism, for example, the fact that Confucianism does not esteem the law as a social regulator of great value may also have a knock-on effect for canon law. It is therefore extremely difficult or even impossible to defend the claim of canon law to essentially serve the public good of the church and the salvation of souls in local churches that consider the law to be a deficient medium of organising and controlling the social. For canon law, this is not merely a sociological problem, it is also an ecclesiological one. It is therefore a matter of considerable interest for canon law scholars to study how global canon law deals with these cultural differences when claiming validity in diverse local settings.

6.2   Conditions of Compliance

Whilst it is enlightening to study phenomena of compliance and non-compliance with laws, it is of specific interest for the sociology of law to examine the *reasons* why individuals or groups are willing to abide by the law. Opinions among sociologists of law differ on this subject. However, they do agree that there are several factors which stimulate compliance. These include a legal community's customs and habits, the legal subjects' social and moral beliefs, and the probability and severity of sanctions imposed in response to breaches of law. These aspects crystallise into three motives, which sociologists of law often refer to as the motive triad of legal

---

[39] See Huels (1987, p. 260).
[40] Huels (1987, p. 274).

compliance. These are fear of sanctions, identification with the group in which legal norms are in operation, and internalisation of norms based on their acceptance. Manfred Rehbinder emphasises that the motives driving people to abide by the law vary from case to case. They depend on the content of a norm, the legal subjects' legal knowledge, their personality structure—for instance on whether someone tends to be motivated by the threat of sanction or not—, on the degree to which the legal subjects internalise norms, and on their legal ethos.[41] Hence, in addition to these widely accepted motivators for conformity, namely the fear of sanction, identification with the legal community, and the internalisation of legal norms, Rehbinder introduces further subjective factors that influence the motivators which are likely to have a persuasive effect on each person in each case, namely knowledge of the law, personality structure, and legal ethos. The reasons why people abide by the law lie in the interplay between these diverse factors. They form a complex bundle of incentives inducing compliant or non-compliant behaviour. In textbooks of legal sociology, these various factors frequently appear in three clusters which sociologists of law present as influential for legal compliance, namely knowledge of the law, the probability of rewards or sanctions, and the attitudes towards the law present in a legal community. These three clusters cover practices of legal socialisation, identification, and internalisation. Sociologists of law believe these diverse motives explain legal subjects' compliance with the law. However, these factors also help to explain legal subjects' non-compliance. This is of particular interest to the sociology of canon law, since these factors might help to identify why canon law is currently suffering from such a serious loss of effectiveness, at least with regard to those legal norms which depend on the legal subjects' decision to abide by them, as I explained in the previous section.

6.2.1 Knowledge of the Law

The sociology of law devotes some attention to the question of whether and in what sense it is necessary to know the law in order to abide by it. Scholars broadly agree that low levels of knowledge of legal norms are indeed a threat to compliance.[42] More controversial, however, is deciding the quantity and the kind of knowledge needed to promote compliance. While sociologists of law consider the legal subjects' basic knowledge of the law to be an essential condition for their compliance, scholars disagree on how to define the precise connection between knowledge and compliance. Karl-Dieter Opp, for example, believes there is a direct gradual correspondence between knowledge and compliance. He is convinced that individuals are more inclined to abide by a law the more familiar they are with it.[43] His approach

---

[41] See Rehbinder (2014, pp. 119–120).

[42] Eg Rehbinder (2014, p. 120).

[43] See Opp (2010, p. 36).

was taken up and modified by Andreas Diekmann. He challenged Opp's gradualist notion by saying that, under certain conditions, even those who are not in possession of detailed knowledge about a legal norm are no less likely to conform to it than those who are better informed. Diekmann refers to cases in which individuals mistakenly consider a certain behaviour to be prohibited. These individuals, who consider a wider range of behaviour to be illegal than a norm actually prohibits and thus have an inaccurate knowledge of the legal norm, are no more inclined to violate the norm than individuals who are precisely informed about the content of the norm. In consequence, it is not in all cases crucial to possess a thorough knowledge of laws in order to ensure their observance. The key point, as Diekmann observes, is that legal subjects do not consider behaviour to be legal when it is not. Accordingly, we should only consider the possession of a rudimentary knowledge of the law to be relevant for the effectiveness of the law if legal subjects erroneously think an action is legal even though it is illegal, but not if they believe an action to be illegal when it is actually legal.[44] Whereas gradualist "the more informed ... the more effective" constructions fail to generally explain the connection between knowledge of the law and compliance with the law, Diekmann's modified approach leaves no doubt that knowledge of the law, even though not necessarily precise knowledge, is indeed a prerequisite for compliant behaviour. From the perspective of the sociology of law, this raises an additional question about the consequences of the legal subjects' declining knowledge of the law in complex contemporary legal systems. After all, in an increasingly complex legal world in which the law is growing in quantity and complexity, we may hardly expect legal subjects to know much of the law.[45] Even legal professionals frequently prove to be well-informed only in those legal fields in which they are experts, while they often have a rudimentary knowledge of the law in other fields. In view of the finding that we may not expect most legal subjects to have much knowledge of the law, it seems reasonable to ask if it is realistic to expect their legal compliance. The sociology of law takes a differentiated view of this. Clearly, whilst it is necessary to somehow know legal norms in order to abide by them, it is frequently not essential to know them *as law*. This is because the content of legal norms often overlaps with other norms, such as social or moral norms. In this light, Klaus Röhl explains that although legal subjects often have a rather meagre knowledge of legal norms, including those relevant to everyday life, they are generally well-informed about what is illegal, because social or moral norms often disapprove of behaviour which is also illegal. Röhl therefore finds that most individuals know at least the basic gist of the law quite well, even though they rarely know the precise content of individual regulations.[46] It is evident, in any case, how much the legal subjects' knowledge of the law varies with respect to the different legal fields. In this vein, Thomas Raiser observes that most individuals are rather well-informed about the basic regulations of penal law, which he thinks is mostly due to the fact that penal

---

[44] See Diekmann (1980, p. 39).

[45] See Luhmann (2014, p. 195); Röhl (1987, p. 259).

[46] See Röhl (1987, p. 265).

law is regularly closely aligned with moral norms common in a society.[47] Legal subjects also frequently have a rough knowledge of constitutional law, even though more on a general and structural level. Very few legal subjects have a detailed knowledge of individual constitutional norms, but many have a basic political education, to which they owe some knowledge of basic rights, the rule of law, or the rules according to which political institutions operate. The media also play a key role in communicating this content. They also often succeed in disseminating knowledge about single legal regulations. Media coverage and public debates also draw the legal subjects' attention to highly conflictive regulations such as the death penalty, abortion, or inheritance tax.[48] Regarding civil law, many legal subjects are well-informed in areas of law that have a strong impact on their everyday lives, such as contract law, tenancy law, or labour law; in other areas of civil law, their levels of knowledge are frequently low. Knowledge about procedural law or administrative law tends to be quite weak, says Raiser. Few individuals are well-informed about how legislation, adjudication, and administration work and have only a rough idea of the organisational structure, duties, and functioning of legal institutions.

If we transfer these observations to canon law, a similar picture emerges. Whilst it is fair to assume that Catholics generally know little about canonical norms, their levels of knowledge vary depending on the legal matter in question. I will try to sketch a short overview by relying on my own experiences in discussing my lectures and talks with students of theology, academic colleagues, and interested Catholics who frequently reveal rather frankly that they know little of canon law—and sometimes are nevertheless rather surprised to discover what they do in fact know. This is the case because many active Catholics know the content of many legal norms through their everyday practice or local conventions. Constitutional issues, for instance, such as the division of church members into laity and clergy and issues of authority deriving from this fundamental division, are part of their everyday knowledge about the way in which the church functions. Practising Catholics are familiar with many regulations on the sacraments, even though they take their knowledge rather from doctrine or practice than from legal norms. As a consequence, many Catholics probably know more about ecclesiastical constitutional and sacramental law, and probably also about the law on the teaching function of the church, than they think they do. However, the situation is different when it comes to the content of canonical norms which are not commonly reflected in doctrinal, moral, or social norms. Most Catholics, for instance, have a rather meagre knowledge of ecclesiastical property law, penal law, or procedural law. Whilst there seems to be barely any knowledge of ecclesiastical procedural law among practising Catholics, they often know some half-truths of ecclesiastical penal law. From my canon law classes I get the impression that there is a widespread view among theology students that the church universally punishes all kinds of transgressions by excommunication. Most students seem to believe, for instance, that anyone who

---

[47] See Raiser (2007, pp. 324–325).
[48] See Raiser (2007, p. 325).

remarries after divorce incurs an excommunication. They define excommunication frequently as the "exclusion from church." These examples show that many Catholics do have some knowledge of penal matters. However, this knowledge is frequently imprecise. Similar observations apply to other legal matters. Most Catholics in Germany only became aware of the existence of ecclesiastical property law after the scandal in the Diocese of Limburg, where the so-called "Bishop of Bling" spent several million euros renovating his bishop's residence. Until then, little was known about ecclesiastical property law—including among those responsible for overseeing the bishop's activities by applying the very same law. Saying this, I do not want to suggest that there were not also equally deliberate and thus well-informed breaches of ecclesiastical property law in the course of the Limburg affair. However, it also seems clear that some breaches of law were indeed caused by a lack of information among the members of those bodies that should have been performing a supervisory function. I say this less as an apology and more as a simple statement of fact, that some committee members only demonstrated an awareness of the norms of ecclesiastical asset management *after* the events had taken place. In this sense, one might say that at least one good thing resulted from the Limburg scandal, namely that it served as an involuntary campaign to educate the German bishops, vicars general, cathedral chapters, and administrators of ecclesiastical goods about the basic principles of ecclesiastical property law. It remains to be seen whether the improved knowledge of property law will have a positive effect on legal compliance in the future. According to the sociology of law, this is possible but not certain. As discussed, some knowledge about the law is indeed a precondition for legal compliance, so that better-quality information may in fact increase the chances of legal compliance. Yet at the same time information does not guarantee an increase in compliance. In this vein Manfred Rehbinder stresses that even the best knowledge of law is useless unless the legal subjects are in fact willing to abide by it.[49] In addition, as Andreas Diekmann emphasises, legal knowledge is not only a driving force behind compliant behaviour, but may in some cases also motivate breaches of law. Diekmann namely observes that some crimes actually require a specialist knowledge of the law to successfully break the law.[50] He cites the example of economic crimes, which are often committed by offenders with a particularly sound knowledge of business and tax law. He gives the example of tax fraud where those committing tax evasion are frequently very well-informed and typically know tax law better than the average taxpayer. Diekmann therefore concludes that knowledge of the law might be a precondition for abiding by the law, but in some cases it is also a precondition for sophisticated legal infringements.

---

[49] See Rehbinder (2014, p. 121).
[50] See Diekmann (1980, p. 40).

6.2.2   *Compliance and Sanctions*

A further motive for compliance with the law is the degree to which one might expect to be rewarded or sanctioned for complying with or breaking the law. In the search for a viable concept of law in Sect. 2.1, I already mentioned the fact that, in line with Niklas Luhmann, I do not understand sanctions as being part of the concept of law, but as being part of the expectations connected with the law. According to Luhmann, law is less about the legal subjects' actual behaviour than about their expectations of legal norms. Yet because legal norms are counterfactual behavioural expectations, they continue to exist even when they are not fulfilled.[51] Hence, it does not fundamentally undermine the law as law if legal subjects occasionally disappoint these expectations by breaking the law. Luhmann observes, "one does not want to do without the expectation of a solid, well-trodden ground, even if one slips once!"[52] Occasional disappointments deriving from the fact that individuals fail to abide by the law even though we expect them to abide by it do not unmake our expectations that the law will generally provide us with solid and well-trodden paths of behaviour. For law, this also means that its enforcement is not as key as one might assume. Even if the authorities fail to consistently enforce legal norms, these norms keep their inherent structure of expectations. It does not harm the character of law as law that the law enforcement authorities do not enforce compliance or impose negative sanctions in each and every case. Permanent enforcement is neither desirable nor necessary, as Luhmann observes. On the contrary, a legal order that seeks the comprehensive enforcement of its legal norms would only confront itself with its own dysfunctionality, as Luhmann maintains, noting, "If the function of law were defined by the enforcement of a prescribed action or a failure to act through coercive power and sanctions, the actual administration of justice would be constantly, even predominantly, concerned with its own inefficiency."[53] A legal system must therefore turn a blind eye to the fact that legal subjects sometimes fail to abide by its norms. It cannot invest all its energy in enforcing the law. However, one should bear in mind that while occasional disappointments are inconsequential for the law, repeated and permanent disappointments can have a deleterious effect, because they can damage the structure of legal expectations as expectations, as Luhmann notes,

> Certainty of expectation is also at risk when conduct, which conforms to expectations supported by law, cannot be assured and when there is not even the slightest chance that expectation can be fulfilled. Law cannot always say: you are right, but unfortunately we cannot help you. Law must at least be able to offer substitutes (punishment, damages, etc.) and to enforce them.[54]

---

[51] Eg Luhmann (1986, p. 22).

[52] Luhmann (2014, p. 25).

[53] Luhmann (2004, p. 164).

[54] Luhmann (2004, p. 164).

In order not to undermine the certainty of expectation which legal subjects associate with the law, it is therefore necessary for measures to be in place that react to the continuous disappointment of expectations. These measures must make clear to anyone engaging in illegal behaviour that they should at least expect to be sanctioned. Karl Llewellyn expresses this figuratively, suggesting that law must prove to be a matter which from time to time shows its "teeth," noting, "The 'legal' has to do with ways and standards which will prevail in the pinch of challenge, with rights and the acquisition of rights which have teeth, with liberties and powers whose exercise can be made to stand up under attack."[55] To avoid becoming toothless, the law must sometimes rely on the authorities to enforce its compliance or sanction non-compliance.[56] Hence, Eugen Ehrlich's thesis about the effectiveness of state law—"The effectiveness of the law of the state is in direct ratio to the force which the state provides for its enforcement, and in inverse ratio to the resistance which the state must overcome"[57]—shows that legal effectiveness is also a matter of overcoming resistance to the law as well as overcoming attempts to evade the imposition of substitutes for legal compliance, such as repressive or restitutive sanctions.[58] Sanctions are therefore important for the law which must defend its structure of expectation. And they are important for the legal community in which these expectations exist. Manfred Rehbinder pays particular attention to this relevance of sanctions for the legal community.[59] It is this group in which breaches of law may cause irritation, because they may lead to cognitive dissonance among the group members.[60] There are three potential responses to this. The first reaction is to take the disappointment of expectation caused by the breach of law as an opportunity to stop having the expectation. The legal norm then becomes ineffective. The second reaction is to ignore the breaches of law or to relativise their significance. This reaction also tends to weaken the effectiveness of legal norms. The third reaction is to take both the law and the breaches of law seriously. However, it then seems necessary to react to the groups' disappointed expectations by compensating for any feelings of aggression towards the guilty party by participating in or witnessing the imposition of sanctions.[61] This option may not only settle the social conflict between the group and the offender, but may also strengthen the sense of solidarity within the group. For this reason, sanctions not only serve to reinforce legal norms and to remind the group of their binding nature, but also reinforce the social forces which integrate legal communities.

---

[55] Llewellyn (1940, p. 1364).

[56] See also Aubert (1952, pp. 263–271, particularly 270).

[57] Ehrlich (1936, pp. 372–373).

[58] On the differentiation between repressive and restitutive sanctions see Durkheim (1960, p. 69).

[59] See Rehbinder (2014, pp. 102–103).

[60] On the concept of cognitive dissonance see Festinger (1957).

[61] See Rehbinder (2014, p. 103).

6.2.3   Limited Sanctions in Church

The sociology of canon law therefore has to face the fact that the effectiveness of canon law depends to some degree on either its ability to overcome the resistance that exists among the ecclesiastical legal subjects towards abiding by the law, or to sanction their non-compliance. However, as an institution which has largely lost its powers of coercion in plural and secular modernity, the church in most countries of the world has very limited options for enforcing its law and few options for punishing non-compliance. The church itself can only exert limited pressure on its members. It lacks a sophisticated Weberian apparatus of coercion. External support is also rare. Nowadays, the state hardly ever helps the church to enforce its law, as it used to do in the past. Some church-state regulations are an exception. The church tax in Germany, for instance, is regularly collected by the state's tax administration, which might also apply coercion to enforce tax collection or punish delinquent tax payers. Here the church can indeed still rely on state support. However, this is an exception. In other cases, the possibility of the church to effectively enforce compliance with the law or sanction its members for non-compliance depends to a great degree on the type of norms concerned, and, above all, on the legal subjects' level of personal dependence on the church as an institution. Whether ecclesiastical authorities are successful in enforcing their legal subjects' behaviour is nowadays first and foremost dependent on the respective church members' personal or contractual connection to the church as an institution. Canonist Urs Brosi observes that church authorities today have only a limited range of opportunities for law enforcement at their command and can only enforce those legal subjects' compliance or sanction their non-compliance effectively whom the authority may remove from an ecclesiastical office or dismiss from their position in church.[62] In this sense, the disciplinary law of clerics, religious, and other ecclesiastical officeholders remains widely effective. In this light, Simon Hecke plausibly points to the intense discussion in canonical circles about whether the church's increasingly ineffective penal law, which is widely failing to sanction ordinary church members, would not be better transformed into a purely disciplinary law pertaining to ecclesiastical officeholders and those which are closely connected with the church as an institution, such as the clergy and the members of religious orders.[63] Also affected by ecclesiastical sanctions are church employees who are subject to ecclesiastical employment law, as well as those Catholics who engage in the teaching function of the church and require their ordinary's permission to preach and teach. Catholics who are thus dependent on the church as an institution are therefore more susceptible to the sanctions of canon law than church members who are largely independent of the institution. For the latter group, it is not merely difficult to move them to act in a way as prescribed by the law, as Eugen Ehrlich observed,[64] but these Catholics also by

---

[62] See Brosi (2013, p. 19); see also Hecke (2017, p. 52).

[63] See Hecke (2017, p. 108).

[64] See Ehrlich (1936, pp. 371–372).

and large no longer feel that canon law applies to them at all. This is not least because the church is unable to establish a consistent connection between breaches of law and sanctions. Whilst the church certainly has the option of sanctioning Catholics, for instance by withdrawing ecclesiastical rights, its scope for doing so is practically limited. One example of a practical limitation to sanctioning church members in Germany consists of increasing levels of anonymity in the large German parishes. It is virtually impossible, for instance, to effectively enforce the key ecclesiastical sanction of exclusion from the sacraments such as from receiving communion, which is one consequence of excommunication (see canon 1331 §1 CIC/1983), if the ministers of sacraments do not know the receivers of the sacraments personally and, consequently, cannot know whether they are in fact subject to this punishment. It is therefore becoming increasingly difficult to enforce ecclesiastical sanctions such as the exclusion from receiving communion in large and vibrant city parishes where ecclesiastical personnel hardly know those attending the church services.[65] Here the church is faced with the fact noted by Niklas Luhmann that "compulsion can only be established if those who control it learn about law infringements".[66] This problem is probably the most significant challenge for legal coercion in church.

Adding to this challenge is that many sanctions in church function merely on the basis of personal belief and the offenders' cooperation, insofar as ecclesiastical authorities frequently depend on the punished individuals freely accepting their sanction and deciding to act according to it. Canon 1352 § 2 CIC/1983 helps to see this. The legal norm directs that offenders may fully or partly pause their observance of a certain penalty—concretely a non-declared *latae sententiae* penalty—if they reside in a certain place where their penalty is not notorious, to avoid creating scandal or damaging their reputation. This shows quite clearly that the legal norm understands the offenders themselves to be responsible for assessing whether it is wise to "self-execute" a penalty under certain circumstances, or if doing so would bring about more social harm than good, in which case they should suspend their observance of the penalty. In church, key punishments such as censures exist to motivate the legal subjects to change their behaviour and to refrain from unlawful action not least by appealing to their conscience. Hence, the execution of these sanctions is often conscience-bound, too. Sociologist Donald Barrett, in 1960, spoke of "the certainty and immediacy of effective sanctions" in church, particularly owing to the fact that canonical penal law addresses the legal subjects' conscience. Barrett found,

> The Code provides for penalties latae sententiae; conscience and the sense of guilt in a member of the Church are stressed; the ever recurrent threat of hell, the ultimate punishment, and the recognition that God demands justice as well as love make the Code's sanctions certain. The immediacy in meaning of such sanctions is guaranteed by the voluntary character of memberships in the Church and the necessary submission thereby to its laws.[67]

---

[65] See Brosi (2013, p. 19).

[66] Luhmann (2014, p. 207).

[67] Barrett (1960, p. 113).

From today's point of view, we may wonder if Barrett's analysis is still applicable. His observation that voluntary membership ensures the legal subjects' submission to canon law seems particularly worthy of discussion. In Sect. 6.3 I will return to the question of whether we may indeed speak of voluntary membership in church and whether ecclesiastical membership necessarily involves church members submitting to ecclesiastical law as a condition of their membership. However, from today's point of view we may also question Barrett's observation that ecclesiastical sanctions succeed in revealing their meaning to church members today, something which Barrett took for granted in 1960. Urs Brosi, in his 2013 textbook on canon law, certainly adopted a different stance when he observed that ecclesiastical penal law was having increasing difficulties creating meaning among modern-day Catholics. Brosi notes,

> For people who believe that receiving the sacraments on a regular basis and being in community with the church is necessary to reach eternal salvation, the ecclesiastical sanctions are effective. But as this belief is decreasing in the modern contexts of the West, the canonical penalties are losing their relevance and hence their power to enforce canon law. Whoever has distanced themselves from the church without fearing for her or his salvation no longer even notice these sanctions anymore.[68]

From this observation one may draw the conclusion that sanctions which rely on the punished Catholics to execute their sanctions themselves today broadly fail to work effectively when those concerned do not freely accept their duty to act in accordance with their sanction.

6.2.4 Cost-Benefit Considerations

As strategies for enforcing the law or sanctions become increasingly unlikely in church, we may come to find that canon law is gradually losing its "teeth," to borrow Karl Llewellyn's image. This makes its observance increasingly improbable, whenever observing the law depends on the legal subjects' decision. This is because, following a key premise in the sociology of law, sanctions are a key motivator of legal compliance. Karl-Dieter Opp consequently assumes that the likelihood of legal infringements decreases in line with the strictness of sanctions.[69] What he means, in any case, are not the actual sanctions—which, as one might note with Luhmann are mostly absent anyway, because the authorities have other things to do than worry

---

[68] Original quote, "Für Menschen, die daran glauben, dass der regelmäßige Empfang der Sakramente und die Gemeinschaft mit der Kirche notwendig sind, um das ewige Heil zu erlangen, verfügen die kirchlichen Sanktionen über Wirksamkeit. Da diese Überzeugung aber im modernen westlichen Lebenskontext am Schwinden ist, verlieren die kanonischen Strafen zunehmend an Bedeutung und damit an Kraft, um das kirchliche Recht durchzusetzen. Wer sich ohne Angst um sein Seelenheil von der Kirche entfernt hat, spürt die gegen ihn ausgesprochenen Sanktionen gar nicht mehr", Brosi (2013, p. 19).

[69] See Opp (2010, p. 36).

about sanctioning lawbreakers—,[70] but the expected sanctions. Legal compliance therefore depends to a notable degree on a legal subject's subjective assessment of the probability of being sanctioned, as well as on their subjective assessment of the sanction as such, namely whether they assess it to be intimidating or fairly unproblematic. Andreas Diekmann observes that there are some empirical grounds for believing that the probability of a sanction is more significant for legal compliance than its potential severity.[71] In a legal system such as canon law, in which the probability of sanctions, as explained above, is low for most church members, there is therefore a rather high probability that legal subjects do not feel particularly induced to abide by the law. However, in practice things might be a little more complicated, as shown by sociological observations on compliance and sanction. One theory on the relationship between compliance and sanction that has received some attention in the sociology of law is a model formulated by Karl-Dieter Opp and further developed by Andreas Diekmann. In his initial work, Opp identified four criteria as essential for compliance with legal norms: the degree to which a person is informed about the law; the degree of what Opp calls "normative variance" ("normative Abweichung"), by which he means the degree to which an individual assesses norms competing with legal norms as binding; the degree of expected negative sanctions for non-compliance with the law; and the degree of expected positive sanctions for compliance with the law.[72] Diekmann augmented and refined these criteria, noting that compliance with the law could also have negative consequences, while non-compliance could have positive effects.[73] In addition, Diekmann also focused on actual opportunities for breaking the law. The more often legally relevant situations arise, he notes, the more frequently legal subjects have a chance to break the law and in fact tend to break it, following the principle that "an open door may tempt a saint." Also of importance are criteria such as the inclination of third parties to report a crime, the clearance rate, and the social stigmatisation of offenders in a given legal community. Taking this model as his point of departure, Diekmann developed a theory for empirically testing legal subjects' willingness to comply with norms. His theory assumes that the inclination of legal subjects to abide by the law depends on their personal assessment of *utility*. Whether legal subjects abide by a law or not depends much on the net benefit accruing to lawbreakers from their breach of law.[74] Here, Diekmann also factors into his observations that there are not only negative but also positive sanctions, rewards for abiding by a legal norm as well as advantages accruing from disregarding it. Every taxpayer who commits tax fraud saves money, and every parking offender saves time finding a parking spot.[75] Diekmann, thus, calculates the "profit" accruing to lawbreakers from breaches of

---

[70] See Luhmann (2004, p. 164).

[71] See Diekmann (1980, p. 144).

[72] See Opp (2010, pp. 36–38).

[73] See Diekmann (1980, p. 41).

[74] See Diekmann (1980, p. 88).

[75] See Diekmann (1980, p. 40).

law by taking the positive sanctions for the breach of law and subtracting the negative sanctions which might apply for it. He factors the positive sanctions for compliance as "costs" which do not apply in the case of breaking the law. By taking the profit and subtracting the costs, he calculates the net benefit of breaking the law. Diekmann's model shows if and when it might be "worthwhile" to break the law. It demonstrates that in deciding whether to abide by or break the law, it is not only—as simpler theories assume—a matter of whether the negative sanctions for a breach of law are high or low,[76] but that we must take a complex bundle of factors into account. By studying the various positive and negative effects which are probable when abiding by or breaking a law, we may for instance find that similar to low negative sanctions, low costs—that is a mere minor loss of positive sanctions that compliance would bring—might have a negative impact on compliance economics. If one benefits greatly from breaking the law, but risks only minor losses from negative sanctions and forfeits only a few advantages that compliance might bring, this results in a clear net benefit from breaking the law.

6.2.5   The Law and Competing Norms

For many legal norms, this net benefit is significant, as Diekmann notes. For example, tax evasion and fare evasion may both be worthwhile undertakings from an economic point of view. Using the example of fare evasion, Diekmann calculated—at the time of his study in the 1970s—that in most German cities the probability of being caught without a ticket and having to face the threat of negative sanctions was extremely low. Diekmann therefore concluded, "Any rationally thinking 'homo economicus' should be a fare-dodger!"[77] Nevertheless, after having studied his empirical data, he found that the violation rates were surprisingly low. The fact that individuals were obviously not overly inclined to dodge the fare, as Diekmann analysed, could either be due to the fact that individuals considered the risk of being caught to be greater than it actually was, or that their moral attitude was also a factor. In his study, Diekmann concluded that morality is evidently more important for the observance of legal norms than the economic ratio of a cost-benefit analysis.[78] Based on this conclusion, he formulated the thesis that compliance with the law and moral beliefs correlate gradually: legally compliant behaviour is more likely if the law reflects the legal subjects' moral beliefs. In a similar vein, Karl-Dieter Opp sees it as a prerequisite for compliance with laws that they do not differ too greatly from the group's everyday normativities. An important factor in explaining the phenomenon of non-compliance is therefore *normative variance*,

---

[76] See Diekmann (1980, p. 18).

[77] Original quote, "Der rational denkende 'homo öconomicus' müßte also schwarz fahren!", Diekmann (1980, p. 73).

[78] See Diekmann (1980, p. 133).

that is the degree to which an individual understands norms other than legal norms as binding which may compete with legal norms for compliance. These other norms that compete with legal norms for compliance are primarily non-legal social and moral norms that are considered binding within a social group. Personal beliefs, such as one's own judgment of conscience, can also produce norms that are incompatible with a law. In legally plural social spaces, competing norms might also include rival laws from other legal systems, for example when state law comes into conflict with religious law. Opp understands the degree of normative variance between our everyday normativities and legal norms as most influential on legal compliance. The greater the degree of normative variance, the lower the chance that legal subjects will abide by the law.[79] The conflicting norms then become the yardstick for the law. They represent alternative conceptions of what is good and what is just. These beliefs form the basis of the legal subjects' evaluation of the law. Whether law is considered legitimate by a group depends on how well it correlates with the ideas of the good and the just prevalent in this group. The more closely the law is related to these ideas, the more legitimate it appears in the legal subjects' eyes. The more clearly it diverges from them, the less likely it is that the legal subjects will accept the law and, in consequence, the less likely it becomes that they will abide by it.

The sociology of law examines the legal subjects' attitudes towards the law within the field of research on *Knowledge and Opinion about Law*. Empirical methods tend to yield the best insights.[80] So far, there have been no such studies on canon law. However, this has not prevented canonists from recording their impressions regarding the attitudes of Catholics towards canon law, as shown by Ladislas Orsy's observation about the increasingly fragile reputation of canon law after the Second Vatican Council.[81] Indeed, this seems to be its core problem in the churches of the northern hemisphere, as evidenced by a number of comments from colleagues who describe the attitude of church members towards canon law as distant. Canonist John P. Beal, for instance, speaks of an "experience of the remoteness of canon law from the everyday life of the faithful".[82] John J. Coughlin refers to phenomena of anomie in church, which he traces back to the "antinomian absence of the proper appreciation of canon law".[83] Werner Böckenförde describes many Catholics' increasingly distanced stance towards the law as the result of alienation between different groups in church. According to him, this process of alienation is not only between the average church members and canon law, but also between the legal subjects and the legislator, as Böckenförde impressively illustrates, noting,

---

[79] See Opp (2010, p. 36).

[80] One "classic" of German-language empirical KOL research is the empirical study undertaken by Theo Rasehorn in 1970 entitled *Zur Einstellung der Unterschicht zum Rechtswesen* [*On the Attitude of the Lower Classes to the Legal System*]: see Rasehorn (1975).

[81] See Orsy (1992, p. 97).

[82] Beal (2011, p. 136).

[83] Coughlin (2011, p. 65).

There is a huge gap between the demands of Rome and the practice in the pastoral field of the church. This gap exists between the priests and the laity, between the bishop and his priests, partially also between the pope and the bishops. People say, 'Fulda is far away, Cologne is far away, Rome is even farther away.' Many clerics and lay people feel conscience-bound to refuse the demands of Rome; and many bishops tolerate this, as long as it does not appear in the newspaper and no one files a complaint about it.[84]

Patricia Goler's comment that canon law is largely meaningless among black Catholics in the United States because they view it as an instrument of a white church and as a law that exclusively favours whites is a further statement about the widespread perception of law among the legal subjects of canon law.[85] The problem of normative variance therefore seems to be particularly serious in church. Alternative judgments of conscience, affective distance, and a lack of identification with canon law are critical issues which impede compliance with canon law. This observation merits an in-depth analysis in the following sections.

6.2.6   Socialisation and Internalisation

The members of a group regularly abide by the group's laws because they identify with the group and the normative beliefs shared by its members. This is in fact an integration mechanism: those who adopt the group's beliefs become members of that group. This happens through the appropriation and internalisation of norms approved by the group. This internalisation process is a phenomenon of socialisation and therefore academically falls under the umbrella of socialisation theory and social psychology. June Tapp is one social psychologist who has specifically worked on the question of legal socialisation as a process of adaptation to social beliefs about the law which members of legal communities appropriate through internalisation. She transferred Lawrence Kohlberg's model of moral development to the field of law and, together with Kohlberg, developed it into a model of legal socialisation.[86] Tapp and Kohlberg identify three different levels of individual orientations with regard to the law, which they understand as phases in legal subjects' legal socialisation. Individuals frequently pass through these phases in the course of their socialisation, although not all individuals reach the final level. As in Kohlberg's model of moral development, the first level in an individual's attitude towards the law is

---

[84] Original quote, "Es tut sich eine Kluft auf zwischen dem von Rom Geforderten und dem, was in der Seelsorge praktisch geschieht. Diese Kluft ist erfahrbar bei Priestern und Laien, auch zwischen dem Diözesanbischof und seinen Priestern, zum Teil auch zwischen dem Papst und den Bischöfen. Es heißt: 'Fulda ist weit, Köln ist weit, Rom ist noch weiter'. Viele Kleriker und viele Laien fühlen sich im Gewissen verpflichtet, die Ausführung römischer Befehle zu verweigern, und viele Diözesanbischöfe tolerieren das, solange es nicht in der Zeitung steht oder zu Beschwerden kommt", Böckenförde (2006, p. 147).

[85] See Goler (1972, p. 295).

[86] See Tapp and Kohlberg (1971, pp. 65–91).

characterised as pre-conventional, which is determined in the first stage by a fear of being sanctioned in the case of non-compliant behaviour. This stage is usually followed by a hedonistic stage, in which compliance with the law is associated with an expectation of reward. This roughly corresponds to the legal judgment of children of kindergarten and early primary school age. On the second, conventional level of legal socialisation, individuals observe the law, first, because they expect and receive social praise for doing so, and second, because they consider it a social requirement to submit to the authority's commands. These stages become well developed among children of later primary school age and teenagers. The tendency for children to conform to norms results, among other things, from the fear of their peers' negative judgment of norm violation. If a group accepts a legal norm, anyone who violates it must fear social disapproval upon violating that norm. According to sociologists working on the question of deterrence in punishment theories, this fear of the anticipated social consequences of breaking the law is a far greater deterrent than the threat of legal punishment itself. Stefanie Eifler notes in this vein that social disapproval and the expectation of personal shame are a more effective means for preventing crime than formal punishment.[87] This is especially the case when individuals may expect disapproval from others whose opinion they hold in particularly high regard.[88] On the third, post-conventional, level, which can (but does not necessarily) develop from young adulthood onwards, legal subjects move beyond the idea of authority. For Tapp and Kohlberg, the first stage of this level consists of individuals developing an awareness of the grounding of law in social contract and of the related significance of the constitutional order and its relevance for social stability and progress. At the second stage of the post-conventional level, legal subjects tend to observe the law if they find it to be legitimate, insofar as it proves to be an expression of a just order in a moral sense. In this stage, the reason for the legal subjects' conformity to the law lies in their personal recognition of the law—an ideal mode of action of the law, as Manfred Rehbinder notes.[89] According to Eifler, assessing whether a legal norm is legitimate or not is more important for legal subjects in the second stage of level three than the threat of punishment for breaking the law, as she observes, "Laws are primarily followed because the actors are convinced of the legitimacy and binding force of legal norms and not because they fear sanctions."[90]

---

[87] See Eifler (2010, p. 101).

[88] See Opp (2010, p. 58).

[89] See Rehbinder (2014, p. 119).

[90] Original quote, "Gesetze werden also in erster Linie befolgt, weil Akteure von der Legitimität und Verbindlichkeit rechtlicher Normen überzeugt sind, und nicht, weil sie eine Bestrafung fürchten", Eifler (2010, p. 100).

6.2.7   Canon Law and Non-Compliance

The levels of legal socialisation in the Tapp-Kohlberg model describe reasons why legal subjects abide by the law. These include the fear of punishment, the prospect of reward, social standing and the fear of the group's disapproval, an understanding of the purpose of the law, and recognition of the legitimacy of the law. At the same time, these motives also reflect the reasons why legal subjects do *not* abide by the law. At the first level of legal socialisation, non-compliance becomes likely if the legal subjects can expect neither punishment nor reward. At the second level, we may expect widespread non-compliance when there is no prospect of the legal subjects receiving praise for compliant behaviour and no threat of social condemnation for non-compliance. At the third level, non-compliance becomes likely when legal subjects are convinced that legal norms are illegitimate. If the law appears illegitimate to them, they will find breaking the law to be justified, and, under certain circumstances, even to be a step required to oppose unjust laws. Bearing these observations in mind, we may ask what these levels mean for canon law. The legal subjects of canon law are Catholics from the age of seven upwards who are in possession of the "efficient use of reason" (canon 11 CIC/1983). Hence, canon law potentially addresses individuals at all stages of legal socialisation. Its observance therefore depends on all of the aforementioned reasons: fear of punishment, the prospect of reward or social recognition, fear of disapproval, an understanding of the purpose of canon law, and the acknowledgement of the legitimacy of the law. If these negative or positive expectations of canon law are missing, it becomes unlikely that the ecclesiastical legal subjects will abide by canon law. I already pointed out that it is rather and increasingly unlikely that ecclesiastical legal subjects may expect to be negatively sanctioned when breaking canon law. The ecclesiastical authorities have only limited options for the imposition of sanctions. As sanctioning requires the authorities' knowledge of a crime and their decision to take action, the threshold for church authorities to punish their legal subjects is frequently too high, with the exception of those crimes such as the sexual abuse of minors which have massive public repercussions. One has to note though that canon law provides the instrument of so-called *latae sententiae* penalties which befall the lawbreaker ipso facto upon committing certain crimes (see canon 1318 CIC/1983). These kinds of penalties apply for offences such as heresy, apostasy, and schism (see canon 1364 §1 CIC/1983), the desecration of the consecrated species (canon 1382 §1 CIC/1983), and abortion (see canon 1397 §2 CIC/1983), and result in a *latae sententiae* excommunication. Clerics entering a civil marriage incur a *latae sententiae* suspension (see canon 1394 §1 CIC/1983). Yet one should note that canon law also directs that offenders are not bound by a *latae sententiae* penalty if they were unaware without any personal fault upon committing their offence that a penalty was attached to it (see canon 1324 §3 in conjunction with §1 no. 9 CIC/1983). Bearing in mind the widespread lack of knowledge of canon law, one may ask in which cases *latae sententiae* penalties are in fact incurred in church if we can take it as given that most Catholics' lack of legal knowledge can hardly be considered to result from personal fault. Whilst probably close to all active Catholics know that the Catholic Church regards abortion as sinful, the vast majority is guiltlessly unaware of the fact that the church also regards it as a crime. Hence, the vast majority of Catholics procuring an abortion do not incur the punishment due to their guiltless lack of knowing about the penalty attached to abortion. This shows that *latae sententiae* punishments, as effective as they may seem at first sight, are upon greater scrutiny rather ineffective in most cases. As hardly any Catholics have personal fault from not knowing of the *latae sententiae* sanctions attached to some ecclesiastical crimes, they do not incur them in the first place. Those who have personal fault in not knowing of the penalty, incur it, but do not know it... Hence, in discussing possible compliance with *latae sententiae* punishments, we have to focus merely on the small group of those Catholics who commit a crime and know of the penalty attached, so that they incur it and also know that they have incurred it; lecturers in canonical penal law at this point in their lectures usually make the joke that this in fact merely applies to canon lawyers. However, whilst canonically educated legal subjects cannot avoid incurring *latae sententiae* punishments upon committing crimes to which these penalties apply, they are frequently free to simply ignore the punishment and also to ignore the consequences connected with them, such as the restriction of the right to receive the sacraments in cases of a *latae sententiae* excommunication (see canon 1331 CIC/1983). As external pressure such as legal enforcement or social condemnation is usually missing or even impossible—in those cases in which no other person knows of the penalty—, it is highly unlikely that these ecclesiastical legal subjects abide by canon law and submit to their penalty. Only a small number of offenders might do so and submit to the penalty, based on their personal belief that they deserve the punishment. Hence, recalling Tapp's and Kohlberg's reasons why legal subjects abide by the law, we may come to find that it is highly unlikely that Catholics abide by canon law due to fear of punishment. Adding to the widespread ineffectiveness of negative sanctions in church, legal subjects may not expect too many positive sanctions for abiding by the law either. One may indeed wonder what the rewards actually are for abiding by canon law. Donald Barrett sums up, "membership in the Mystical Body, participation and communication with other members, security in a life with meaning beyond immediate gratification."[91] However, one may ask how many contemporary Catholics feel they are endowed with these goods because they observe *the law,* and how many feel deprived of these goods if they break ecclesiastical law. As abiding by or breaking the law does not influence church membership and frequently does not even diminish the rights that Catholics enjoy in church, it is difficult to connect Barrett's "rewards" with legal compliance. Hence, Barrett's list reveals that there are hardly any direct advantages to observing canon law. Church members at the first level of legal socialisation thus have little incentive to observe canon law whenever they have the choice to do so or to refrain from abiding by the law. A similar finding applies to the conventional level of legal socialisation, at least in most local churches of the northern hemisphere.

---

[91] Barrett (1960, p. 113).

Conventional conformity to norms depends on praise or disapproval by the group and by the group's relevant authorities. Conversely, if a group holds the law in low esteem, observance becomes unlikely. Legal subjects tend to ignore laws when nobody, including the relevant authorities, expects their compliance. This applies to many canonical norms. Often neither those third parties who are important to the church members nor ecclesiastical "authority figures" expect others to comply with ecclesiastical laws. We might call to mind by way of example the obligation to receive confession at least once a year (see canon 989 CIC/1983). Hardly any Catholics in my culture face the expectation to observe this legal norm, not even by the ecclesiastical pastoral staff. Hence, nobody may expect the observance of this law to find someone's praise nor non-observance to meet with disapproval. Those who go to confession annually will receive little praise from fellow Catholics for doing so. And hardly anyone will disapprove of their non-observance of the obligation to confess if they do not do so. Consequently, neither feelings of shame nor guilt will arise in those who violate the legal obligation if they—like the majority of practising Catholics in northern countries—do not comply with their annual duty to go to confession. This has a detrimental effect on many legal subjects' inclination to abide by the law. Simon Hecke goes one step further. He actually finds that "deviation from the canonical norm is the 'general norm'".[92] Although it is doubtful whether this is universally true, it is certainly the case for many legal norms, including the obligation to go to confession. The social norm in German parishes, for instance, is to refrain from going to confession, because confession is widely connected with religious trauma. Many members of the post-war generation of Catholics who were still obliged to go to confession regularly frequently experienced this as highly traumatic,[93] often connected with spiritual abuse and abuse of power, and sometimes even with sexual abuse. There is therefore a maximum degree of normative variance between canon 989 CIC/1983 and the widespread belief among German Catholics that it is advisable to avoid going to confession. Consequently, compliance with this legal norm among German Catholics is most unlikely. If this high degree of normative variance is the norm, then there is nobody who confronts legal subjects who break the law with any consequences. Instead, those who comply with it become the ones more likely to have to explain their actions. In German parishes, in any case, those Catholics who actually follow the legal obligation of annual confession are more likely to raise fellow Catholics' eyebrows than those who refrain from doing so. A similar finding emerges at the post-conventional level of legal socialisation. Legal subjects at this level will predominantly disregard canon law if the law deviates from their normative beliefs, because they assess the law to be unjust whenever it departs from internalised moral or social norms. One example of this is the widespread practice in Germany of distributing communion without further ado to Protestant partners in mixed confessional marriages during a Catholic

---

[92] Original quote, "Abweichung von einer kirchenrechtlichen Norm 'allgemeine Norm' ist", Hecke (2017, p. 47).

[93] See Moser (1976).

Eucharist, which is common even in congregations which know about the confessional status of these non-Catholic Christians. This is because most ministers of communion as well as local parish members do not consider the restrictive legal regulation of canon law (see canon 844 §4 CIC/1983) to be just and therefore feel justified in breaking it or even obliged to do so.

6.2.8 Structures of Normative Variance

The ways in which many Catholics approach confession or communion are two examples of how a significant normative variance between legal norms on the one hand and moral or social norms on the other hand may weaken compliance with the law. Of course, every legal system has its own comparable examples. However, normative variance is of particular interest to the sociology of canon law, primarily because it is not only a widespread phenomenon in church, but also because of its structural dimension. Insofar as canon law has fundamentally and consistently distanced itself from social beliefs about a whole range of issues prevailing in many local churches, it is fair to think of normative variance as having become structurally solidified with regard to many normative issues. On the one hand this is because canon law has decoupled itself from the contemporary understanding of state law, and on the other hand because global canon law only has a rather tenuous relationship with the local churches. Both of these arguments merit some further explanation, which I will give in the following. First, to no small degree, normative variance between canon law and other norms essential to many Catholics is due to the premodern structure of canon law. This premodern structure contradicts the way in which ecclesiastical legal subjects who are simultaneously citizens of modern democratic constitutional states conceive of the law in general. Canon law therefore finds itself increasingly confronted by Catholics claiming the freedoms they associate with secular state law in church, too. Many church members want the church to grant them similar freedom rights to those they enjoy in liberal society and the secular state: freedom of conscience, freedom of speech, and a wide range of participation rights.[94] The fact that canon law operates at a lower standard of freedom rights compared to contemporary liberal orders creates a high degree of normative variance between canon law and state law. This makes compliance with canon law structurally improbable. Second, compliance with canon law is also marked by cultural dissonances. These create a distance between ecclesiastical laws and locally effective norms of the social. As early as the 1970s, as I already mentioned, Patricia Goler questioned whether, from the perspective of black American Catholics, canon law as "white law" could claim binding force for black Catholics. She observed, "With each advance of black self-consciousness, there comes a corresponding sense that the laws and authorities are white laws and

---

[94]Eg Beal (2011, pp. 140–141); Essen (2013, p. 217).

white authorities and that they are not legitimate for black people."[95] According to Goler, the non-observance of Roman canon law by black Catholics in the United States is due to the fact that the relevant legal and cultural norms are largely incompatible. It would no doubt be possible to find similar incompatibilities in relation to other Catholic groups and cultures. In the global church, it is particularly problematic that canon law has a global claim to validity, but demands compliance locally. In the local churches, in any case, canon law as the evident result of central European legal thought clashes with local beliefs about the law, especially in the non-European churches.[96] This frequently results in high degrees of normative variance. However, and most surprisingly, canon law studies has devoted relatively little thought to this issue so far. Simon Hecke remarks that one may identify the Second Vatican Council as the historical context in which the church started to recognise that modern societies are complex and that having a global church permeating through complex societies makes things even more difficult. Whilst the church in the meantime has learnt to conceive of itself as a global church, Hecke finds, it has yet to learn to understand its law as global law.[97] So far, it has only done so insofar as canon law claims global validity for all Catholics worldwide. Yet, thus far, the legislator seems to have given little thought to the fact that it is theoretically insufficient and also detrimental for the effectiveness of global canon law if the Roman legislator merely transplants legal norms grown in a European civil-law context into the local churches all over the globe.

6.2.9   Choice of Law and Forum Shopping

This is not without consequence for the effectiveness of canon law. The normative variance between canon law and competing norms which Catholics have internalised make the observance of canon law highly improbable. Church members who are unconvinced by canon law are in fact encouraged to break the law because they need not fear punishment most of the time, but more importantly, neither do they need to fear any disapproval from fellow Catholics for doing so. Yet there is a further motive which legal scholar Jacques Vanderlinden identified by examining how contemporary legal subjects experience freedom and pluralism. He found that many legal subjects of today no longer feel they are a subject at the mercy of a legislator, but have become self-confident citizens of a global world who can therefore at least to some degree decide to which legal system they subject themselves. Vanderlinden notes, "The essential pluralist point is that the individual is not just the anonymous object of State law, but also the autonomous subject who chooses between the

---

[95] Goler (1972, p. 295).

[96] See Huels (1987, p. 260).

[97] See Hecke (2017, p. 109).

various laws of the social networks to which he belongs."[98] Those who make full use of the plurality of modern-day global life are no longer inevitably destined to follow a certain law. Instead, their experience of the law is very much more malleable. The widespread practice in private international law of choosing between several jurisdictions, known as "forum shopping," is an example of how global legal pluralism enables legal subjects to choose their preferred laws.[99] Legal systems of non-state origin, which Jean Carbonnier calls "sub-law",[100] such as contract law, transnational law, or canon law, are particularly vulnerable to selection by the legal subjects. The latter in particular, due to its paucity of coercion, is especially dependent on its legal subjects' decision to comply with it or not. Nowadays, however, legal subjects usually take this decision of their own free will on the basis of their belief in a justice system. Compliance with canon law therefore increasingly ties in with whether its legal subjects accept it as legitimate law or not. Jürgen Habermas notes, "The *de facto validity* of legal norms is determined by the degree to which such norms are acted on or implemented, and thus by the extent to which one can actually expect the addressees to accept them."[101] This verdict, quite evidently, applies to canon law, too.

However, contrary to what Carbonnier's "sub-law" implies, it is not necessarily the case that legal subjects will routinely choose state law over other laws whenever they find themselves addressed by various and competing legal claims. A study from Israel may serve as an illustration. As part of their survey for the *Israeli Democracy Index 2016*, Ella Heller, Chanan Cohen, Dana Bublil, and Fadi Omar asked their Jewish interviewees how they would react in the event of a conflict between Halacha—that is Jewish religious law—, and state law, specifically a state judicial decision.[102] Only 28% of the respondents preferred Halacha to secular law, while 64% preferred state law. Here, it is of course necessary to differentiate between religious groups. While 97% of ultra-Orthodox respondents gave priority to the Halacha, only 6% of secular Jews did so. The responses of other groups—religious Zionists, traditional religious, and traditional non-religious groups—were between these values. In the middle of the spectrum, the response of traditional religious respondents was fairly well balanced: 40% voted for the primacy of religious law, 44% for secular state law. This result is certainly noteworthy as it suggests that the middle ground of Jewish-Israeli society is undecided on the primacy of religious or secular law. The interviewers also asked Arab Israelis whether they would rather follow their own religious law or state law in the event of a conflict. Here, 48% preferred religious law, with only 44% preferring state law—a result that might be rooted in the problematic political situation of Arab Israelis in Israel. This shows that Israeli law has problems of legitimacy in the Arab population, and that Arab Israelis

---

[98] Vanderlinden (2002, p. 180); see also Tamanaha (2008, pp. 375, 385).

[99] See Tamanaha (2008, p. 389); Seinecke (2015, pp. 37–40).

[100] Original quote, "Unterrecht", Carbonnier (1974, p. 137).

[101] Habermas (1996, pp. 29–30).

[102] See Heller et al. (2016, pp. 83–85).

are more likely to recognise religious law. However, these results vary with regard to the religious orientation of the interviewees. While Muslim respondents overwhelmingly preferred religious law (56%), Christian (62%) and Druze respondents (56%) were mostly in favour of secular law. The more religious the respondents considered themselves to be, the more likely they were to say they would abide by religious law in the event of a conflict between religious and secular law. These data are as interesting for the general sociology of law as they are for the sociology of religious law. For the sociology of religious law, they point to the relationship between an individual's religious belief and their readiness to follow religious law; thus, the *Israeli Democracy Index* shows a gradual correlation between individual piety and individual inclination to abide by religious law. It would be interesting to ask if one can make broader generalisations based on this observation. We may in fact ask if highly devout Catholics are more willing to abide by canon law than active but less devout church members. A separate empirical study would be necessary to draw reliable conclusions in this regard in order to examine whether there are more general correlations between individual piety and personal readiness to abide by religious law which also apply to Catholics. However, besides this finding, the observation based on the *Israeli Democracy Index 2016* shows that legal pluralism does not necessarily decide whether legal subjects will choose to follow state law whenever conflicts between state law and religious law arise. In fact, the findings underline the observation that in conflicts between competing legal orders, the type of law likely to win the argument is that which the legal subjects regard as being more legitimate. This result points strongly to the relevance of legitimacy with regard to legal compliance, a conclusion of key significance for canon law.

6.3   Effectiveness and Validity

In summary, we can say the following about the ecclesiastical legal subjects' compliance with canon law: neither with respect to the legal subjects' knowledge of the law nor with respect to the likelihood of sanctions nor with respect to many Catholics' ideas of legitimacy is canon law currently in a position to make its observance highly likely, at least in those cases in which abiding by the law depends on the legal subjects' individual decision. Whilst many legal norms, such as the norms of constitutional law, are fairly effective as they reproduce ecclesiastical structures by way of a quasi-automatism, those legal norms which depend on the legal subjects' decision to abide by the law are in tendency rather ineffective. Their observance is unlikely and becoming ever more improbable, the more the legal subjects' legal knowledge decreases, the more constrained the church authorities' range of sanctions becomes, and the greater the normative variance between canon law and the everyday norms as internalised by Catholic individuals and groups become. As modernity progresses, canon law successively fails to be a normative medium for influencing the legal subjects' behaviour and their social reality.

6.3.1 Non-institutionalised Law

In his recent book on the legal formation and structure of canon law, however, Simon Hecke states that this problem makes the mere question of legal effectiveness pale into insignificance. The issue is about far more, as Hecke finds, namely the *institutionalisation* of canon law and therefore about processes of stabilisation and restabilisation, which attribute the law with binding force in the first place. In light of the current conditions, Hecke doubts whether canon law can still succeed in institutionalising itself and thus create a binding force which binds all Catholics. He observes that there is continuing public discourse inside and outside the church about the divergences between behavioural expectations maintained by ecclesiastical doctrine and canon law, and the church members' concrete behaviour. This continuous criticism, as Hecke finds, massively obstructs the institutionalisation of canon law among the ordinary church members—the non-ordained Catholics and those who are not ecclesiastical officeholders.[103] These ordinary Catholics, as Hecke finds, no longer contribute to the institutionalisation of canon law. The processes of stabilisation and restabilisation of canon law, which give the law its binding force, take place far from their reality. Canonical norms are of minor or no significance for them; they do not accept the roles which the law ascribes to them; and they pay minor or no attention to the status functions deriving from the law. The law, even when it exists in fact and is formally in force, is therefore based on a claim to have binding force which, for many Catholics, is completely meaningless. However, one may wonder what the consequences are that arise from this finding. Hecke believes it necessary to rethink who still belongs to the core carrier group ("Trägergruppe") of canon law, as the group of Catholics upon whose shoulders the law primarily rests. Hecke also refers to these pillars of canon law as those agents who institutionalise canon law.[104] They form the group which stabilises and restabilises the law. This group has changed considerably and irreversibly in the modern era. Whilst in the premodern *res publica Christiana*, society as a whole could be regarded as the carrier of canon law, we might attribute this function today merely to active members of the Catholic Church.[105] Canon law itself acknowledges this reduction. Canon 11 CIC/1983 states in this respect that mere ecclesiastical laws are exclusively binding for Catholics, that is those who were baptised in the Catholic Church or received into it. Canonical theory, however, still envisages a somewhat broader circle of obligation for norms founded in divine law: according to ecclesiastical doctrine, divine law binds all human beings where natural law is concerned, and all Christians regardless of their confession where the law of revelation is concerned. Yet it is evident that today the church is incapable of practically imposing its legal norms upon legal subjects outside the Catholic Church. Hence, the carrier group upon which canon law rests consists merely of Catholic Christians. However,

---

[103] See Hecke (2017, p. 45).

[104] See Hecke (2017, p. 47).

[105] See Hecke (2017, pp. 40–41, 58).

according to Hecke, this general claim is also increasingly difficult to defend sociologically. He suggests instead that we make a distinction between those Catholics who are part of the church hierarchy and ecclesiastical officeholders, and those ordinary Catholics who are not. The latter group, as Hecke sees it, may be subjects of canon law, but they do not in fact belong to the carrier group of canon law anymore.[106] From the perspective of organisation theory, this is an oddity that requires some explanation. Hecke gives an explanation with reference to Niklas Luhmann's studies on the church as an *atypical* organisation. One typical characteristic of organisations is that they set the conditions for their own membership. Individuals or groups can only belong to an organisation if they submit to its membership conditions. And only those who accept these conditions can remain in the organisation. Jürgen Habermas similarly emphasises that "membership must rest on an (at least tacit) act of agreement on the member's part."[107] Those who no longer accept the membership conditions can leave the organisation; and the organisation expels those members who refuse to accept its membership conditions. These bilateral membership decisions are a constitutive feature of organisations. The church, however, functions differently. Luhmann explored this point in greatest depth in his book *Funktion der Religion* [*Function of Religion*]. The church does not allow its members to decide whether to stay or leave the church, because it assesses membership according to the principle "once a Catholic, always a Catholic" ("*semel catholicus semper catholicus*"). For this reason, formal church membership does not really tell us anything about whether the church members in fact *want* to belong to the church.[108] Church membership therefore also says little about the church members' willingness to submit to the conditions of church membership. For Luhmann, this means that belonging to the church is not specified. What he means by this is that ecclesiastical authorities are not in the position to connect their decisions with the church members' decisions.[109] Consequently, atypical with regard to the general functioning of organisations, ecclesiastical authorities' decisions are often not very relevant for ordinary church members. Luhmann uses doctrinal teachings by way of illustration by noting that the ecclesiastical magisterium is widely unsuccessful in generally connecting their doctrinal teaching with the church members' decisions. Whilst both doctrine and individual decisions may be expressions of the Catholic faith, the connection between official doctrine and personal faith is rather vague. It is not therefore possible to conclude with any certainty from the church members' behaviour whether they accept the magisterium's teaching or not. Ultimately, it remains largely unclear what significance doctrinal statements have for Catholics as members of the church as an organisation. Luhmann goes on to explain that the church has sought to counter this disconnect between the ecclesiastical authorities and the ordinary church members by dividing

---

[106] See Hecke (2017, p. 47).

[107] Habermas (1996, pp. 124–125).

[108] See Luhmann (1977, p. 294).

[109] See Luhmann (1977, p. 295).

the church into different groups of church members. The church distinguishes between roles for the ordained and ecclesiastical officeholders on the one hand, and roles for its ordinary members on the other hand.[110] In the case of ordinary members, one also has to make a further distinction between those Catholics who are purely formal members of the church as an organisation and merely show their membership, for example, by paying church taxes—Luhmann has the German situation in mind—, and the active church members.[111] Simon Hecke now applies this division of church members into classes to the carrier group shouldering canon law, as he finds that we may not expect ordinary Catholics at one remove from the church to provide any constitutive support for canon law.[112] However, as Hecke goes on to observe, we might not even expect this from the active members either. Instead, this task falls essentially to the church hierarchy and ecclesiastical office-holders. Other church members make virtually no contribution anymore to the institutionalisation of canon law. While the legislator creates laws which he sees as binding for all Catholics, these laws are no longer generally institutionalised with regard to those to whom they pertain. From a sociological point of view, this has direct consequences for the validity claim of canon law. Sociologically, one may argue that canon law can in fact no longer be regarded as law which is binding for the whole church, since it lacks general institutionalisation. It only acquires legal form through and for those members of the hierarchy and for ecclesiastical officeholders. One may therefore argue that contrary to what the law generally claims, canon law in the present day is merely what Hecke calls "Amtskirchenrecht," a law which is institutionalised merely by the official church and merely binds members of the official church. However, as I have said, canon law still claims validity for all the baptised who formally belong to the Catholic Church and it also claims to bind all the baptised regardless of their confession through the law of revelation and all human beings irrespective of baptism through natural law. In doing so, canon law claims a reach which is far greater than what can be justified sociologically. Hecke finds this claim to be rather unrealistic. To illustrate his point, he conjures the vivid picture of the church cultivating a phantom pain, by observing that canon law has created a phantom validity claim, noting,

> In modern society, the carrier group of canon law will soon merely consist of the members of the Catholic Church; today ... [it consists] merely of the members of the 'narrower' or 'professional organisation of church ministry'. The reactions of the church to this develop-ment have certain similarities with consecutive symptoms of losing a limb or amputation in human beings, so-called 'phantom pains' or 'phantom limbs'. On the one hand, the church acts as if it still senses pain in 'body parts' which are already gone and are not really part of the 'body' anymore (the major 'part' of the non-members); on the other hand, [the church acts, addition by the author] as if it assumes that certain 'body parts' for supporting canon

---

[110] See Luhmann (1977, p. 299).

[111] See Luhmann (1977, p. 300).

[112] See Hecke (2017, pp. 45, 59).

law are still there which have in fact also been lost … (the major part of the 'ordinary' church members).[113]

6.3.2   Validity Through Reception

This finding is rather alarming for current canon law theory, which strongly relies on the idea that the church as a whole is a unity, not only as a communion of faith, but also as a legal community. Canon law theory believes that canon law is dependent on that community, both for the formation of the law and for its continuation. Canonical theory expresses this in its distinct theory of *receptio legis*, which emphasises the need for the ecclesiastical community's affirmative response to the creation of norms, not merely for reasons related to the effectiveness of the law, but also for its validity. Although ecclesiastical legislators may validly enact ecclesiastical laws without the legal subjects' participation, their act of promulgation must be complemented by the legal subjects' reception of law for the law to come into being and to remain the valid law of the church. If reception is fully missing, the law lacks validity. Canonists love to refer to the example of the Apostolic Constitution *Veterum sapientia* on the Promotion of the Study of Latin when explaining this effect. John XXIII promulgated this law in 1962 to increase the use of Latin in theological education.[114] The constitution advised all lecturers in theology to teach the main theological disciplines in Latin and to use Latin textbooks for their instruction. The constitution even ordered the gradual replacement of any lecturers who could not manage to adjust to Latin teaching. Canonist Bertram Griffin laconically remarks with respect to the effects of that papal law, "A few professors tried this for about a week and then gave up."[115] The Catholic universities and theological faculties never made any efforts to enforce the law or replace those who did not abide by it. So *Veterum sapientia* became one example of a papal law that was not received by its addressees, as it was ignored by nearly all theological scholars and had next to no effect on theological training. Those scholars who were used to teaching in Latin continued to do so; those who had never used Latin in their classes before did not take up the practice. Hence, the law did not change a single legal subject's

---

[113]Original quote, "Die Trägergruppe des kanonischen Rechts umfasst in der modernen Gesellschaft bald nur noch die Mitglieder der katholischen Kirche; heute … sogar nur noch die Mitglieder der sog. 'engeren' bzw. 'beruflichen Organisation kirchlicher Arbeit'. Die Reaktionen der Kirche auf diese Entwicklung weisen gewisse Ähnlichkeiten zu Folgeerscheinungen des Verlusts bzw. der Amputation von Gliedmaßen beim Menschen, nämlich sog. 'Phantomschmerzen' bzw. 'Phantomglieder', auf: So handelt die Kirche zum einen so, als empfinde sie Schmerz noch in 'Körperteilen', die bereits abgetrennt und eigentlich nicht mehr zu ihrem 'Körper' zu zählen sind (der große 'Teil' der Nichtmitglieder); zum anderen so, als gehe sie davon aus, dass bestimmte, zur Unterstützung des kanonischen Rechts faktisch ebenso verlorene 'Körperteile' noch vorhanden sind … (der große 'Teil' der 'einfachen' Kirchenmitglieder)", Hecke (2017, p. 102).

[114]*Acta Apostolicae Sedis, 54*, 129–135; on this issue also Müller (1978, pp. 5–6).

[115]Griffin (1984, p. 25).

behaviour. We may therefore consider it to have been fully ineffective and consequently may assume that it never entered into force in the first place, although it was correctly enacted in a formal sense.

Canonists do however discuss whether there is truly an invalidating effect on the law connected with non-reception. Some voices disagree with the relevance of the legal subjects' acceptance of a law for its validity.[116] After all, canon 7 CIC/1983 only cites the act of promulgation as being constitutive of legal validity by regulating, "A law is established when it is promulgated." The canon evidently makes no reference to the legal subjects' response to a law in the context of its emergence. Adding to this observation is that the Code explicitly directs how the community has to respond to laws which a legislator lawfully enacts, as the law itself obliges Catholics to abide by legal norms. Canon 212 §1 CIC/1983 commands that the church members must "follow with Christian obedience those things which the sacred pastors, inasmuch as they represent Christ, declare as teachers of the faith or establish as rulers of the church." As the law belongs to those matters which ecclesiastical legislators "establish as rulers of the church," Catholics are obliged to abide by the law obediently as part of their Christian duties. Their response to a lawful command is therefore fairly restrained, as it includes merely their obedience and does not accommodate individual decisions on the acceptance or non-acceptance of laws.[117] Other canonists, however, leave little doubt that the legal community's reception of a law is important for the validity of the law,[118] although clarification is necessary to identify the point at which this begins. One may doubt that the general non-observance of a law results in its immediate invalidity, as this reading is indeed incompatible with canon 7 CIC/1983, which only mentions the act of promulgation as essential for the emergence of a law. For this reason, Ladislas Orsy distinguishes between the mere legal validity of a law, which it acquires as the result of a correct legislative act, and its *existential* validity, which the law receives upon the legal subjects' acceptance and reception of the law. For Orsy, this existential validity is of crucial importance for the law because, as he finds, "No matter how valid the law can be legally, if it is rejected existentially it will not shape the life of the community."[119] Since its impact on the social is of essential importance for laws, Orsy introduces the idea of vitality into the concept of law. According to Orsy, only law which is vital insofar as it influences the social practice of the church deserves to be called "law." Norms which are mere law on paper lack their existential validity and will therefore eventually fail to be regarded as law. Canonist Hubert Müller draws a similar conclusion when noting that the legal community's acceptance might not be relevant for the emergence of a law, but that it most certainly is for the

---

[116] Eg Lüdecke and Bier (2012, pp. 25, 30).

[117] See Lüdecke and Bier (2012, pp. 30, 79).

[118] Eg Müller (1978, pp. 10–11); Orsy (1980, p. 42); Demel (2010, p. 260).

[119] Orsy (1980, p. 44); see also Orsy (1984, p. 68).

continued existence of a law.[120] If a legal community does not receive a law, this law ultimately faces desuetude. It is destined to lapse into obsolescence.

We may understand these theoretical observations on the necessity of *receptio legis* for the law to become vital as seamlessly connecting with the sociological observation that at present, canon law is borne merely by the official church as a carrier group and is only institutionalised with regard to that group. What Orsy and others theoretically note with regard to the legal community refusing to lend the law its vitality finds its sociological expression in the widespread non-institutionalisation of canon law among most Catholics. One may deal with this finding in two ways. One may either change the theory of canon law to limit its scope to the smaller group of Catholics representing the official church and serving as the carrier group of canon law. Or one may reform the law in a way that increases the probability of it receiving more wide-ranging support from ordinary church members. Whatever happens in the future, the current situation is a phantom situation, as Simon Hecke has described it. It presents a globally valid Catholic canon law with all pomp and circumstance, but widely fails to ensure the effectiveness of this law among ordinary members of the Catholic Church. Canon law thus threatens to become largely "zombie law," a term used by constitutional scholars to describe laws which have become unenforceable but nevertheless maintain a shadow existence as law in books.[121] In cases in which its reception is at stake and dependent on the acceptance of the ordinary Catholics, canon law tends to be dead letter which fails to shape the life of the church and to impact the social reality of ordinary church members.

Bibliography

Aubert, V. (1952). White collar crime and social structure. *American Journal of Sociology, 58*, 263–271.

Barrett, D. N. (1960). Penal values in canonical and sociological theory. *The American Catholic Sociological Review, 21*, 98–116.

Beal, J. P. (2011). Something there is that Doesn't love a law: Canon law and its discontents. In M. J. Lacey & F. Oakley (Eds.), *The crisis of authority in Catholic modernity* (pp. 135–154). Oxford University Press.

Böckenförde, W. (2006). Zur gegenwärtigen Lage in der römisch-katholischen Kirche: Kirchenrechtliche Anmerkungen. In N. Lüdecke & G. Bier (Eds.), *Freiheit und Gerechtigkeit in der Kirche. Gedenkschrift für Werner Böckenförde* (Forschungen zur Kirchenrechtswissenschaft 37, pp. 143–158). Echter.

Brosi, U. (2013). *Recht, Strukturen, Freiräume: Kirchenrecht* (Studiengang Theologie 9, überarbeitet und mit einem Beitrag zum deutschen Staatskirchenrecht ergänzt von I. Kreusch). Theologischer Verlag Zürich.

Carbonnier, J. (1974). *Rechtssoziologie* (Schriftenreihe zur Rechtssoziologie und Rechtstatsachenforschung 31). Duncker & Humblot.

---

[120] See Müller (1978, p. 8).

[121] Eg Wasserman (2021).

Coughlin, J. J. (2011). *Canon law: A comparative study with Anglo-American legal theory*. Oxford University Press.

D'Antonio, W. V., Davidson, J. D., Hoge, D. R., & Gautier, M. L. (2007). *American Catholics today: New realities of their faith and their church*. Rowman and Littlefield.

Demel, S. (2010). *Handbuch Kirchenrecht: Grundbegriffe für Studium und Praxis*. Herder.

Diekmann, A. (1980). *Die Befolgung von Gesetzen: Empirische Untersuchungen zu einer rechtssoziologischen Theorie* (Schriftenreihe zur Rechtssoziologie und Rechtstatsachenforschung 47). Duncker & Humblot.

Durkheim, É. (1960). *The division of labor in society* [1893] (G. Simpson, Trans.) The Free Press.

Ehrlich, E. (1936). *Fundamental principles of the sociology of law* (W. L. Moll, Trans., with an introduction by R. Pound). The Harvard University Press.

Eifler, S. (2010). Die Definition der Situation und die Befolgung oder Inanspruchnahme von Gesetzen. In G. Wagner (Ed.), *Kraft Gesetz: Beiträge zur rechtssoziologischen Effektivitätsforschung* (pp. 91–117). Springer.

Essen, G. (2013). Nachholende Selbstmodernisierung? Katholische Kirche und politische Öffentlichkeit. *Theologie der Gegenwart, 56*, 208–220.

Festinger, L. (1957). *A theory of cognitive dissonance*. Stanford University Press.

Francis. (2016). Apostolic Letter issued *Motu proprio Come una madre amorevole*, 4 June 2016. *Acta Apostolicae Sedis, 108*, 715–717.

Geiger, T. (1964). *Vorstudien zu einer Soziologie des Rechts* (mit einer Einleitung und internationalen Bibliographie zur Rechtssoziologie von P. Trappe). Luchterhand.

Goler, P. A. (1972). Must canon law be color blind? *Catholic Lawyer, 18*, 293–299.

Griffin, B. F. (1984). Introduction to the jargon of canon law. *The Jurist, 44*, 19–27.

Habermas, J. (1996). *Between facts and norms: Contributions to a discourse theory of law and democracy* (W. Rehg, Trans.). The MIT Press.

Hahn, J. (2017). *Das kirchliche Richteramt: Rechtsgestalt, Theorie und Theologie* (Beihefte zum Münsterischen Kommentar 74). Wingen.

Hahn, J., Schüller, T., & Wode, C. (2013). *Kirchenrecht in den Medien*. UVK.

Hecke, S. (2017). *Kanonisches Recht: Zur Rechtsbildung und Rechtsstruktur des römisch-katholischen Kirchenrechts*. Springer.

Heller, E., Cohen, C., Bublil, D., & Omar, F. (2016). *The Israeli democracy index 2016* (K. Gold, Trans.). The Israel Democracy Institute.

Huels, J. M. (1987). Interpreting canon law in diverse cultures. *The Jurist, 47*, 249–293.

John XXIII. (1962). Apostolic constitution *Veterum sapientia* on the promotion of the study of Latin, 22 February 1962. *Acta Apostolicae Sedis, 54*, 129–135.

Llewellyn, K. N. (1940). The normative, the legal, and the law jobs: The problem of juristic method. *Yale Law Journal, 49*, 1355–1400.

Lüdecke, N., & Bier, G. (2012). *Das römisch-katholische Kirchenrecht: Eine Einführung* (unter Mitarbeit von B. S. Anuth). Kohlhammer.

Luhmann, N. (1977). *Funktion der Religion*. Suhrkamp.

Luhmann, N. (1986). *Die soziologische Beobachtung des Rechts*. Suhrkamp.

Luhmann, N. (2004). *Law as a social system* (Oxford socio-legal studies, F. Kastner, R. Nobles, D. Schiff & R. Ziegert, Eds., K. A. Ziegert, Trans.). Oxford University Press.

Luhmann, N. (2014). *A sociological theory of law* (M. Albrow, Ed., E. King-Utz & M. Albrow, Trans.). Routledge.

Mezey, N. (2001). Law as culture. *Yale Journal of Law & the Humanities, 13*, 35–67.

Möllers, C. (2020). *The possibility of norms: Social practice beyond morals and causes*. Oxford University Press.

Moser, T. (1976). *Gottesvergiftung*. Suhrkamp.

Müller, H. (1978). *Das Gesetz in der Kirche "zwischen" amtlichem Anspruch und konkretem Vollzug: Annahme und Ablehnung universalkirchlicher Gesetze als Anfrage an die Kirchenrechtswissenschaft*. Minerva.

Neudecker, G. (2013). *Ius sequitur vitam—Der Dienst der Kirchengerichte an der Lebendigkeit des Rechts: Zugleich ein Beitrag zur Vergleichung des kanonischen und staatlichen Rechtssystems* (Tübinger Kirchenrechtliche Studien 13). LIT.

Opp, K.-D. (2010). Wann befolgt man Gesetze? Entwicklung und Probleme einer Theorie. In G. Wagner (Ed.), *Kraft Gesetz: Beiträge zur rechtssoziologischen Effektivitätsforschung* (pp. 35–63). Springer.

Orsy, L. M. (1980). The interpreter and his art. *The Jurist, 40*, 27–56.

Orsy, L. M. (1984). Reception and non-reception of law: A canonical and theological consideration. *Canon Law Society of America Proceedings, 46*, 66–70.

Orsy, L. M. (1992). *Theology and canon law: New horizons for legislation and interpretation.* Liturgical Press.

Raiser, T. (2007). *Grundlagen der Rechtssoziologie* (4th ed.). UTB.

Rasehorn, T. (1975). Zur Einstellung der Unterschicht zum Rechtswesen. In E. Blankenburg (Ed.), *Empirische Rechtssoziologie* (pp. 103–115). Piper.

Rehbinder, M. (2014). *Rechtssoziologie: Ein Studienbuch* (8th ed.). C. H. Beck.

Röhl, K. F. (1987). *Rechtssoziologie: Ein Lehrbuch.* Heymann.

Rottleuthner, H., & Rottleuthner-Lutter, M. (2010). Effektivität von Recht: Der Beitrag der Rechtssoziologie. In G. Wagner (Ed.), *Kraft Gesetz: Beiträge zur rechtssoziologischen Effektivitätsforschung* (pp. 13–34). Springer.

Seinecke, R. (2015). *Das Recht des Rechtspluralismus* (Grundlagen der Rechtswissenschaft 29). Mohr Siebeck.

Shapiro, M. (1981). *Courts: A comparative and political analysis.* The University of Chicago Press.

Tamanaha, B. Z. (2008). Understanding legal pluralism: Past to present, local to global. *Sydney Law Review, 30*, 375–411.

Tapp, J. L., & Kohlberg, L. (1971). Developing senses of law and legal justice. *Journal of Social Issues, 27*, 65–91.

Vanderlinden, J. (2002). Religious Laws as Systems of law. In A. Huxley (Ed.), *Religion, law and tradition: Comparative studies in religious law* (pp. 165–182). Routledge.

Verband der Diözesen Deutschlands. (2015). Grundordnung des kirchlichen Dienstes im Rahmen kirchlicher Arbeitsverhältnisse, 27 April 2015. Retrieved June 22, 2021, from www.dbk.de/fileadmin/redaktion/diverse_downloads/VDD/Grundordnung_GO-30-04-2015_final.pdf

Wagner, G. (2010). Kraft Gesetz: Überlegungen zur Kausalität von Rechtsnormen. In G. Wagner (Ed.), *Kraft Gesetz: Beiträge zur rechtssoziologischen Effektivitätsforschung* (pp. 145–159). Springer.

Wasserman, H. (2021). Zombie Laws. In *Florida International University legal studies research paper no. 21-02.* Retrieved 24 October 24, 2021, from https://ssrn.com/abstract=3778122

Chapter 7
Conclusion

Abstract In modernity, it has become ever more difficult to claim that the church as a whole, as the community of all Christian faithful, is responsible for institutionalising canon law. Many church members widely ignore the law. They disregard the roles attributed to them by the law. Status functions as provided by the law have become meaningless to them. From the perspective of the sociology of canon law, these observations support the finding that the ordinary members of the church no longer contribute to institutionalising canon law. Instead, it has become the ecclesiastical hierarchy who mainly serve as "carrier group" of the law. Canon law is therefore slowly developing into mere law of the "official church." Despite this sociological finding, it continues to claim validity with regard to other members of the church, too, even though these members—in a sociological sense—have stopped being carriers of the law. This claim is somewhat dangerous as it contributes to destabilising canon law and confers on it some characteristics of "phantom law" or "zombie law."

Keywords Institutionalisation · Loss of effectiveness · Loss of validity · Carrier groups · Law of the official church · Phantom law · Zombie law

7.1 A Short Outlook

From a sociological perspective, there is little more to say in a basic study such as my book, if one does not venture beyond the descriptive approach represented by a sociology of law in a narrower sense. However, for a sociological jurisprudence of canon law, which seeks sociological insights with the aim of improving canon law, my conclusion does mark the starting point at which further work might commence. In itself, my study does not seek to pursue such a programme despite it being, as I noted at the outset, a genuine task of canon law studies to confront the legal reality of the church with sociological findings and use them as the basis for normative considerations. It is only in taking this additional step towards a sociological jurisprudence of canon law that the sociology of canon law can bond with theology to tackle the ecclesiological challenges of canon law. Only here does it seek to identify what kind of law the church actually requires, and whether the Catholic

Church sees itself as a community embracing all Catholics not merely as a community of faith but also as an institution endowed with its own law. This work follows on seamlessly from the discussion about legal effectiveness and legal validity in which I engaged towards the end of my study, as the tension between facticity and validity of canon law has major repercussions for ecclesiology. After all, canon law bases its broad validity claim on ecclesiology. In this light, it is of dramatic importance for the church if the validity claim of canon law proves sociologically unattainable as modernity progresses. If it is true that canon law is essential for the earthly church, as the Second Vatican Council at least implied in number 8 of its Dogmatic Constitution *Lumen gentium*—which canonists traditionally cite to find that the concrete earthly church requires a legal frame—then the transformation of canon law into a phantom law or zombie law is not only a problem of legal effectiveness, it is also an ecclesiological challenge. A church which defines itself as being founded on a dysfunctional phantom law eventually runs the risk of becoming a phantom church. Viewed in this light, the fundamental connection between church and canon law is ecclesiologically treacherous. The legal nature of the church, if postulated as a necessity, does not permit the reduction of canon law to a purely organisational law that is only functionally binding for members of the hierarchy and ecclesiastical officeholders. Thinkers who accept the argument traditionally drawn from *Lumen gentium* that the church must have a legal form must view these socio-legal findings with alarm. For the sociological jurisprudence of canon law, which is devoted to the improvement of canon law, this observation means pursuing legal reforms that serve the re-institutionalisation of canon law as the law of the *whole* church. If, on the other hand, as one might also propose, the church can get by with having a law which merely serves the official church as a frame of organisational regulation, it must revise the ecclesiological legal theory traditionally based on *Lumen gentium* number 8. This would necessitate abandoning the link between legal theory and ecclesiology in favour of a more functional view of canon law. A development like this would not necessarily lead to the detheologisation of canon law, but it would necessitate correcting the broad validity claim of canon law as grounded in ecclesiology. However, my study does not delve any deeper into these matters. It is merely a still image which depicts the state of canon law as it is now. How and whether the church may heal the gap between the validity and facticity of its law is a wide-ranging topic, sizeable enough to fill another book. This topic will most likely occupy canonists intensively in the years to come.

7.2   A Summary in Theses

7.2.1   A Sociology of Canon Law

Canon Law Studies as Theology

1. My study understands canon law studies as a theological discipline. Its task is to interpret the church as an institution in its legal constitution as the earthly realisation of the heavenly church. Canon law studies is practical theology because it studies the legal structure of the church as the practical embodiment of the heavenly church.

Theology with Legal Methodology

2. Canon law studies inter alia uses legal methods to study canon law. As legal exegesis, it works with hermeneutical and linguistic methods. As legal dogma, theory, and philosophy, it analyses the reasoning behind law, its principles, and relation to justice. As legal history, canon law studies works historically. In the sociology of canon law, it develops sociological theories and uses theoretical and empirical methods of social research, taken from general sociology, the sociology of law, and the sociology of religion.

Theoretical and Empirical Sociologies

3. Sociology studies the law theoretically and empirically. In order to benefit from the findings of the sociology of law as empirical science, the sociology of canon law must overcome the Neo-Scholastic hostility towards empirical research that still permeates theology and canon law today.

Law as Doctrine, Law as Practice

4. Like all sociologies of law, the sociology of canon law must mediate between sociological ("law as practice") and normative doctrinal approaches to law ("law as doctrine"). To achieve this, it requires canonists trained in dogma—in a legal and theological sense—*and* sociology.

Orthodoxy and Orthopraxy

5. Insofar as the practice of the church has a theological relevance, canon law studies has to mediate between ecclesiastical doctrine and practice. Modern canonical thought must consider both orthodoxy and orthopraxy not only to understand the law as ecclesiastical practice but also to connect it convincingly with ecclesiastical doctrine.

Descriptive and Normative Sociologies

6. One may study the reality of canon law using a descriptive approach (*sociology of law* in a narrower sense). A descriptive approach to the sociology of canon law documents and analyses the reality of canon law. As *sociological jurisprudence*, the sociology of law also pursues normative goals. The sociological jurisprudence of canon law uses its findings as the basis for normative considerations about how to improve canon law.

Theoretical Approach of this Study

7. My study adheres to the descriptive paradigm of the sociology of law. It develops an interpretive theory of the sociology of canon law. To achieve this, my study refers to existing socio-legal theories. It examines these theories to identify how they contribute to understanding canon law. I verify whether my theoretical approach does indeed reflect the reality of canon law by drawing on empirical findings from the sociology of law and the sociology of religion.

7.2.2   Law Through the Lens of Sociology

Law and Social Reality

8. The sociology of law studies groups and their law. It studies the influence of law on the social reality of communities and societies and the influence of their social life on the law.

Monistic and Pluralist Sociologies of Law

9. Monistic approaches devote their attention solely to state law, because the state dominates the field of law in modernity. Pluralist approaches to law also accept other groups, such as confederations of states, contracting parties, or religious communities, as producers of law. A pluralist understanding of law is therefore well-suited to approaching religious law such as canon law.

The Problem of Panjurism

10. However, pluralist approaches are susceptible to some arbitrariness because they do not consistently succeed in differentiating between law and non-legal norms which influence the social ("panjurism"). Pluralist thinkers must therefore define clearly which norms they mean when they speak of "law."

Law as a Coercive Order

11. Max Weber stressed the coercive character of law. Current sociology of law only partially accepts his premise. Everyday legal life demonstrates that law

generally forms an often invisible basis for social interaction, functioning for the most part without being challenged and largely without coercion.

Low-Level Coercion of Canon Law

12. Canon law is particularly notable for its low level of coercion. The church has no policing function, and can only rely on the coercive power of the state in very rare cases. One might even argue that a low level of coercion is a theological necessity: because canon law supports the faith—and faith is by definition a free act—canon law must refrain from constraining the legal subjects' freedom substantially.

Law as Behavioural Expectation

13. Niklas Luhmann understands law as communication based on the binary codification "legal"/ "illegal." Law is formed through the institutionalisation of expectations regarding "legal" behaviour. Luhmann, thus, does not define "law" as a mechanism for controlling behaviour but as norms generating expectations with regard to "legal" behaviour. These expectations are counterfactual insofar as individuals maintain them even in cases in which they are disappointed.

Law as Institutionally Bound Doctrine

14. One may link Luhmann's approach to approaches that understand law as institutionally bound doctrine. While all social norms have doctrinal features, the law relies on institutions to provide doctrinal consistency and to provide legal subjects with the justiciability of its norms: institutionalised legal procedures determine what is lawful, thereby providing the legal subjects with decisions regarding what is lawful and (re)producing doctrine. Based on these observations, we may define law as follows: Law is a knowledge system which produces justiciable norms endowed with the option of institutional contestation.

Dominance of State Law

15. Contemporary individuals associate the concept of law primarily with state law. When studying non-state law, the sociology of law is therefore highly interested in the relationship between this law and state law. The sociology of law often studies non-state law through comparison with state law. Canon law also acquires clearer definition through this comparison. However, this is merely a matter of methodology, not of legal theory, as canon law is grounded in the church, not in the state.

7.2.3 Functions of the Law

Order and Conflict Theories of the Law

16. Order theories of the law understand law as a power for organising the social: law assigns authority and defines roles; assigns rights and duties to the legal subjects; offers them institutional frameworks to legally organise their social affairs; stabilises exchange relations; and provides instruments for systematic conflict resolution. Canon law fulfils these functions for the church. Unlike order theories, conflict theories see the primary function of the law in its merit to avoid and solve conflict.

Primacy of the Ordering Function

17. The potential of the law so solve conflict comes to light when there is conflict over the law and its power to create order. One may therefore find the ordering function of the law to be its primary function. Law creates order—and does so in a number of ways, inter alia by avoiding and solving conflict.

Law and Conflict

18. Nevertheless, "law and conflict" is an independent field in the sociology of law. It studies various features of legal conflict management: legal counselling, the working of bodies for the administration of justice, and institutional conflict resolution through mediation, arbitration, and adjudication.

Counselling, Police, Conflict Resolution

19. Like secular law, canon law is a specialist field, the understanding of which requires expertise conveyed to the legal subjects in the form of legal counselling. The church does not possess a police force to enforce ecclesiastical decisions; this begs the question whether and under what conditions canon law can be effective without the support of a law enforcement agency. The focus of ecclesiastical justice research is on extrajudicial and judicial conflict resolution such as mediation, arbitration, and adjudication.

Adjudication in Conflict

20. Adjudication plays an important role in modern legal systems as a key instrument of conflict resolution. Yet judicial systems face a problem of legitimacy. This is because judicial decisions create "winners" and "losers," which does not necessarily defuse conflicts and can even exacerbate them. To counter this problem, adjudication frequently resorts to mechanisms of mediation, which promise to have a pacifying effect.

Amicable Settlements

21. One may discover the same strategy in ecclesiastical procedural law. The legislator prefers amicable settlements and peaceful conflict resolution over adjudication. Ecclesiastical penal law maintains that ordinaries are to initiate penal proceedings only if fraternal correction, warning, or other pastoral measures have proven ineffective for the purposes of sufficiently restoring justice, reforming the offender, and repairing the scandal (see canon 1341 CIC/1983).

Misuse of Amicability

22. However, when courts or law enforcement authorities attempt to find amicable solutions by referring to mediation elements and proposing extrajudicial settlements, they may end up suppressing conflicts rather than resolving them. In the abuse scandal of the church, it has become clear that many ecclesiastical authorities misused "amicability" to refrain from rigorously prosecuting offenders.

Clerical Justice and Male Justice

23. Judicial research also challenges ecclesiastical adjudication on its specific version of class justice. Whilst the sociology of law has traditionally focused on class justice as a social issue, the sociology of canon law has to address the problem of "clerical justice" as a justice system based on mostly clerical judges, insofar as canon law restricts the service of laypeople as ecclesiastical judges. As clerical justice, canonical adjudication is also predominately male justice.

7.2.4 Law and Legal Validity

Law Born of Power, Power Born of Law

24. Modern law is positive law. It comes into force by virtue of decision. This raises the question of power in a dialectical sense for the sociology of law: as power generated through law and as law generated through power. The sociology of canon law must analyse the power of canon law and of those who generate the law. These debates have been evolving slowly, as ecclesiastical authorities tend to hamper debates about power in church by veiling power in the terminology of "service."

Changeability of Positive Law

25. The fact that positive law applies by virtue of decision indicates that it is changeable. This characteristic of law also applies to positive canon law. Some voices have raised the objection that so-called "divine law" is unchangeable. However, since the divine will only transforms into legal norms through

human legislation, these norms are also changeable—not arbitrarily, but in accordance with the current state of theological knowledge about how God's will expresses itself in history.

Change and Legal Learning

26. Frequent and recurring breaches of law are an opportunity to consider changes to the law. Breaches of law can therefore initiate legal learning. Nevertheless, legal learning can be problematic, as legal change can destabilise legal orders. The challenge is to change legal norms in a way which allows the legal subjects to adjust their former expectations of the law and redirect them to the new legal norms with as little disappointment as possible.

Consistency and Destabilisation

27. Changes to fundamental canonical norms can destabilise the ecclesiastical order. Consistency can ensure stability. One may therefore see the low level of flexibility in canon law as a strategy for maintaining stability in the ecclesiastical order. From the perspective of the sociology of law, however, one has to note that refusing to reform the law can both stabilise and destabilise, especially in cases in which legal stagnation creates problems of legitimacy.

7.2.5 Validity and Legitimacy

Legitimacy as Acceptance

28. The law draws its legitimacy from its legal subjects' recognition, their acknowledgement, or acceptance of the law as a legitimate source of social order. The same applies to canon law. The sociology of canon law observes that the recognition of canon law is often in dispute.

Acceptance Issues of Validity Reasons

29. Problems of recognition often relate to the validity reasons of law, as one may demonstrate with regard to laws rooted in revelation and nature. Revelation and nature are unsuited as the basis for legal validity in secular and pluralist groups. As the church also becomes increasingly pluralised, the magisterium's findings about which norms derive from revelation and nature are no longer self-evident to many church members.

Power as a Source of Validity

30. Revelation and nature as validity reasons of law in pluralist groups frequently morph into "power" arguments in order to decide which of their interpretations should become legally binding. Hence, revelation and nature can continue to

serve as validity reasons of modern law if they draw on power to determine what God's will is for humanity and what is right according to nature. However, there is still a problem of recognition. Modern legal subjects recognise power only in the form of legitimate authority, as shown in Max Weber's reflections on charismatic, traditional, and legal authority.

The Rule of Law and Social Contract

31. As the modern age progresses, it is primarily legal authority that is acceptable. Legitimate power must be restricted and controlled by the law. The legal subjects tend to accept legal authority because law provides them with a rational framework within which to pursue their own interests. The idea that the recognition of authority can be in one's own interests links Weber's theory with the theory of the social contract. No longer is it the content of common beliefs that serves as the basis of law; it is the general consensus that it is in one's own interests to forego some personal freedom and submit to a common order.

Law Through Consensus

32. Consensus theories are a recent variant of contractual theories. Jürgen Habermas alludes to consensus as reached in rational discourse as the basis for the validity of law. Legal norms that prove to be broadly acceptable in a discourse free from domination are worthy of recognition based on the presumption of their correctness. Habermas sees the crux of consensus theory not in the achievement of a de facto consensus, but in the fact that consensus is conceivable. With regard to law, it is therefore important to ensure that conditions are in place for the emergence of law that legal subjects can rationally accept.

Fictitious Consensus

33. However, as the modern age progresses, consensus about the law is becoming increasingly unlikely. Law is a specialist field that exists at one remove from the legal subjects' everyday reality, placing consensus out of reach. In order to establish acceptance of the law, consensus is replaced by a rhetoric of consensus, which conceals the lack of consensus. This strategy can be convincing as long as it is not contradicted by fundamental dissent. Dissent is a major problem for canon law, because there is evident dissent in many legal matters, such as celibacy, the exclusion of women from ordination, or the lays' limited share in ecclesiastical governance.

Legitimation Through Procedures

34. Fictitious consensus about the law is generated through procedures such as legislation and application of the law that meet the demands of the rule of law. However, this creates a problem of recognition, especially in the case of obviously contingent majority decisions on the law. Yet the legal subjects

tend to accept majority decisions despite their obvious contingency if decision
making has expectable results and provides opportunities for participation.

Participation Through Representation

35. In complex societies or communities, participation usually takes place through
representation. The recognition of a majority decision then depends on whether
the decision-making body is considered a legitimate representative body for
those for whom the body makes the decisions. This is problematic for the church
because, as a consequence of its hierarchical organisation, members of the
clergy are those primarily involved in the creation and application of canon
law. The extensive non-participation of the laity undermines the recognition of
canon law.

The Canonical Rule of Law

36. In addition, from the point of view of recognition, it proves to be problematic
that the church fails to grant the rule of law as rigorously as is common in other
constitutional legal systems. This problem is not sufficiently remedied simply by
pointing out that the church is not a constitutional state. Whilst this is true, it
does not change the fact that church members expect comparable standards from
the church and its law.

Legal Protection and Control of Power

37. At present, canon law fails to guarantee thorough legal protection. Fundamental
rights in church do not enjoy the level of protection to which citizens of liberal
states are accustomed. Church authorities are confronted to a lesser extent with
instruments for the containment of power. The pope is not even bound by the
law. Conditional decision-making programmes, such as legislation, do not have
a reliable legal basis and are difficult to understand and impossible to control.
One may suspect growing anti-juridism to have its roots in many Catholics'
view that in church, illegitimate power produces law and illegitimate law produces power.

7.2.6 The Effectiveness of the Law

Compliance and Sanctions

38. Law is effective when it leaves its mark on the social reality of a legal community. Legal norms are effective when the legal subjects abide by them or when
their non-compliance is sanctioned.

Different Types of Compliance

39. It is important, in any case, to differentiate between different types of norms. Compliance is different depending on whether norms are commands, prohibitions, permissions, exemptions, authorisation rules, or procedural norms. Whilst prohibitions, for instance, strive for maximum compliance, quantity does not play a significant role with regard to norms which provide legal subjects with institutional mechanisms for legally organising their social affairs.

High Effectiveness

40. The effectiveness of canon law is high whenever canonical norms reproduce their effectiveness quasi-automatically. This is for instance the case with most constitutional norms which automatically reproduce the hierarchical structure of the church largely independently of ecclesiastical legal subjects' individual decisions whether to support this effect of the law or not.

Low Effectiveness

41. The effectiveness of canonical norms is low whenever abiding by the law depends on the legal subjects' decision. The legal subjects often ignore prohibitions or commands. Only rarely does this result in the imposition of negative sanctions. Legal subjects are choosing to use norms which provide them with institutional mechanisms for legally organising their affairs ever less frequently. Procedural norms are in use in the marriage annulment and penal cases treating sexual abuse of minors, but are mere law on paper in most other cases.

Conditions for Legal Compliance

42. In order to understand the reasons why many canonical norms prove to have a low degree of effectiveness, it is necessary to examine the conditions for legal compliance. The sociology of law identifies a host of factors, including the legal subjects' knowledge of the law, their expectation of sanctions, and their ideas of legitimacy with regard to the law.

Knowledge of the Law

43. It is not necessary to know the law *as law* for it to be effective. But it is necessary for legal subjects to have a rudimentary familiarity with its content. Many active church members know some basic regulations of canon law, particularly from constitutional law, sacramental law, and the law on the teaching function of the church, mostly from everyday practice. However, they are largely oblivious to other norms, such as property law, most criminal law, and procedural law.

Negative Sanctions

44. No law can be enforced consistently, canon law being no exception. Hence, legal claims often remain unfulfilled. However, there must be a chance for

negative sanctions to act as substitutes for the fulfilment of claims in the event of a breach of law, so that the legal community's disappointment does not translate into lowered expectations with regard to the law.

Limited Sanctions in Church

45. The church has no coercive apparatus to enforce compliance with the law or to effectively subject most of its members to negative sanctions. In most Catholic groups, pressure to abide by canon law is low. Ecclesiastical authorities often fail to notice breaches of canon law or are reluctant to impose sanctions. When they do impose sanctions, this often only affects legal subjects bound to the church through ordination, membership in a religious order, or employment.

Compliance Based on Recognition

46. The sociology of law observes that compliance with the law depends to a large extent on the legal subjects' recognition of the law. Beliefs that a regulation is justified are often more important for its observance than cost-benefit calculations about whether to abide by or break the law.

Normative Variance

47. It is therefore a problem affecting the effectiveness of law when legal norms come into conflict with other norms recognised by the legal subjects ("normative variance"), such as competing legal, social, or moral norms. Many ecclesiastical legal subjects tend to experience a considerable degree of normative variance between canon law and other norms of key value for them, including norms of secular law, because canon law does not adhere to the constitutional standards which legal subjects are used to as citizens of contemporary democratic orders.

7.2.7   Effectiveness and Validity

Law of the Official Church

48. From the perspective of the sociology of canon law, most ordinary church members no longer contribute to the institutionalisation of canon law. Instead, it is merely the clergy and ecclesiastical officeholders that serve as the carrier group of canon law today. Canon law—formerly the law of all church members—has transformed into being a mere "Amtskirchenrecht," as Simon Hecke observes, a mere law of the "official church."

Phantom Validity Claims

49. As a consequence, as Hecke points out, current canon law works with a phantom validity claim. It claims validity for legal subjects who, from a sociological point

of view, are no longer part of its carrier group. With regard to those groups where non-institutionalised law claims validity, canon law becomes phantom law or zombie law.

Starting Point for Further Studies

50. This poses an ecclesiological problem, namely whether canon law is essential for the earthly church, as the Dogmatic Constitution *Lumen gentium* number 8 insinuates. If one regards the law as essential for the church, a church which is no longer integrated by phantom law threatens to become a phantom church. Further studies which transcend the descriptive approach of the sociology of law and follow the normative aims of a sociological jurisprudence of canon law might investigate whether this is in fact the case and whether this state of affairs can be changed.

The manufacturer's authorised representative in the EU is Springer
Nature Customer Service Centre GmbH, Europaplatz 3, 69115 Heidelberg,
Germany. If you have any concerns regarding our products, please
contact ProductSafety@springernature.com

Printed and bound by CPI Group (UK) Ltd, Croydon, CR0 4YY
29/04/2026
02099458-0007